I0057220

BIGGER GOVERNMENT

The Future of Government Expenditure
in Advanced Economies

BIGGER GOVERNMENT

The Future of Government Expenditure
in Advanced Economies

MARC ROBINSON

Arolla Press
2020

Copyright © 2020 Marc Robinson

All rights reserved. No part of this book may be reproduced or used in any manner whatsoever without the express written permission of the publisher except for the use of brief quotations in book reviews and for certain other noncommercial uses permitted by copyright law.

First published 2020 by
Arolla Press
www.arollapress.com

ISBN: 978-2-9701401-2-2 hardback
ISBN: 978-2-9701401-3-9 paperback

Library of Congress Control Number: 2020906175

Cover design: Elizabeth Heissler Design
Page layout: Catherine Williams, Chapter One Book Production, UK

Printed in the United States of America, the United Kingdom and Australia.

ADVANCE PRAISE FOR *BIGGER GOVERNMENT*

"This deeply-researched and brilliantly-argued book is an honest, clear-minded assessment of the fiscal future that awaits advanced countries in response to changes in health care, income support, infrastructure deficits and other powerful drivers of public spending. Robinson's mastery of program details and socioeconomic trends makes this study essential reading for national leaders and public finance specialists."

Allen Schick, Senior Fellow, Brookings Institution and Professor Emeritus, School of Public Policy, University of Maryland

"This book represents a path-breaking original contribution to our understanding of the future of public finances in advanced economies. It challenges traditional dogmas on drivers of public spending and instead suggests that irrespective of political leaning of governments, advancements in health care technology, delayed actions on climate change and long-term care will drive public spending through the roof in coming decades in advanced countries. This book is a wake-up call for policy makers to take action now on emerging challenges or face the wrath of electorates in justifying higher taxes in future. It is a must-read book for policy makers, practitioners, scholars and students."

Anwar Shah, Senior Fellow, Brookings Institution; Director, Governance Program, World Bank Institute (2004-2009) and Director, Center for Public Economics, SWUFE, Chengdu/China

"Financial pressures emanating from health, long-term care and climate change will translate into higher government spending irrespective of ideological orientations of governments. Marc Robinson underpins his thesis with impressive empirical evidence and deliberate arguments why alternatives appear unlikely. Hard stuff for all foes of big government."

Gerhard Steger, Austrian Federal Budget Director (1997-2014)

"Marc provides valuable 'contrarian' insights into the three major causes for future increases in government spending ... 'Bigger Government' provides a well-researched alternative way of looking at the future of government spending."

Barry Anderson, former US Assistant Director for Budget and Acting Director of the Congressional Budget Office

"This book by an internationally renowned expert in public expenditure management provides a compelling analysis of major recent and future drivers of government spending in advanced economies. ... The book is a wake-up call for policymakers, who need to think early and proactively how to contain and finance these escalating costs. It offers a number of suggestions, but also calls for more reflection and analysis on the very difficult policy trade-offs that these trends pose. In my view, a must-read!"

Teresa Ter-Minassian, Director, Fiscal Affairs Department International Monetary Fund (2001-2008)

"Budgeting is often understood as a result of political strategies and struggles ... but when democratic representation works well, public budgets are in the long run determined by basic societal trends and citizens' needs. Marc Robinson's book invites us to take a journey to explore these fundamental trends. With a very pragmatic approach he takes stock of numerous theories and research on different areas of public spending and gives us a broad-based and lively insight into what the future might hold."

Martin Kelleners, Director, Ministry of Finance, Germany; Chair, OECD Network of Senior Budget Officials

ABOUT THE AUTHOR

Marc Robinson is a senior consultant who has advised more than thirty countries, on all continents and at all stages of development, on budgeting reforms. During his career, he has been a senior civil servant, a professor of economics and a staff economist at the International Monetary Fund. Dr. Robinson has published over thirty books and articles on government budgeting issues. He frequently participates as an invited speaker on budgeting topics at conferences and symposiums held by diverse entities such as the OECD, European Union, APEC, NATO and national ministries of finance. He is a member of the OECD Advisory Panel on Budgeting and Public Expenditures. His website is www.pfmresults.com.

CONTENTS

LIST OF FIGURES

LIST OF BOXES

INTRODUCTION

This book is about the future of public spending in advanced economies* over the time horizon of the next 30 years. Its central proposition is that government is set to get considerably bigger. All advanced countries can, other things being equal, expect to see large, permanent increases in government expenditure – increases of at least 7 percent of gross domestic product (GDP) in a majority of countries. This will not be the consequence of the political triumph of "big government" advocates. Rather, the dramatic rise will result from external forces and pressure points that will impact heavily on government spending, irrespective of the ideological orientations of governments.

Health, climate change and long-term care will be the main areas where governments in all countries will find themselves with little choice but to spend more than they do today. In some, but not all, countries, pensions and infrastructure will add to the pressure.

Health will represent by far and away the largest area of long-term expenditure growth. The need to strengthen capacity to fight future

---

*   "Advanced economies" means higher-income countries with sophisticated modern economies. Per capita income on a PPP basis, advanced economy status and size are the selection criteria for inclusion in the statistical and other coverage of this book. Concretely, this means that the following 22 countries are in principle included: Australia, Austria, Belgium, Canada, Denmark, Finland, France, Germany, Ireland, Israel, Italy, Japan, the Netherlands, Singapore, South Korea, New Zealand, Norway, Spain, Sweden, Switzerland, the United Kingdom and the United States. With the exception of Singapore (for which data tend to be limited), all are members of the Organisation of Economic Cooperation and Development (OECD). Excluded on the practical grounds of size are countries with very small populations such as Iceland and Luxembourg.

pandemics will play only a secondary role in this. More important will be the impact on spending of the rapid expansion of the technological capabilities of medicine.

Very large long term increases in government spending will pose a major problem for future governments and for all mainstream poles of political opinion.

On the one hand, those who are staunchly opposed to bigger government will face a conundrum. To be credible, they will be compelled to propose substantial reductions in the scope of government – such as far-reaching reductions in eligibility for income support or in the coverage of health services – merely to prevent government growing bigger. Vacuous claims about the scope to contain spending merely by cutting waste will not be sufficient.

Those at the other end of the ideological spectrum will not have it any easier. The financing challenge created by the external forces and pressure points identified in this book will be formidable, even before considering the additional costs of expansions in the scope of government favored by many progressives, such as the introduction of a universal basic income or free tertiary education. It is an illusion to think that, as certain snake oil peddlers suggest, very large increases in public spending can be financed by borrowing most of what is required or by simply printing money. But raising taxes is politically difficult, and is *extremely* difficult in those nations, such as France and the Scandinavian countries, where taxes are already high.

Political conflict over the level of government spending will intensify. Because of the coronavirus pandemic, this will happen much earlier than would otherwise have been the case. Government spending has surged in response to the economic crisis induced by the pandemic. As soon as the world economy starts to recover, political swords will be drawn in a battle over whether expenditure should be cut back to pre-crisis levels or should instead remain permanently higher in order to give governments greater scope to meet the needs and challenges of the future.

This book does not enter, for the most part, into debates about the appropriate role or scope of government. It is not concerned with questions such as whether certain countries should, on moral or pragmatic grounds, adopt a more or less generous approach to the relief of poverty. Even though the analysis pays particular attention to the future of health expenditure, it does not address controversies concerning the expansion of coverage of health services, such as whether the US should move to universal health coverage or whether universal dental care should be introduced in countries such as Australia and Switzerland. Debates about these questions are important for the future of government and are central to democratic politics. But they are not the focus of this book. The analysis which follows is, instead, concerned with forces that will impact government spending independently of philosophical preferences about the scope of the welfare state or about the appropriate role of government more generally.

Our analysis of future spending trends takes a close look at certain "usual suspects" that many consider to be pushing advanced countries in the direction of increased public spending. One of these is mass technological unemployment, which some claim will force governments to spend much more on income support for a large body of permanently unemployed or precariously employed citizens. Another is the *cost disease* – a long-time favorite of many economists – which supposedly continually forces up the cost of many government services.

Also examined are certain forces that might work in the opposite direction to relieve pressure on government spending. One of these is potential savings from the aggressive adoption of new-generation digital technologies. There are optimists who consider that artificial intelligence, robots and other related technologies are capable of delivering such enormous reductions in the costs of providing health and other government services that budgetary pressures on governments will be contained or even reversed. They are wrong, and we will discuss why.

Quite a large part of this book is about health. This is for two reasons. One is that there are multiple competing theories about the drivers of health spending, and there is no way of properly understanding long-term expenditure trends without first assessing the validity of each of these theories. The other is that, as mentioned above, the analysis suggests that health will be the largest area of long-term growth in spending.

The structure of the book is as follows:

Chapters 1 to 7 examine the long-term dynamics of expenditure in the main relevant areas. Background to this analysis is provided in Chapter 1, which outlines past trends in public expenditure and the pressures on government budgets in recent decades. The following two chapters focus on health expenditure, starting (in Chapter 2) with an analysis of the dynamics that have driven spending growth in the past, and then moving on to what the future holds (Chapter 3). Chapter 4 focuses primarily on long-term care and pension expenditure, where population aging is the key external force at work. Chapter 5 analyzes the spending implications of the challenge of global warming. The pressure on governments in many countries to deal with accumulated infrastructure deficits is the subject of Chapter 6. In Chapter 7 we ask whether there might be another major external force that needs to be taken into account – concretely, whether technological change and a mutating labor market are likely to compel government to greatly increase income support expenditure.

Chapters 8 to 10 focus on the potential responses to the long-term expenditure pressures which have been identified. The first issue addressed, in Chapter 8, is whether increased taxes might be avoided by using borrowing and/or money creation by central banks. Chapter 9 looks at the potential to mitigate the spending pressure by making efficiency savings – that is, expenditure reductions which "trim the fat" without affecting the range and scope of services provided by the state. This sets the scene for discussion, in Chapter 10, of the most fundamental decision which governments will be obliged to make over the long-term: how far are they willing and able to reduce future tax increases by making "compensatory" expenditure cuts which scale back the services and benefits which they deliver to citizens.

Note: Government Expenditure

"Government expenditure" in this book refers to expenditure undertaken by what is known in public finance statistics as "general government" (IMF, 2014: 18). General government is the public sector excluding public enterprises and government banks. Expressed differently, general government is that part of the public sector financed mainly by taxes and other compulsory charges and levies. (By contrast, public enterprises are in large measure financed by sales revenue.) General government includes social security funds.

Although much government expenditure is authorized through government budgets, a considerable portion is outside the budget ("off-budget" spending). This includes, in many advanced countries, most social security spending. Whether or not government expenditure is included in the government's budget is irrelevant to the analysis in this book. Any references to, for example, pressures on government budgets is only shorthand – the analysis does not assign any significance to the distinction between on-budget and off-budget government expenditure. Similarly, references to budget deficits or surpluses should be taken to refer to the general government budget balance.

General government expenditure encompasses the combined expenditure of all levels of government. This book does not address the manner in which spending pressures will affect different levels of government. This is not a matter about which it is possible to generalize, because the assignment of expenditure responsibilities between national and sub-national governments differs so much between countries. In some countries, for example, health is an exclusively national government responsibility, while in others, states or regions carry much of the burden. For this reason, in this book we focus on government as a whole, all levels combined.

Government finance statistics inevitably raise questions of accounting choices. Debt, for example, can be measured in multiple ways, including gross debt, net debt and net financial worth. There are also a number of different measures of expenditure. This book essentially avoids discussions of such accounting issues, which can rapidly become boring without shedding much extra light on the issues at hand. The measures of expenditure which are used in the statistics cited are generally either conceptually the same, or very close. The precise accounting definitions may be obtained by referring to the data sources.

1. BIG SPENDERS OR MISERS?

The coronavirus pandemic and consequent economic crisis led to a massive surge in government spending in advanced economies from 2020. Governments and central banks took exceptionally aggressive action to counter economic fallout from what several world leaders dubbed the "hidden enemy." In the United States, Congress quickly approved a $2 trillion relief plan. Even governments as renowned for their hostility to fiscal profligacy as Germany opened their purse strings wide. "Whatever it costs" became the slogan on everyone's lips.

As this shows, it is sometimes possible – when faced with a sufficiently grave crisis – to obtain broad political agreement on the need for governments to spend generously to limit the damage and subsequently expedite the recovery process. This is as it should be. In the face of a severe downward economic spiral, only government is in a position to spend to support citizens who have lost their livelihoods, prevent aggregate demand from collapsing and forestall widespread business bankruptcies.

Any such consensus on the need for higher spending cannot, however, be expected to last long. Outside crisis conditions, there are few political issues more contentious than the size of government. A deep gulf separates those who believe that government spends far too much from those who believe that it spends too little. Even if temporarily bridged in times of severe crisis, this gulf invariably reopens quickly as soon as conditions start to normalize.

Disaccord on government spending has been particularly pronounced in recent years. On one side of the debate are those who believe that years of cuts to spending – "austerity" as they often label it – have had disastrous consequences across the board, including:

◆ An erosion of healthcare quality and access, whether through long waiting times (e.g. the UK), shortages of essential pharmaceuticals (e.g. France), or the refusal of public health authorities to pay for expensive but highly effective new drugs (many countries);

◆ Dilapidated and inadequate transport and other public infrastructure (e.g. Germany, France, the UK and the United States);

◆ A crisis in access to social care which has left increasing numbers of very elderly citizens – together with many of the disabled – without essential residential care services or necessary domestic support;

◆ Growing difficulties in recruiting essential categories of public sector workers as a result of uncompetitive pay and conditions – especially for nurses and other health sector workers (e.g. France, Denmark and the UK);

◆ Loss of military capacity to resist aggression as a result of years of contraction of the budgets of the armed forces in many countries (e.g. Germany).

To the anti-austerity camp, the need for a substantial boost to government spending was clear well before the coronavirus pandemic shone a spotlight on the deficiencies of public health services. For this camp, spending "whatever it costs" is more than a slogan for the short term. Its members believe that governments must in coming years spend what is needed to properly tackle the fundamental challenges facing society today – such as climate change – while brushing aside obstruction from small-minded "bean-counters".

To those on the other side of the public expenditure debate, the proposition that crisis spending should be other than strictly temporary is shockingly misguided. They consider that it will be essential that, when societies and economies are back on the path to recovery, government expenditure is brought back to – or below – pre-crisis levels. Unsustainable levels of government debt will, they believe, make this imperative.

It is easy to understand their reasoning. Governments will unquestionably incur considerable additional debt in fighting the impact of the coronavirus pandemic. For the very few advanced countries with low pre-pandemic levels of government debt, this may be unproblematic. But governments in most advanced economies went into the coronavirus pandemic with debt levels that were already very high, and which had increased greatly over the preceding decades. In the United States, for example, federal government debt exceeded $23 trillion in 2019. With the debt of state and local governments added, this represented more than $67,000 for every resident of the country. In Japan, per capita government debt was even higher, at $93,000. The same broad story applied elsewhere, as the examples in Figure 1.1 show. While the appropriateness of the particular measures of debt used in these comparisons may be debated,[1] there is no arguing that pre-coronavirus pandemic debt levels in most advanced countries were – barring war conditions – unprecedented.

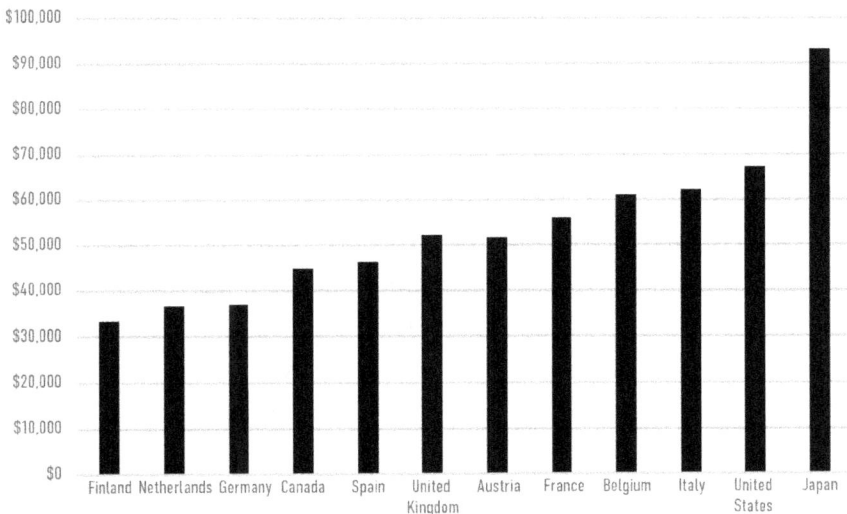

Source: OECD.Stat (Figure for Japan is 2017)

Figure 1.1
Gross Government Debt Per Capita: Selected Advanced Nations (2018)
US Dollars (Purchasing Power Parity Basis)

Viewed from this perspective, it seems clear that large *permanent* increases in government expenditure in the aftermath of the coronavirus pandemic would put many countries on a sure road to ruin. This suggests that, once normality returns, the focus should be on reducing debt by reducing spending.

Fear of debt-fueled economic ruin is not the only source of deep opposition to bigger government. There is also the widely held notion that big government undermines economic growth and living standards. Many conservative economists consider that there is a direct trade-off between the size of government and GDP (Lucas, 2003). There is even economic literature purporting to numerically estimate the "optimal" size of government in each country – which invariably turns out, in these calculations, to be well below current levels.[2]

When the world eventually starts to emerge from the pandemic-induced crisis, the debate on the appropriate size of government will be back with a vengeance. Progressives will push for permanently higher spending, arguing that the time has come to address crucial social, environmental and economic challenges. They will be vigorously opposed by a coalition comprising, on the one hand, political conservatives committed to smaller government as a matter of principle and, on the other hand, those whose fear of debt leads them to call for the rapid withdrawal of stimulus spending. In the United States, a clear precedent for such a coalition can be seen in the recommendations on government spending made in the wake of the 2007-2008 global financial crisis (GFC) by the Simpson-Bowles Commission, a bipartisan commission on deficit reduction established in 2010 by President Obama. Even though the American economy was at the time still in severe recession, the Commission recommended prompt efforts to bring back federal government expenditure to 21 percent of GDP and to then keep it *permanently* below that level.

The debate on appropriate long-term levels of government expenditure in advanced economies is one rooted, in the final analysis, in profound differences in values and ideology. However, while values matter, so do facts and analysis. This is where this book aims to make a contribution. Its simple premise is that it is impossible to meaningfully debate the appropriate size of government without first carefully analyzing the external forces and pressure points that bear upon government budgets over the long term. Expressed differently, trends in government expenditure are not only the consequence of political choices about how expansive or limited the role of government should be, but also the result of a range of forces that are beyond the control of politicians but which have huge impacts on government budgets.

It is, however, not possible to properly analyze the future without first understanding the past. With this in mind, this chapter sets the scene by reviewing the long-term evolution of government expenditure in advanced countries prior to the pandemic-induced economic crisis of 2020.[3]

◆ ◆ ◆

Government expenditure has over the long term grown enormously everywhere. In the United Kingdom, for example, total government spending as a proportion of GDP almost tripled over the 20th century (Clark and Dilnot, 2002). In the United States, a similar expansion in the expenditure of all levels of government took place between 1930 and 2012 (Schuyler, 2014). The same story, with variations in timing, played out everywhere else.

Looking specifically at the period from the end of World War II to the present, we can identify three broad phases: the expansion phase, the retrenchment phase and the phase "between the two crises" – where the latter refers to the period starting with the recession induced by the 2007-2008 global financial crisis (GFC) and continuing up to the pandemic-induced crisis of 2020.

The Expansion Phase

In the decades following World War II, government expenditure grew greatly in all advanced countries.[4] This was driven principally by the extension of the modern welfare state, which brought greatly expanded levels of social protection and health coverage, and better public education.

If we look at total government *non-interest* expenditure, which provides the best perspective on underlying spending trends during this period,[5] we see that in the great majority of countries the expansion phase culminated with a spending peak at some point in the 1980s or 1990s (see Figure S1.1 and Figure S1.2 in the statistical annex).[6] In Germany, for example, spending grew from 27 percent of GDP in 1950 to a peak of 51 percent in 1995. In Ireland, it increased from 25 percent to a peak of 48 percent (1982), and in New Zealand it grew from 20 percent to 38 percent (1991). The United Kingdom and Ireland peaked earliest, in the early 1980s. In most other countries, the peak occurred in the subsequent decade.[7]

The United States was different. There, the expansion phase came in the late 1950s and 1960s, when the limited American version of the welfare state was created under presidents Kennedy and Johnson.[8] Following that burst of reforming energy, government expenditure was essentially stable from the 1970s right through to the GFC (see Figure S1.3, statistical annex).

The Retrenchment Phase

After expenditure peaked – at different times in different countries – advanced economies moved into the retrenchment phase, when the growth of government expenditure stopped everywhere.[9] In most countries, this phase in fact brought a sustained post-peak decline in spending. In countries such as the UK, Netherlands, Finland and Sweden, the decline was cumulatively large. (In the Netherlands, for example, non-interest expenditure/GDP fell from an average of 52 percent in the 1980s to 46 percent in the 1990s.) In other cases – including Austria and Spain – spending fell more modestly.[10]

In a mere handful of countries – Australia, France and the United States – expenditure remained essentially stable rather than falling.[11]

The retrenchment phase was first and foremost a reaction to the emergence of a major debt problem. From the mid-1970s, government debt increased rapidly in a large majority of advanced countries, including the US and most of Europe.[12] It kept increasing, in most cases, for the best part of two decades. In the US, gross government debt grew from 41 percent of GDP in 1974 to 72 percent in 1993. Much larger increases occurred elsewhere: in Belgium, for example, debt escalated from 54 percent in 1974 to 134 percent in 1992. As debt burgeoned, governments felt a growing need to tackle the problem with deficit-reducing expenditure and revenue measures. Even the very few countries that did not experience explosions in public debt – such as Australia – took fright and implemented preemptive measures to ensure it would not happen (in Australia's case, a rule setting a ceiling on expenditure as a proportion of GDP).

Why did debt shoot up? Budget imbalances were an important part of the problem. In many countries, taxes had not increased sufficiently during the expansion phase to fully cover the increased spending – something that was not always obvious at the time because government revenues were abnormally buoyant during the decades of post-war boom. Then came the global recession of the mid-1970s, which ushered in several decades of slow growth and weak revenue. Additional damage was inflicted by a large rise in the interest rates[13] governments were obliged to pay on their debt. With the world in the grip of "stagflation" – a toxic combination of recession and high levels of inflation – central banks restricted the growth of the money supply and forced interest rates up to kill inflation.

Other more specific factors also contributed to the debt problem in particular countries, such as the big surge in spending the German government was obliged to undertake after reunification in 1990.

Phase Three: Between the Two Crises

During the third phase, which stretched from 2008 to the beginning of 2020, government expenditure *in underlying terms* remained – in all but a handful of countries – significantly below the peak attained during the expansion phase. It was essentially stable in many countries and increased somewhat in others.

The words "in underlying terms" are crucial here. The GFC triggered a worldwide recession, the full fury of which was felt in 2008-2009, and from which advanced countries subsequently made only slow – and in some cases incomplete – recoveries in the years before they were once again knocked flat by the coronavirus pandemic. The GFC-induced recession led to large *temporary* increases in government expenditure. These took the form partly of the automatic increases in unemployment benefits and certain other types of expenditure which always occur during recessions. To this was added substantial deliberate stimulus expenditure as well as – in the few countries which counted this in their official government expenditure statistics – the costs of government bailouts of banks.[14]

This temporary spending did not, for the most part, constitute a broad permanent shift to bigger government. What was going on below the surface during this third phase can be seen when we look at *underlying* spending – in other words, at what was happening setting aside temporary recession-linked expenditure. A simple way of doing this is to compare government spending levels[15] in 2007, just before government budgets were impacted by the GFC, with those of a decade later, when economies had more or less recovered (see Appendix 1.1).[16] When we do this we see that, with the exceptions of Ireland and Israel, advanced countries divide more or less evenly into two groups: those where underlying spending levels changed little (see examples in Figure 1.2) and those where there was some increase in underlying expenditure (examples in Figure 1.3).[17]

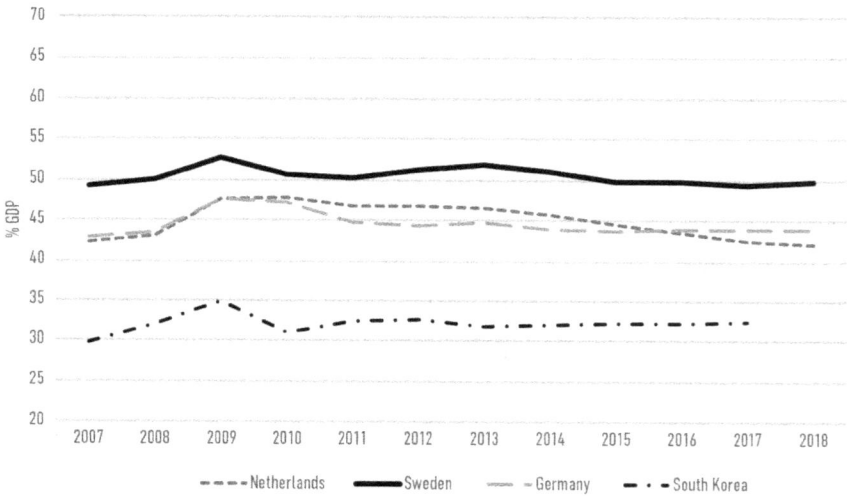

Source: OECD.Stat

Figure 1.2
Government Expenditure/GDP Before and After the GFC (A)

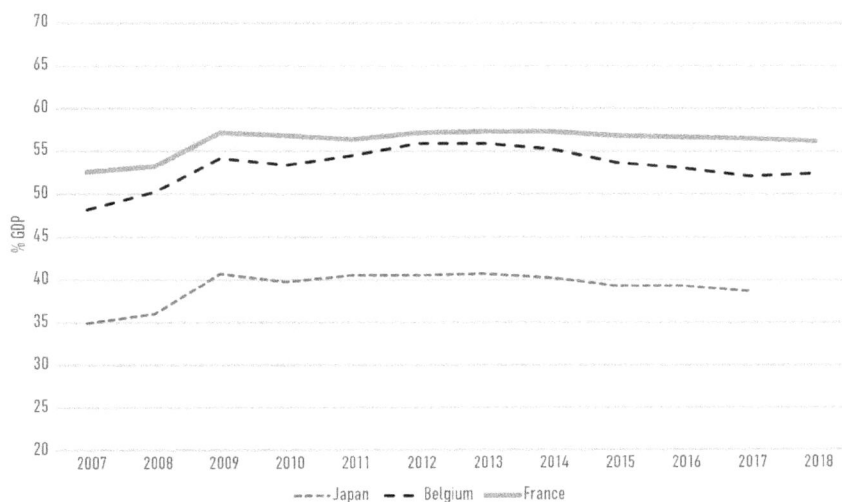

Source: OECD.Stat

Figure 1.3
Government Expenditure/GDP Before and After the GFC (B)

Data from the same source show that even in those countries where spending increased, it remained in almost all cases lower – and in many cases considerably lower – than at its historic peak back in the pre-GFC era. France, where spending at the end of this third phase exceeded the previous peak in the 1990s, is one of the rare exceptions. Another exception is the United States, where spending remained at broadly the same (relatively low) level it had been for many decades (Figure S1.4, statistical annex).

As mentioned above, there are two countries – Ireland and Israel – where spending levels prior to the pandemic-induced crisis were significantly lower than they had been immediately before the GFC. In Ireland they were *much* lower. The Emerald Isle was one of the countries that had suffered most as a consequence of the harsh austerity treatment meted out by the European Commission (with the acquiescence of the IMF) to member nations receiving international bailouts. The spending cuts it was obliged to implement as a condition for assistance were deep indeed.

The GFC brought with it a very large and rapid increase in debt levels in the majority of advanced countries. A good part of this additional debt had nothing to do with government expenditure but represented the high cost of government bailouts of banks and major enterprises (such as the auto industry bailouts in the United States between 2008 and 2014). In the US, government debt was in 2011 54-70 percent higher (depending on which measure of debt you use) than it had been immediately before the GFC. By 2014, it was 62-79 percent higher. In the UK, the increases were even bigger: 102-128 percent by 2011 and 121-162 percent by 2014. Debt increases in France were more "modest," at 35-58 percent and 56-128 percent respectively.[18]

In this bleak situation, there was one big positive factor: the dramatic fall in interest rates. This had the effect, approximately speaking, of preventing the burden of interest payments from rising, despite the big increase in debt. Governments were thereby saved from a repeat of the problem they had confronted from the mid-1970s, when the impact of the increasing debt was amplified by sharply rising interest rates.

International Differences in Government Expenditure

Notwithstanding the universally large long-term growth in government expenditure, advanced countries differ greatly in their levels of total government expenditure, as can be best seen by looking at recent pre-crisis levels (Figure 1.4).

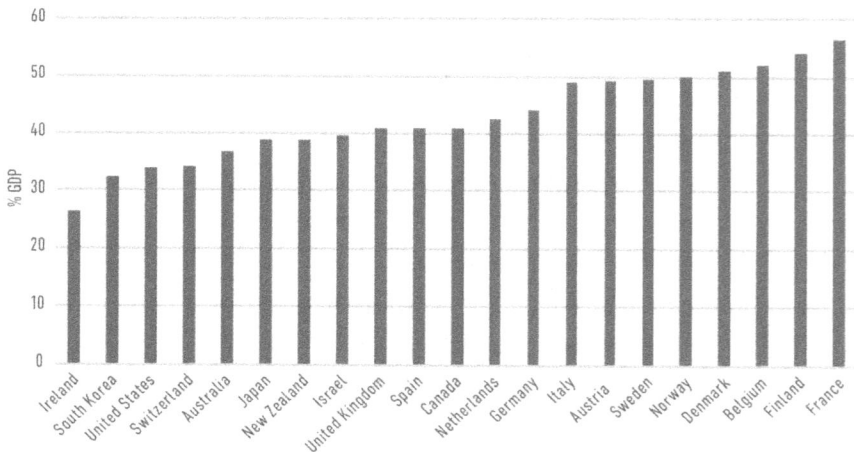

Source: OECD.Stat: US figure from Bureau of Economic Analysis.

Figure 1.4
Government Expenditure/GDP (2017)

The main explanation of the differences between nations is the scope of their respective welfare states. Retirement income is in some countries mainly paid by the government, where in others private pension schemes and savings play a big role alongside public pensions. Pensions and unemployment benefits are in certain countries income-based (i.e. you get more in old age if your income was higher during your working life), whereas elsewhere the general principle is that these and other welfare payments are paid at a standard "safety net" rate. The role of the state in healthcare provision also varies considerably: even though almost all advanced countries have systems of universal health coverage, there are differences in the extent to which the state finances that coverage.

At one end of the spectrum are countries such as the United States and South Korea that have never constructed complete modern welfare states like those elsewhere. In the land of the stars and stripes, welfare benefits are limited and particularly ungenerous, universal health coverage does not exist and public education is often particularly poor. South Korea, which has made an impressively rapid transition from developing country to advanced status, still has an under-developed social protection system that has, notoriously, left large numbers of its elderly citizens in dire poverty. Ireland's present particularly low level of government expenditure reflects the scale of the cuts to spending inflicted under the country's bailout program.

At the other end of the spectrum are the most comprehensive welfare states, of which the Netherlands, Denmark and Sweden are examples. Welfare benefits are generous and comprehensive, and include substantial child allowances to families. Poverty rates are correspondingly low. Childcare is either free or heavily government-subsidized. Education is free right up to and including university level, where students can also receive living expenses. Taxes are high, but so are government services and benefits.

International comparisons of spending are, however, fraught with traps. For example, the relatively low figures for Australia and Switzerland are misleading because, in each, certain elements of the welfare state are financed through systems of compulsory contributions that do not count as government expenditure.[19]

Budgets Under Pressure

Since the end of the post-war expansion phase, budgeting has been tough for governments in all advanced countries. Spending cuts made during the retrenchment phase were far from easy and expenditure policy decisions remained exceedingly difficult. Budgets continued to be under considerable strain during the subsequent phase between the two crises.

Why has money been so tight? Much of the explanation is that there have, throughout, been two major sources of expenditure pressure making life miserable for those charged with putting together budgets.

The first of these has been health. Health expenditure, which represents a large part of government budgets, has grown consistently and substantially virtually everywhere in the advanced world (see Figure 1.5).

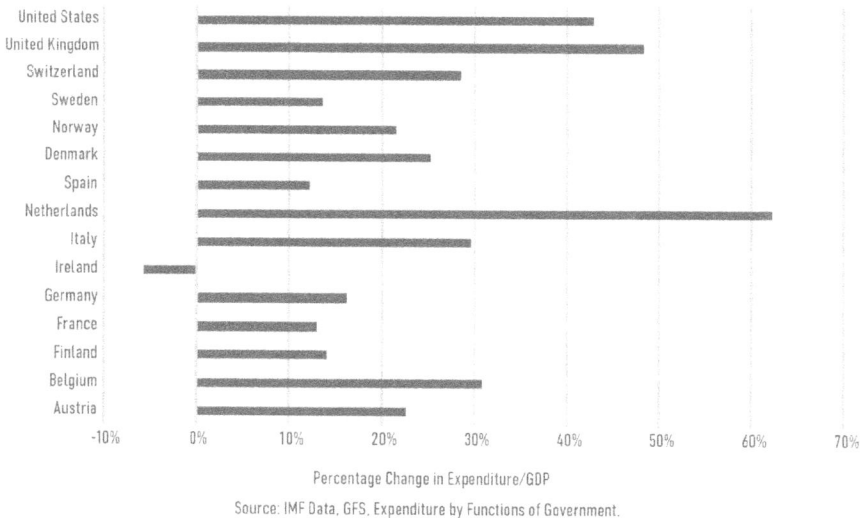

Percentage Change in Expenditure/GDP

Source: IMF Data, GFS, Expenditure by Functions of Government.

Figure 1.5
Change in Government Health Expenditure (1995-2018)
Percentage Change in Expenditure/GDP

(The sole exception[20] to this has been Ireland, where health spending was cut along with everything else during the bailout period following the GFC. Ireland is, in a sense, an exception that proves the rule, because the cuts made to health expenditure in Ireland were tiny relative to those made to other areas of government expenditure – see below).

The other area of pressure was old-age pensions, where expenditure has also grown greatly in a large majority of advanced countries. Figure 1.6 tells the story.[21]

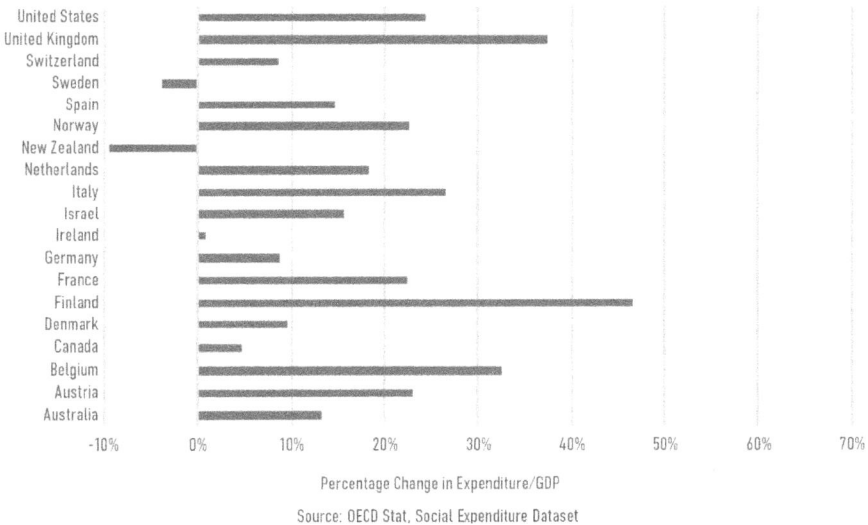

Percentage Change in Expenditure/GDP

Source: OECD Stat, Social Expenditure Dataset

Figure 1.6
Change in Government Age Pension Expenditure (1995-2015)
Percentage Change in Expenditure/GDP

Ballooning health and pension expenditure have put such intense pressure on government budgets as to prompt large reductions in expenditure elsewhere. This is highlighted in Figure 1.7, which shows what happened to spending outside the areas of health and social protection (of which age pension expenditure is part) over the past two decades (Figure 1.7).[22]

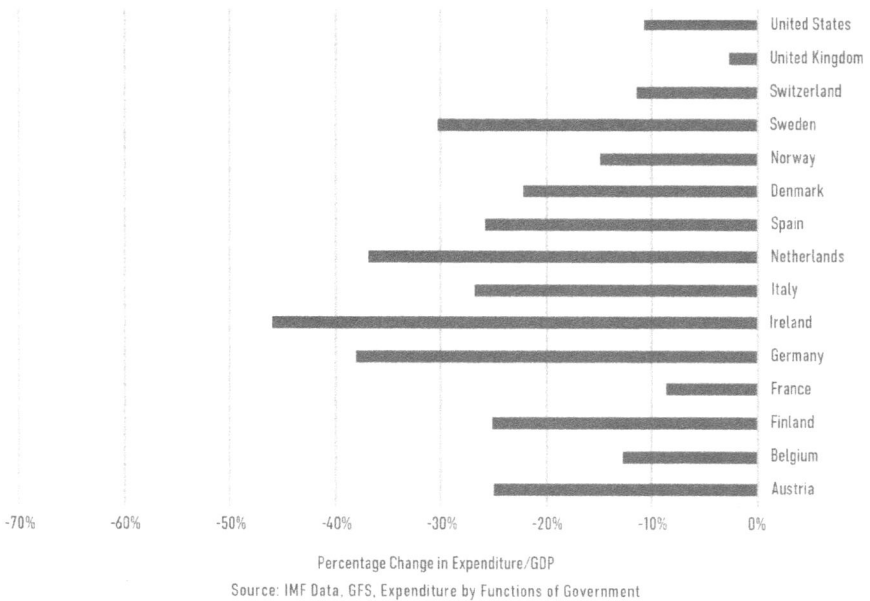

-70%   -60%   -50%   -40%   -30%   -20%   -10%   0%

Percentage Change in Expenditure/GDP
Source: IMF Data, GFS, Expenditure by Functions of Government

Figure 1.7
Change in Total Government Expenditure ex Health and Social Protection (1995-2018)
Percentage Change in Expenditure/GDP

If we were to peer into this aggregate data, we would see that most categories of government expenditure – including education, housing, economic affairs and general public services – have been significantly squeezed. Defense expenditure has also been cut considerably almost everywhere.

In only a couple of notable areas – the environment, and public order and safety – has spending increased over this time period in a substantial number (approximately half) of advanced countries.

Social protection has not gone untouched. To the contrary, welfare benefits have been pared back in most countries. Many governments have reduced access to, and levels of, unemployment benefits. Disability benefits, including those paid under occupational injury schemes, have also been scaled back, in some cases through tougher medical tests. Governments have not sat passively while pension spending has shot up. Rather, they have sought to dampen the pressure by raising the retirement age and reducing pension levels – although often through reforms with delayed impact.

The net result is that, within total social protection expenditure, spending on the non-elderly has tended to fall markedly. Spending on the elderly has generally increased, because big increases in the elderly population have outweighed reductions in pension and other benefits (see Figure S1.5 in the statistical annex).

Sweden was mentioned above as one of the countries with the most generous modern welfare states. But in Sweden also there have been significant cuts to the welfare state. In that country, the retrenchment phase – ushered in by a severe economic crisis in the early 1990s – saw deep cuts to welfare spending. Measures taken included the introduction of patient contributions for medical treatments, the reduction of benefits paid under the country's sickness insurance system and the replacement of the defined benefits pension system with a defined contribution system. Further scaling back of welfare benefits has occurred since that time, including further significant cuts to sickness benefits during the 2000s. While Swedish welfare expenditure may be well above the advanced country average today, it is considerably lower than it was at the end of the 1980s.

Reforms to unemployment insurance in France in 2019 provide another example. France is one of the countries where unemployment benefits are paid for an initial period of unemployment at a high proportion of previous earnings, before being reduced to a lower "safety net" level. In these reforms, the duration of the initial period was reduced markedly, such that benefits are now cut to safety net levels after six months of unemployment. France was, in this respect, following what Germany did in 2005, as part of a series of so-called Hartz reforms to labor market and welfare policies. These reforms were driven by labor market policy as well as budgetary considerations.

Despite the large long-term growth in health expenditure, health services have been under intense pressure in many countries. In response to acute financial pressure, public hospitals in many advanced countries have drastically reduced average patient stays, squeezed pay, cut back on equipment and supplies, and deferred maintenance. Britain's National Health

Service has been in a state of rolling crisis for years, with long waiting lists, decaying hospital infrastructure and an inability to fill many staff positions because of poor pay and working conditions (Atkins et al, 2019). In France also, it is no exaggeration to say that the hospital system has been in crisis in recent years. Many major hospitals have been chronically overloaded, with patient numbers vastly in excess of capacity and patients frequently waiting for hours on stretchers in corridors. The system was in 2018-2019 hit by a wave of departures of staff doctors, disillusioned with the lack of resources, extreme pressure of their working days and the chronic lack of adequate time to meet the needs of individual patients. Professional burnout was said to be endemic.[23]

Even in Denmark's supposed welfare paradise, the hospital system has been under intense strain. A severe shortage of nurses and other professional staff, driven partly by poor pay and partly by "rationalization," has forced hospitals to take extreme measures such as sending mothers home a couple of hours after giving birth and drastically shortening hospital stays after major operations.[24]

This was the fragile state in which public health systems found themselves in many advanced countries when, in 2020, the coronavirus pandemic hit the advanced world. It is unquestionably the case that acute budgetary pressure was one significant factor behind the poor state of readiness of most countries to face a perfectly predictable infectious disease pandemic (see Chapter 3).

Health is not the only area where many governments have made spending cuts that are manifestly unsustainable over the longer term. Capital expenditure, including spending on vital infrastructure, has been another (see Chapter 6). Nurses and doctors are, moreover, not the only public sector workers who have seen their pay either fall in real terms or lag behind community standards. Among the other victims have been academic staff in public universities.

On the political far left, all of this has been continually denounced as a deliberate assault on the welfare state by governments supposedly dominated by "neoliberal" ideology, and whose agenda is to downsize the state. This is, at least in most countries, a wild exaggeration. If we add together the three main categories of welfare state expenditure – education, health and social protection – expenditure is higher today in a majority of advanced countries than it was two decades ago, and is *substantially* lower in only a couple (see Figure 1.8). The most important development has not been the reduction of total welfare state spending but, rather, reallocation *within* welfare state spending. Money has been shifted from many areas of welfare spending in order to fund the increased spending on health and age pensions.

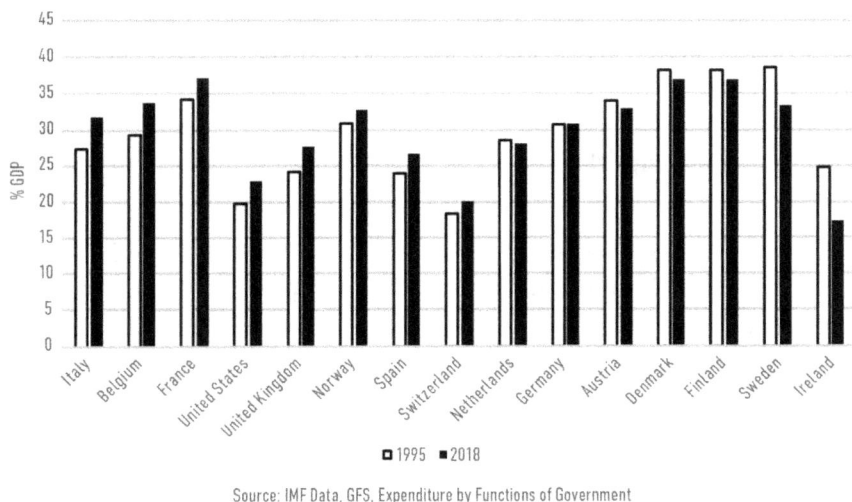

□ 1995 ■ 2018

Source: IMF Data, GFS, Expenditure by Functions of Government

Figure 1.8
"Welfare State" Expenditure/GDP (1995 vs 2018)
Sum of Education, Health and Social Protection Expenditure/GDP

In much of the advanced world, and particularly in continental Europe, there is a strong political consensus around – and deep community support for – the fundamental principles of the welfare state. Any political force seriously attempting to dismantle the structure of government education, health care and social protection would – except, perhaps, in the United States – do so at its peril. Nevertheless, the welfare state is under intense pressure today, first and foremost because of the pressure of health and pension spending.

What explains the financial stress that much of government has experienced in recent decades, and what does it mean for the future? There is no mystery behind the pressure of sharply increased age pension expenditure, which is mainly due to population aging (see Chapter 4). But what about rising health expenditure? When criticized for the increasingly intolerable pressure on the public health system, governments often respond by pointing out that they have in fact substantially increased health spending over time. They are not wrong – health budgets have indeed increased considerably. The problem is that increases in government health expenditure have not kept up with the rising demand for health services. The question is why. Is it population aging? Or some other factor or combination of factors?

This raises other associated questions. For how much longer will it be possible to cope with these types of expenditure pressures by the means that have been employed in recent decades? For how much longer will it be possible to keep squeezing capital expenditure and the pay of nurses and others? How much more can conceivably be shaved off social protection expenditure without threatening the core principles of the welfare state?

To all of these questions must be added the issue of new sources of spending pressure – such as the fight against global warming and, potentially, more pressure on income support in the new economy.

All this can be summed up in one big question. Will it be possible to contain the growth of government expenditure in coming decades, or are we headed inexorably for a new expansion phase – an era of bigger government?

Appendix 1.1: Government Expenditure as a percentage of GDP during the Phase "Between the Two Crises" (2007–2018)

	2007	2008	2009	2010	2011	2012	2013	2014	2015	2016	2017	2018
Ireland	35.94	41.84	47.05	65.08	46.57	42.05	40.35	37.45	28.96	27.58	26.3	25.74
Israel	42.13	42.83	42.79	41.1	40.43	41.04	40.98	39.59	38.35	38.59	39.51	
Austria	49.24	49.87	54.14	52.84	50.9	51.21	51.65	52.43	51.14	50.27	49.17	48.49
Netherlands	42.34	43.11	47.58	47.86	46.79	46.75	46.52	45.74	44.61	43.58	42.5	42.16
United Kingdom	40.9	44.4	47.31	47.56	45.92	45.74	43.94	43.01	42.2	41.39	40.98	40.84
New Zealand	38.31	41.17	41.76	47.37	43.47	42.13	40.22	39.84	38.97	39.02	38.81	
United States	37.43	39.82	43.26	43.17	42.05	40.23	39.01	38.34	37.93	38.21	37.95	
Sweden	49.28	50.01	52.7	50.76	50.25	51.3	51.95	51.08	49.76	49.8	49.44	49.88
Germany	42.82	43.57	47.58	47.26	44.71	44.3	44.69	43.96	43.71	43.89	43.93	43.87
Italy	46.79	47.83	51.16	49.89	49.38	50.79	51.06	50.9	50.26	49.04	48.91	48.58
Denmark	49.59	50.41	56.54	56.67	56.43	57.95	55.82	55.22	54.53	52.66	51.16	51.41
Canada	39.34	39.59	44.28	43.9	42.38	41.72	40.91	39.16	40.83	41.35	41.02	41.32
Australia	34.67	36.99	38.37	36.93	37.2	36.33	36.6	36.73	37.42	36.74	36.71	
Spain	39.03	41.16	45.78	45.63	45.83	48.1	45.56	44.85	43.73	42.2	40.99	41.34
South Korea	29.67	32.01	34.88	31	32.35	32.73	31.76	31.98	32.3	32.26	32.44	
Switzerland	30.73	31.28	33.2	32.98	32.9	33.23	34.23	33.77	34.01	34.23	34.15	
France	52.57	53.3	57.15	56.88	56.29	57.11	57.23	57.21	56.8	56.73	56.46	56.13
Japan	35	36.07	40.69	39.74	40.64	40.61	40.76	40.2	39.33	39.26	38.74	
Belgium	48.25	50.28	54.15	53.34	54.52	55.87	55.83	55.27	53.73	53.09	52.13	52.38
Finland	46.8	48.26	54.76	54.75	54.38	56.2	57.5	58.11	57.04	55.92	54.19	53.14
Norway	41.42	40.19	46.06	44.94	43.76	42.89	43.97	45.79	48.8	50.77	49.94	48.69

Source: OECD.Stat (accessed 9 March 2020)

2. WHY HAS HEALTH SPENDING RISEN SO FAST?

Health has long been an area of great upward pressure on government spending. In many advanced economies, the ratio of government health expenditure to GDP has more than doubled since 1970.[1] The sharp rise has made health care the second biggest sector of government spending almost everywhere.

Underlying the dramatic increase has been the continual rise in total (government plus private) health expenditure. Across the advanced world, per capita total health expenditure has increased at a faster rate than per capita income, leading to huge increases in the proportion of GDP devoted to health (see Figure 2.1).

The rise in total health expenditure has also pushed up government health spending. Today, in the great majority of advanced economies, government accounts for 70 percent or more of health expenditure.[2] The figure is in excess of 80 percent in Germany, Sweden, the United Kingdom, Japan, Belgium and Denmark. Even in the US and South Korea, which are outliers in their relatively high degree of reliance on private financing, government is today responsible for around half of total health expenditure.[3] Over the past 50 years, the government share of overall health spending has increased substantially in many countries and has fallen almost nowhere.[4]

The widespread expectation that the trend of rising government health expenditure will continue has led to pervasive fears that the cost will be unsustainable. This belief makes it critical to the future of public finances

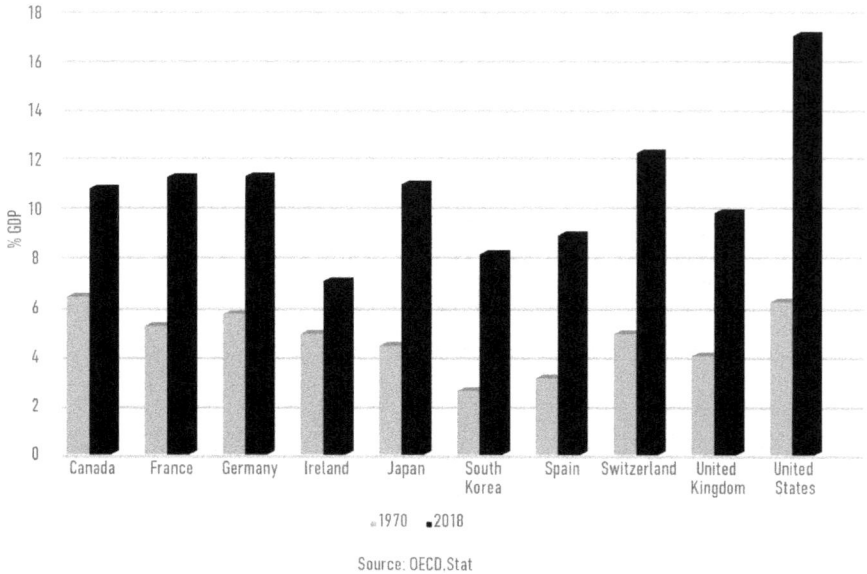

Figure 2.1
Total Health Expenditure/GDP: Selected High-Income Countries

to know whether health spending can indeed be expected to continue rising in coming decades.

Understanding future trends in health expenditure is impossible without properly understanding the past – in particular, without being clear about the forces at work over recent decades. With this in mind, this chapter looks at what has driven the long-term upward movement of health expenditure. The chapter provides the foundations for an explicit analysis, in the following chapter, of what the future holds.

To gain insight into the forces at work, we will look closely in this chapter at two overlapping areas in which total health expenditure has risen most: chronic conditions and pharmaceuticals. What emerges clearly is the dominant role of technological innovation – in particular, of the continual development of new treatments – in driving up spending. Technological innovation has increased health expenditure overall, although many innovations do indeed save money.

This chapter also discusses other factors that have contributed to the pressure on spending. One of these is population aging, the impact of which has been controversial.

In both this and the next chapter, the spotlight is on the forces at work across the developed world as a whole, as opposed to factors specific to individual countries. This is because the same fundamental forces have been at work everywhere, irrespective of the role of country-specific factors such as differences in the design of health systems (see Box 2.1).

Box 2.1 The Impact of Differences in the Design of National Health Care Systems

Differences in the design of national health systems are important in understanding why the level of health expenditure differs considerably between countries. Such differences largely explain, for example, why the United States manages to spend so much more of its national income on health than all other advanced countries (17.2 percent of GDP in 2017 versus around 10 percent on average elsewhere). The United States is the world leader in wasteful administrative costs, excessive medical practitioner remuneration, high pharmaceutical prices and medical over-servicing – and at the same time achieves appreciably worse health outcomes than most other advanced countries (Garber and Skinner, 2008; Anderson, Hussey and Petrosyan, 2019; Topol, 2015; Schneider et al, 2017; Papanicolas, Woskie and Jha, 2018; Mueller, Hagenaars and Morgan, 2017). This is the direct result of a health system that gives too much free play to the profit motive, with government playing too little of a regulating and coordinating role. If the United States were somehow able to radically restructure its health system to make it more like the systems that operate in much of Europe, overall health expenditure could ultimately be lower and health outcomes better. But such reform appears to be politically impossible.

Waste, overcharging and over-servicing are, of course, not confined to the United States. In every country in the world, government could make savings by improving the efficiency of health services – including, in some cases, by making structural reforms to the design of their health systems.[5] Flaws in the way health systems are designed and managed do not, however, explain the large long-term increase in health spending in all advanced countries, and it is not

the case that spending could have been stabilized merely through
better system design and greater efficiency. As Figure 2.1 shows,
even countries that have health systems with much stronger built-in
cost-containment mechanisms – such as France and the UK – have
seen massive long-term increases in spending. This tells us that
there are other, more fundamental forces which have been pushing
up health expenditure everywhere. It is these forces which are the
principal focus of our analysis.

Chronic Conditions

The treatment of chronic conditions has seen the largest increases in expenditure over recent decades.[6] There have been significant rises both in cost
per case and in the numbers of people suffering from diagnosed chronic
conditions (what is known as the *prevalence* of chronic conditions[7]).

Chronic condition prevalence today has reached levels far in excess of
anything witnessed previously. For example, in Australia in 2014-2015, an
estimated 50 percent of the population suffered from at least one of eight
major chronic conditions and approximately half of those suffered from at
least two conditions (AIHW, 2016). In France at that time, 35 percent of
the population was receiving ongoing treatment for one or more chronic
conditions (Assurance Maladie, 2016: 5).

Chronic conditions have become much more common.[8] Between 1990
and 2016, the prevalence of diabetes in high-income countries grew by 41
percent. For chronic kidney disease (CKD), prevalence grew 34 percent;
for osteoarthritis, 41 percent; and for dementia, 63 percent. For cancer,
incidence – which measures the numbers of *new* cases of a given condition
occurring during the year and which is for this category of disease a better
measure of trends[9] – increased 46 percent. Only for cardiovascular disease
(CVD) are the figures less shocking, with an 11 percent increase in prevalence (and a 3 percent growth in incidence).

"Multi-morbidity" – a descriptor for individuals who suffer from
two or more chronic conditions[10] – has also become much more widespread (Academy of Medical Sciences, 2018). In the United States, for
example, the RAND Corporation estimated that in 2014, 42 percent of

the population – equivalent to approximately two-thirds of persons with chronic conditions – was multi-morbid (Buttorff, Ruder and Bauman, 2017; AHRQ, 2010).

Not only are more people suffering from chronic conditions, but those affected require, on average, much more medical treatment than the rest of the population. The 35 percent of the French population mentioned above as receiving treatment for chronic conditions in 2014 accounted for 61 percent of the expenditure of the country's national health system (Assurance Maladie, 2016: 5). In England, approximately 70 percent of expenditure on health and long-term care in 2012 went on people suffering from chronic conditions (DOH, 2012). This is hardly surprising: the long duration of treatment received by many patients with chronic conditions comes at a high cost. The lifetime cost in the United States of medical treatment for a patient diagnosed with type 2 diabetes at the age of 40 has, for example, been estimated at $124,600 (Zhuo et al, 2014).

The considerable long-term increase in the prevalence and cost per case of treating chronic conditions has been mainly due to four key developments:

◆ A dramatic fall in quick deaths prior to old age;

◆ Marked increases in the average duration of treatment and (for that and other reasons) cost per case;

◆ Adverse lifestyle trends (mainly increased obesity);

◆ Population aging.

Technological innovation – in the form of the development of new and better medical treatments – has played a pivotal cross-cutting role in this story, contributing to all but the third of these. We discuss each of these developments in turn.

1. Fewer Premature Quick Deaths Means More Chronic Disease

Throughout history, most human beings died prematurely – i.e. prior to old age – from diseases that killed them quickly. Many died in childhood.

The so-called "conquest" of infectious diseases, largely accomplished between the end of the 19th century and the 1950s, ended this situation. From then on, many more people lived on to develop non-infectious diseases, increasingly of a chronic nature, in adulthood. Advances in medical treatments (in particular the development of vaccines and antibiotics) played a crucial role in this shift from infectious to non-infectious diseases. But so did major improvements in underlying health, particularly as a consequence of public health reforms (such as improved sanitation and food regulation) that greatly reduced exposure to infectious diseases.

Box 2.2 The Coronavirus Pandemic

References to the "conquest of infectious disease" may sound absurd in the light of the wave of deaths triggered by the coronavirus pandemic of 2019-2020. The pandemic is a grim reminder that the threat to humanity from infectious disease will never be completely eliminated – something which has implications for the future which will be considered in the next chapter. It nevertheless remains the case that the premature deaths from infectious disease have been, by historical standards, very uncommon in advanced countries over the past half-century, and that this will probably continue to be the case in the future.

In more recent times, however, falling rates of premature quick death from certain *non-infectious* diseases have been the main force increasing the number of people who live on to become chronic disease sufferers. Fewer people now die prematurely after short periods of illness from cardio-vascular disease (CVD) or cancer.

The fall in premature CVD mortality has been particularly striking. CVD remains, along with cancer, one of the top two causes of death. Today, however, CVD deaths are heavily concentrated amongst elderly people and have become far less common in the rest of the population, something that the "raw" CVD mortality statistics hide. Falling rates of premature CVD mortality become clear if one looks instead at the "age-standardized" mortality rate, which shows how mortality has evolved, setting aside changes in the age structure of the population (see Box 2.3). Measured in this way, there have been dramatic reductions in CVD mortality, particularly for heart attacks and strokes, in all advanced countries since it peaked (with variations in timing between country) in the period between 1950 and the early 1970s. For example, between 1979 and 2015, age-standardized CVD mortality fell by 76 percent in Australia,[11] 68 percent in France, 72 percent in Japan, 73 percent in the UK and 59 percent in the US.[12]

Box 2.3 Age-Standardized Measures

Age-standardized measures of mortality, prevalence and incidence adjust for (i.e. exclude) the impact of the increased percentage of elderly persons in the population by netting out that part of changes in these rates associated with changes in the population age structure. They do this by calculating what the relevant measure would be if the proportion of the population in each age bracket had remained unchanged over time, based on age-specific mortality, prevalence or incidence rates.

Behind these trends is the fact that far fewer people below the age of 65 are today having heart attacks, strokes and other CVD crises, and that, if they do, they are much less likely to die than before.[13] The huge reduction in premature CVD mortality has been due primarily to advances in medical treatment. Positive health-behavior changes, such as the large fall in the number of smokers,[14] have been important but appear to have made a lesser contribution (see Appendix 2.1). The quite extraordinary progress that medicine has made in this area is exemplified by advances in the treatment of ischemic heart disease (coronary artery disease). These advances include the development of preventative treatments (e.g. statins and antihypertensive drugs), radically improved acute treatments for patients actually suffering heart attacks or at imminent risk of doing so (e.g. thrombolytic drugs, coronary bypass procedures, angioplasty and stents) and treatments (mainly pharmaceutical) designed to minimize the risk of further crises (Weisfeldt and Zieman, 2007).

While less spectacular than the reduction in CVD mortality, premature quick death from cancer has also fallen significantly. The (age-standardized) cancer mortality rate in high-income countries as a whole fell substantially over the period 1990-2016 (by 20.5 percent), notwithstanding that incidence (again age-standardized) rose (by 7.4 percent).[15] Major advances in treatment methods are, once again, the main reason. Technological advances have led to large increases in the survival rates for common cancers such as melanoma, breast cancer, ovarian cancer and colon cancer.

This is not to deny the contribution of behavioral changes to reducing mortality. The impact of the decline of smoking in reducing the incidence of lung cancer has been particularly important because survival rates for this form of cancer have not, as yet, increased greatly.

As a result of these trends, many people who would in the past have died prematurely and quickly from CVD and cancer – or, in earlier times, from infectious diseases – are now living longer and developing, later in life, chronic conditions such as diabetes, dementia and CKD.[16]

2. Longer Duration, More Expensive Treatment of Chronic Condition Sufferers

In addition to these increases in the number of people developing chronic conditions, cost *per case* has risen because an increasing number of patients are receiving longer-term, often expensive, treatments for their conditions. Technological innovation has been the primary driver. Today, chronic conditions are commonly treated with pharmaceuticals, and innovation through new pharmaceuticals has played a major role in pushing costs up. This is particularly true of the treatment of cancer. In the US, for example, the prices of newly launched cancer drugs are estimated to have increased annually by 10 percent in real (post-inflation) terms between 1995 and 2013 (Howard et al, 2015).

The role of technological innovation in driving up pharmaceutical prices is discussed further below. But advances in medical technology have also had a big impact on health spending by extending the *duration* of treatment for chronic conditions. The development of better treatments has extended the life expectancy of sufferers of a number of conditions, as well as greatly improving their quality of life. However, it has often done so at the price of continuous lifetime medical treatment (see Box 2.4). Long-term preventative treatment for CVD is a case in point – as may be illustrated by the example of hypertension, which has become one of the most common chronic conditions in rich countries today. In France, for example, 18.6 percent of the population was being treated with antihypertensive medication in 2014 (Santé Publique, 2017: 258). In the same year, one-third of the US adult population suffered from diagnosed hypertension, and a large portion of those involved were taking antihypertensive medication on a continuing basis (NCHS, 2017). Hypertension was one of the four medical conditions for which spending grew most rapidly in the United States over the period 1996-2013 (Dielman, 2016: 2644).

Box 2.4 Longer Life Expectancy and Treatments for Chronic Diseases

There are many chronic diseases for which medical science has developed new and improved therapies that have considerably extended patient life expectancy, but which require ongoing long-term treatment. Type 1 diabetes is an example: with regular pharmaceutical treatment and careful management, life expectancy for sufferers of this condition has increased by decades (Miller et al, 2012; Livingstone et al, 2015).[17] In the case of HIV, whereas prior to the development of antiretrovirals patients could expect to live for 9-11 years after diagnosis, today, with ongoing treatment, they have an essentially normal life expectancy. Patients with severe CKD now live considerably longer, whether following transplants or whether treated by improved dialysis technology (Braun, 2012). US data show, for example, an increase in life expectancy for a representative 36-year-old man on hemodialysis of 4.3 years (to 11.5 years) over the period 1996-2013 (Neild, 2017). Medicine has also substantially increased the life expectancy of sufferers of a number of rare diseases such as cystic fibrosis (see below).

When medical technology prevents premature deaths from CVD and cancer and extends the life expectancy of people suffering from certain chronic conditions, it leads to an increase in the number of people who subsequently develop *other* chronic conditions. The increasing number of CVD survivors in the population is particularly important here, because long-term chronic CVD significantly increases the risk of developing other conditions such as CKD and dementia (AIHW, 2017).

Diabetes and HIV are also major contributing factors to CKD (Tucker et al, 2014). Diabetes frequently leads to CVD, and probably increases the risk of developing dementia. There is also some evidence to suggest that chemotherapy may hasten the onset of certain forms of dementia. This tendency of chronic conditions to breed other chronic conditions is a key reason for the increasing number of "multi-morbid" patients referred to above.

3.   Adverse Lifestyle Trends

The third factor driving up spending on chronic conditions has been obesity. The continuing increase in the numbers of obese people has been a major reason for the increase in the incidence and prevalence of type 2 diabetes (Eckel et al, 2011) and has significantly affected the prevalence of other chronic conditions such as CKD. The effect on health expenditure has already been substantial (Buchmueller and Meliyanni, 2015; Finkelstein et al, 2009; Thorpe, 2005).

In the United States, 40 percent of the population is today obese (Hales et al, 2017), as is approximately 16 percent of the population of European Union nations (Eurostat, 2016). In the period 1980-2008 alone, the percentage of obese people in the population is estimated to have doubled in Western Europe and increased almost threefold in the United States (Finucane, 2011). Almost everywhere in the advanced world, this trend continues. Obesity has probably already been a contributing factor to recent small declines in life expectancy in the United States (opioid abuse being the most important single factor).

The rise of obesity, associated with poor nutrition and insufficient exercise, means that it is no longer true that health behavior trends are on the whole positive, as was the case in the 1970s and 1980s. This has implications for the future prevalence of chronic disease and for health expenditure.

4.   Population Aging and the Rise of Chronic Conditions

Population aging – the progressive increase in the percentage of elderly and very elderly people in the population – has also contributed to the wave of chronic conditions affecting modern societies. Elderly people are more likely to suffer from these conditions than are younger people. The incidence of diabetes among the 70-plus age group in high-income countries is, for example, twice that for people in the 15-49 age group.[18] Multi-morbidity is particularly common amongst the elderly. Age-standardized measures of trends in the incidence/prevalence of chronic conditions make the association with population aging clear (see Box 2.5).

Box 2.5 Trends in Age-Standardized Prevalence/Incidence of Chronic Conditions

Percentage changes in the age-standardized prevalence/incidence of selected chronic conditions in high-income countries as a whole over the period 1990-2016 are as follows:

◆   CKD prevalence: -4.9 percent (as against +34 percent on an unstandardized basis).

◆   Diabetes prevalence: -1.9 percent (+41 percent).

◆   Osteoarthritis prevalence: +6.7 percent (+41 percent).

◆   Dementia prevalence: -0.6 percent (+63 percent).

◆   CVD incidence: -25.2 percent (+3 percent).

◆   CVD prevalence: -18.3 percent (+11 percent).

◆   Cancer incidence: +7.4 percent (+46 percent).

These statistics might be read as indicating that population aging has been the real cause of the increasing prevalence of chronic conditions, rather than technological innovation or other forces. But this would be the wrong way to look at the matter, because population aging has itself been, to a considerable extent, the consequence of technological innovation. The main force driving population aging has been, until relatively recently, increased *longevity* (see Box 2.6). The increase in longevity that has occurred since the end of World War II has been large and historically unprecedented, due in large measure to medical advances (Lichtenberg, 2017; Cutler, 2004; Bunker, 2001).

Particularly important has been the pivotal role of medicine in reducing CVD mortality (see above), because it is the reduction in premature CVD deaths that has been the single most important factor in boosting longevity (Chernew et al, 2016, Mathers et al, 2015; Klenk et al, 2016)[19]. Medical advances have also contributed to the increase in longevity in a range of other ways, including by extending the life expectancy of those suffering from a number of other chronic diseases. One intriguing and persuasive theory is that the earlier progress in drastically reducing deaths from infectious disease – to which, as we have seen, technological advances made a major contribution – contributed to the impressive post-war increase in longevity by boosting the percentage of genetically slower-aging people in the population.[20]

Box 2.6 Longevity

"Longevity" is used in this book to refer to average life expectancy in old age. One often-used measure of longevity is average remaining life expectancy at age 65. By contrast, "life expectancy," when the term is used without any qualifier, means average expected years of life *at birth*. Longevity is therefore not the same as life expectancy. Life expectancy may increase without any increase in longevity – for example, as a consequence of reduced child and infant mortality (as happened in the 19th and first half of the 20th centuries). Increased life expectancy therefore does not *necessarily* lead to population aging, whereas increased longevity does.

Population aging must, nevertheless, be acknowledged as having also played an independent role in the rising presence of chronic conditions, because the increase in the percentage of elderly and very elderly people in the population is not solely attributable to advances in medical technology. Increased longevity is also partly due to non-technological factors such as the decline of smoking. Longevity is, moreover, not the only force behind population aging. *Fertility-rate effects* have also contributed, even if their contribution has until relatively recently been less important than increased longevity. Fertility-rate effects refer to changes in the percentage of elderly persons in the population arising from past fluctuations in the number of children born to the average woman – at present, this means the delayed impact of the post-war baby boom and the subsequent major falls in fertility rates.

Some health analysts have in the past dismissed the association between population aging and chronic disease, based on what is known as the "compression of morbidity" theory. As originally formulated (Fries, 1980, 2011), this theory asserted that increased longevity had no impact on the prevalence of chronic conditions. This is because the increase in longevity over time was supposedly accompanied by a postponement of the average age at which serious chronic conditions started to develop. The theory was, in other words, that there has been a long-term trend for elderly people to become intrinsically healthier at any given chronological age.

The evidence suggests that this theory – which is discussed further in Appendix 2.4 – was valid in the past but ceased to be so by the later decades of the 20th century. A body of national studies suggests that there has in recent decades been no trend for people to develop chronic conditions at a progressively later stage of life.[21] Comprehensive data on chronic condition prevalence/incidence for high-income countries over the period 1990-2017 show the same thing.[22] Recent US research (Silberman et al, 2015) has even suggested that the onset of chronic conditions may start much earlier (at 45.5 years on average in their sample) than imagined by proponents of the compression of morbidity theory. All this means that dismissing the link between population aging and the rising prevalence of chronic conditions ceased to be a tenable position a long time ago.

The role of population aging as a force increasing health expenditure more generally is a question to which we will return toward the end of this chapter.

❖ ❖ ❖

Up to this point, we have focused principally on the reasons for the large increase in the prevalence of chronic conditions – that is, for the long-term increase in the percentage of the population suffering from, and being treated for, chronic conditions. The evidence indicates that multiple forces have been at work, with technological advances in medicine playing a particularly important role. The growing burden of chronic conditions on health expenditure is, however, not only due to increased prevalence. It also reflects rising costs per case due to the development of more expensive treatments. We now turn to the most important aspect of this – the rise in pharmaceutical prices.

Rising Pharmaceutical Prices and Expenditure

Increasing spending on pharmaceuticals is a major part of the story of rising health expenditure. "From the 1980s onwards," as the OECD has noted, "the growth and use of new drugs [has] resulted in rapidly increasing pharmaceutical spending" (Belloni et al, 2016).

The prices of some new pharmaceuticals are stunning. For example, Ravicti and Carbaglu (both of which prevent a build-up of nitrogen in the bloodstream) cost $793,632 and $585,408 respectively per patient per year in the United States (2016), while Lumizyme (which treats a progressive muscle weakness that can lead to heart and respiratory failure) costs $626,400 per patient year (AHIP, 2016). Immunization against human papilloma virus (HPV) with Gardasil (the first vaccine (2006) developed against this disease) costs around $570 in the US for the required three doses and £450 in the UK. The cost of immunizing large target populations with such expensive new vaccines is considerable.

Pharmaceutical companies – particularly the "big pharma" multinationals – attract bitter criticism for these high prices. There is no doubt that these companies seek, as profit-driven entities, to exploit the monopoly pricing power conferred by patents to the maximum extent they are able.[23] Prices are particularly high in countries, such as the US and Switzerland, where restraints on the pricing freedom of pharmaceutical companies are relatively weak. By contrast, in the increasing number of advanced countries where governments negotiate hard with pharmaceutical companies on the prices of new drugs before approving them, new drug prices – although generally not disclosed publicly – are often significantly lower.[24] Notwithstanding these price variations, the fact is that in most cases the prices of new pharmaceuticals are significantly higher everywhere than were the prices of typical traditional drugs when, decades back, they first came onto the market. This is because, whatever the role of price gouging might be, there are two fundamental underlying forces pushing up the prices of new pharmaceutical-based treatments.

Complexity and Rising Pharmaceutical Prices

The first of these forces is the increasing complexity of new product development. New complex-molecule "biologics" are orders of magnitude more difficult and expensive to develop than traditional chemically synthesized small-molecule pharmaceuticals (see Box 2.7). The majority of new drugs, and almost all new vaccines (such as Gardasil) are biologics. According to the McKinsey Global Institute (2014):

> Large-scale biotech [pharmaceutical] manufacturing facilities cost $200 million to $500 million or more to build, compared with similar-scale small-molecule facilities that may cost just $30 million to $100 million, and they can take four to five years to build. These facilities are costly to run, too, with long process durations, low yields, expensive raw materials, and, not least, the need for a team of highly skilled experts to operate them.

Box 2.7 Biologics

A biologic is a pharmaceutical made in a laboratory from a living organism, as opposed to a process of chemical synthesis (used for traditional pharmaceuticals). Consistent with this, European legislation defines a biologic as 'a medicine that contains one or more active substances made by or derived from a biological source.' Biological sources include micro-organisms, animal cells and human cells. Some biologic medicines mimic proteins made naturally in the human body. Examples include insulin, growth hormones and growth factors that control blood-cell production. Other biologic medicines are modifications of proteins occurring naturally in the human body, enhanced in the laboratory to improve bioavailability, specificity and effectiveness. The best-known examples of these are antibodies, which bind to the surface of cells in the body and are used extensively in the treatment of cancer. Biologic proteins are

much larger and more complex molecules than traditional chemical
medicines. This means they cannot in many cases be manufactured
as a pill and need to be administered via an injection.

Increased complexity has pushed up pharmaceutical development costs.
According to a 2016 estimate by a Tufts University team, the average cost
of developing a successful new drug today is $2.6 billion, up from $868
million in 2001 (DiMasi, 2016). The Tufts estimate of the cost of developing a successful drug quite reasonably takes into account the costs of
the many failed attempts – that is, the costs of developing drugs that were
never approved. But even if one looks only at the costs of bringing specific
new drugs successfully to market (i.e. excluding the costs of the failures),
costs commonly exceed $500 million (Simon and Giovannetti, 217: 25).

Fierce controversy reigns over estimates such as those produced by
the Tufts study, with critics of big pharma claiming that they are greatly
exaggerated. The basic message that development costs have increased
considerably is, however, certainly true. Increased risk of failure has also
contributed to rising costs. Today, it is more likely than in the past that,
after years of development and vast expenditure, a potential new drug will
not work properly and will fail to get regulatory approval (Scannell et al,
2012). Tougher contemporary regulatory regimes for the approval of new
pharmaceuticals – which are necessary for the protection of patients –
have also contributed to increased development cost and risk.

The Problem of Scale

Complexity is, however, not the whole story. Across the economy as a
whole, there are many products that are complex but nevertheless inexpensive. The computer chip is a striking example. The complexity of
the microprocessors (CPUs) in personal computers sold today is quite
breathtaking, but their prices start at under $100. This is achieved by mass
production. Intel, the company dominating the market, produces over a
hundred million CPUs annually in twelve mega-plants around the world.
This allows it to spread the massive R&D costs of developing new types
of chips over huge volumes of sales, while at the same time delivering

remarkable savings in manufacturing costs – a striking example of what economists refer to as "economies of scale."

Many of the complex new pharmaceuticals that have arrived on the market in recent times face precisely the opposite production conditions. Their production volumes are quite small because they target conditions affecting only a relatively small numbers of patients. This makes it impossible to spread high development and production costs over very large sales volumes. Unlike computer chips, they do not benefit from economies of scale. When the costs of developing a new pharmaceutical are high but the potential market is relatively small, high prices are the inevitable result.

So-called "orphan drugs" illustrate the problem. Orphan drugs are pharmaceuticals developed to treat rare diseases. These are diseases that affect only a very small percentage of the population (under the European Union definition, no more than 0.05 percent of the population).

Cystic fibrosis (CF) is one rare disease for which a number of orphan drugs have been developed. CF affects only around 70,000-100,000 people worldwide. Up to the 1980s, CF was untreatable and most of those afflicted died before reaching adulthood. The first CF drug developed was Pulmozyme (1993). This breakthrough pharmaceutical greatly alleviates CF symptoms in most sufferers and has played a major role in increasing patient life expectancy (now an average of more than three decades). Its cost is, however, high. In the US, the annual cost of treatment with Pulmozyme, which remains under patent, is $24,000-$40,000 (2016 prices). (This is, incidentally, an amount representative of the average annual cost at that time – $32,000 – of orphan drug treatment for treatable rare diseases in general (ICVIA Institute, 2017)).

Pulmozyme's cost is, however, dwarfed by the price of one of the newer CF drugs – Kalydeco (2012), which costs around $300,000 per patient per year in the United States (£182,000 in the UK). The very high cost of Kalydeco further illustrates the inverse relation between prices and patient numbers, because it is a treatment targeting a much smaller group of patients than Pulmozyme (it is effective for only approximately 5 percent of CF sufferers). For those patients, it is much more effective.

The astronomic cost of such a drug means that, even with very small patient numbers, the total cost to the health system is large. In the UK, for example, treating all eligible patients (370 of them) with Kalydeco would in 2012 have cost £67 million annually, equivalent to more than half of that year's budget (£130 million) for the treatment of all (approximately 10,000) British CF patients (IRDiRC, 2015: 26). Because, moreover, patients taking Kalydeco can be expected to live longer than the average CF sufferer, the increase in lifetime treatment cost per patient is greater than the increase in the annual treatment cost.[25]

Another example of a recently developed (2016) orphan drug with an astronomic price is Nusinersen. This is a continuing treatment for spinal muscular atrophy – a condition that occurs in about one in 10,000 babies. It costs $625,000-$750,000 in the first year and about $375,000 per year subsequently.[26]

Not only are prices of orphan drugs high, but they remain higher for longer than other pharmaceuticals. This is because of the extended patent rights conferred upon such drugs by governments in most advanced countries, as part of a range of incentives introduced in the 1980s and 1990s to encourage pharmaceutical companies to develop more drugs for rare diseases. (Incentives also include subsidies such as tax concessions and research grants.)

The Impact of High Prices

The impact on total healthcare expenditure depends not only on the price of new pharmaceuticals but also on the number of expensive new drugs receiving approval and the total number of patients being treated with them. These numbers have been growing rapidly.

In the US, complex new pharmaceuticals (broadly captured under the label "specialty drugs"[27]) were estimated to account in 2016 for 43 percent of pharmaceutical manufacturers' sales revenues (up from 26 percent in 2010), despite accounting for less than 2 percent of the volume of prescription drugs sold (QuintilesIMS, 2017: 6).

Orphan drugs are not the only type of expensive new pharmaceutical, but the number of new orphan drugs arriving on the market is quite impressive. There were 32 new orphan drug approvals in the United States and EU each year on average in the period 2010-16 (IRDiRC, 2018). By 2017, total orphan drug approvals in the US reached 650, and in 2016 they made up 41 percent of new drugs approvals. Even though each individual orphan drug by definition treats only a relatively small number of patients, the overall percentage of the population treated by orphan drugs generally is significant and growing, with total expenditure on this type of drug increasing accordingly. In the US, annual expenditure on orphan drugs doubled in real terms over the period 2007-13, increasing from 4.8 percent to 8.9 percent of total pharmaceutical expenditure (Divino et al, 2016).

One of the reasons why spending has increased so fast is that the majority of orphan drugs need to be prescribed for years or even decades. This is because rare diseases have in most cases been impossible to cure or prevent, because nearly all are primarily genetic diseases (see next chapter). Orphan drugs therefore have generally only been able to provide long-term treatment of symptoms.

The trend of increasing prices for new pharmaceutical treatments – whether for rare or more commonplace conditions – is firmly established. It is during the patent period that pharmaceutical companies have the greatest pricing power. Irrespective of the actual cost of production, pharmaceutical companies that have developed a new drug which is more effective than its predecessors will, during that period, demand a price premium. They will expect to be rewarded for the superior outcomes the new drug produces – an expectation captured in the contemporary notion of "value-based pricing." The new drug will then cost the government and insurers more. It may be highly cost-effective from a social point of view and may even be cost-saving to patients (e.g. because lost earnings from sickness are greatly reduced). But in the great majority of cases, its higher cost for national health systems and insurers will exceed any future savings these payors might realize (e.g. from lower future treatment costs for patients who have been cured).

After patents expire, other companies are, in principle, free to manufacture and sell "generic" versions of the drug. Prices *may* then fall, and in the past have often fallen significantly. This means that the upward pressure on pharmaceutical prices depends in part on the *rate* of development of new treatments, relative to the number of established treatments for which patents are expiring. The market presence of generics for ex-patent pharmaceuticals has increased greatly in most advanced countries over recent decades, usually with active government encouragement. Generics have, thus, been a useful moderating force on pharmaceutical prices.

There is, however, reason to fear that generics may be a less significant restraining force on prices in the future and that pharmaceutical prices may tend to fall less after patent expiry than has been the case. The greater complexity of many new pharmaceuticals makes it harder for competitors to enter the market, and the limited market for many newer drugs further constrains potential competitors. Already, it seems to be the case that when only one or two generic manufacturers enter the market for such a pharmaceutical, they are inclined to reach an understanding with the original manufacturer, so as to keep the drug price at an elevated level advantageous to them all. (This is an example of what economists refer to as oligopolistic collusion.)

Many of the higher-priced pharmaceuticals developed over recent decades have been very effective. A good example is the orphan drug Imatinib, which came on the market in 2001 for the treatment of chronic myeloid leukemia (CML) – a disease which, like CF, affects only around 100,000 people worldwide. Imatinib requires several years of treatment at a worldwide average price of around $26,000 per year. Whereas previously, 10-year life expectancy was less than 20 percent, CML sufferers treated with Imatinib can expect to live close to a normal lifespan (Bower et al, 2016).

However, not all expensive drugs developed over recent decades deliver such impressive results. Some deliver only marginal extensions to lifespan at high additional treatment costs, and some add no value at all. Well-managed national health systems around the world have been striving hard to ensure that the government does not pay for new drugs that do not pass the cost-effectiveness test. Health insurers are trying to do the same thing. Many countries are, for example, doing what Germany has done since 2011, which is to assess all new drugs and approve higher prices only for those for which there is convincing evidence they will deliver additional benefit for the patient (Busse and Blümel, 2014). There is also an emerging trend towards outcome-based payment arrangements, under which national health authorities or health insurers pay for the new pharmaceutical only if, and to the extent that, they actually deliver additional benefits (Simon and Giovannetti, 2017). But even when decisions about which new drugs will be paid for are guided by the strictest value-for-money criteria, it has proven impossible to avoid paying historically high prices for many new pharmaceutical treatments. Only by systematically denying citizens access to highly effective new treatments could this be avoided.

Technological Innovation That Reduces Treatment Costs

The review of trends in pharmaceuticals and the treatment of chronic conditions highlights the many ways in which technological innovation increases health expenditure, both by increasing cost per case and by increasing the numbers of people being treated. Technological innovation does not, however, only work to increase expenditure. Far from it. There has always been a great deal of technological innovation that generates savings.

Take the case of cataract surgery. Over past decades, the cost of cataract surgery has fallen dramatically — in the US, for example, by 85 percent over 1985-2002 (Brown et al, 2013). In parallel, the effectiveness of the procedure has greatly improved and risk to the patient much reduced. Cataract surgery is today a relatively straightforward outpatient procedure, typically requiring about 15 minutes of actual surgery and two hours in a clinic. In the 1970s, by contrast, it required hospitalization for up to three days. At that time, it was a sufficiently complex and risky procedure to be reserved for only the worst cases.

Asthma is a similar story. The average cost of treating an asthma patient has fallen markedly because far fewer doctor consultations and hospitalizations are now required, primarily as a result of the development of highly effective pharmaceutical treatments – both short-acting treatments to manage asthma attacks and long-term control medications that greatly reduce the number of attacks.

A particularly stunning example of cost-reducing treatment

innovation is the re-purposing of aspirin, approximately two decades ago, as an exceptionally cheap and effective drug for lowering the risk of further attacks for heart attack and stroke patients.

These examples, which can easily be multiplied many times over (Topol, 2015: 295-98), illustrate the way in which medical advances have not infrequently led to major reductions in the cost per case of treating specific conditions.

Taking a broader perspective, the main mechanisms through which technological innovation has worked to reduce health expenditure are:

◆ The development of new, lower-cost surgical techniques

◆ The development of new cost-reducing medical equipment

◆ The reduction in cost of existing types of medical equipment that become smaller and more portable over time

◆ The arrival on the market of new pharmaceuticals that greatly reduce the time input and/or complexity of treatment by doctors or other medical personnel

◆ Earlier and more accurate diagnosis

◆ Reductions in overhead costs of health service providers due to new technologies used across the entire economy.

The example of cataract surgery, referred to above, illustrates a number of these mechanisms. The principal reason for the remarkable improvement in *productivity* (see Box 2.8) in this form of surgery was the adoption of ultrasound to dissolve patients' damaged lenses, in the place of surgical extraction. This was made possible by the prior invention of medical ultrasound machines. Productivity was further improved, and costs pushed down, by the subsequent transformation of ultrasound probes from massive machines, which only hospitals could afford, to simple, cheap handheld devices. Cataract surgery is today one of the most commonly performed surgical procedures, so the impact of the huge fall in cost per case has been large.

Box 2.8 Productivity Growth

The term "productivity" is used by economists in a number of different ways. In this book, it is used strictly in reference to the quantity of inputs – such as the amount of labor, raw materials or equipment – required to produce a unit of product (such as a medical treatment). Productivity increases if, as a result of technological change or some other reason, fewer inputs are required per product. A particularly useful measure of productivity – "labor productivity" – refers to the amount of labor required per product. Thus, when technological innovation greatly reduces the time a surgeon takes to carry out a cataract surgery, there is a major improvement in labor productivity. Enhancements to the *quality* of a product are not considered to be productivity improvements when the term productivity is used in this way.[28]

Notwithstanding the pressure created by increases in pharmaceutical prices in general on total health expenditure, in plenty of cases the invention of new drugs has significantly reduced treatment costs. An example is the recent development of a new heat-stable oral rotavirus vaccine, which not only has a lower price but saves on refrigeration costs and is cheaper to administer to the patient. The long-term shift in the treatment of cancers from costly surgery to chemotherapy and radiotherapy-based treatments has also resulted in significantly lower costs per case for some (although certainly not all) cancers (Lee, Roehrig and Butto, 2016).

Earlier and more accurate diagnosis reduces cost per case in those cases where treating a disease earlier means that it is less difficult to treat. But in addition to reductions in cost per case, earlier and more accurate diagnosis can generate savings when it leads to a higher success rate, and this in turn avoids the need for substantial subsequent expenditure on the treatment of secondary conditions or on long periods of palliative care.

Finally, "back-office" support services in the health sector have benefited from the same type of productivity gains as the rest of the economy. In particular, information technology has been widely applied to achieve savings in administrative areas such as patient records, billing and supply chain management (Buntin et al, 2011; CBO, 2008). Significant scale economies have also been through the construction of larger, better-designed hospitals.

Certain of these mechanisms have been behind one of the most important sources of savings in costs per case over the long term: shifts in "treatment setting" (BLS, 2017). This refers to the gradual migration of many treatments from the hospital inpatient setting to outpatient clinics and doctors' surgeries, and sometimes even to patients' homes – resulting in considerable savings. These mechanisms made possible the shift of cataract surgery from hospitals to outpatient facilities and have done the same for many other types of surgery (e.g. hernia operations). They also facilitated the transfer of some cancer treatment from hospitals to stand-alone clinics, sometimes with considerable savings. They are also the reason why kidney dialysis, which in the past was exclusively carried out in hospitals, is these days frequently home-based (NHS, 2013: 18). Technological change – and not, as is sometimes suggested, the drive of bean-counters to cut costs irrespective of the impact on service quality – has been the prime driver of these shifts in treatment setting.

Clearly, therefore, the health sector has seen considerable, ongoing productivity growth – even if measuring that productivity growth poses major conceptual and practical difficulties (see below).

Technological innovation thus has both raised and reduced costs. So far, the forces driving up costs have considerably outweighed those reducing them, giving technological innovation an overall expenditure-increasing bias. Why this has been the case is considered later in this chapter.

The "Cost Disease" Theory

In sharp contrast to this story of technological innovation as a key determinant of the evolution of health expenditure is an influential alternative explanation of rising health expenditure that views the health sector as the victim of the "cost disease" (see Box 2.9). In 2012, William Baumol, the economist who developed the cost disease theory, published a book entitled *The Cost Disease: Why Computers Get Cheaper and Health Care Doesn't.* According to Baumol, health care is a technologically "stagnant" industry with very low productivity growth. The industry is nevertheless obliged to increase the remuneration of its workforce over time in line with economy-wide wage movements. However, with little or no productivity growth to offset these increases in remuneration, health care finds itself faced with continually rising costs that make its services progressively more expensive (i.e. their prices rise faster than the rate of inflation — in economic language, they rise in 'real' terms). More expensive healthcare services lead in turn to increasing total health expenditure. Baumol's theory thus purports to explain increasing health expenditure by the operation of a mechanism that has nothing to do with spending on new and better treatments.

Box 2.9 The Logic of the Cost Disease Theory

The logic of the cost disease theory is relatively simple. Imagine an economy comprised of a number of stagnant industries and a number of "dynamic" industries.[29] The stagnant industries are personal services industries, such as hairdressing, which are very labor-intensive, where every service is provided by human beings and where it is impossible to compress the labor time required to deliver a service by automation. As a result, labor productivity growth in these industries is zero – meaning the number of hours of work required to produce a product remains unchanged. Baumol's classic example was a live music performance, where he observed there could not and never would be any productivity improvements reducing the amount of labor input required to play a Mozart string quartet (Baumol and Bowen, 1966).

On the other hand, the dynamic industries that comprise the rest of the economy are industries where, as a result of automation, the number of hours of work taken to produce a product is continually falling. Labor productivity is, in other words, constantly increasing.

This is where the impact of increases in remuneration come into play. Over time, real wages – that is, wages adjusted for inflation (approximately speaking, increases in employee purchasing power) – in the dynamic industries increase as labor productivity

increases. (In presenting the cost disease theory, Baumol assumed
that real wages grow at the same rate as labor productivity.[30])
Notwithstanding this, the products of the dynamic industries do not
become any more expensive, because wage increases are paid for
by rising productivity.

However, increasing real wages pose a problem for the stagnant industries. A refusal to increase wages would, over time, make
it impossible for the stagnant industries to recruit staff. The cost
disease theory therefore assumes that the stagnant industries
match the wage increases being paid in the dynamic industries. The
problem is that, without the growth in productivity necessary to pay
for them, these pay rises increase the costs of the services produced by the stagnant industries. These services, therefore, become
continually more expensive. Plenty of real-world examples of this
process can be cited, such as the rising prices of haircuts and live
concert tickets.

Baumol viewed health care as one of the economy's stagnant industries
because he considered it to be a highly labor-intensive industry in which
there is limited scope to reduce the labor content of services. He illustrates
this with the example of consultations with the family doctor. Such consultations always take an average of, say, 20 minutes and cannot be compressed
without quality being sacrificed. This means, in Baumol's interpretation,
that labor productivity growth over time is essentially zero. Put this absence
of productivity growth together with the fact that the real remuneration of
doctors rises gradually along with economy-wide increases in living standards, and the inevitable consequence is that the price of a consultation
with the family doctor continually increases in real terms. Baumol considered that most other health services – including, for example, surgery – are
affected by the cost disease in essentially the same way.

Baumol did not suggest that there was absolutely no productivity
growth in the healthcare industry. He did, however, assert that productivity growth was very low – much lower than that of the economy as a whole.
Nor did he claim that wages in the healthcare sector necessarily increase
at the same rate as wages elsewhere in the economy (or that they necessarily increase at the rate of economy-wide labor productivity growth[31]).

He recognized that, in practice, healthcare industry remuneration may lag over certain sustained periods. But these qualifications do not affect the essential point, which can be reformulated in the following way: *if real wages in the healthcare industry grow faster than the – supposedly very low – rate of healthcare industry productivity growth, healthcare services will become progressively more expensive.*

There is an additional component to the cost disease theory. This component is essential to the theory because a process that makes healthcare services more expensive cannot by itself, even in theory, explain rising total health expenditure. After all, the fact that a particular type of service becomes more expensive does not mean that consumers will necessarily spend more on it. They may respond to higher prices by buying significantly less of the service concerned, in which case total spending may even fall. But as Baumol notes, this is not true for health care. Increases in healthcare prices have a quite limited impact on the amount of healthcare services people use. Generally speaking, when people need medical treatment, they will not forego it because it is somewhat more expensive than it was a few years ago.[32] It is this unresponsiveness of the demand for healthcare services to price changes that explains why progressively more expensive healthcare services would lead to increased total healthcare expenditure.

Baumol made bold claims for the cost disease theory. Not only did he assert that it was the number-one driver of rising health spending. He went further to declare that there was no other factor that "appears to constitute a major source of the continuing and rapid rise in healthcare costs." It is remarkable that, in this context, he did not even mention the continuing arrival of new and better treatments as one of the other factors that might potentially explain rising spending.

Why Baumol Was Wrong

The most fundamental problem with Baumol's reasoning is that focusing on what has happened to the cost of specific *services*, such as a hospital stay or a consultation with the family doctor, is entirely the wrong way of viewing the matter. The correct way of looking at health productivity is in terms of *cost per case*. This means looking at the set of services required to treat each specific condition and how they collectively determine the overall cost of treating a patient for that condition (Scitovsky, 1967; Newhouse, 1992; Atkinson, 2005). Suppose, for example, that the development of a new, more effective treatment means that treating a patient for a condition that 50 years ago typically involved several (or even many) trips to the doctor today only requires a single consultation, at which a highly effective and relatively inexpensive pharmaceutical treatment is prescribed. Cost per case will have fallen significantly, productivity will have risen and any talk of the "cost disease" would be misplaced. It would be irrelevant that the cost *per visit* of consulting a doctor is higher now than it was half a century ago.

This type of productivity improvement, with reductions in the number of consultations required to treat a condition, has been commonplace. It has been the consequence not only of the development of more effective new treatments. Improved *diagnostic* technology has also helped, by enabling doctors to more frequently administer the appropriate treatment right from the start.

It is not only in doctors' offices that technological innovation has often worked in this way to significantly reduce the time it takes medical professionals to treat cases. The same is true in hospitals. Consider, for example, the treatment of heart attacks. In the 1960s, 95 percent of heart attack patients had hospital stays of 21 days or more. Today, the average stay is less than a week, even though post-discharge survival rates have significantly improved. This dramatic shortening of the period of hospitalization has meant huge labor savings.

Psychiatry has seen similar striking changes. Whereas 50 years ago, depression was commonly treated (when it was treated at all) by regular therapy sessions, today antidepressants are usually used. Although widely criticized, and no doubt overused, these drug therapies have been shown to be at least as effective as the old, more labor-intensive treatment approach.

With large labor productivity gains of this type in many areas of medical practice, the fact that medical personnel earn today significantly more per hour or per consultation than in the past tells us nothing whatsoever about productivity and certainly does not constitute evidence of the cost disease mechanism.

The inappropriate focus on the cost of services rather than on the cost of cases (treatments) is a key reason why, historically, official statistics have misreported productivity growth in the health sector (see Box 2.10).

Box 2.10 Measuring Productivity in the Health Sector

Historically, official statistics measured productivity in the health sector on the basis of services rather than treatments, which unsurprisingly led them to report that the health sector has exceptionally low productivity growth. For some time, it has been recognized that this approach is conceptually flawed and that productivity should be measured on the basis of treatments (Atkinson, 2005). A number of leading public-sector statistical organizations – such as the Bureau of Labor Statistics and the Bureau of Economic Analysis in the US (BLS, 2017; Dunn, Rittmueller and Whitmire, 2015) – have been working to develop more appropriate accounts for the health sector. This effort will ultimately produce better productivity measures, although a number of difficult measurement issues are still being worked through (Sheiner and Malinovskaya, 2016).

Closely related to the inappropriate focus on the cost of services was Baumol's misconception of health care as a highly labor-intensive industry, similar to education, hairdressing or live music. This is a misconception widely held by adherents to the cost disease theory – as exemplified by one vocal cost disease enthusiast and *Forbes* columnist who has claimed that "the vast majority of the cost of any medical care system is the time of the people in it. From the assistant nurse type who empties bedpans and feeds patients their soup through to those very expensively trained and very well-paid specialist doctors."[33] But this is completely untrue. Although good data are hard to find, remuneration of health workers probably accounts for less than half of the cost of health treatments.[34] Even in hospitals, only around 60 percent of costs is attributable to the remuneration of doctors, nurses and other health workers, with the rest accounted for by the costs of equipment, supplies, infrastructure and other non-labor inputs.[35] Health care has, moreover, become progressively less labor-intensive over time, with medical equipment playing an increasingly important role. Like other service industries, health care is certainly much more labor-intensive than manufacturing and agriculture. But it is less labor-intensive than, say, education, where the cost disease effect has been quite pronounced (see Appendix 2.2).[36]

Baumol's characterization of health care as a technologically "stagnant" industry, blighted by low productivity growth, is thus entirely incorrect. It is regrettable that many economists continue to take it for granted that health-care productivity growth is close to zero (e.g. Autor and Salomons, 2017).[37]

It cannot be emphasized too strongly that, when thinking about why health expenditure rises over the long term, we must abandon any notion that the problem is an absence of productivity growth. While we are still not good at measuring productivity growth in the healthcare industry, common sense alone makes it clear that such a description is totally wrong. Productivity growth in the industry – in the specific sense of reductions in the labor or other input requirements needed to treat a patient – is very real and substantial.

Box 2.11 Econometric Evidence for Low Productivity in the Health Sector?

Several economists claim to have produced econometric (i.e. statistical) evidence that the rate of productivity growth of the health sector is – even when viewed from the cost-per-case perspective – extremely low. However, they base their analysis of health-sector productivity on a truly bizarre definition of productivity, according to which productivity refers to the efficiency with which *unchanged* treatments are delivered.[38] This definition demands, for example, that the productivity of cataract operations be measured by estimating what it would cost today to carry out a cataract operation using precisely the same treatment technique as was used in the 1960s. This is a definition of productivity that excludes savings in cost per case delivered through the substitution of lower-cost new treatment methods. It is equivalent to insisting that productivity growth in the passenger transport industry over the past two centuries should be measured by estimating changes in the cost per passenger kilometer of horse-drawn transport, ignoring the dramatic reduction in costs from the introduction of trains, cars and planes.[39]

Has the Cost Disease Nevertheless Played Some Role?

The fact that health care is, manifestly, *not* a technologically stagnant industry does not rule out the possibility that the cost disease mechanism plays some role in pushing up health spending. In principle, the cost disease will contribute to rising spending if healthcare productivity growth – even if significant – is lower than the average productivity growth of the economy as a whole. This is because, stripped of the extreme assumptions of the simple version presented by Baumol, the cost disease theory can be expressed in terms of the propositions that (on certain simplifying assumptions[40]):

◆ Products of industries with below-average productivity growth become progressively more expensive over time (i.e. their prices increase faster than inflation).

◆ Products of industries with above-average productivity growth become progressively cheaper (their prices increase less than inflation).

This tells us that if we go back quite a long time in the economic history of most advanced countries – to the time when manufacturing and agriculture were the dominant industries – the cost disease was unquestionably a major factor in rising health spending. Because, unlike service industries as a whole, manufacturing and agriculture have been so easily automated, they have historically experienced very rapid productivity growth. So during the epoch when these industries accounted for a large percentage of national product, productivity growth in health care (and in other service industries) *must* have been well below that of the economy-wide average.

But the situation is different today. Modern advanced economies are dominated by services (see Appendix 2.2). The productivity growth of service industries, thus, is the main determinant of economy-wide average productivity growth. In this context, it is not at all clear that productivity growth in the healthcare industry has – over, say, the past 30-40 years – been below that of the rest of the economy and, if it has been, by how much.

New Technology and Health Expenditure

The view that "the largest single factor driving spending growth [is] greatly expanded capabilities of medicine brought about by technological advances in medical science" (CBO, 2008) is one held today by a majority of health economists. Statistical analysis also highlights the central role played by technology.[41]

However, as we have seen, technological innovation works both to increase and to reduce health expenditure. On the one hand, the ongoing development of new and better treatments exercises a powerful upward pressure on spending. But at the same time, technological change delivers significant productivity gains. The ongoing battle between these expenditure-increasing and expenditure-reducing impacts of technological innovation is the main determinant of the evolution of health expenditure. The crucial point is that the expenditure-increasing impact of technological innovation has over time considerably outweighed its expenditure-reducing impact, giving technological change an overall *expenditure-increasing bias.*

Why is it that technological innovation has had this powerful overall expenditure-increasing bias in the health sector? Answering this question is essential to any analysis of what the future holds.

The first part of the puzzle is understanding why the upward pressure on spending from the development of new and better treatments is so strong. Much of the explanation for this lies on the demand side, in the nature of the powerful, long-term, *needs-focused expansion* of health services. This expansion has been directed to meeting health-treatment needs that have either previously been unmet or have increased for demographic, epidemiological or other reasons. Like basic food and shelter, and unlike many of the other goods and services we consume, health care is a *need*, rather than merely a *desire.*[42] But the most distinctive feature of health care is that there is always a huge reservoir of unmet need for new and better health treatments (what economists call large "latent demand"). This is because, despite the ongoing impressive progress of medicine, the treatments available for many diseases and conditions are only partially effective. They fail to work for many patients or are only partially successful in alleviating symptoms and suffering. There are, moreover, conditions that remain essentially untreatable.

To individual patients suffering from conditions hitherto untreatable or only partially treatable, new treatments that can save their lives or greatly reduce their suffering and disability have enormous value. So when, as a result of technological innovation, new and better treatments become available, there is almost immediately considerable demand for their use, even when they are expensive. Citizens who are able to pay for the new treatments themselves are willing to do so. But more importantly, the great majority who rely upon national health systems or health insurance to pay for treatment put pressure on payors to fund the new treatments and make them available for everyone who needs them. So do their doctors. Either way, when the new treatments are truly cost-effective, they will eventually be funded (Thorpe, 2012: 413).

This is the most fundamental reason why the development of new and better treatments has such a powerful expenditure-increasing impact, outweighing the significant savings realized as a result of productivity-enhancing technological innovation.

A "balloon" effect is also at work. Squeeze a balloon on one side, and it pops out on the other side. In the same way, when medicine is successful in reducing mortality from one type of disease, people live longer and eventually develop other types of diseases and conditions. Medical product innovation then shifts to focus more on these other diseases.

Historically, there was another major source of unmet need for medical services. This was the inability of many citizens to afford medicine. In the past, a major driver of the needs-focused expansion of health services in advanced countries was therefore the broadening of health coverage to citizens who previously had limited access to health care for financial reasons. But in almost all rich countries the move to universal health coverage was largely accomplished quite a long time ago, the United States being the main exception.[43]

The permanent reservoir of unmet healthcare needs means that the primary focus of technological innovation in health has always been upon the development of new and better treatments. Technological innovation to reduce treatment costs is not neglected, but has always been secondary to the goals of saving more lives and reducing pain and suffering.

In short, on the demand side, the growth of health expenditure has been driven primarily by the fact that people gain, on the whole, great benefits from new treatment technologies – even if we accept the significant incidence of over-servicing in modern medical systems. Over-servicing cannot explain the rate of growth of health spending, and even if it were possible to completely prevent over-servicing, this would not remove the strong demand-side pressure (see Box 2.12). Even in the United States, with its exceptional levels of wasteful spending, careful analysis by Cutler (2004: 153) finds that "it is almost certainly the case that increases in medical spending have been worth it."

Box 2.12 Market Imperfections and the Excessive Use of Medical Services

Economists have an ingrained tendency to focus on so-called "market imperfections" – departures from the textbook competitive market model – to explain the real or apparent malfunctioning of specific industries. In the case of the health sector, there are two key market imperfections. The first is so-called "information asymmetry." This means that doctors have the expertise, whereas patients do not have the knowledge required to judge the relevance or quality of their treatments. The second market imperfection arises from the fact that, due to health insurance or government provision, patients pay either nothing or much less than the full cost of the treatments they receive. Together, these two market imperfections give medical practitioners considerable power to determine the treatments that are delivered, giving them scope to over-service to raise their incomes (or to mollify demanding patients and thereby reduce the risk of being sued). Such over-servicing is referred to as

the problem of "supplier-induced demand." These market imperfections also result in some patients demanding and receiving more
medical services than they actually need – so-called "moral hazard"
These problems are real ones (Einav and Finkelstein, 2017; Topol,
2015; Cutler, 2004), and those who seek to deny or minimize either or
both of them – such as Gladwell (2005) with respect to moral hazard
– are doing a disservice to the policy debate.

One of the important challenges in designing and managing
health systems is that of how to contain these pressures for the
excessive use of medical services without greatly exacerbating
under-servicing, which is also a major problem (Cutler, 2004). It
is, nevertheless, an illusion to believe that market imperfections
are the fundamental reason why health expenditure has risen so
substantially, or that dealing with them is the recipe for stabilizing
health spending. Particularly misguided are those "free-market"
economists who believe that greatly increasing the role of the price
mechanism – in particular by requiring patients to pay significantly
more each time they visit the doctor – is the answer to the problem of
rising health expenditure.

Rising living standards also play a key role on the demand side, by financing
the adoption of new medical treatments. As real incomes have risen, individuals and society collectively have consistently proven able and willing
to allocate an increasing share of income to purchasing new and better
health treatments to save, prolong or improve the quality of their lives.
It is, after all, an entirely reasonable social choice to devote an increasing
share of resources to purchasing better health, particularly when the most
elementary needs – such as food and basic shelter – are no longer a preoccupation for most people in advanced countries. The extensive government
support for orphan drug development, and regulatory permission given to
pharmaceutical companies to maintain higher prices for longer periods of
time for these drugs, are manifestations of this social choice.

When government is responsible for a large portion of health expenditure, this social choice has played out in a specific way. Faced with the
arrival of new and better treatments that cost more, governments have
responded – often in a very discontinuous manner – by increasing the
relative size of the health budget. They may have occasionally cut health

spending, especially at times when public finances have been particularly strained (e.g. in the wake of the 2007-2008 global financial crisis). But such restraint has been temporary, and sooner or later the upward movement in spending has recommenced. On the other hand, when lower-cost treatments or processes have become available, the response has rarely been to use the savings to cut total government health expenditure. Instead, the additional "fiscal space" provided by such savings has generally been used to respond to citizens' demands for more and better treatments.

Many economists have a different view as to the way in which rising real incomes contribute to the long-term increasing ratio of health expenditure to GDP. They subscribe to the notion that health is a so-called "superior good." A superior good, also known as a "luxury good," is one which we want to consume a lot more of when our income rises, so much so that we spend an increasing portion of our incomes on it. Champagne is a good example: many people enjoy it so much — or derive such a sense of prestige from drinking it — that if their pay were to double, they would drink three or four times more champagne. But to think of health treatments as luxury goods similar to champagne defies common sense. An individual whose pay doubles is highly unlikely to choose to splurge by tripling their dose of antihypertensive medication, or to have another coronary triple bypass or two just because they enjoyed the first one so much. The fact that, over the long term, health expenditure/GDP has grown with rising real incomes in advanced societies has nothing whatsoever to do with the supposedly luxury nature of health care. (The superior good theory is discussed in more detail in Appendix 2.3).

So much for the demand side. Supply-side factors also play a role in the upward pressure on spending associated with the development of new and better treatments, because new medical treatments are often more expensive than the treatments they replace. One of the reasons for this is the increasing complexity of the underlying science.

As the examples discussed in this chapter have highlighted, new medical treatments are often expensive because of the complexity and heterogeneity of the diseases and conditions they target, and because of the radical and discontinuous nature of much of the product innovation in health. What this means can be seen by comparing new product development in the health sector with that of a particular manufacturing sector: land transport. In that sector, there is a quite limited number of different product types (cars, buses, trains, etc.). Technological innovation may seem impressive but in fact it has been relatively narrow in the sense that there are few significantly different basic technologies used in, say, cars. The fact that vast numbers of cars of essentially the same technology are produced enables huge scale economies to be realized. Almost all technological innovation has been gradual and incremental. Today's cars represent essentially an evolution of the cars of a century ago, and they still have a lot of common technology. (Even electric cars are not a particularly radical innovation – the technology has been around for a long time and has just got better.) One of the reasons for this is that throughout history, cars and other forms of land transport have always been almost entirely successful in meeting user needs. Unlike health care, it has never been the case that there are large groups of people for whom cars, buses or trains do not work, and for which the industry has had to seek to develop radically different means of transport. The fact that today the land transport sector may be moving toward more radical technological changes, such as the introduction of autonomous vehicles, simply underlines the relatively incremental nature of past technological innovation.

Medicine is nothing like this. The range and diversity of medical treatments, and that of their underlying technologies, is enormous. Product innovation is characterized by discontinuous shifts in technology on many fronts – not only for new treatments developed for previously untreatable conditions, but also treatment substitution (replacement of an old treatment by a newer one). Waves of new treatments arrive that employ fundamentally different technologies from those used by the treatments they replace.

Although new medical treatments often generate downstream healthcare expenditure savings – because, for example, curing or preventing a condition can save on future costs of treating symptoms – it is not very common that such savings are sufficient to offset the cost of a new treatment. It seems that even many vaccines cost more than they save in downstream health expenditures, notwithstanding that vaccination offers great value for money from a broader social point of view.[44]

These demand and supply factors explain why the ongoing development of new and better treatments creates such strong upward pressure on total health expenditure. But there is another key point, concerning the productivity gains that technological innovation has so often delivered in the healthcare industry. As discussed above, productivity growth can, approximately speaking, only work to reduce costs per treatment if it is greater than the productivity growth of the economy as a whole. This means that the only way that healthcare productivity growth could fully offset the sizable upward spending pressure from the development of new and better treatments would be if the productivity growth in health care was *much* greater than productivity growth in the rest of the economy.

To understand why this is the case, we need to go back to Baumol's reasoning. Setting aside his unjustified characterization of health care as a technologically stagnant industry, the core proposition suggested by the "cost disease" theory is that if productivity growth in the health care industry is less than productivity growth in the economy as a whole, health care will become progressively more expensive over time.

Flipping this reasoning tells us that productivity growth in the healthcare industry can only be expected to reduce costs per case if it exceeds the rate of productivity growth in the rest of the economy. This in turn means that, if the ongoing upward pressure on spending due to the constant arrival of new and better treatments is quite large, productivity growth in the healthcare industry could only be expected to offset this upward pressure if it were *much* greater than the economy-wide rate of productivity growth.[45] This has manifestly not been the case.

Multiple forces have, then, been at work to give technological innovation an expenditure-increasing bias. Whether this will remain true in the future is considered in the next chapter.

Population Aging and Rising Health Costs

Up to this point, the role of population aging in increasing health expenditure has been mentioned only briefly, in relation to the increasing prevalence of chronic conditions. This lack of focus on the elderly might seem strange, given the widespread belief that population aging has been the principal factor pushing up health spending. This is a belief that seems common sense. After all, per capita health expenditure is, at any point, much higher for elderly people (65-plus) than it is for younger people, and is higher again for the very elderly (80-plus). It seems to follow that the growth in the percentage of elderly and very elderly people in the population must *greatly* increase per capita health expenditure.

This "common sense" view of the impact of aging was behind horror forecasts produced by governments and international organizations back in the 1980s, when serious discussion of the fiscal impacts of population aging first got under way. These forecasts predicted that health spending would rise very rapidly as a direct consequence of the impact of population aging (see, for example, OECD (1988)).

This view of the impact of aging on health spending was, however, rejected by influential health economists at the time as wildly exaggerated. Remarkable as it may seem, some of these economists even went so far as to dismiss population aging as *totally* irrelevant to rising health expenditure.[46] Aging, they asserted, was a "red herring" that distracted attention from the real drivers of higher spending (Zweifel, Felder and Meiers, 1999).

How is it that these economists could have taken such a seemingly illogical position?

The reason is they believed *increased longevity has no impact on per capita health expenditure.* (Recall that increased longevity refers to longer average life expectancy in old age.) Some took this view under the influence of the "compression of morbidity" theory discussed earlier — a theory which, as noted, we now know not to be valid with respect to recent times. More commonly, however, they based their position on what has become known as the "proximity to death" (PTD) effect.

In its pure form, the PTD effect asserts that, on average, annual per capita health expenditure is not determined by a person's age, but by how many years they are away from the end of their lives (see Appendix 2.4 for further explanation). If this were true, increasing longevity would have no effect on health expenditure because, even though it increases the percentage of elderly people in the population, it does not increase the percentage of people who are any given number of years away from death.

One significant fact about health expenditure provides a measure of support for the PTD effect. This concerns the timing of the period of intensive use of medical services (mainly acute treatment, much of it in hospital) that people tend to experience late in life, and which accounts on average for quite a substantial fraction of lifetime health spending (perhaps around one-quarter[47]). Research has shown that this peak occurs not at a certain average chronological age (such as, say, 76) but, rather, in the last year or two before death.[48] (For those who live until 72, for example, it occurs on average within the period when they are between 70 and 72. For those who live until 82, it is between the ages of 80 and 82.) As longevity increases, the average age at which the peak in acute treatment spending occurs is therefore postponed. This postponement of the age at which health expenditure peaks greatly weakens the impact of increasing longevity on health expenditure.

The PTD effect, even in its pure form, does not imply that population aging has had absolutely *no* impact on health expenditure. Longevity is not the only factor behind population aging. Fertility-rate effects – the impact of past variations in the numbers of children per woman – also play a role. Insofar as population aging results from fertility-rate effects, its impact on health expenditure is not neutralized by the PTD effect. But this is a minor qualification. Until relatively recently, the role of fertility-rate effects in population aging has been distinctly secondary, and increased longevity has been the most important force at work.[49, 50]

There is no inconsistency, therefore, between subscribing to the "pure" version of the PTD effect and taking the view that population aging has in the past had some impact, but only a *minor* impact, on health spending. It is possible, in other words, to deny that increasing *longevity* has any impact on expenditure while accepting that *population aging* does have an impact insofar as it is the consequence of fertility-rate effects rather than of increased longevity. This is, in effect, the position that many health economists have taken. A concrete example of what is meant by "minor" is given by an OECD estimate – based explicitly on the assumption that longevity has no impact on health expenditure – that population aging contributed only about one-eighth of the annual average growth in real per capital health spending across the organization's member countries from 1995 to 2009 (de la Maisonneuve and Oliveira Martins, 2014).[51]

This line of reasoning, however, has a big problem, as does its conclusion that the past contribution of population aging to the rise of health expenditure has only been "minor." The problem is that the assumption upon which it is based – that increased longevity has absolutely no effect on spending – is wrong. Certainly, the PTD effect is real. However, the "pure" version of the effect is manifestly incorrect. It is not true that chronological age has zero impact on spending and that all that matters is proximity to death. The clearest evidence is the fact that increased longevity has contributed to increased spending on long-term continuing treatment of chronic conditions. This is important given the major role played by chronic conditions in pushing up health spending. Further evidence that increased longevity affects spending is provided by research on the "age-based rationing" effect (see Appendix 2.4). The fact that increasing longevity postpones the late-life peak in spending proves only that health expenditure is *partly* determined by the number of years away from death. It does not prove that chronological age has no impact on spending.

A further reason for disputing the view that population aging has had only a "minor" impact on spending lies in the way in which aging and advances in medical treatments interact. Discussion of this point will, however, be left for the next chapter.

This analysis suggests two conclusions about the past role of population aging. First, the view that aging has been the main force driving up health expenditure is, as most health economists agree, incorrect. Second, notwithstanding this, it is wrong to dismiss its impact as minor. Secondary, yes; minor, no.

How one views the past has important implications for how one views the future. The tendency of some health economists to continue to regard population aging as a "red herring" risks prompting them to take a somewhat too rosy view of the likely impact of the much more rapid population aging now underway across the advanced world and which will continue in the coming decades. We will return to this in the next chapter.

◆ ◆ ◆

The analysis in this chapter has underlined the role of technological innovation as the main force driving the long-term evolution of real per capita health expenditure. Demographic trends and lifestyle trends play a role, but they are secondary. Technological innovation does not, however, work in a unidirectional manner. It has both expenditure-increasing and expenditure-reducing impacts, and it is the net effect that is crucial. In the next chapter, we focus on the manner in which these forces are likely to operate in coming decades.

Appendix 2.1: The Role of Medical Advances in Reducing CVD Mortality

Together with the results of research carried out by Cutler (2004), an examination of statistics on CVD incidence and mortality rates in high-income countries (now available in the Global Health Data Exchange database) sheds light on the roles of medical advances and non-medical factors, such as improvements in health behaviors, in reducing CVD mortality. During 1990-2016, there was a 25 percent fall in age-standardized CVD incidence (which had already fallen prior to 1990). Over that period, the age-standardized CVD mortality rate – which measures the proportion of the total population who die each year from the various forms of CVD, adjusted for changes in the age structure of the population – fell by 51 percent. The fact that the mortality rate fell by twice as much as incidence means that there was a very large increase in in the proportion of people who survive such events (the survival rate).

Logically, most of the contribution to reduced CVD mortality of developments that are unrelated to advances in medical treatment, such as reduced smoking and other positive trends in health behavior, should be captured in the fall in CVD incidence. On the other hand, the impact on mortality of advances in the medical treatment provided to patients following CVD events such as heart attacks and strokes will show up in increased survival rates. It therefore seems reasonable to assume that much of the increase in survival rates is due to medical advances (including technologies that facilitate earlier detection of disease).

However, even the improvement in survival rates significantly understates the impact of advances in medical technology, because it only captures the impact of treatment occurring after a CVD event such as a heart attack. It consequently does not recognize the contribution of improved "primary prevention" treatment – defined as medical treatment intended to prevent disease from developing in the first place (such as statins) – which combat mortality mainly by lowering incidence. This means that the 25 percent reduction in age-standardized CVD incidence must in some significant measure have been the consequence of the advances that have occurred in primary prevention treatments and cannot be wholly attributable to improvements in health behaviors and similar non-treatment factors.

A number of studies have been carried out on the causes of the reduction in mortality rates for coronary heart disease (the main form of CVD) in major advanced countries over the final decades of the 20th century. Most of these studies attribute at least 40 percent of the decline to improved medical treatment, and something around 50-60 percent to risk factor reduction (such as reduced levels of cholesterol, blood pressure and smoking, as well as increased exercise) (Palmieri et al, 2010; Unal et al, 2004; Ford et al, 2007; Bennett et al, 2006) – although one US study estimates the contribution of improved treatment at 55 percent (Cutler, McClellan and Newhouse, 1999). Once again, however, this underestimates the impact of medical advances because of the significant contribution to risk-factor reduction by improved primary preventative treatment. Overall, it seems reasonable to view these studies as supporting, in the specific case of coronary heart disease, the view that advances in treatment (including primary preventative treatment) have been the most important reason for the fall in mortality.

Appendix 2.2: Is the Baumol Effect at Work Today?

If health care is compared with manufacturing and agriculture – as Baumol does – it is easy to conclude that healthcare productivity growth must be relatively low. Historically, the main reason for high labor productivity growth in manufacturing and agriculture has been the impact of automation – that is, machines taking over tasks previously carried out by human beings. Although machines now play a much more important role in health care than they did, say, a hundred years ago, this has less often than in other industries been in the form of direct automation. In clinical applications, what machines have more often done is change the treatment technique, thereby making certain tasks previously carried out by human beings redundant (in the way in which ultrasound dissolution of damaged lenses made surgical extraction unnecessary in cataract procedures, or chemotherapies replaced surgery in many types of cancer treatment). Machines have also often assisted humans in carrying out clinical tasks rather than replacing them.[52] (Automation has been more extensive in administrative and support services, such as health-record management.)

Comparing productivity growth in health care with that in manufacturing and agriculture is a convincing way of demonstrating that the Baumol effect must have been important, say, a century ago, when those industries dominated the economy. Today, however, it is other service industries that account for most of the output of advanced economies, and manufacturing and agriculture account for only a relatively small portion of GDP (typically 20-30 percent). This means that if we want to know whether the Baumol effect is still at work in the contemporary economy, the main thing we need to know is how the productivity growth of the healthcare industry compares with that of other service industries. Therefore, the fact that healthcare industry productivity growth is still well below that of manufacturing does not, contrary to what some appear to think (Erixon and van der Marel, 2011), mean that the cost disease is still at work.

How does healthcare productivity growth in recent times compare with that of other service industries? The problem here is that, as noted, we do not have reliable measures of the true productivity growth of the healthcare sector or, for that matter, of some of the other key service industries in the modern economy. Moreover, factors such as limits on the scope for automation have in the past applied equally or more to at least some of the other major service industries.

There are a number of statistical studies that claim to test for the role of the Baumol effect in health care in recent times. However, without going into detail, the methodologies these studies employ are not such as to give confidence in their findings.

Appendix 2.3: Is Health Care a Superior Good?

The view that health care is a "superior good" is widely held amongst economists, Including some as eminent as Fogel (2008) and Baumol (2012). Nevertheless, it does not stand up to serious scrutiny.

The proper definition of a superior good is a specific good or service with an income elasticity exceeding one. This means that for every 10 percent increase in real income, the quantity (number of units) of that good or service that is consumed increases by more than 10 percent. It follows from this definition that, if a specific good or service is a superior good, and its price remains constant, then as income increases a larger percentage of income will be spent on that good or service.

Superior good status can only be a property of specific health treatments (treatments for specific conditions), not of total healthcare consumption. The superior good concept cannot be applied to aggregate spending on a large category of goods and services, the composition of which is changing dramatically over time – in the case of health, due primarily to the arrival of new treatments.

But if we think about demand for most specific health treatments – such as, for example, treatment for diabetes or acute treatment for a stroke – it makes no sense that it would be a superior good. Assuming that an individual already has access to a specific treatment that they require, they will not generally wish to consume more of that treatment as their income rises. Their demand for the treatment is essentially determined by medical need and the advice of their treating medical professional. (The only obvious exceptions to this are discretionary treatments like cosmetic surgery.) In formal terminology, this suggests that demand for nearly all specific health treatments is income-inelastic (i.e. not very responsive to increases in income).

Nevertheless, affordability does play some role in demand – the lower incomes are, the more treatments individuals or society collectively may be obliged to forego. Because of this, demand for health treatments is somewhat responsive (rather than totally unresponsive) to increases in income (i.e. in formal language, it is why at least some health treatments are "normal goods").

This commonsense reasoning is supported by the results of most "cross-sectional" statistical analysis of household health expenditure, which compares health spending of households at different income levels at a given point in time – although such analysis is not without its problems.[53]

If the income elasticity of most health treatments is significantly less than one, the percentage of income spent on each specific treatment would tend to fall as income rises. The most important reason this does not happen is that there is so much additional spending on new and better treatments. But the willingness to spend more on new treatments that previously did not exist is something quite different from the superior good concept.[54]

The fact that the percentage of national income spent on health care has risen in line with rising income does not therefore constitute evidence that health care is a superior good.

Some economists have claimed to have demonstrated the superior good status of health care by means of cross-sectional comparisons of countries. These compare countries that have different levels of real per capita incomes and find that those with higher incomes tend to spend a higher proportion of GDP on health care. However, it is well established that cross-sectional comparisons do not, for a range of reasons, prove the superior good theory (Parkin, McGuire and Yule, 1987). One of these reasons is that for cross-sectional country comparisons to test the superior good hypothesis, the prices of treatments would need to be the same across countries. But this is manifestly not the case. For example, the price of pharmaceuticals is not the same, in significant measure because pharmaceutical companies set prices based on what they think the market will bear in the country concerned.

Appendix 2.4: Increased Longevity and Health Expenditure

The main focus of research and debate on the question of population aging and health expenditure has been the impact of increased longevity. Researchers have looked closely at what has happened over time to the "age profile" of health expenditure as longevity has increased. The age profile of health expenditure refers to the positive relationship that exists, at any given point in time, between age and health spending. (Simplifying, it may be thought of as an upward-sloping curve on a graph that plots average per capita spending against age.) The "horror" forecasts made several decades ago projected health expenditure on the assumption that the age profile of spending remains constant over the long term as longevity increases.

What does it mean to assume that the age profile of health expenditure remains constant as longevity increases? Suppose that 50-year forecasts of health expenditure were prepared in, say, 1990. Suppose further that at that time the age profile of spending was such that annual health spending on the average 40-year-old was $1,000, whereas the figure for the average 65-year-old was $3,000 and for the average 80-year-old $6,000. The assumption of a constant age profile means (approximately speaking) that in preparing the 50-year forecasts, it would be assumed that during the forecast period – right up to 2040 – real per capita health spending for the average 65-year-old would continue to be three times higher than that for the average 40-year-old, and real per capita health spending for the average 80-year-old six times greater. It will be obvious that forecasts assuming that the age profile of spending remains constant necessarily project huge increases in health expenditure as a consequence of population aging.

Research has, however, made it clear that the assumption of a constant age profile of health expenditure is not valid. It has become apparent that the age profile of spending has changed with increasing longevity in a way that attenuates the impact on health expenditure.

The Proximity to Death Effect

The main reason why the age profile of expenditure has changed is the "proximity to death" (PTD) effect. As noted in the main text, it has been clearly shown that the timing of the period of intensive use of medical services that people on average experience toward the end of their lives does not in general depend on age but instead on proximity to death. Thus, as the longevity of the population increases, this period of peak health expenditure occurs on average at an older chronological age. This has the effect of "flattening" the age profile of spending, so as to reduce the impact of increasing longevity on health spending.

The "pure" version of PTD takes this mechanism to the extreme by asserting that, as longevity increases, the age profile of health spending flattens so much that there is no increase in per capita health spending, notwithstanding the increase in the elderly population.

The pure version of the PTD effect can be illustrated by a thought experiment in which we assume that the population is divided equally between two groups of people, half of whom live until 72 ("group A") and half of whom live until 82 ("group B"). On the assumption that only proximity to death matters, annual average health spending for group A at age 70 would be the same as average annual health spending for group B at age 80 – because each group is two years away from death. The same would be true if we compared the two groups at, say, ages 65 and 75 respectively (12 years away from death). The difference between the two groups would therefore be that annual average spending increases less rapidly with age for the second group than for the first. If then, by some miracle of increasing longevity, everybody in group A were suddenly also to live until the age of 82, all that would happen is that the rate at which their health spending increases with age would slow. Their average annual spending at any given age would now be significantly less than it was when their lives were shorter. For example, their average annual spending at the age of 70 would, now that they live 10 years longer, be the same as it would have been at age 60. The result is that this group's increased longevity has no effect on health spending.

As discussed in the main text, the "pure" version of the PTD effect is an extreme position that is not justified by the evidence. A sounder position is that the PTD effect flattens the age profile of spending somewhat, but not sufficiently to prevent increased longevity from increasing health spending.

There is emerging evidence of another mechanism which works to stop the age profile of spending flattening to the extent assumed by the pure version of PTD. This is the impact of age-based rationing as longevity increases. Age-based rationing means that doctors tend to limit the amount of acute treatment that they provide to elderly patients who they believe to have reached an age at which they probably have few years of life left – and, conversely, that they "treat patients more aggressively if they think the result will pay off for a longer time span." Doctors may, for example, be much less inclined to recommend punishing chemotherapy to a 75-year-old cancer patient than to a 55-year-old cancer patient. (Patients themselves not infrequently take a similar view, being less willing to suffer radical treatments at an advanced age.) However, as longevity increases, doctors' (and patients') perception of the probable remaining lifespan of elderly patients at any given age increases. They come, for example, to think of the average 75-year-old patient as still in all likelihood having a decade or more ahead of them. They are consequently less likely to adopt a passive "low intervention" approach to bear on the treatment of such a patient. Thus, as longevity increases, the point at which "age-based rationing" of health treatments starts to happen is postponed until more advanced ages (Breyer, Lorenz and Niebel, 2012; Felder, 2013). Age-based rationing works in the opposite direction to PTD. As longevity increases, its effect is to raise the average annual spending on patients of any given age.

Compression of Morbidity

"Compression of morbidity" is a different theory about why the age profile of health expenditure cannot be expected to remain constant as longevity increases. In its original form, this theory focused on the duration of a supposed period late in life during which people tend to be afflicted with chronic disease. It assumed that, approximately speaking, the average person's lifespan can be divided into two phases – a largely disease-free period, followed by this period of chronic disease. The theory was that, as longevity increased over time, the age of onset of the period of chronic disease was postponed by more than the age of death. As a result, as longevity increased, people on average were spending a smaller proportion of their lives in chronic ill-health and a larger percentage of their lives disease-free – hence the term "compression of morbidity". People were, in other words, becoming intrinsically healthier at any given chronological age.

This hypothetical period of chronic disease must not be confused with the period of intense end-of-life medical treatment that is the focus of the "proximity to death" theory. Many people experience many years of chronic disease requiring long-term ongoing treatment, starting well before the end-of-life treatment peak.

In discussing the compression of morbidity theory, the distinction between recent and historical trends is crucial. Point-of-time comparisons between the start of the 20th century and the later decades of the century (e.g. the 1980s) have established beyond doubt that there was a significant delay in the onset of chronic disease over the historical long term (Fogel, 2004). But it is more recent *trends* in the onset of chronic conditions – i.e. trends from the later decades of the 20th century to the present – which are relevant in discussing the impact of population aging on chronic condition prevalence in recent times, and therefore to the subject matter of this book.

The findings of the research (cited in the main text) indicating that there has been no further ongoing compression of morbidity in recent times makes sense when we consider that most of the forces identified in earlier research as having given rise to the long-term historical compression of morbidity are no longer at work. These were forces that essentially arose during developments taking place quite a long time ago – in particular, the "conquest" of infectious diseases (childhood exposure to which gives rise to chronic conditions later in life); the end of widespread malnutrition; and environmental improvements (Fogel, 2004).

The impact of these forces is now largely exhausted (and the obesity plague is currently working in the opposite direction).

Health economists who continue today to assert the relevance of the "compression of morbidity" theory mostly have in mind a quite different version of the theory. This is what is more accurately referred to as the "compression of disability" theory, which holds that the age of onset of *serious functional disability* has been progressively postponed as longevity has increased. The evidence for this version of the theory is very mixed. But the question of whether the age of onset of functional disability is being postponed is irrelevant to the issue of the relationship between increased longevity and the prevalence of chronic conditions. As Lindgren (2016) notes, any postponement of the age of onset of serious functional disability is probably in large measure the consequence of the success of improved medical treatment in reducing the level of disability experienced by those suffering from chronic conditions, by slowing the progress of these conditions and ameliorating symptoms (see also Costa, 2005).

Those who have in the past entirely denied the impact of population aging on real per capita health expenditure have often relied mainly on the "compression of morbidity" theory, and not primarily on the "proximity to death" effect, or have failed to distinguish clearly between them. Only a major postponement of the onset of chronic disease would completely neutralize the impact of increasing longevity on health expenditure. But the "proximity to death" effect does not suggest any postponement in the age profile of increased spending on the ongoing long-term treatment of chronic conditions. It suggests only the postponement of much acute health expenditure. The "proximity to death" effect operating alone is therefore only capable of reducing, rather than eliminating, the impact of increased longevity on spending.

3. THE FUTURE OF HEALTH EXPENDITURE

Having looked at the past, we now turn to long-term trends in future government health spending. Here, the potential impact of policy changes looms large. In the United States, the introduction of universal health coverage – something to which much of the Democratic Party is strongly committed – would likely increase government expenditure by at least $1.38 trillion annually, equivalent to 6 percent of GDP.[1]

In other advanced countries, where universal health coverage is already a reality, no realistically imaginable single policy change would have such huge expenditure implications. Even something like the addition of universal dental cover would be inexpensive by comparison[2]. Nevertheless, the cumulative impact on government health spending of multiple future policy changes that increase or restrict health service coverage, or make other changes, could over time be substantial.

These types of policy changes are not, however, the subject matter of this book. What we are concerned with is, rather, the long-term evolution of government expenditure independent of the impact of future discretionary policy changes. This chapter therefore sets to one side the potential implications for spending of explicit decisions to expand or reduce the scope of government-provided health service coverage, and of other major policy measures. It does so to focus on a single question: *what will happen to total government health expenditure in advanced countries over the next 30 years, assuming unchanged policies?*

Unchanged health policies would certainly not result in unchanged spending. As in the past, powerful external forces will shape the direction of health budgets as surely as trade winds nudging along sailing ships on the high seas. The key external forces that have shaped spending in the past – the arrival of new and better treatments, population aging, productivity savings from technology, and changing health behaviors – will continue to operate in the future. Some of these will make themselves felt more (or less) strongly than in the past. Other forces, such as the health effects of climate change and a heightened awareness of the threat of infectious disease pandemics, will also come into play.

The initial focus of this chapter is the likely evolution of *total* health spending. As in the last chapter, we distinguish between expenditure-increasing forces and expenditure-reducing forces. Analyzing each of these leads to an assessment as to whether over the next three decades the growth of total health expenditure can be expected to accelerate or slow down — or even come to a halt, as some optimists suggest.

After this analysis, we focus specifically on *government's* share of health expenditure. Will government spending simply move in tandem with total spending? Or are there external forces at work that might significantly increase or reduce government's share of total health expenditure in some countries? Answering these questions leads to conclusions about the overall direction of government health expenditure over the next 30 years and beyond.

When we look ahead, there is one external force that looks set to dwarf all others — technological innovation. The health sector today is in the early stages of two major and closely linked technological transformations. The first is a bioscience revolution, centered on advances in molecular biology that are furnishing medical science with an increasingly detailed knowledge of the molecular mechanisms of disease. The other transformation is the application to health of new-generation digital technologies that are, in one form or another, changing the whole economy. These two technological transformations overlap in the growing field of bioinformatics, the main focus of which is the application of advanced computing to biosciences — for example, to analyze massive patient databases in search of a better understanding of the typology and causes of diseases. These major transformations will have far-reaching consequences for health spending. Some of them will be expenditure-increasing and some expenditure-reducing. We start by looking at the expenditure-increasing transformations.

Bioscience Advances and the Expanding Capabilities of Medicine

The continual development of new and better treatments that expand the "capabilities of medicine" has been the most important single force driving up health spending over the long term. Will this continue?

The bioscience revolution holds so much promise as to suggest that the answer is a resounding "yes." The foundations of this revolution were laid by the Human Genome Project, completed in 2003, which sequenced most of the human genetic code. Since then, rapidly expanding scientific knowledge has provided medicine with a growing armory of tools, such as whole genome sequencing of patients and diagnostic testing of pathogens and tumors by means that include DNA sequencing. The potential for these dramatic advances in molecular biology to further expand medicine is enormous.

A key area in which this expansion is currently under way is precision medicine, including customized medicine. Because of their potential impact on health spending, we focus on these in detail in this section.

Precision Medicine

Precision medicine refers to treatments geared to the specific genetic, lifestyle, environmental or other relevant characteristics of the patient. The main form of precision medicine draws on the field of pharmacogenomics to develop *precision pharmaceuticals* targeting patients whose conditions are characterized by specific "molecular signatures" (see below) such as particular gene mutations. Precision pharmaceuticals are not generally personalized, in the sense of being developed specially for the individual patient. Most are, rather, designed to treat groups of patients who share the same problematic molecular signature.

The term "personalized medicine" is not used in this book because, as noted by the US National Research Council (2011), it gives the false impression that *all* the treatments covered by the term are "developed uniquely for each individual patient."[3] For this reason, the NRC recommended that the term "precision medicine" replace "personalized medicine." Treatments unique to individual patients are referred to here as "customized medicines." Customized medicines are therefore one type of precision medicine, but most precision medicines are not customized medicines.

Precision pharmaceuticals are expensive for the same reason that orphan drugs are expensive: they are complex and they target groups of patients that are in most cases much smaller than those targeted by traditional pharmaceuticals. But the potential market for precision drugs collectively is enormous and their future cost impact correspondingly large.

The coming decades will bring an explosion in the development and use of precision pharmaceuticals. The potential benefits of these new types of drugs arise from the fact that, at the level of molecular biology, many non-infectious diseases are highly heterogeneous – they vary considerably. What have to date been labelled and treated as single diseases are in many cases groups of diverse medical conditions that do not respond, or respond equally well, to the same pharmaceutical treatment. Obtaining better results requires more targeted drugs that distinguish better between patients.

One way to look at this is by contrasting infectious and non-infectious diseases. Defining and treating infectious diseases is in principle straightforward. Each infectious disease is unambiguously defined by its biological causes – its *pathogenesis* – which in this case means the bacteria or virus causing the infection. Once the pathogenesis of the disease is known, the choice of treatment is usually clear. A test establishing the bacteria or virus involved is, therefore, generally sufficient both to provide a conclusive diagnosis and determine the appropriate treatment. Frequently, however, no such test is necessary, because the symptoms of many infections are sufficiently distinctive for their pathogenesis to be identified based on those alone.

Most non-infectious diseases are not like this. Identifying and testing patients to establish the pathogenesis of diseases such as chronic kidney disease, diabetes and cancers from which they are suffering has usually not been possible. Because of this, these and most other non-infectious diseases have traditionally been *defined*, as well as diagnosed, not on the basis of their biological causes, but by reference to their "clinical features" – physical manifestations such as skin blotches, high blood pressure, abnormalities identified in blood tests, obesity and other patient symptoms and characteristics.

For example, cancers have until recently been defined primarily based on the location and observable characteristics of the tumor. Breast cancer – to take a representative case – has been classified as a distinctive form of cancer because it occurs in a specific location (the breast), and is sub-classified into types of breast cancer such as "ductal" and "lobular" on the basis of where in the breast the tumors are located.

Similarly, diabetes is defined by the presence of sustained high blood sugar levels, and the more specific diagnosis of the type of diabetes – e.g. type 1 (insulin-dependent, normally childhood onset) or type 2 (non-insulin-dependent, usually adult onset) – is usually based on insulin tests, supplemented where considered appropriate by other tests and observations of patient characteristics such as obesity.

The problem is that classifying and diagnosing non-infectious diseases based on clinical features does not, in many cases, give doctors a terribly good basis to select the treatment that will work best. What medical practitioners have typically done has been to use a diagnosis based on clinical features as the basis for delivering a "one size fits all" treatment. This means, concretely, that the patient is initially given the standard "first-line" pharmaceutical or other treatment for the diagnosed disease. When, as is not infrequently the case, this treatment does not work or work well, other treatments are tried until (hopefully) something works. In the case of type 2 diabetes, for example, doctors commonly start a patient on Metformin, see how effective it is and then add or replace it with other drugs if it does not adequately control the patient's condition. This trial-and-error approach is taken because the doctor does not have the diagnostic tools to reliably judge how well Metaformin will work.

The fact that there is great variability in the response to standard pharmaceuticals of patients with the "same" diagnosis is a good indication that there are actually significant differences in the underlying nature of the diseases affecting them – that their pathogenesis is not uniform. That such differences exist is further suggested by the variability of patient characteristics and disease progression. For example, not all patients diagnosed with type 2 diabetes are obese and unfit. Some are thin, well-exercised and have none of the usual risk factors. It is hardly surprising then that, at the individual patient level, doctors have difficulty predicting the rate of progression of type 2 diabetes and sometimes even find it hard to identify risk factors in the patient.[4]

Advances in molecular biology provide the explanation – making it clear that, at the molecular level, what appears like the "same" disease often takes diverse forms. The biomolecular characteristics of these diseases – their "molecular signatures" – frequently differ considerably from one patient to another.

This is true even for some non-infectious diseases, the causes of which are in a sense the simplest – namely, "single-gene disorders" that are purely genetic in origin and arise from a single faulty gene. Cystic fibrosis (CF), for example, is always caused by mutations in the CFTR gene. But not all CF cases are the same, nor do they respond uniformly to specific treatments. Approximately 2,000 possible mutations of the CFTR gene can give rise to CF. The "molecular signature" of CF differs between individuals with respect to which of these mutations, or combinations of these mutations, are present. Depending on which mutations are involved, the impact of the disease and the appropriate treatment may differ significantly.

A great many non-infectious diseases have even more varieties at the biomolecular level. They are "multifactorial" (a.k.a. "complex") conditions. The genetic contribution to multifactorial conditions usually does not come from a single gene, but from multiple genes. To further complicate matters, many of these conditions are caused not by genes alone, but also by the way in which lifestyle, the environment and other factors impact on the individual's molecular biology. For such multifactorial conditions, genetic defects create susceptibility to disease, but do not by themselves make the disease inevitable. By making what are known as "epigenetic" changes, lifestyle, environmental and other external factors contribute to the development of diseases in individuals. Epigenetics refers to biomolecular characteristics at the cellular level that control the way an individual's genes operate but which are not themselves part of the genes.[5]

The molecular signatures of multifactorial diseases are thus considerably more complex than those of single-gene disorders. The molecular signatures of any one of these multifactorial diseases may vary considerably between patients and sub-groups of patients. Autism is a good example. To date, hundreds of different types of genetic defect contributing to autism have been identified, with more undoubtedly remaining to be discovered. The majority of the genetic defects concerned are, in isolation, associated with only a low risk of autism, meaning that (with limited exceptions) inheriting one faulty gene is not enough to develop autism. Most individuals with a form of autism have inherited a number of them (Robert et al, 2017; Griesi-Oliveira and Serité, 2017). And it is not only genes involved – epigenetic factors also play a role in the development of autism in some patients.

This variability at the biomolecular level explains why, beyond certain core symptoms, considerable variations in behavioral abnormalities are exhibited by patients with autism. Even though it has been possible to define a number of major sub-types of autism based on behavioral characteristics, many patients do not fit neatly into these sub-types, which is why psychiatrists label autism as a "spectrum" of conditions (autism spectrum disorder). It is also the fundamental reason why patients typically "will not have the same responsiveness to the same medication."[6]

Almost all of today's most widespread chronic conditions are multifactorial. In the case of so-called type 2 diabetes, for example, "the emerging picture is one in which a large constellation of genetic factors (from many hundred to a few thousand, according to some empirical estimates) work in concert with environmental and demographic factors" (Merino and Florez, 2018: 148). In other words, not only are a large number of possible mutations of different genes involved, but so are a large number of possible epigenetic factors that cause genes to malfunction. This enormous heterogeneity in the molecular signature of type 2 diabetes (and also in certain other types of diabetes) largely explains the variability in patient responsiveness to drugs, as well as in symptoms and disease progression. The degree of heterogeneity is so great as to call into question the usefulness of the term "diabetes." Certain experts suggest that the term will eventually disappear from the medical lexicon, to be replaced with a number of more detailed and specific diagnoses.

Dementia is similarly diverse (Fenoglio et al, 2018), as is chronic kidney disease. For many cancers, it is broadly the same story. Different patients who, according to the traditional disease taxonomy, suffer from the "same" form of cancer – such as ductal breast cancer – often display different molecular signatures, and this changes the effectiveness of specific treatment options.

This forms the background to precision pharmaceuticals. The core promise of precision pharmaceuticals is the treatment of patients with drugs designed to address the specific molecular signature of the condition that affects them. Treatment is preceded by diagnostic testing of the patient for the presence of so-called "biomarkers" – i.e. indicators of the specific molecular signature of disease. If the relevant biomarkers are detected, the precision drug is administered.

Keytruda (approved in 2014) is an example of a precision pharmaceutical. It is a drug used to treat patients suffering from a certain class of tumors – including the most common type of lung cancer – that manifest themselves in different parts of the body but share common genetic characteristics. Keytruda was pathbreaking because it was the first cancer drug targeted at solid tumors on the basis of a biomarker, without regard for the traditional location-based cancer classification (lung cancer, skin cancer, etc.). It is expensive: treatment costs $150,000 per year.

In addition to matching pharmaceuticals to the molecular signatures of diseases, precision medicine also offers the means of developing pharmaceuticals that avoid adverse "pharmacogenetic" interactions – that is, adverse reactions to drugs caused by unusual genetic or other biomolecular characteristics of specific patients (Topol, 2015: 174).

One of the first precision pharmaceuticals – Herceptin (a breast cancer therapy) – was approved as far back as 1998. Herceptin is designed to treat the sub-set of patients whose breast cancer is caused by the malfunction of a specific gene (ERBB2). Despite this pioneering example of an effective precision pharmaceutical, it is only recently that substantial numbers of precision pharmaceuticals have come on the market. By 2017, the US Food and Drug Administration had approved several dozen, and it is clear that increasing numbers will become available over coming years. Many of the recently approved precision pharmaceuticals are cancer drugs. However, precision pharmaceuticals are also emerging for widespread multifactorial chronic conditions such as diabetes (Merino and Florez, 2018: 143).

The burgeoning development of precision pharmaceuticals has been made possible by the impressive recent advances in molecular biology and bioinformatics. These advances are increasingly making it possible to identify the molecular signatures of disease in specific patients, initially through genetic sequencing and now through other techniques such as epigenetic profiling. The ever-widening understanding of the genetic, epigenetic and other biomolecular factors triggering disease is derived from the analysis of huge databases of patient biomolecular profiles using techniques such as "genome-wide association studies," which apply advanced computing to identify causal patterns otherwise impossible to see. Tests for the presence of the relevant biomarkers have also only become possible because of these advances in molecular biology.

Diseases that are purely genetic – together with those with a particularly large genetic component (like some cancers) – offer the greatest immediate potential for the development of precision pharmaceuticals. For this reason, the development of orphan drugs is a rapidly developing focus of precision medicine. (As mentioned in the last chapter, most rare diseases are purely genetic and a large proportion are single-gene disorders.)

Kalydeco, the specialized cystic fibrosis (CF) drug, is a prime example of an orphan drug for a single-gene disorder that also qualifies as a precision medicine, because it is targeted at patients who have specific identifiable mutations of the relevant gene. Kalydeco works only for patients who have one of a small number (33 at time of writing) of the approximately 2,000 different mutations of the CFTR gene giving rise to CF. For individuals with these specific mutations, Kalydeco is very effective,[7] because it is the first CF drug that treats the underlying causes of the disease rather than merely alleviating its symptoms.

The potential impact on health expenditure of the development of increasingly large numbers of precision pharmaceuticals is enormous.

Even the development of more precision pharmaceuticals for rare diseases has a big potential impact on spending. Notwithstanding the impressive progress in the development of orphan drugs, treatments currently exist for only about 5 percent of the more than 7,000[8] rare diseases identified by medical science. Although each individual rare disease affects only a tiny part of the population, the numbers of people suffering from rare diseases is significant collectively. In France, for example, government estimates put the figure at 4.5 percent of the population, while in the United States, estimates suggest around twice that percentage (QuintileIMS, 2017).

The risk of an explosion in expenditure on precision pharmaceuticals for rare diseases needs, however, to be qualified in one important way. There is a real possibility that *gene editing* (see Box 3.1) will in future provide effective, low-cost treatment – and even permanent prevention – for many diseases that are purely or primarily genetic.

Even if this happens, expenditure on precision drugs will still increase enormously in coming decades, because gene editing is not capable of providing cures for the most widespread non-infectious diseases and, in particular, for the chronic conditions that already account for such a large portion of health spending. Why? Because most of these conditions are multifactorial, with a large component of epigenetic causation.

Box 3.1 Gene Editing

Gene editing – not the same as gene therapy[9] – permits targeted modification of human genetic code (Doudna and Sternberg, 2017). By correcting disease-producing mutations, it can in principle totally cure genetic diseases. Even more exciting is the prospect that "germline" gene editing will radically reduce the prevalence of genetic diseases by editing undesirable mutations out of stem cells in human embryos so as to prevent them causing disease not only in the baby concerned, but in its descendants.

Gene editing has greatest applicability to purely genetic diseases

such as cystic fibrosis, where it has already been used in the laboratory to remove and replace the faulty CFTR gene, opening up the
exciting possibility of cures for many rare diseases. It also has good
prospects for curing some cancers. However, it has a long way to go
before it can move out of the laboratory and into hospitals. Significant
question marks about its efficacy remain, together with major issues
concerning its potential application for germline gene editing.

The development of large numbers of expensive new precision drugs for a
multiplicity of forms of chronic diseases such as diabetes, chronic kidney
disease, Alzheimer's[10] and other forms of dementia will increasingly
expose the treatment of these common conditions to the same forces that
make orphan drugs so expensive – complexity and the absence of scale
economies due to relatively small numbers of patients.

It seems quite possible that the revolution in molecular biology will
also open the door to new successes in the treatment of mental illness.
Mainly because of the biomolecular complexity of mental illness, the
development of new psychiatric drugs has in recent years proven exceedingly difficult, to the extent that certain major pharmaceutical companies
have exited the field entirely. But as the example of autism spectrum disorder suggests, there is hope based on precision medicine strategies. If so,
the potential for the relief of human suffering will be enormous, but so
potentially will be the cost.

New-generation digital technologies – especially artificial intelligence
– are being applied to the search for new precision pharmaceuticals, as
well as to new approaches to testing them. Gene editing is also providing
multi-purpose tools that greatly assist the process of developing new pharmaceuticals. However, while these technologies are capable of lowering *per
drug* research and development costs, their overall effect is likely to be to
increase pharmaceutical expenditure by accelerating the rate at which new
precision pharmaceuticals arrive on the market.

The patent system will also contribute significantly to the high prices
of new precision pharmaceuticals. Even in cases where the development
and production costs of new pharmaceuticals are relatively modest, the

patent system guarantees that, if they are effective, they will command high prices for decades. This means the *rate* at which new pharmaceuticals are developed has a major impact on total expenditure. The role of the patent system will be particularly important if the coming decades turn out, as can be expected, to be a period when repeated waves of new precision pharmaceuticals come on the market.

The rise of precision pharmaceuticals will also bring with it a major increase in spending on biomolecular diagnostic testing, such as various forms of DNA sequencing, RNA sequencing, comparative genomic hybridization and epigenetic profiling. Spending will increase, despite the fact that, over the decades to come, costs per test can be expected to fall significantly. This will be because savings from falls in cost per test will be outweighed by a huge expansion in the number of tests carried out. Almost every precision drug will be accompanied by a diagnostic test to establish the presence of relevant biomarkers. Biomolecular tests will also be used increasingly for preventative purposes – that is, the testing of people who have not yet developed diseases or symptoms. Not only will there be more testing, but tests will become more complex, covering progressively more dimensions of each individual's cellular biology.

Precision pharmaceuticals will have a major impact on the costs of treating chronic conditions, even if the prevalence of chronic conditions such as diabetes, dementia and cancer does not change. But it seems highly likely that prevalence will indeed increase over coming decades, and that the impact of precision pharmaceuticals on health spending will be even greater as a consequence.

Chronic condition prevalence can be expected to increase for three reasons. The first is population aging, which is discussed below. The second lies in trends in health behaviors. The rate of obesity seems certain to continue increasing, pushing up the prevalence of diabetes, CKD and other chronic conditions.[11] OECD projections suggest that obesity will increase across advanced countries generally (OECD, 2017a). Another recent study estimates that fully half of the American children who were aged between two and 19 in 2016 will be obese by the time they are 35 (Ward et al, 2017). Although the obesity crisis could in principle be resolved through preventative measures to address the root problems of excessive nutrition, industrial junk food and physical inactivity, it is hard to be optimistic about society's collective capacity to make the major changes required. The tide is unlikely to be turned only through measures designed to encourage individuals to change their behavior (in the way that the problem of smoking was attacked), and it is difficult to see governments taking the draconian action required against the highly processed food industry.

Some are more optimistic about future trends in health behaviors. They base this optimism on the increasing number of people with a strong commitment to healthier living, stretching from organic foods to fitness regimes (Comtesse, 2017). But this trend is particularly concentrated in the educated professional elite and there is little evidence to suggest that it will become the norm across society as a whole.

A third reason to expect chronic condition prevalence to rise is the impact of medical advances themselves. Paradoxically, advances in the treatment of chronic conditions work, both directly and indirectly, to increase prevalence. They do so directly because patients being treated for specific chronic conditions tend to live longer, thereby swelling the prevalence count for the condition concerned. They do so indirectly, because the longer patients live with chronic conditions, the more likely they are to develop other chronic conditions – to develop "multi-morbidity," as discussed previously.

Customized Medicine

Small production scale resulting in high treatment costs is even more of a problem for *customized* medicine, which refers to treatments produced *uniquely* for individual patients.

Customized pharmaceuticals are one type of customized medicine. They include customized immunotherapies,[12] which boost the capacity of the immune system of the patient in order to fight disease. A pioneering example of a customized immunotherapy is Provenge, a treatment for advanced prostate cancer, approved in 2010 and which costs approximately $100,000 per treatment. Customized immunotherapies like this are produced by extracting cells from the patient's own immune system and processing them (sometimes using gene editing) to create what is effectively a patient-specific pharmaceutical. The processed cells are then re-introduced into the patient's body where they strengthen the immune system so that it does a better job of recognizing and fighting the cancer or other targeted disease.

Another example of a customized pharmaceutical is Strimvelis, approved in Europe in 2016 for the treatment of the very rare "bubble boy" syndrome, caused by a single-gene mutation that disables the immune system. Its "list" price is €594,000 per treatment. Strimvelis also works by treating the individual patient's blood cells – in this case, by using gene therapy to insert a functioning copy of the gene concerned.

Customized pharmaceuticals are, once again, different from other types of precision pharmaceuticals. The precision pharmaceuticals discussed earlier – such as Keytruda, Herceptin and Kalydeco – are not unique products for individual patients. Once developed, such precision pharmaceuticals become off-the-shelf products used for all patients with the relevant biomarkers. Provenge and Strimvelis, by contrast, are tailored uniquely to the patient.

Customized *regenerative medicine* (see Box 3.2) is another rapidly developing field. Here, "customized" medicine involves treating patients by means of the infusion or transplantation of replacement cells, tissues and organs developed using patients' own biological material (or in some other way specific to that patient). Organ transplants using organs grown from patients' own cells ("autologous" transplants) are a particularly promising field. Autologous bladder transplants have already been carried out. Liver and kidney transplants are likely to follow quickly. Autologous transplants have a higher success rate than conventional transplants using donor organs ("homologous" transplants) because they avoid the problem of transplant rejection, when the body's immune system fights against "alien" genetic material. They thereby also avoid the need to treat transplant patients with anti-rejection therapies, which, by suppressing the immune system, create their own risks.

Box 3.2 Regenerative Medicine

The aim of regenerative medicine is to replace or regenerate human cells, tissues or organs to restore or establish functionality lost due to age, disease, damage or congenital defects. When this is done using the patient's own biological material, it constitutes a form of customized medicine. One approach to customized regenerative medicine is to trigger the regeneration within the body of damaged tissues and organs that were previously irreparable by means, for example, of the harvesting and use of adult stem cells. Another is the use of replacement tissues and organs grown in the laboratory, including by means of 3D "bioprinters."

Customized regenerative medicine will push up health costs significantly for at least two reasons. One is that the customized nature of such treatments means that they will never be cheap. The other is that the potential demand is enormous. The current large unmet demand for organ transplants provides particularly clear evidence. Everywhere in the world, the limited supply of donor organs means that many people who need transplants never receive them. The removal of this replacement-organ supply bottleneck through the use of autologous transplants would enormously increase the number of transplants. The high prevalence of CKD makes it certain, for example, that there will be many more kidney transplants.

In coming decades, regenerative medicine will become extensively used for rejuvenation purposes, to slow down the process of aging and extend human lifespans. It will therefore overlap with the growing field of *anti-aging medicine.* This brings us to the broader question of the impact of population aging on health expenditure.

Aging and Health Expenditure

We are now in the midst of a sharp acceleration of population aging across most of the advanced world, with the percentage of the population of high-income countries aged 65 and over projected to increase from 17 percent to 27 percent between 2015 and 2050 (UN, 2019a: 240-41). The percentage of those aged 80 or over is projected to more than double. This has led many non-specialists to believe – wrongly – that aging has become the principal force pushing up health spending. Specialists, by contrast, take precisely the opposite view, and consider that population aging will play only a minor role in increasing spending. Proponents of this school of thought include the OECD, which in its long-term health expenditure projections sees aging as likely to account for only about one-seventh of the projected total increase in health spending in its member countries over the period 2010-2060 (de la Maisonneuve and Oliveira Martins, 2014).[13]

The problem with the OECD's long-term health expenditure forecasts is that they are underpinned by the most extreme version of the "proximity to death" effect – specifically, the assumption is that "health care spending is only driven by the proximity to death and not by an increase in the average age of the population." The OECD is, in other words, asking us to believe that even though people will in the future live longer in old age than they do today, this will not increase average annual per capita health spending by a single dollar (so that the small impact of aging on health expenditure arises *solely* from fertility-rate effects). But this is, as discussed in the last chapter, an unrealistic assumption. A more appropriate basis for forecasting would be a model which recognizes that increasing longevity does in fact increase spending, notwithstanding that its impact is attenuated by the proximity to death effect.

The recognition that increases in longevity will have some expenditure-increasing effect over coming decades is not, however, the only reason to believe that the impact of population aging on spending will not be "minor." Two other relevant considerations point in the same direction.

The first is that "fertility-rate effects" are now playing a more important role in population aging than increases in longevity. As noted, fertility-rate effects describe the way in which past changes in the number of children per woman affect the proportion of elderly people in today's population. Concretely, much of the rapid population aging we are witnessing at present is due to the progressive movement of the baby boomer generation into old age, compounded by subsequent falls in fertility rates.

In many (but not all) advanced countries, fertility-rate effects will be the main force driving population aging for several decades to come.

The second reason is that population aging and technology can be expected to work together to push spending up. The arrival of new medical treatments tends to increase per capita health expenditure on elderly people more than on younger people, for the simple reason that older people use more medical services. The combination of population aging and the pressure of medical advances on treatment costs thus has a "double whammy" impact on spending (Dormont and Huber, 2012). As Meijer et al (2013) put it, "the most important driver of health expenditure growth, medical technology, interacts strongly with age and health, i.e. population aging reinforces the influence of medical technology on health expenditure growth and vice versa." This point is missed if population aging and technology are viewed as entirely separate forces.[14]

The interaction between population aging and technology will become even more important because new precision medicines and customized regenerative treatments will be disproportionately used to treat elderly patients. The dynamic will be further reinforced if major advances are made in the field of anti-aging medicine.

Although the bioscience revolution will be the main force pushing up health spending in coming decades, population aging will therefore play a somewhat greater role than in the past. Dismissing the future impact of population aging as "minor" is unrealistic. Quantifying exactly what its impact will be in specific advanced countries would require modelling that is beyond the scope of this book. It seems, however, safe to say it will be greater than forecast by the OECD. This is a view which, incidentally, is shared by the IMF.[15]

The Challenge of Infectious Diseases

The coronavirus pandemic which hit the advanced world in 2020 put health systems, and particularly public hospitals, under extreme pressure. Government health expenditure has risen sharply everywhere. In no other area has the slogan "whatever it costs" been a more apt description of the response to the crisis.

This surge in health expenditure will, however, be mainly temporary. Given the nature of the SARS-CoV-2 virus, scientists are confident that a vaccine can be developed relatively rapidly. There is also a good chance that pharmaceutical and other treatments for COVID-19 will soon become available. The powerful new tools developed by the bioscience revolution have strengthened the capacity of humanity to fight back against this type of unseen enemy.

When the worst of the coronavirus pandemic is finally behind us, attention will shift to the longer-term implications for health systems and for government health expenditure. The key question will be what needs to be done, and what money needs to be spent, to protect ourselves better against future pandemics.

The coronavirus pandemic was not a freak event like a giant meteorite hitting the planet. Infectious disease experts have been warning for years of the risk of the emergence of precisely this type of pandemic.[16] Government officials were also well aware of the danger. Thus in January 2019, the US director of national intelligence warned that "the United States and the world will remain vulnerable to the next flu pandemic or large-scale outbreak of a contagious disease that could lead to massive rates of death and disability, severely affect the economy [and] strain international resources."[17] There have, moreover, been multiple past "close shaves" including the 2009 H1N1 influenza pandemic, the Ebola-Reston outbreak in Virginia in 1989, the Marburg virus in Germany in 1967, the Hendra virus in Brisbane, Australia in 1994, and the 2014 Ebola incident in Dallas, Texas. A serious pandemic was only a question of time.

Health systems were nevertheless poorly prepared to deal with this entirely predictable eventuality. Stocks of essential equipment and supplies, including ventilators, key pharmaceuticals, face masks and other personal protective equipment (PPE) were inadequate, and ran out quickly. There were far too few isolation wards and specialist facilities, and no capacity to rapidly deploy tests on a sufficient scale. Health workers were in many cases inadequately trained and prepared to handle pandemics.

Many avoidable deaths – of health workers as well as patients — have resulted from this lack of preparedness. In a sense, however, humanity has been lucky, because the mortality rate of COVID-19 (the disease caused by the virus) is relatively low. Things would have been infinitely worse if we had, say, faced a virus as contagious as SARS-CoV-2 but as lethal as smallpox, Ebola or even SARS. And there might have been less confidence about the rapid development of a vaccine if the virus had been of a more complex and/or unusual type.

There are a number of reasons why health systems were poorly prepared. Prominent among them was the acute financial pressure under which public hospitals have for some time been operating (see Chapter 1). Here, the writing was on the wall well before 2020. During the winter of 2017-18, for example, cash-starved public hospitals in the United Kingdom ran out of ventilators, oxygen cylinders, and face masks, in the face of a normal seasonal wave of influenza.[18] France faced a similar position a year earlier, at which time a senior health official who subsequently became national director general of health warned in a confidential memo that the seasonal flu epidemic would have a "significant and avoidable human cost" because "hospitals, already in crisis … have no elasticity to absorb variations of activity."[19] Several years earlier, moreover, France had made the disastrous decision for budgetary reasons in 2013 to abandon most of the country's centrally managed strategic stock of medical face masks.[20] In the United States, the fact that hospitals were not maintaining adequate stocks of PPE and other specialist equipment was documented in several studies and official reports prior to 2020 that explicitly identified budget pressures as a major contributing factor to the problem (OIG, 2018: 17; Popescu and Leach, 2019).

A senior US Treasury official once described government as "a gigantic insurance company (with a sideline business in national defense and homeland security)." Pandemic risk is one of the risks against which government should be providing proper insurance cover. But for cover to be provided, society must pay the required insurance premium. This means paying, amongst other things, for adequate emergency stocks of PPE and other vital equipment; specialist facilities; regular training and simulation exercises to maintain staff readiness; and the maintenance of local industry capacity to rapidly ramp up production of needed equipment, pharmaceuticals, tests and other supplies in the event of an emergency (Patel et al, 2017). With the coronavirus pandemic, humanity has paid a steep price for having skipped the premium payments.

This is unlikely to happen in future. Governments of all advanced countries can be expected to spend considerably more in coming years to strengthen and maintain the capacity of their health systems to respond to future pandemics. There is no easy way of putting a figure on what this will cost, but data on past limited capacity-building efforts suggests that the cost will be considerable (e.g. Patel et al, 2019).

Apart from pandemics, there are two other scenarios in which infectious diseases might become a higher priority for health systems in advanced countries. One is that outbreaks of insect-borne diseases such as dengue, yellow fever, malaria, and Zika – and "vector-borne" diseases more generally – become rampant in parts of the developed world because of global warming (IPCC, 2018; USGCRP, 2018). The other scenario is that the growth of antibiotic resistance paves the way for a large increase in the incidence of untreatable infectious diseases – potentially (in the words of the former chief medical officer of England) "putting medicine back in the dark ages"[21].

Both of these appear to be significant risks. With respect to the impact of climate change, scientific opinion appears to have become progressively gloomier about the potential impact on the prevalence of vector-borne diseases in advanced countries as well as the developing world (e.g. Ryan et al, 2019; Lee and Farlow, 2019). The unexpected dengue fever outbreak in Japan in 2014 – bringing with it the first domestic dengue cases for 70 years – gave considerable concrete grounds for concern. Southern parts of Europe and the United States are also in the front line for the future emergence of this problem. It therefore seems quite probable that climate change will bring with it both increased treatment and vaccination costs, although it is not easy to estimate how significant these costs might be.

Antibiotic resistance may pose an even greater risk. Here, much depends on the degree to which advances in biosciences help in the development of new antibiotics. Also important will be how successful we are in discouraging practices that accelerate the development of antibiotic resistance, including excessive and inappropriate use of antibiotics in medicine and animal husbandry. Nevertheless, it is not possible to make confident predictions concerning the implications of antibiotic resistance for the long-term evolution of health expenditure.

◆ ◆ ◆

The preceding review of upward pressures on health spending in coming decades makes it clear that the bioscience revolution can be expected to lead to the development and use of many new treatments. Humanity can look forward to a period of particularly rapid expansion of the "capabilities of medicine." Many of the new treatments will either target relatively small numbers of patients or be tailored to specific individuals. Their costs will tend to be high because of technical complexity and the absence of scale economies. High cost per case will combine with widespread utilization of these new treatments to impact heavily on total health expenditure. Population aging will add to the upward pressure on spending, in part because it will magnify the impact of technological innovation. More will also be spent on strengthening and maintaining capacity to fight infectious disease pandemics.

There is every indication that this upward pressure on spending will be quite powerful. Without some major countervailing force, health expenditure/GDP will grow more rapidly than in the past. Is it, however, possible that savings arising from the use of new-generation technologies will provide such a countervailing force?

Will Digital Technologies Save the Day?

New-generation digital technologies – including artificial intelligence (AI), advanced robotics,[22] cloud computing and the internet of things – offer exciting possibilities for savings in the health sector. Diagnostic systems based on AI and machine learning, automated triage systems, intelligent hospital monitoring systems, "wearables," apps and attachments to smart phones capable of carrying out medical tests – all of these and more appear poised to significantly change medical practice. One thing particularly striking about these new technologies is that so many of them are focused on *clinical* tasks (tasks involved in diagnosing and treating patients). This represents a major break from the past, when the main application of information technology was for administrative and support tasks, such as the management of medical records and billing.

Some confidently believe that savings from the use of new-generation digital technologies will be so great that the upward movement of health spending will finally be halted (e.g. Comtesse, 2017). This simple view fails, however, to take proper account of the strength of pressure on spending resulting from the continuous arrival of new treatments and the willingness of individuals and society to finance these new treatments from rising real per capita incomes. As we have seen, these expenditure-increasing impacts of technological innovation can be expected – taken in isolation – to push health expenditure up significantly more rapidly than national income. It follows that, to stabilize or reduce health spending as a proportion of national income, cost savings from new-generation digital technology would need to be large enough to pay for the bulk of the increased spending arising from the expanding capabilities of medicine. Is it realistic to expect that new-generation digital technologies will deliver savings of this magnitude?

New Technology and Healthcare Productivity

The most direct way in which new-generation digital technologies can potentially reduce health expenditure is by increasing productivity – that is, reducing the inputs required to treat any given medical condition – thereby reducing cost per case. Suppose, for example, that due to technologically driven improvements in efficiency, the average cost of treating a heart attack case was reduced by, say, 15 percent, that of treating osteoarthritis fell by 20 percent, and that there were similar reductions in the cost of treating the majority of other medical conditions. The resulting savings would do much to absorb the cost of the introduction of new and better treatments.

The most exciting prospect for raising productivity is increased automation, particularly of clinical tasks. One area where there is significant scope for automation is diagnostic information gathering. Even with currently demonstrated technology, machines are capable of taking over a significant part of the work of taking patient histories, monitoring patients (both in and outside hospitals) and carrying out tests and clinical examinations. A range of clinical support tasks are also ripe for automation – for example, through the use of robots for lifting and transporting patients in hospitals.

McKinsey (MGI, 2017) estimates that, based on currently demonstrated technology, there is potential for net cost savings from automation of 11 percent in hospital emergency departments. Applying similar methodology to that employed by McKinsey, Darzi (2018) has estimated that in the United Kingdom the following time savings could be realized: 23 percent for National Health Service doctors; 31 percent for general practitioners ("family doctors" in US parlance); 29 percent for nurses and health visitors; 25 percent for scientific, therapeutic, and technical staff, and so on. This, according to Darzi, implies potential cost savings in the order of £12.5 billion.

Some progress is also being made in automating diagnosis itself and some of the tasks involved in treating patients. Certain component tasks of surgery (e.g. suturing) can now be performed by robots, and more will undoubtedly follow. AI-based diagnostic systems have performed impressively in diagnosis based on pattern recognition using big data (e.g. skin cancer and pneumonia from images; Parkinson's disease from analysis of voice patterns), and it looks likely that a significant part of the work of radiologists will be automated in years to come.

Automation is not the only way in which new digital technologies can increase productivity. As in the past, productivity gains will sometimes arise as the indirect consequence of technological innovation primarily aimed at improving the *quality* of medical treatment. The current use of surgical robots is one example. The main role of these robots is not to automate surgery, but rather to serve as tools to assist surgeons. In the case of the Da Vinci surgical robot, for example, the surgeon controls the robot, which reproduces his or her movements using micro-instruments, making smaller and more accurate movements inside the patient's body. Despite the fact that the robot is not replacing the surgeon, hospitals have achieved significant cost savings because more precise surgery reduces the rate of post-operative complications and the average post-operative hospital stay.[23]

The same is potentially true with respect to the use of AI-based diagnostic systems. At present, machines are not permitted to take over the diagnostic role. Rather, AI is being deployed to suggest diagnoses (and sometimes also to present treatment options) to medical practitioners. The doctors make the final diagnosis and decide which treatment will be used. Even in this restricted role, these systems have significant potential to improve productivity. In the first place, they can enable doctors to make diagnoses more quickly in complex cases, thereby saving time. Secondly, they can cut wasteful expenditure on inappropriate treatment by reducing the rate of incorrect diagnosis. This is already happening in areas such as the analysis of mammograms, where misdiagnosis by radiologists is not uncommon (Harwich and Laycock, 2018).

Another source of productivity savings is the increasing use of "digital first triage" systems (see Box 3.3). These systems improve productivity principally by economizing on highly skilled labor, both by reducing the number of unnecessary doctor appointments and by diverting patients from doctors to nurses for conditions which the latter are competent to handle.

Box 3.3 Digital First Triage Systems

In these systems – one of the better-known of which is that developed by Babylon Health (Razzaki et al, 2018) – a bot or app interrogates the potential patient about his or her symptoms, and then advises whether there is a need to see a doctor or whether, alternatively, it will suffice to see a nurse or pharmacist. The bot or app will also tell the patient if none of this is necessary and that they should either treat themselves (e.g. take a pain killer and go to bed) or do nothing. This can potentially have a large labor-saving impact by reducing the currently high number of doctor appointments that are unnecessary because the patient does not in reality require treatment.[24] As for diverting patients from doctors to nurses, US experience has demonstrated that there is significant scope to do this without any loss of quality of care for less complex cases (Topol, 2015: 264-6).

Productivity gains may also arise from better patient adherence to treatment regimes, such as when apps help patients to remember to take their medication (Topol, 2015: 220-24).

What does the future hold for productivity gains driven by digital technology? Technological enthusiasts consider the potential to be virtually unlimited. They suggest that 80 percent of what doctors currently do will be automated (Khosla, 2012). Some even envisage "major hospitals... where robots diagnose, prescribe, and make surgical interventions" (Johannessen, 2019).

Such predictions are representative of the broader techno-enthusiast view that the economy as a whole is moving rapidly towards a machine takeover, in which most of what humans currently do will be automated. However, for reasons discussed in detail in Chapter 7, this interpretation of current trends is not credible. Human labor is unlikely to be broadly replaced by machines over this book's timeframe – or any time soon after. In predicting a machine takeover, the techno-enthusiasts grossly underestimate the magnitude of the obstacles confronting the development of artificial intelligence. They fail to grasp the complexity, and consequent difficulty, of automating much of what humans do (including things that seem very simple). AI systems, for example, cope very poorly with the unexpected and non-routine, and are good only when focused on very narrow tasks. Common sense and any concept of "relevance" remain beyond them.

In the specific case of health care, there are considerable obstacles to the automation of many of the tasks that form part of the treatment of patients. Medical practice involves a great deal that is unexpected and non-routine, and the ability to assess relevance and apply common sense is extremely important. "Today's AI is narrow and not capable of the holistic thinking and complex judgment required for many clinical tasks" (Loder and Nicholas, 2018). This is why the so-called "AI chasm" – the gap between concept and practical application – is particularly large in the health sector (Keane and Topol, 2018).

Surgery graphically illustrates these points. It is precisely because of the difficulties AI faces in dealing with the unexpected and non-routine, and its inability to make quick common-sense decisions, that it will be a *very* long time before the main work involved in carrying out a successful surgical procedure will be automated. Completely automated surgery – as opposed to robots carrying out limited surgical tasks – is pure science fiction.

It is also hard to see diagnosis and treatment decisions being wholly automated in anything other than the distant future. While AI excels in narrow diagnostic tasks such as the identification of skin cancers, much diagnostic work requires a considerably broader perspective than pattern recognition. Systems designed to carry out more challenging diagnostic tasks – such as Watson Oncology, the IBM system for diagnosing cancer – are much less reliable.[25] These systems will improve, and it can be expected that some diagnostic work will be automated. Fully robotized diagnosis appears, however, less likely.

This is not to downplay the great potential for AI-based diagnostic systems, working to support human doctors, to improve medical practice. Human doctors also make incorrect diagnoses and even the very best doctors are unable to master more than a small fraction of the vast body of medical literature and knowledge.

Will Costs Per Case Fall Across the Board?

How large are the savings in cost per case that new-generation digital technology is likely to deliver? Given the potentially large productivity gains, it might be thought that reductions in cost per case will also be substantial. This overlooks, however, a critically important point – productivity gains in an industry do not *necessarily* reduce the cost of producing that industry's products. As discussed, Baumol's cost disease theory suggests that the impact of productivity gains on product costs depends on how the productivity gains achieved in the industry concerned compare with those realized in the rest of the economy. Once again, the theory says, approximately speaking, that:

◆   Products of industries with below-average productivity growth tend to become progressively more expensive (their prices increase faster than inflation).

◆ Products of industries with above-average productivity growth become progressively cheaper (their prices increase less than inflation).

The reason, as we have seen, is that industry productivity growth that is merely in line with the economy-wide average tends to be absorbed in wage increases, as real wages rise in line with productivity. This implies that productivity gains from new-generation digital technology cannot be expected to lead to lower costs per case across the board unless future productivity growth in the healthcare industry is *faster* than productivity growth in the economy as a whole.

Moreover, with substantial additional spending on new and better treatments, future healthcare productivity growth would need to be *much* faster than productivity growth elsewhere in the economy if it were to deliver reductions in cost per case large enough to offset that additional spending and thereby to halt the upward movement in health expenditure/GDP.

Is it realistic to expect that the productivity gains in the healthcare industry will be much larger than those realized across the rest of the economy? The problem is that even if future productivity gains in the healthcare industry are impressive, new-generation digital technology can be expected to also deliver large productivity gains across the rest of the economy. New-generation technologies will have – and indeed already are having – a major impact not only on manufacturing and agriculture but also on other service industries. McKinsey (MGI, 2017), for example, projects potential economy-wide increases in the rate of productivity growth in the range of 0.8-1.4 percent per annum.

It might be thought that as labor costs constitute a substantial part of overall treatment costs (probably around half) in the healthcare industry, they offer the potential for particularly large productivity gains. However, service industries, many of which are relatively labor-intensive, account in most advanced economies for 70-80 percent of GDP. Although the labor-cost component is higher for health care than for some other service industries, it is also lower than for others – including major industries such as education and professional and business services.

Moreover, the nature of the healthcare industry makes it more challenging to implement some of the new technologies than in other major service industries. These technologies are most readily applied to routine or highly structured activities carried out in predictable environments. For this reason, the service industries with the greatest potential for direct labor savings include trade and transport, food services, and finance and insurance. Health care is tougher because there is such a large degree of variability in the diseases and conditions affecting patients, and in other patient characteristics that may alter the choice and mode of treatment. Fully automated diagnosis and surgery are, for these reasons, even more technologically difficult to achieve than self-driving vehicles, meaning that the scope for the new productivity-enhancing technologies in the healthcare industry is less than for the economy as a whole.

The complexity of much health treatment affects not only the technical feasibility of implementing new-generation digital technology, but also the cost of the systems required. It reduces the scope for using "off-the-shelf" technology solutions and components. AI and other systems for health care often need to be heavily customized, which – given the complexity – raises costs.

A safe assumption is therefore that the main impact of productivity gains from digital technology will be to slow down somewhat the rise of health expenditure. Those who look to large technologically driven reductions in cost per case to stem the tide of rising health expenditure/GDP will be disappointed.

Box 3.4 Stabilizing Health Spending by Squeezing Healthcare Worker Remuneration?

Even if productivity growth is no greater in health care than in the rest of the economy, cost per case could still fall if healthcare workers are denied wage rises that workers elsewhere in the economy receive. Squeezing wages, in other words, also offers potential for offsetting to some extent the costs of new and better treatments. This strategy, however, has limited mileage because it necessarily results in growing recruitment problems – as illustrated by the increasing inability of the British National Health System over the past decade to fill vacant clinical positions.[26]

Other Potential Savings

Perhaps, however, all is not lost. Digital technologies will deliver savings through channels other than their impact on costs per case. One is prevention, where digital technologies are already giving individuals and physicians an enhanced capacity to monitor health status and make behavioral changes that can prevent the emergence of disease. Techno-enthusiasts wax lyrical on the possibilities here. Some foresee a shift in the focus of the health system from "diagnose and treat" to "predict and prevent" (Darzi, 2018). Others seem to imagine that we are about to enter a new era where, armed with DIY technology, most people will pursue healthy lifestyles and active disease prevention with great dedication – becoming, in Topol's purple prose, "chief operating officers" in charge of their own health. A second, related, channel for potential savings is earlier disease detection – for example, through easy, self-administered tests using smartphones or other digital technology (see Box 3.5). The idea here is that, by detecting a disease earlier in its progression, it will be possible to treat it more cheaply (something often, but not *always*, true).

Three points, however, suggest we should moderate our expectations about the magnitude of savings from prevention and earlier diagnosis.

The first is that the more systematic monitoring and testing necessary to achieve earlier diagnosis will also have the "perverse" effect of greatly increasing the number of people receiving medical treatment. Many people today should be receiving treatment for conditions but are not doing so because their conditions have not been diagnosed. As Cutler (2004) notes, "undertreatment of chronic disease is a pervasive feature of all medical systems." To the extent that new technology reduces the problem of under-diagnosis, the resulting increase in the number of people being treated will in all likelihood lead to a net increase in health expenditure.

The second point is that there is a great deal of wishful thinking about the likely impact of prevention through the improvement of health behaviors. It is naïve to think that providing more real-time information will be sufficient to address the social and psychological factors that are so often the basis of unhealthy behaviors – such as work and domestic stress, difficult-to-break habits, psychological problems, unemployment and demoralization. The fact that successful professionals have taken enthusiastically to self-monitoring devices and fitness regimes does not mean that everybody else will follow.

The third point is that success in disease prevention is not the same as the elimination of disease. Most people will eventually develop serious diseases requiring substantial medical attention, no matter how virtuous their health behavior may have been and how successful they may have been in avoiding the earlier emergence of preventable diseases. This means that, whatever the contribution new technology may make to disease prevention by giving early warning of health risks, "diagnose and treat" will always remain central to the medical system.

Box 3.5 Do-It-Yourself Medicine

Another way in which new technology can achieve labor-cost savings for the health system is by encouraging patients to themselves carry out certain medical tasks – such as monitoring and testing through "wearables" or apps connected to their smart phones. Some label this "do-it-yourself" (DIY) medicine. Others call it, disparagingly, the IKEA model of medicine. The critics are right to the extent that simply transferring work from the doctor to the patient, in the way that IKEA transfers the task of assembly to the hapless consumer, is not a true productivity gain because it is not a saving from the point of view of society as a whole. It is nevertheless clear that many of the new technologies will save substantial time for the patient – who will, for example, no longer have to visit the doctor or hospital for certain tests or treatments – as well as for the treating professionals. In these cases, their use will indeed represent a true social saving.[27] The prospects for DIY medicine have, however, been subject to much unjustified hype by techno enthusiasts. Some declare that we are about to enter a new era when "empowered" patients will become "masters of their own health," in the process reducing doctors to a secondary supportive role (Comtesse, 2017).

If this were true, it would undoubtedly result in huge savings in the health budget. However, no amount of sophisticated technology will transform untrained citizens into medical experts.

Notwithstanding the importance of improved prevention and earlier diagnosis, it is unrealistic to expect that either or both of these will deliver expenditure savings of the magnitude required to prevent the ongoing increase in health expenditure/GDP.

Slowing the Increase?

The expenditure-increasing impact of technological innovation can thus be expected to continue to outpace its expenditure-reducing impact. Even the savings delivered by new-generation digital technology – as substantial as they are likely to be – will not be sufficient to offset large increases in spending on new and better treatments. Indeed, one can realistically assume the rate of increase of health spending as a proportion of national income will increase.

This, moreover, is a fundamentally good thing. The prospective increase in spending will pay for major improvements in the scope and quality of medical treatments. Better treatments will be developed both for widespread chronic conditions and for rare diseases. Treatments will be developed for conditions that are at present largely untreatable. Paying more to benefit in this way from the increasing capabilities of medicine will be an entirely rational social choice.

We should not, however, take a relaxed view of rising spending. Far from it. The upward pressure of expenditure on new and better treatments, coupled with pressure from population aging and adverse lifestyle trends, will make it more essential than ever to take all possible measures to minimize waste and inefficiency and achieve maximum value-for-money.

Facilitating the adoption of the new-generation digital technologies will be particularly important. Even if these technologies are not able to halt the increase in health expenditure/GDP, they can help to slow it somewhat. Large potential productivity gains must not be blocked by the professional self-interest of medical professionals, inadequate public investment or other obstacles.

Redoubling efforts to ensure that medicine is as evidence-based as possible is also necessary. Some medical tests – for example, mammograms and prostate cancer screening (Topol, 2015: 198-200) – do not pass a benefit/cost test, and some of the new drugs marketed by pharmaceutical companies deliver no additional benefits to patients. Unnecessary duplication of expensive equipment, excessive numbers of specialists creating demand for their own services, too many hospital beds – all these and other problems bedevil health systems. Governments and insurers are generally well aware of them and have progressively implemented measures to tackle them. But more needs to be done.

In some countries – such as the United States – the only way of attacking the magnitude of waste is to fundamentally change the design of the health system. In most advanced countries, this is not necessary, but significant ongoing reforms are required.

Some argue that it is also important to dial back the excessive "medicalization" of natural human processes, including death itself. They point particularly to sometimes extravagant expenditure on end-of-life health treatment. Others take the argument further, critiquing spending in areas such as anti-aging medicine. This is not an easy issue, because extending life may be seen as a legitimate objective and something we are prepared to pay for, both as individuals and society. The issue is arguably more one of benefit versus cost, and is therefore no different from the judgment that needs to be made in relation to all new treatment technologies: are the benefits sufficient to justify the additional cost?

With ongoing upward pressure on health spending, these issues will continue to preoccupy health administrators, governments and society as a whole. However, it would, once again, be a mistake to think that waste, inefficiency and over-servicing are the fundamental reasons health expenditure has increased in advanced countries, or that vigorously tackling these problems will be sufficient to put a lid on spending. It would also be a mistake to believe that more systematic preventative health efforts – as important as these are – will stop spending from rising.

Containing spending is, in any event, not the fundamental objective. The fundamental objective is, or should be, to ensure that citizens benefit from the expanding capabilities of medicine, to the extent that the benefits of new treatments (or preventative interventions) exceed their costs. In this context, to focus exclusively on over-servicing and waste would be to overlook the extent to which people who need treatment currently miss out because of a failure to diagnose or a failure to treat properly. Future health policy should be as much concerned with tackling under-servicing as with cost-containment.

Government's Share of Future Health Expenditure

What does the continuing rise of total health expenditure as a proportion of national income mean for government health spending *assuming unchanged policy*? In almost all advanced countries, universal health coverage (see Box 3.6) is the basic underlying principle of health policy. If this remains the case, then the central question is: what will it cost government to maintain universal coverage?

In countries where government itself pays most health service costs, the answer is obvious: government health spending must rise at broadly the same rate as total health expenditure. The only way to avoid this would be to shift an ever-increasing proportion of health service costs from governments to citizens – for example, by increasing "co-payments" or reducing the range of services covered. However, as discussed further below, beyond quite narrow limits, this would undermine the principle of universal coverage.

Box 3.6 Universal Health Coverage

Universal health coverage is defined by the World Health Organization as ensuring that all people and communities can use the promotive, preventive, curative, rehabilitative and palliative health services they need, of sufficient quality to be effective, while also ensuring that the use of these services does not expose the user to financial hardship. Such a definition raises issues – for example concerning the scope of health services covered. But the basic idea is clear enough.

In almost all advanced countries, the gradual advance towards universal health coverage was one of the most important social reforms of the 20th century. Although countries such as the UK and Japan largely accomplished this reform many decades ago, in a surprising number of advanced countries the process was completed only relatively recently.[28] Today, the United States is the only advanced country without a system of universal health coverage – although the much-contested reforms of the Obama presidency sought to move the country closer to that objective.

For health coverage to be universal, government needs to intervene to ensure the health-financing system accomplishes two basic forms of redistribution. The first is from the healthy to the sick and the second is from better-off citizens to those who are financially least well off. The second is necessary for the obvious reason that, without it, many low-income people would not have access to health services. The first form of redistribution, on the other hand, is about social risk sharing – "social solidarity" as it is sometimes called. The basic rationale is that, because health is a need and because the occurrence of ill-health is in significant measure a matter of chance, it is necessary to share the costs of health services so as to ensure that those who have the misfortune to suffer illness or injury are able to receive treatment without being financially ruined.

What about systems that deliver universal coverage but that nevertheless rely primarily on private health insurance? It might be thought that under such systems, governments can avoid the pressure to spend more on health. But this is not the case. Not, at least, if the commitment to universal health coverage is maintained.

Ensuring universal coverage under a system based on private insurance requires two things. First, "adverse selection" must be prevented from undermining social risk sharing (see Box 3.7). Second, people who cannot afford to pay for health insurance must be covered. This can be accomplished mainly by government paying their health insurance premiums or directly paying for their treatment.

Box 3.7 Adverse Selection and Health Insurance

Adverse selection happens when people who need to make extensive use of health services purchase health insurance but many healthy people don't. It also happens when health insurance companies operate policies designed to attract the healthiest clients and avoid enrolling sicker ones. Adverse selection undermines the principle of social risk sharing, essential for universal health coverage.

Dealing with adverse selection is the most fundamental policy problem in health systems based on private insurance (Geruso and Layton, 2017). Broadly speaking, to ensure universal coverage in a system based on private insurance, in the face of the problem of adverse selection, it is necessary to do what the Swiss and the Dutch do. This is to make health insurance compulsory, subsidize premiums for those who can't afford them, ban insurance companies from refusing clients and maintain a system of "risk sharing" between insurers so that those with a disproportionate number of high-cost clients receive financial compensation through transfers from insurers with a disproportionate number of low-cost clients. Without such government intervention, the problem of adverse selection becomes worse over time as health expenditure/GDP rises and health insurance premiums increase, encouraging more people to drop cover.

In a system based on private insurance, increasing health expenditure/GDP means rising health insurance premiums. Rising premiums mean that health insurance becomes unaffordable to an increasing number of people and the cost to government of guaranteeing access to health services progressively increases. The result is, if there is a commitment to the maintenance of universal health coverage, government health spending will increase at an even faster rate in coming decades in countries with systems based on private insurance than in countries where government pays for most health services.

Future trends in income inequality are a crucial additional factor. If the share of national income flowing to, say, the bottom 20 percent of households were to fall significantly, government would need to spend even more to subsidize health insurance for low-income families. Continuing wage stagnation, of the sort seen in the United States over many decades (see Chapter 7), would therefore push government health spending up more rapidly in countries where government subsidizes health insurance for low-income people.

The United States is the "odd man out" among advanced economies in not having a system of universal health coverage. Approximately 40 percent of the population is, however, covered by the two government health insurance programs – Medicare (for the aged and some disabled people) and Medicaid (for the poor). Essentially the same dynamic applies: to maintain the existing level of coverage in the face of rising health costs will necessarily cost the government more.

Can government health spending be reduced by measures that promote efficiency without threatening existing levels of service coverage? One of the means governments have employed to contain health expenditure has been to demand that individual citizens pay more of the costs – to increase what are known as "out-of-pocket" payments. Co-payments – e.g. the requirement that every patient pay some amount towards the cost of each visit to the doctor – are an example. Another, widely used since the 2007-2008 global financial crisis, is to require patients to pay a portion of the cost of prescribed pharmaceuticals (Belloni et al, 2016). The rationale for such out-of-pocket payments is not just cost-cutting. Their proponents see them primarily as a tool for reducing excessive use of health services (so-called "moral hazard," as discussed in Chapter 2). The idea is that if, for example, a patient has to make a contribution to the cost of seeing a doctor, he or she will be less likely to rush to see their local physician at the first appearance of minor symptoms.

The impact of out-of-pocket payment requirements has been extensively researched. Above relatively low levels, they tend to deter significant numbers of people who need medical services from obtaining them (Trivedi, Moloo and Mor, 2010; Farbmacher, 2009; Newhouse et al, 1981). Increasing them as a means of containing future growth in spending would therefore directly undermine the principle of universal health coverage.

Another means of containing spending growth is to allow treatment waiting lists to grow. An example is in England, where budgetary restrictions on the National Health Service have led to people waiting many months, or even more than a year, for surgery.[29] (A handful of other advanced countries, such as Italy, have always had unacceptably long waiting lists.) Allowing waiting lists to lengthen is not a solution, but rather a means of deferring the problem. Its inevitable consequence is that the waiting lists become an increasingly powerful pressure point, and that ultimately government is compelled to inject significant extra funding into the system to bring waiting times down.

On the other hand, in the context of rising financial pressures, it is both reasonable and appropriate for governments to look hard at which health services they pay for as part of the universal health coverage entitlement. It is astonishing, for example, that prior to a decision by the Macron government, the French national health system paid for homeopathy – basically, a form of voodoo medicine. Controversy may also arise concerning the extent to which, if at all, government should finance anti-aging medicine, including regenerative treatments for the elderly.

A growing refusal of governments to fund highly effective new precision medicines on the grounds of cost would, however, be inconsistent with the principle of universal coverage – and more broadly with the notion of "unchanged policy." As more of these expensive new treatments become available, governments will continue to find themselves fighting a rearguard action. They may delay paying for them or they may insist on clear proof of their efficacy. Ultimately, however, they will be obliged to pay for those that work.

Box 3.8 Expenditure Limits?

One approach to containing government spending on health is the use of *expenditure limits* – basically, quantitative limits on health expenditure set on a yearly or multi-annual basis. Germany pioneered this approach in the early 1990s, France picked it up in 1996 in the form of a target maximum for health expenditure and it has recently been recommended by an expert committee in Switzerland (RGE, 2017). Properly designed, this approach has merit in a health

system that is predominantly government-financed because, by
setting a quantitative limit on spending, it strengthens the incentives
to find productivity gains and other savings. But both experience and
logic make it clear that quantitative limits are "impractical in the
long term" (Busse, 2017: 890; Rebba, 2014) as they do not provide a
means of holding back upward spending pressure other than in the
short term. Gradually but significantly raising such limits over time
is impossible to avoid.

The Future of Government Health Expenditure

The analysis in this chapter suggests that the pace of development and pro-
liferation of new and better treatments will increase markedly in coming
decades. The upward pressure on health expenditure from technological innovation will increase substantially. Population aging will add to
this upward pressure, as will the need to develop better capacity to fight
infectious disease pandemics. Although productivity gains from new-generation digital technology will no doubt be impressive, these technologies
cannot be expected to generate sufficient savings to offset this rising
spending. As a result, the long-term trend of rising health expenditure/
GDP will not only continue but will accelerate.

The implications for government expenditure are clear. Irrespective of
the division of health expenditure between government and private individuals in specific countries, government health expenditure will need to
rise. A failure to increase government spending would of necessity mean
growing inequality of access to health services, undermining the principle
of universal health coverage.

It is intrinsically difficult to say what this means in quantitative terms.
However, as explained in Box 3.9 below, there are reasonable grounds to
believe that health expenditure will increase in all advanced countries
by at least 4 percent of GDP by 2050. These figures are conservative. Not
only will this increase be permanent, but it is to be expected that health
expenditure/GDP will continue to increase over the even longer term.

As has been emphasized throughout, this assumes unchanged policy.
It does not, in other words, take into account the impact of any possible

future decisions by governments to expand or reduce the scope of health service coverage (e.g. a move to universal health coverage in the United States, or large increases in co-payments in European national health systems.) But it also assumes continuing vigorous efforts to achieve efficiency savings, including through the use of new cost-reducing technologies as they become available.

Irrespective of precisely how large the spending impact of accelerated technological innovation turns out to be, it is clear that health expenditure will be one of the areas of greatest pressure on government budgets. Indeed, as we will see, it can be expected to be the largest single persistent area of pressure on future government budgets.

Box 3.9 Long-Term Health Expenditure Forecasts

The most methodologically solid long-term forecasts of government health expenditure for advanced countries generally are those prepared by the OECD. (This is despite the fact that, as noted earlier, these forecasts probably somewhat understate the impact of demographic aging.) The OECD projects increases in health expenditure averaging 6.3 percent of GDP for its member countries over the 50-year period 2010-2060. For individual countries, the projected increases range from 5.8 percent (Belgium) to 7.6 percent (South Korea) (de la Maisonneuve and Oliveira Martins, 2014).[30]

Forecasts prepared by the IMF are also useful. These project that government health expenditure in advanced countries will increase by 3.8 percent of GDP over the 35-year period 2015-2050, and by 6.4 percent by 2100 (Clements et al, 2015). The OECD and IMF forecasts are quite close. Taken together, they suggest increases in the order of 3.5 percent of GDP by 2050 and 6 percent of GDP over the coming half-century (2020-2070) for advanced countries on average.

(In the case of the US, this is broadly consistent with Congressional Budget Office projections showing an increase in government health spending of 4.1 percent of GDP over the 30-year period 2019-2049 (CBO, 2019a).)

These projections are in a certain sense quite plausible, because they are broadly consistent with past trends. This is not surprising because they assume, approximately speaking, that the impact of technological innovation on health spending will be the same as it has been in past decades.[31] (Although, in the case of the IMF projections, the assumption is in effect made that, post-2050, the impact of technology on spending will actually lessen.[32]) This assumption of the continuation of the "status quo" is the most common approach taken in health expenditure forecasting by governments and experts.

The European Commission has coordinated the preparation of forecasts for its member countries that are significantly more conservative. However, these forecasts lack methodological credibility and look more like wishful thinking on the part of the governments concerned.[33]

The analysis presented in this chapter argues that technological innovation is accelerating and that this will have a major impact on health expenditure. If this is correct, the increase in public health expenditure will be larger than suggested by the OECD and IMF forecasts. How much larger? It is impossible to say. There is no credible methodology for quantifying the likely impact on spending of the technological transformations currently gathering pace. Nevertheless, it seems a safe guess to suggest that – even with the continuing aggressive pursuit of efficiency savings – the annual average increase in government health expenditure/GDP will be at least, say, 15 percent greater than suggested by the "status quo" forecasts of the international organizations. Further support for this assumption is provided by the need to strengthen the capacity to deal with infectious disease pandemics. This raises the forecast increases in average health expenditure/GDP for advanced countries to 4 percent over the next 30 years, and close to 7 percent over the 50-year timeframe.[34] Fifteen percent faster growth in health spending is a conjectural figure, but given the strength of the forces that are now starting to push up health spending, it seems conservative. For this reason, and because of the tight range of the OECD forecasts[35], it is further suggested that no advanced countries will experience spending growth lower than 4 percent over the coming 30 years.

4. THE IMPACT OF AGING

The impact of population aging looms large in discussions about trends in government expenditure. In the last two chapters, we considered its contribution to increasing health expenditure. In this chapter, we turn to two areas of expenditure that are much more sensitive to population aging: long-term care and pensions. These comprise a considerable portion of what is referred to as "social protection" expenditure.

The process of population aging has been under way in advanced societies for some time (see Figure 4.1[1] and Figures S4.1 and S4.2 in the statistical annex), driven both by the long-term trend of declining fertility rates and by the unprecedented increase in longevity (life expectancy in old age) since the end of the World War II. More recently, the process has accelerated in most countries as more and more of the "baby boom" generation have joined the ranks of the retired.

Alarm bells were being rung as far back as the 1980s about the implications of population aging for public finances. The costs of government-funded pension schemes were the main concern. It was obvious even prior to then that large increases in pension expenditure would be the inevitable consequence of aging and of the declines in the age of retirement that occurred in the post-war years (Lee, 2003: 186). And that is exactly what happened: over the period 1980-2015, public pension spending increased by 1 percent or more of GDP in most advanced countries – and much more than that in many countries (see Figure 4.2).

Governments did not, however, sit on their hands in the face of the pension threat. Almost all advanced countries significantly modified

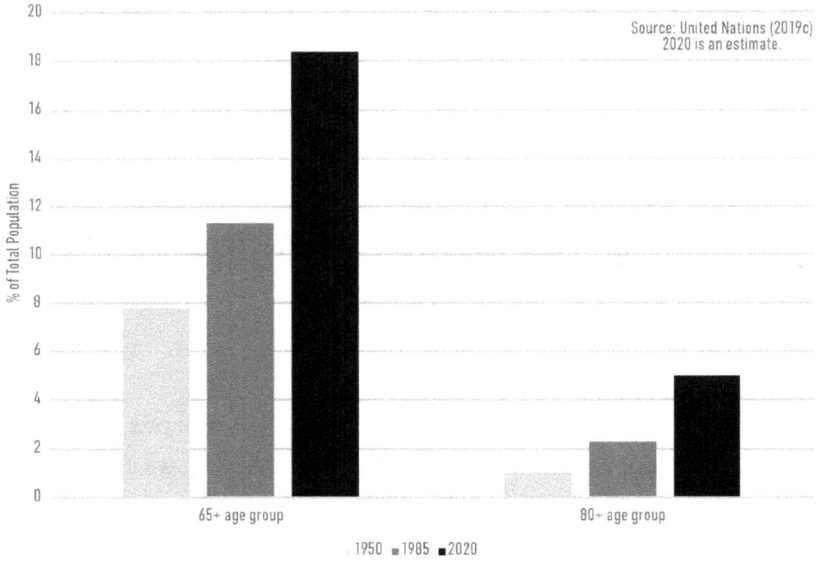

Figure 4.1
Population Aging: High-Income Countries (1950, 1985 & 2020)
Percentage of Population in Elderly Population Groups

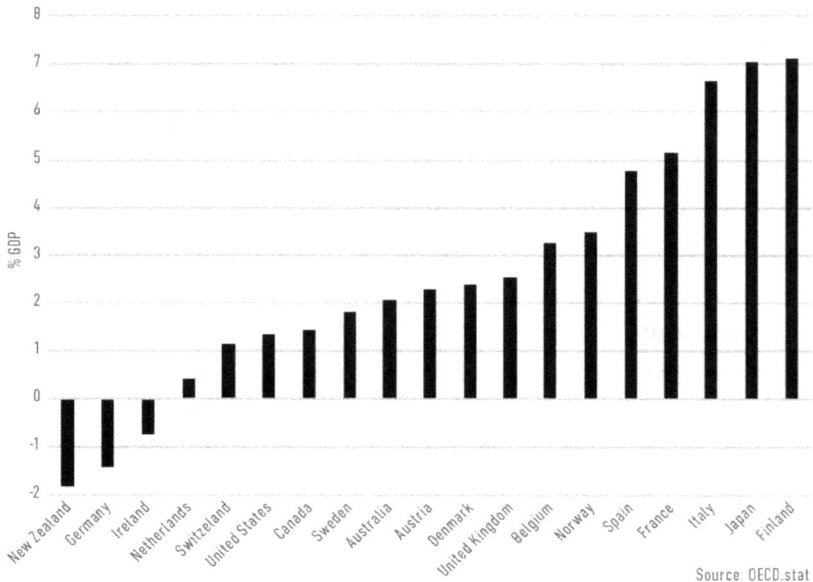

Figure 4.2
Change in Expenditure on Age Pensions (1980-2015)
Increase (Fall) in Pension Expenditure/GDP

the design of their public pension systems to address, at least in part, the problem. Nevertheless, many still continue the process of pension system reform.

In more recent times, the issue of long-term care expenditure has become the focus of concern, reflecting the fact that over the past decade it has become one of the fastest-growing areas of government expenditure (OECD, 2019a: 161).

What do the coming three decades hold for pension and long-term care expenditure? Will these be areas where the powerful external pressure of population aging will force governments to substantially increase spending? These questions are the focus of this chapter.

Future Population Aging

Let's look firstly at the demographic background. Notwithstanding the uncertainty affecting all population projections, there is no doubt that the size of both the 65-plus group (the "elderly") and the 80-plus group (the "very elderly") will increase greatly in all advanced countries over the 30-year time horizon.[1] Figure 4.3 shows the United Nations' projections.[2]

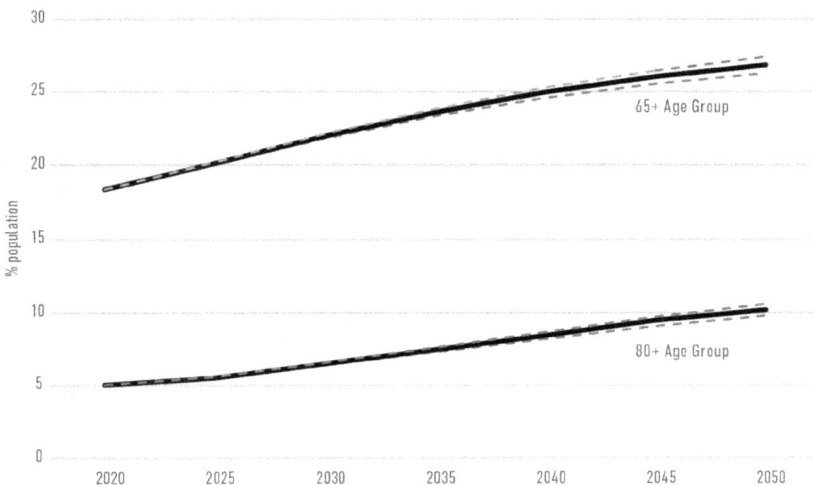

Source: United Nations (2019a).

For each age group, the median, lower and upper 80 % prediction interval projections are shown

Figure 4.3

Population Aging: High-Income Countries

Range of Projections of Percentage of Population in 65-plus and 80-plus Age Groups

Most striking is the projected doubling of the 80-plus age group's share of the population of high-income countries. Other official forecasts show broadly similar trends (see Figures S4.3-S4.6, statistical annex).[3]

Almost everywhere, the pace of population aging looks like being most rapid over the next 10-20 years, slowing somewhat thereafter. This broadly reflects the timeframe of the particularly rapid aging currently under way due to the baby boom effect.

Longer-term projections beyond 2050 suggest these increases in the elderly part of the population are not temporary. Although over the next half-century population aging is likely to slow down – and even to plateau in some countries – the 65-plus and 80-plus part of the population looks like remaining permanently much higher than at the start of the 21st century.[4]

Population decline – which has already started in Japan – will be something some advanced countries are also likely to experience even within the 30-year timeframe. South Korea is at the tipping point, and several other countries may join it over the coming decades.

Long-Term Care

Although the primary policy focus over past decades has been on pension spending, long-term care (LTC) is the area of government expenditure where the pressure of population aging will be felt most broadly across advanced countries over the next 30 years and beyond (see Box 4.1). Historically, the modern welfare state has largely failed to provide adequate care for those with major disabilities. This failure now leaves governments exposed to increasingly irresistible pressure to expand the role of the state in response to the rapid growth of severe age-related disability.

Box 4.1 Long-Term Care

Long-term care refers to assistance provided to people with disabilities sufficiently severe that they are unable to carry out many routine daily activities unassisted. Although LTC often includes a certain element of medical care, it is not primarily a medical service. Much of it is provided to elderly people suffering from age-related disabilities, including physical frailty and dementia. The other client group is working-age adults and children who suffer from a range of disabilities, mental or physical, which mean they require ongoing care.

LTC comes in two major forms: home-based care and institutional care (such as care for the elderly in nursing homes). Many more people receive home-based care than institutional care. Most advanced countries nevertheless spend more on institutional care because it costs much more per client. This is the main reason why many advanced countries have, in the face of growing expenditure pressure, sought to shift care as far as possible away from the institutional setting towards the home.

Everywhere in the advanced world, population aging has over recent decades increased the share of the population requiring LTC. But this has been only a foretaste of what is to come. The large projected increases in the elderly population – and particularly in the ranks of the very elderly – will entail nothing short of an explosion in demand for services over the next 30 years. By contrast, the non-elderly population requiring LTC services is unlikely to change greatly.

A handful of advanced countries – the Netherlands, Japan and the Nordic nations in particular – have acted already to address the problem through the creation of comprehensive, primarily publicly-financed care systems. Governments in these countries spend 2 percent of GDP or more on LTC. The Netherlands is the biggest spender, at 3.7 percent of GDP in 2017. Japan illustrates the way in which demographic pressure can change the politics of LTC provision. Japan felt the pressure of population aging earlier and more intensely than any other advanced country. By the 1990s, the inadequacy of LTC provision for the elderly had become the "number one public issue" in Japan and it was in this context that public policy shifted dramatically, resulting in the introduction in 2000 of the country's current comprehensive system (Curry, Castle-Clarke and Hemmings, 2018).

Outside this small group of countries, governments play a more limited role in this vital area. In countries where the predominant view is that the cost of LTC is a burden that should be borne principally by individual citizens and their families – such as Australia and the United States – government spending on LTC is less than 1 percent of GDP.

The following analysis suggests that, irrespective of their starting points, all advanced countries will almost certainly see increases of at least 1 percent of GDP in government expenditure on LTC over the coming three decades. In percentage terms, LTC may well be the fastest growing area of government expenditure.

This immediately raises the question of why population aging should have such an outsized impact on LTC spending when its impact on health expenditure is, as we have seen, more muted. However, before addressing this issue, it is important to shine light on another major factor driving up LTC costs for both elderly and non-elderly clients. This is the "cost disease."

LTC and the Cost Disease

As outlined in Chapter 2, the Baumol "cost disease" refers to the way in which services provided by industries with very low productivity growth become progressively more expensive over time.

As discussed previously, the proposition that cost disease has been one of the main factors behind the long-term rise in health spending does not stand up to rigorous analysis. LTC is, however, a completely different matter. It is a classic example of a labor-intensive service that is exceedingly difficult to automate and that consequently experiences very low productivity growth. Unlike health, LTC and other forms of personal care have seen very few labor-saving changes in techniques or treatments. Official forecasts assume, realistically, that this will continue to be the case.[5]

Is it possible this will change as a result of the future large-scale deployment of robots to substitute for human care staff? There is undoubtedly scope for their use. As in hospitals, they will be increasingly deployed in tasks such as lifting and moving people. "Social" robots – robots that interact with people to stimulate and entertain them or reduce loneliness – will also play a useful role (robotic "pets" for dementia patients are an example). However, much of the human content of care is irreplaceable. Although there are techno-enthusiasts who think that robots with near-human social capabilities are just around the corner, the reality, as discussed in Chapter 7, is that advances in artificial intelligence sufficient to produce robots capable of emulating human-level social interaction are a distant prospect. It is therefore much more likely that in the LTC sector robots will be used over the next three decades principally in ways that complement, rather than substitute for, humans. Their role will primarily be to improve the quality of the service rather than to reduce costs. They will no more "solve" the cost disease problem in LTC than did the invention of the television when it made it possible to put elderly nursing home residents in front of daytime television.

Productivity growth in the LTC industry will, therefore, probably remain extremely low relative to that in the broader economy, and the industry will continue to be afflicted by the cost disease.

The Impact of Population Aging

Official projections assume, without exception, that the projected further aging of advanced societies over coming decades will bring commensurately large increases in the percentage of the population requiring LTC. This reflects the fact that demand for LTC is much more strongly impacted by population aging than is the demand for health services (Meijer et al, 2013: Martikainen et al, 2012; McGrail et al, 2000; Yang, Norton and Stearns, 2003; Spillman and Lubitz, 2001). This may seem surprising, since it might be thought that the "proximity to death" (PTD) effect would operate, as with health expenditure, to greatly mitigate the impact of increased longevity on LTC spending on the elderly.

We know that a substantial portion of the elderly who receive institutional LTC are people who spend periods of no longer than several months in care institutions *in the year prior to death*.[6] If all LTC clients were like this, then increases in longevity would simply postpone the chronological age at which these stays occur, so that LTC spending on the elderly would be unaffected by increases in longevity.

All LTC clients are not, however, like this. Most importantly, LTC clients suffering from dementia are *nothing* like this. The probability of developing dementia at any given chronological age has changed little over recent decades (see Chapter 2) and seems unlikely to change in the predictable future. Future demand for LTC for dementia patients is thus unlikely to be mitigated by the PTD effect. This is the single most important reason why "unlike acute [healthcare] expenditures, long-term care expenditures still increase significantly with age after controlling for the expensive final years of life" (Meijer et al, 2013).

All this would change if there were to be a medical breakthrough in the treatment of Alzheimer's and other major forms of dementia — a possibility which cannot be completely dismissed. But the complexity of these conditions, and the lack of success so far in developing new treatments, give little grounds for optimism. However optimistic one might be with respect to the scope for substantial progress in the treatment of other widespread chronic conditions, such as diabetes (see Chapter 3), dementia looks like a much tougher nut to crack. It is realistic to assume that any progress will be slow and limited.

The consequences of this for total LTC spending on the elderly are enormous. With projected large increases over the next three decades in the number of people living to very old age, the percentage of the population who will develop dementia during their lives will increase enormously. This will, moreover, have a disproportionate impact on spending. Care for dementia victims is particularly costly, both because those affected often require years of care and because, once dementia progresses beyond the mild stage, home-based care becomes increasingly impractical and a shift to expensive institutional care unavoidable.[7]

The longevity-induced increase in LTC spending on elderly people suffering from dementia can therefore be expected to greatly outweigh the expenditure-reducing effect of the postponement of stays in institutional care for other elderly people. The balance of forces at work is already evident in the way in which dementia has emerged as the most important single condition driving institutional LTC (Agüero-Torres et al, 2001).

To this must, of course, be added the impact on spending of population aging arising from the fertility-rate effects – in particular, the continuing impact of the baby boomer generation over the next couple of decades.

The impact of population aging on LTC spending will probably be amplified in many countries by the continued shrinking of the supply of "informal" care – that is, of long-term care provided free, essentially by family members (e.g. OECD, 2019: 232; RCAC, 2019: 31). Past low fertility rates mean that the elderly of the future will typically have fewer children to look after them when they need care. Today's high female labor market participation also means that the adult daughters of the elderly will in most cases be working and unable to provide full-time informal care to the extent provided by previous generations of women.

This prospective reduction in informal care provided by children is expected to be partly offset by another demographic trend: the ongoing reduction in the gap in life expectancy between men and women. If this trend continues, as demographers mostly think will be the case, there will be some reduction in the number of elderly women living alone without a partner and consequently in need of formal care (OECD, 2011; Wittenberg, 2016). However, most analysts consider this will be insufficient to fully outweigh the reduced supply of informal care (e.g. Bell, Rutherford and Wright, 2013: 72-74).

What does all this mean in quantitative terms? Official projections (see Figures S4.7-S4.9, statistical annex) suggest that, over the next 30 years, government spending on LTC will increase by at least 1 percent of GDP in most advanced countries. There are nevertheless a few countries where projected increases are somewhat less (such as France, with a projected increase of 0.6 percent).

There is good reason to believe, however, that these official estimates understate the increases in spending that will occur in the great majority of countries, because it is highly likely a major policy shift towards governments playing a much bigger role in financing the cost of LTC for the elderly will occur. Other than in the handful of countries that already have primarily publicly funded comprehensive care systems, there is an almost universal perception of a growing crisis of under-provision due to governments failing to shoulder their responsibilities in this area. When coupled with the growing voting power of the elderly, this is generating irresistible pressures on governments to spend more.

The problem is not simply that many more elderly people will need LTC. It is the nature of the risk that people face. While a majority of people will never need institutional LTC for *very* long periods, a significant minority of people face the catastrophic situation of requiring long years of expensive institutional care. Dementia victims – some of whom fall prey to these cruel conditions even before reaching retirement age – are the prime case in point. But they are not the only ones. Older people with severe disabilities arising from other chronic conditions can also find themselves requiring institutional care for very long durations.

Most advanced societies have already seen a sharp rise in the number of people facing this catastrophic scenario, who also suffer ruinous financial consequences as a result. Either they are unable to afford care at all or – if they are middle class – they are obliged to run down all of their assets (including selling their home) and use the proceeds to pay for care until the money runs out.

One can, in this context, contrast two alternative views of the government's role in LTC. One is the view that government's only concern should be to help those who do not have the means to pay for their own care, so that any and all assistance provided by government should be subject to tough income and assets tests. The alternative view is that government has an additional important responsibility, which is to ensure society-wide risk-sharing, just as it does with respect to the risk of ill health. Underpinning this is the view that, with every human being facing an unknown risk of catastrophic disability involving very long periods of expensive care, it is appropriate that everyone is insured against this risk, with the costs of care (at least above some threshold) being paid from a common pool of funds.

If the insurance principle is to apply to LTC, then both experience and economic theory make it clear that it is not possible to rely on voluntary private insurance to do the job (Nuffield Trust, 2019a). Experience in the United States and Germany (Fernandez and Nadash, 2016; Curry, Schlepper and Hemmings, 2019) clearly demonstrates that, if such insurance is left to voluntary decisions in private markets, only a small, well-off portion of the population will purchase cover. It is therefore necessary to cover this risk in the same way that nearly all advanced countries cover health risks – that is, via either tax financing or *compulsory* insurance (public or private). Voluntary private insurance can, at most, play only a supplementary role in financing a higher standard of care for those who choose to pay.

The view that government's role in LTC should be governed by the risk-sharing principle has been clearly articulated by France's President Macron, who has declared that the risk of requiring long-term care should be designated explicitly as one of the life risks covered by his country's social security system.[8] The narrower means-focused approach is, by contrast, one that has tended to dominate policymaking in countries such as Australia (PC, 2011; Aged Care Sector Committee, 2016).

There is, then, a strong policy case for a substantial increase in the social financing of LTC. The focus of this book is not, however, on what governments *should* do, but rather upon what they will increasingly find themselves *forced* to do because of powerful external forces and pressure points. What is important from this perspective is that in those many countries where LTC provision for the elderly is perceived as seriously inadequate, political pressure to do better is becoming intense.

France is a particularly relevant example, because it is, as mentioned above, one of the minority of countries where expenditure growth over coming decades is projected, *on an unchanged policy basis*, to be less than 1 percent of GDP. In that country, government LTC benefits, even when supplemented by voluntary insurance, leave a large financing gap (Fernandez and Nadash, 2016). Benefits are seriously inadequate, even for those with the most limited personal resources, who are most dependent on care (Fizzala, 2016). As a consequence, LTC has become a major political pressure point, leading the Macron government to commit itself to a major change of direction. New policy directions floated in a 2019 government report (Libault, 2019) include a large reduction in costs borne by those in institutional care and a substantial improvement in the quality of service. The report notes that this will require considerable government expenditure, not least because many of the country's existing aged nursing homes are dilapidated. Although the precise directions of future government policy have not, at the time of writing, been decided, it is clear that they must mean a substantially larger increase in spending than forecast in official projections.

England provides another illustration of just how powerful the pressure has become in recent years for major expansion of government's role – and government expenditure – in aged LTC (see Box 4.2).

Box 4.2 The Long-Term Care Crisis in England

Political pressure for major change in the system of elderly long-term care has become intense in England. While the Scottish government introduced a system of free personal care for the elderly in 2002 (Bell, 2013), England has maintained a system "widely regarded as unfair, complex, confusing and failing to meet growing care needs in the population" (Nuffield Trust, 2019b). A multi-party House of Lords committee recently described the system as a "national scandal." The inadequacy of the system was compounded by severe funding cuts in the wake of the global financial crisis.

Today, there is almost universal recognition – including by all major political parties – that LTC for the elderly in England is under-funded, and that a significant increase in government spending will therefore be required (Green, 2019). Concern is particularly focused on the need to "better protect individuals from catastrophic risk" (House of Lords, 2019) – or, as it is more colloquially expressed, to protect those who draw the short straw in the "dementia lottery." While a range of proposals for reform are being debated, there is extensive support for the adoption of some variant on the Scottish system (e.g. Darzi, 2018), potentially with additional protections against catastrophic risk.[9] Bottery et al (2018) estimated the costs of various reform options for England. Their estimates indicate that moving to free personal care would alone require an increase in government expenditure of 48 percent over the decade from 2020/21. Brexit will aggravate the problem because, as with nursing, England has been very dependent on immigrants to meet the labor force requirements of this poorly paid industry.

In March 2020, press reports indicated that the British Health Secretary (minister for health) was considering the imposition of a 2.5 percent social care tax on persons over the age of 40 in order to fund future LTC provision.

The growing political pressure for additional government spending in countries such as France and England echoes the earlier experience of Japan, where the introduction in 2000 of a new LTC system was preceded by a period during which the inadequacy of care had moved to the center of the political stage.[10]

Adding to these pressures in almost all countries is the growing pressure to increase workforce remuneration. Long-term care workers are generally poorly paid. The near-universal result has been growing recruitment difficulties and continuous hemorrhaging of the existing workforce (Colombo and Muir, 2016; OECD, 2011; Curry, Schlepper and Hemmings, 2019). This is why, for example, the French government report mentioned above identifies the "revaluation of aged care work" as one of the three main aims of reform. However attractive it might be for LTC providers and governments to artificially hold down the costs of LTC through poor pay and, in some cases, heavy reliance on immigrants to fill the jobs, it will simply not be possible to provide the level of service needed in the future without making employment in this sector less unattractive. The impact on government expenditure will not be limited to countries that currently do a particularly unsatisfactory job of providing LTC, but will affect advanced countries generally.

A further factor generating pressure on governments to spend more on LTC is the way in which, in the absence of adequate care, public hospitals have become de facto long-term care institutions. Patients who should be discharged and provided with LTC are kept in hospital because the care they need is unavailable. Caring for such people in hospitals is more expensive than providing even institutional LTC in nursing homes, and the extra pressure this applies to health budgets is considerable (Darzi, 2018; Fernandez and Nadash, 2016).

This analysis makes it clear that official projections of future government spending on LTC are too conservative. This is not because these projections are methodologically flawed. It is because they assume the continuation of current policy, whereas it is overwhelmingly likely that political pressure will force major changes of policy in the great majority of advanced countries.

Government (and compulsory insurance) expenditure on LTC can therefore be expected to increase everywhere by a minimum of 1 percent of GDP over the 30 years to 2050. In many countries, the increase will be appreciably larger than this. This will represent a *permanent* increase in expenditure, because the population aging that advanced nations will experience over the next three decades is an essentially permanent phenomenon.

This does not assume that governments will in future foot the entire bill for LTC. It assumes only that political pressure will oblige governments to assume financial responsibility for catastrophic LTC risk – in other words, that they will generally move to pay for LTC beyond some threshold level for those who face prolonged care needs due to dementia or other grave disabilities. Some will go beyond that. However, the magnitude of the fiscal pressures facing governments will create strong incentives to contain the increase in spending, and certainly to avoid paying for all LTC for everyone.

Questions might be asked about how the pressure for action will play out in the United States, where the politics of welfare are so different from those of most other advanced countries. It is, perhaps, less certain than elsewhere that in the United States government will step up its role in LTC provision over coming decades. Arguably, however, the politics are much more favorable to such an expansion of the role of the state than, for example, to the extension of health coverage to those who can't afford health insurance. Private health insurance works, more or less, for a large majority of Americans. Private provision of LTC does not, by contrast, work for a large part of the growing elderly population. Almost everyone is exposed to catastrophic LTC risk as they age.

Age Pensions

In principle – "other things being equal," as economists are prone to saying – pension spending is more sensitive to population aging than is long-term care. For this reason, and because of the huge problem that rising pension expenditure has created for government over recent decades, it seems natural to assume that age pensions will be one of the main sources of pressure on government budgets over the coming half-century. The story is, however, not quite as simple as that.

It is true that government pension expenditure/GDP will increase almost everywhere for the next 10-20 years, reflecting the continuing impact of the baby boom generation. During this period, rising pension expenditure will continue to loom large as a source of fiscal pressure. In the longer term, however, pressure will ease off in many countries. Official projections (see Figures 4.4 and 4.5) suggest that, although in a majority of advanced countries government pension expenditure/GDP will be higher in the middle of the century than today, this is not the case everywhere. Expenditure is actually projected to be significantly lower in France, Denmark and Japan and to be approximately the same in Sweden and Australia.[11] Moreover, even longer-term projections – which are, of course, particularly uncertain – point to a larger number of countries where pension expenditure is projected to be declining after the middle of the century.[12]

What this means is that it is not possible to include the impact of demographics on age pension expenditure in the list of external forces and pressure points which will force up government expenditure *everywhere* in

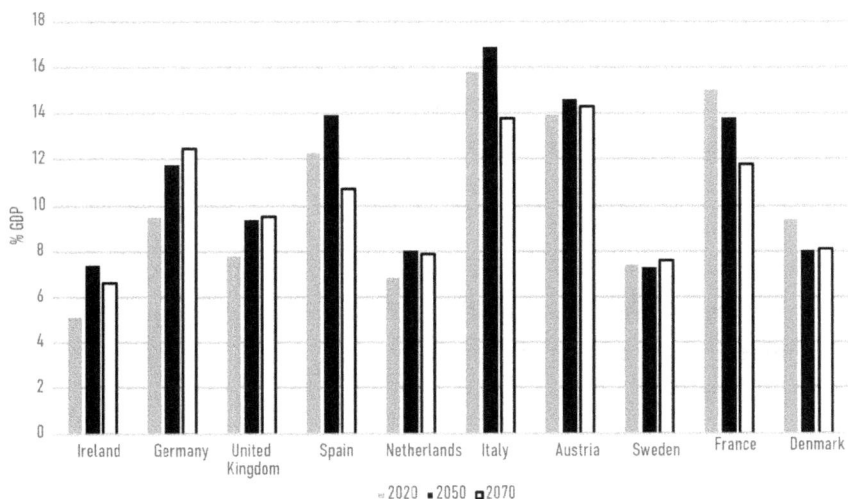

Source: 2019 Stability and Convergence Programs and EC (2018) (baseline scenario).

Figure 4.4
Projections of Government Pension Expenditure: Selected European Nations

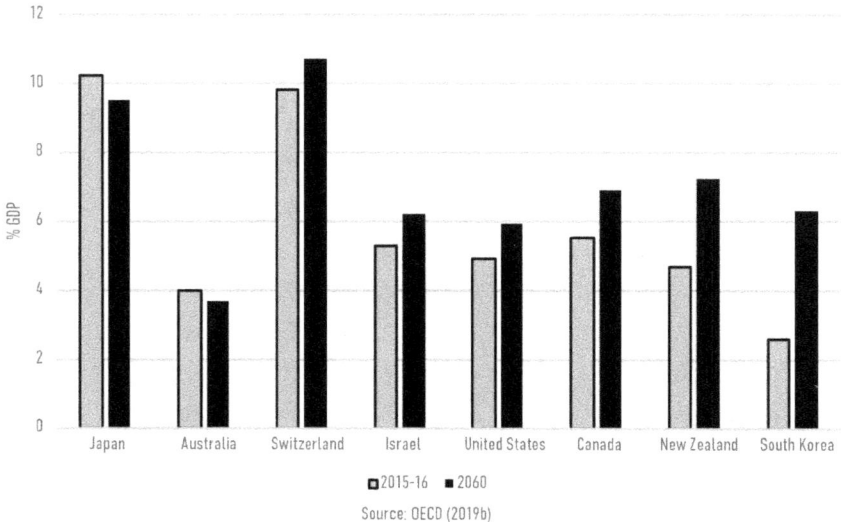

Figure 4.5
Projections of Government Pension Expenditure: Selected Non-EU Advanced Nations

the advanced world between now and 2050. This is, rather, a factor which will be at work in some countries – most spectacularly, South Korea – but not in others.

How could this be? A key part of the explanation is the delayed effects of policy changes that governments have made over recent decades. Governments in most advanced countries have taken steps to raise retirement ages, trim benefit levels and limit entitlements in other ways. Generally speaking, they have managed the delicate politics of pension reform by providing that these measures would come fully into force only many years after they were legislated and only on a quite gradual and progressive basis, meaning that their full financial impact will only be completely realized some decades into the future (see e.g. EC, 2018a: 76-77; PBO, 2019).

Education

Although the focus of this chapter is expenditure pressures arising from population aging, it is not possible to discuss this topic without acknowledging that the flipside of population aging is declines in the younger section of the population and that these may also have implications for public spending. The main area concerned is education spending.

Education is, together with social protection and health, one of the three biggest areas of government expenditure in all advanced countries[13] and accounts for spending generally in the range of 3-7 percent of GDP. According to UN population projections, advanced countries can generally expect to see declines in the proportion of their populations in the 0-19 age bracket in the range of 1-3 percent between 2020 and 2050 (UN, 2019b). However, although this might suggest that some small reductions in education expenditure should occur over the coming three decades across all or most advanced countries, this is not what is in fact likely to happen and it is not what those official forecasts suggest.

Thus, of 10 advanced European Union countries that have prepared consistent forecasts of government education expenditure for the period 2020-2050, only half project declines in education expenditure/GDP, and for three of these, the projected decline is essentially trivial (0.1 or 0.2 percent of GDP).[14] A key reason is that it is generally anticipated that participation rates in non-compulsory education (tertiary education and, in most advanced countries, the later years of high school) will continue to increase. Increased participation will, in other words, offset the impact of demographics. In addition, expenditure on school and pre-school education – which accounts for two-thirds or more of government education expenditure in nearly all advanced countries[15] – is, as discussed in Chapter 9, impacted by the Baumol cost disease.

We will consequently disregard education spending in our outline of major spending trends, in effect assuming education spending/GDP will be generally stable across advanced nations in the coming three decades. (A qualification to this, to be discussed in Chapter 10, is the possibility of technology-generated savings in tertiary education.)

5. DECISIVE ACTION ON GLOBAL WARMING: WHAT WILL IT COST?

Climate change will in the quite near future become one of the most irresistible external pressures on government spending in advanced economies. This will prove to be true irrespective of differences of political ideology. Global warming is the most pressing challenge facing humanity today. It is imperative that decisive action be taken to address the problem of greenhouse gas emissions.

Scientific opinion on the scale of action needed has strengthened over recent decades as climate science has advanced and the impact of global warming to date has become increasingly evident. In 2018, the Intergovernmental Panel on Climate Change (IPCC) urged that policy should be guided by the goal of preventing temperatures rising on average by more than 1.5°C beyond pre-industrial levels, and affirmed that achieving this goal would require a transition to net zero emissions ("net zero"). Consistent with this, governments in a growing number of advanced countries have committed themselves – in many cases through legislation – to the goal of net zero by 2050. Net zero is a more demanding emissions reduction target than those embodied in international agreements and previous government policy commitments. But whatever the precise magnitude of the targets for net emissions appropriate to the threat humanity faces, the challenge is a major one.

The proposition that climate change will soon become an irresistible external pressure on government budgets might appear surprising given the depth of irrational climate change skepticism which is to be found on the hard right of politics in many advanced countries and which even dominates governments in some. The politics of climate change are, however, changing. With the profoundly damaging consequences of global warming – unprecedented heat waves, massive forest fires and increasingly common extreme weather events – becoming clearer by the day, climate change denial will become increasingly politically untenable. Only a shrinking minority of voters will be prepared to deny the reality staring them in the face. Political leaders will feel irresistible pressure to spend substantially to tackle the problem. It is indicative of the direction of the tide that in the United States, forward-looking Republican strategists now realize that their party risks suffering enormous electoral damage unless it moves away from its present stance of refusing to acknowledge either the human impact on the climate or the gravity of the situation.[1]

Climate change denial is, in any event, as much a generational as an ideological phenomenon. Whatever some elderly politicians may think, there will be few among the coming generations of politicians in any major party – including parties on the right – who doubt that climate change represents a grave challenge for humanity. Unfortunately, this transformation of the politics of climate change is not happening quickly enough, given that the world needs bold government action immediately. The political transformation will, nevertheless, happen much more rapidly than many expect.

The Spending Response

As this transformation gathers pace, the governments of advanced countries can be expected to spend more in four areas: adjustment assistance, climate-impacted public services, compensation for developing countries and government contributions to the *climate investment effort*. The first three are, as discussed below, not likely to prove particularly large in relation to the total size of government budgets. It is the fourth that will have the biggest impact on aggregate government expenditure.

The term "climate investment effort" describes the investments that will need to be made by businesses, households and government over the next three decades and beyond to limit global warming and to cope with the damage it causes. The largest component will be investments in the *abatement* measures required to drastically reduce carbon and other greenhouse gas emissions, and increase carbon capture and storage, to achieve the goal of net zero emissions. Most important here are the investments needed to decarbonize the economy, requiring what the International Energy Agency (IEA/IRENA, 2017) describes as an "energy transition of exceptional scope, depth and speed," including more rapid scaling up of renewables, electrification and wide-ranging energy efficiency measures. In addition, significant non-energy investments (particularly to support modifications of agricultural practices) will be needed.

A second, closely associated component of the climate investment effort will be a large boost to research and development (R&D) into relevant technologies. Here, both government and the private sector have major roles to play.

The final component will be substantial *adaptation* investment – that is, investment in infrastructure to cope with, and reduce the damage caused by, higher temperatures. The construction of improved urban drainage systems to handle elevated flood risk due to higher precipitation is an example, as is the installation of new and improved coastal defenses.

The share of the total society-wide climate investment effort funded from government budgets, and the size of the total investment effort itself, depend on policy decisions governments will make.

This chapter advances two main propositions. The first is that, if the most effective policy mix were chosen to tackle climate change, the additional budgetary spending required from governments over the coming decades, although substantial, would not be huge in the overall context of the budget. Concretely, it would probably be below 1 percent of GDP annually.

The second proposition is that, in practice, governments are almost certain to end up spending significantly more – regrettably, without achieving better or faster results. The main reason is that political leaders will, for political reasons, make excessive use of subsidies aimed at inducing businesses and households to undertake the abatement and adaptation measures tied to their own business operations and modes of living and working. This will not only unnecessarily raise government spending but may also increase the total social costs of the climate investment effort. Government climate-related spending could easily be double the 1 percent figure as a result.

The structure of the chapter is as follows. The first part focuses on the choices that will determine the magnitude of government spending on the climate investment effort. We start with the question of government support for energy and other climate-related R&D. After that, the climate investment effort concerning the government's own services and operations is discussed. The analysis then turns to spending on subsidies intended to induce businesses and households to undertake their own investments.

In the second part of the chapter, the focus turns to the other forms of government spending needed in response to the climate change challenge – adjustment assistance, climate-impacted government services and compensation for low-income countries. This leads to conclusions about the appropriate role and scale of government spending as part of the overall strategy for tackling global warming.

Following that, we turn to revenue: concretely, to a discussion of the potential of revenues from carbon pricing to help relieve spending pressures. The chapter concludes with a brief digression on a topic relevant to the context of the book as a whole – whether the energy transition, and environmental sanity more generally, are compatible with continued economic growth or whether it is time for humanity to turn the page on the era of continuous economic expansion.

The Climate Investment Effort – the Role of Government Expenditure

The two areas where government expenditure has an indisputably central role to play are, firstly, climate-related R&D and, secondly, abatement and adaptation measures pertaining to the government's operations and services.

The first requires only brief discussion as there is a consensus economic case for substantial government spending on basic scientific R&D

of all types. The case is based on the fact that most of the benefits of technological advances generated by basic research are not captured by those who carry out the research but by others who profit from its application without having paid for it. This reduces the commercial incentives to undertake basic research and means that, without government funding, there will be too little such research. The case for generous government funding is particularly strong in the case of R&D capable of contributing to resolving the problem of climate change, whether through the development of renewable energies, energy efficiency, carbon capture and storage or other means (Nordhaus, 2013).

However, as important as an increased R&D effort is to tackling climate change, the additional government spending will not make much of a dent in the budget. Government funding of energy-related R&D is so small relative to GDP that it could be increased 10-fold, or more, without making an appreciable difference to aggregate government spending.[2]

Government's Own Operations and Services

Government abatement and adaptation investments pertaining to its own operations and services will have a much bigger budgetary impact. With respect to *abatement*, public buildings and public transport will be the two areas where the largest investments will be needed. The carbon footprint of schools, public housing and other public buildings will need to be drastically reduced by improving insulation, installing low-carbon heating and cooling systems and taking a range of other measures. Significant extensions of public transport systems – which in most advanced countries are substantially subsidized from government budgets – will be required, particularly in countries such as the United States, where they have traditionally been poor.

Responsibility for much *adaptation* investment will also fall directly on government, because much of it is collective infrastructure that the government must provide. It will, for example, be the role of government to undertake the public works necessary to cope with increased flood and erosion risks in urban, river system and coastal settings. The same is true of many of the infrastructure investments required by elevated levels of other natural risks (e.g. forest fires, landslides in Alpine areas previously held stable by permafrost). Reforestation of public lands is also a task for government. The transport network generally, including road systems, will need upgrading to make it resilient to higher temperatures.

However, if government's abatement and adaptation investments were restricted to its own operations and services, its spending would be only a relatively small fraction of the total cost of the society-wide climate investment effort. This is because the lion's share of the total abatement investment needed across advanced societies – including in energy efficiency, electrification and building renovation – is investment that businesses and households need to undertake in respect to the industrial equipment they use, buildings they own, vehicles they drive and other aspects of their own operations and lifestyles. Although the situation will be somewhat different with respect to adaptation investments, with government having direct responsibility for a larger portion of the required investment spending, this is less important because total (public and private) spending on adaptation will probably be considerably less than that required on abatement.

Box 5.1 Public Enterprises and the Climate Investment Effort

In those advanced countries where much of the electricity industry remains in government hands – such as France – it might be thought a large portion of the required energy sector abatement investment will need to be paid for by government. This is on the assumption that government will need to pay for extensive improvements required to electricity transmission and storage systems (including substantial investment spending on the development of so-called SMART electricity networks) and for the construction of extensive increased renewable energy generation capacity.

This, however, is not the case. Electricity systems in such countries are run by public enterprises, and public enterprises in advanced countries are very largely self-financing through commercial charges on their customers rather than financed from the government budget. The focus of this book is future pressures on government budgets, and public enterprise expenditure is therefore not relevant unless – and only to the extent that – those enterprises tap funding from the government's budget. Because this is (apart from public transport) not the normal situation, for the purposes of our analysis here, public enterprises can be treated as part of the private sector, along with other businesses.

What, then, is it likely to cost governments in advanced countries to undertake the climate-driven investments related to their own operations and services, as well as to substantially increase support for relevant R&D, in the coming decades? We don't really know, because of the limited work done on estimating the costs, the inherent difficulty of making such estimates and the level of uncertainty in the science of climate change. However, a rough calculation drawing on the best available estimates of economy-wide costs (see Appendix 5.1) suggests it is unlikely that the extra spending required would exceed 1 percent of GDP annually. This might seem surprising. But 1 percent of GDP is a great deal of money.

Subsidizing the Private Sector Climate Investment Effort?

The bigger question for public finances is what role government will play in financing the large investments households and businesses – the private sector – need to make as part of the climate investment effort. This raises the question of the best means of inducing the private sector to make the massive effort required, and to do it within the urgent timeframe of the next three decades. How, for example, can government best persuade individuals to give up gasoline (petrol) cars and switch to (improved) public transport, electric cars or other potentially zero-emission modes of transport? What is the best way of achieving the phasing out of coal-fired electricity generation? What about all of the thousands of other types of investments and other measures households and businesses need to take to improve energy efficiency, decarbonize and cut other greenhouse gas emissions?

Increasingly, the default response of political leaders is that subsidies and regulation are the best means of persuasion – with subsidies receiving particular emphasis. A good example is the $1 trillion 10-year "clean energy" subsidy program proposed by a US Democratic Party primary candidate, Elizabeth Warren, in September 2019. This program envisaged spending of approximately one-half of 1 percent of US GDP per year on a wide range of tax credits, grants and other subsidies to households and businesses to promote zero-emission vehicles, zero-carbon houses and buildings, and renewable energy.

Even more effusive with respect to the role of subsidies of various forms was the Green New Deal (GND) resolution introduced into the US House of Representatives in July 2019. This resolution called for the across-the-board use of grants, loans and guarantees for "providing and leveraging ... adequate capital" for communities, households and businesses "working on Green New Deal mobilizations" – including extensive assistance to industry, with a particular emphasis on assisting local and community businesses and farmers. Linked to this were proposals to use industry assistance as an instrument of trade policy, with government export subsidies for clean-energy products.

Enthusiasm for government subsidies as a cornerstone of the fight against global warming is not confined to the left. On the conservative side of politics as well, at least in Europe, political leaders are increasingly proposing more subsidies.[3] The trend is towards a new politics of climate change in which politicians use the size of their proposed spending packages – and in particular of proposed spending on subsidies – as the main means of showing voters the seriousness with which they view the problem.

The political logic of this is obvious, because the enthusiasm of politicians for subsidies is the flip side of their reticence towards carbon taxes (see Box 5.2). Politicians have become convinced that carbon taxes – especially carbon taxes on motor fuels – are politically toxic. And with good reason. In France, the populist *gilets jaunes* movement that started in late 2018 was triggered by increases in the carbon tax on motor fuels. In elections in Australia, Austria and elsewhere, incumbent government leaders have not hesitated to opportunistically exploit, in hard-fought election campaigns, fears of more expensive gasoline (petrol) driven by carbon taxes. In this context, loudly calling for higher carbon taxes looks like electoral suicide.[4]

Box 5.2 Carbon Taxes

A carbon tax is a tax imposed on fossil fuels at rates proportional to their carbon content, based on a standard universal price per tonne of carbon dioxide emitted. It is applied to coal, gasoline, diesel, gas and all other fossil fuels, at rates that depend on the intensity of carbon emissions associated with each.[5]

Carbon pricing may also be imposed in the alternative form of a system of tradable emissions permits (so-called "cap and trade" systems). In theory – although not entirely in practice – the two forms of carbon pricing are equivalent.

The case for carbon pricing is based on the fact that those responsible for carbon emissions are inflicting a cost on society without paying any compensation. The carbon tax transforms the social cost of emissions into a cost borne directly by the emitter, thereby creating "price signals" that force people to take into account the social cost of emissions. This provides powerful incentives for emitters to take abatement measures, and for consumers to prefer goods and services with lower carbon footprints.

Many advanced countries already have carbon taxes and other forms of carbon pricing. However, the carbon prices on which these are based are in almost all cases much lower than the levels economists estimate would be necessary to achieve sufficiently rapid reductions in rates of emissions.[6] A further problem is that in most countries carbon pricing does not apply to all fossil fuels.

The lack of support for carbon taxes is regrettable because, notwithstanding their political advantages, subsidies are generally speaking a poor way of addressing climate change. The best way of inducing the private sector to make the necessary climate investment effort is a strategy based primarily on a combination of carbon pricing and regulation. Such a strategy requires that carbon prices be increased substantially in the short term and then progressively raised further over the coming years. It requires also the deployment of appropriate regulations, especially in the forms of:

◆ *Technology phase-out mandates,* such as bans on new coal-fired power stations, the installation of home heating systems using fuel oil, or the purchase of new gasoline cars (Tvinnereim and Mehling, 2018).

◆ *Energy efficiency and emissions standards,* an example of which is rules banning the sale of refrigerators that do not meet a minimum efficiency standard.

Box 5.3 What Role for Regulation?

The appropriate degree of reliance on carbon pricing and regulation respectively can be debated. Economists with the greatest degree of faith in market mechanisms tend to be skeptical of the use of regulation, pointing to the distortions it often creates. There are, however, good reasons to believe that an approach reliant entirely on carbon pricing, with very little role for regulation, would require astronomically high carbon prices, and that a more efficient approach is to combine realistically high carbon prices with appropriate but aggressive regulatory instruments (IPCC, 2018: 152-153; High-Level Commission on Carbon Prices, 2017). But the question relevant to the subject matter of this book is how much use to make of subsidies, rather than the correct balance between carbon pricing and regulation.

Subsidies can legitimately play a certain limited role, as discussed below. As a general rule, however, it should be left to households and businesses to pay the cost of adapting houses and buildings, constructing new renewable energy power-generation plants, replacing their gasoline cars with electric vehicles, installing solar panels and batteries, and a host of other abatement and adaptation measures that specifically concern them.

Consider the goal of decarbonizing road transport. The best means of achieving this would be to combine substantial and progressively increasing carbon taxes on gasoline and other hydrocarbon fuels, with an announcement that the sale of new hydrocarbon-based vehicles will be largely banned at an appropriate point (e.g. in 10 years). How does such an approach compare with the alternative of forgoing the carbon tax and using generous subsidies? A subsidies-based approach in this case essentially means the government heavily subsidizing the purchase of electric cars (and other potentially zero-emissions vehicles when and if they become available), as well as slashing the cost of public transport. This would, however, constitute a much less effective way of reducing emissions, because the carbon tax has multiple advantages over the use of subsidies.

One advantage is that higher taxes on hydrocarbon fuels create incentives for greater use of *all* actions by citizens that reduce the use of carbon-based road transport – including home-based work (e.g. telecommuting), carpooling, biking, walking, electric cars and public transport. Subsidies, by contrast, encourage only the latter two alternatives. A second advantage of the carbon tax is that it puts greatest pressure on drivers who use their cars the most and who drive large gas-guzzlers, whereas a subsidy on the purchase of an electric car is paid indiscriminately to those who drive a great deal and those who drive only occasionally.[7] A third advantage is that a carbon tax creates strong incentives for a shift away from carbon-based electricity generation, which is essential if the potential benefits of a shift to electric-powered transport – cars, buses or trains – are to be realized.

This example points to a general problem with subsidies: that of coverage. To be able to make subsidies for *not using* carbon-based energy function as well as a tax on *using* carbon-based energy, it would be necessary to subsidize each and every significant way of avoiding or minimizing the use of carbon-based energy. This is, in practice, impossible. There are many ways of not using carbon-based energy that are impossible to subsidize. Any subsidies-based approach will therefore inevitably leave important gaps in the incentives it creates for households and businesses to undertake appropriate abatement measures. As Nordhaus (2013) puts it, "in the end, it is much more effective to penalize carbon emissions than to subsidize everything else."

The other big problem with the subsidies approach is the difficulty of setting the level of the subsidy. A carbon tax requires only the setting of a single uniform price per tonne of carbon. Subsidies, on the other hand, have to be set at different rates for a multiplicity of different measures promoting energy efficiency, renewable energy, carbon capture and storage, and other forms of abatement. They become even more complicated when the subsidy may take different forms – such as a tax credit rather than a grant. The challenge is magnified by the rapidity of technological progress, as a result of which the costs of many renewables and abatement technologies have been falling fast. In principle, any subsidies provided for these technologies should be reduced in line with these falling costs. In practice, governments have all too frequently made long-term commitments to subsidies that are too high.

This problem has arisen time and time again when governments have used subsidies to encourage renewables. One of the most spectacular examples is the way in which Germany mismanaged subsidies designed to encourage solar power. Legislation introduced in 2000 introduced 20-year guaranteed tariffs for solar electricity at rates that have turned out to be excessive, given the rapidly falling cost of solar electricity. The cost of this subsidy is in this case not borne by the government budget but is paid via a surcharge on electricity customers – the main reason why the average retail price of electricity in Germany is among the highest in the world.

Similar bungling has characterized government policy designed to promote decarbonization of the electricity industry in the United Kingdom. As in Germany, a primarily subsidies-based approach to the promotion of renewables has proven to be grossly inefficient, with the result – according to an official review conducted in 2017 (Helm, 2017) – that "the cost of energy is significantly higher than it needs to be to meet the government's [decarbonization] objectives ... and to ensure security of supply." The setting of subsidy rates for different forms of renewables turned out to be all wrong, with the greatest incentives created for "some of the most expensive technologies first." Offshore wind, for example, was grossly over-subsidized. As the 2017 review points out, the unduly high electricity prices that have resulted "risk undermining the broader democratic support for decarbonization."

This is not to say there is no case whatsoever for the use of subsidies. They have a clear role to play in promoting equity – for example, in the provision of grants or loan guarantees to low-income homeowners to finance insulation or other energy-efficiency measures. There is also a plausible *in principle* case for the use of government subsidies to encourage the commercialization of promising new technologies. The argument is that many technologies need to be given a good kick start in order to become commercially viable, and that government subsidies can do this. (More specifically, the argument is that they need scale economies and extensive learning-by-doing to achieve low prices and high quality.) However, as plausible as the theoretical argument for this type of subsidy might be, governments have in practice often done a bad job of putting the idea into practice and have, as a consequence, paid subsidies that are much higher than needed. Government should therefore think carefully before introducing subsidies for the promotion of specific technologies.

In summary, when it comes to inducing households and businesses to undertake the required climate investment effort, government subsidies should be used in only a limited and sparing manner, with any deployment of this instrument being justified on very specific policy grounds. Carbon pricing and regulation should do the heavy lifting. To put it bluntly, the stick will in this case work much better than the carrot.

Making the economic case for a subsidies-lite approach does not, however, change the politics. It is inevitable that governments will, for political reasons, rely far too heavily on subsidies to influence private-sector decisions. This is already the case and will be even more so in future. In coming years, as governments increasingly feel the political heat on climate change and feel compelled to demonstrate that they are acting boldly to tackle the problem, they will react by greatly ramping up reliance upon handouts. This will not only greatly increase the budgetary cost of achieving net zero, but will be an inefficient way of tackling the problem that will unnecessarily raise the cost to society as a whole of achieving the energy transition.

Other Climate-Related Government Spending

Apart from the climate investment effort, there are, as mentioned, three other areas where government spending can be expected to increase over coming decades in response to global warming.

The first is *adjustment assistance*, which refers to help provided to those adversely affected by climate change, the decline of fossil fuel industries and other structural changes in the economy arising from the transition to net zero. Adjustment assistance is likely to mainly take the form of retraining, early retirement benefits,[8] and other assistance for workers who lose their jobs. There will also be some assistance to hard-hit regions, to individuals obliged to move (e.g. from flood-prone areas[9]) and a limited amount to companies. However, even if relatively generous, these forms of adjustment assistance are not likely to have a large total budgetary cost (see Box 5.4). Very few regional communities in advanced economies are still primarily dependent on coal mining or other fossil fuel extraction industries. These industries are, moreover, today highly capital intensive and employ few people. (There are said to be as many lawyers in the US "coal state" of Kentucky as there are coal miners.[10]) Job losses resulting directly from the shift to net zero will be minor compared, for example, to those seen in manufacturing in many countries over recent decades.

Box 5.4 Adjustment Assistance in Germany

In January 2020, the German government announced a major adjustment assistance program to phase out the use of coal power over the following 15-18 years. At the time the program was announced, over one-third of electricity generation in the country came from burning coal – considerably more than in most advanced countries.[11] The value of the assistance package announced was Ð44 billion – which, spread out over the 15-18 year period, is equivalent to less than 0.1 percent of GDP annually. Even this should be put in context, as the assistance package is approximately the same in value as subsidies paid by the German government to support coal mining in the country in the two decades prior to 2018.[12]

Compensation for low-income countries is a second area of potential increased spending. Advanced countries, which have historically benefited from carbon-based economic development, undeniably have a duty to compensate the world's least developed countries if the latter are to be asked to forgo the same development path. This is, however, a moral imperative rather than an irresistible external force on government spending. The governments of advanced countries have not to date indicated a great willingness to spend big on climate-related support for developing countries and it is not clear this will dramatically change in future. It is therefore not realistic to factor in large amounts of compensation for low-income countries in the list of external pressures on spending that are the focus of this book.

There may, however, be at least one exception: compensation to halt deforestation. It is clear that mere exhortations will not stop countries like Brazil and Indonesia from destroying the huge tropical forests that have been rightly described as the lungs of the world. A core component of any solution to this problem must be large financial compensation to such countries for foregoing the economic benefits from logging and use of the land for agriculture. In this case, substantial compensation from advanced countries makes sense in the most narrowly selfish terms, given the very substantial contribution of deforestation to global carbon emissions (around 10 percent of emissions).

How much it would cost on a continuing basis to protect the giant forest regions of the world has not been reliably estimated. The amounts concerned are, however, unlikely to be huge. In 2009, the Brazilian government put forward a proposal to save the Amazon, based on the creation of a fund with advanced-country financing to the tune of USD21 billion. Even if this sum were multiplied several hundred (or even thousand) times in order to protect tropical forests across relevant developing countries generally, the cost to the budgets of advanced countries as a whole – assuming the burden was shared broadly – would not be large enough to substantially jack up aggregate government expenditure. Once again, any spending of this sort would be a footnote compared with the costs of the climate investment effort.

Finally, there is the question of how much more governments will find themselves obliged to spend on a continuing basis on climate-impacted public services such as health care and emergency services to cope with the continuing consequences of a hotter climate. The question warrants deeper analysis than it appears to have received to date. However, it would seem that once again the spending concern will, although substantial, not be so large as to significantly shift aggregate government spending as a proportion of GDP.

The question of the impact of climate change on the incidence of infectious diseases in advanced countries was discussed in Chapter 3. Floods, forest fires, landslides and other natural disasters will certainly oblige governments to spend a great deal more on the relevant emergency services, as well as on the adaptation infrastructure discussed earlier. There will also be extra spending in some other areas. However, even though all this additional spending taken together will be considerable in absolute (dollar) terms, there is no reason to believe it will be large relative to the biggest-ticket items in government budgets.

Government Budgets and Global Warming

The above analysis is, it must be admitted, crude and at many points speculative. There is a need for more detailed, high-quality analysis by researchers of the expenditure implications for governments of climate change. What the analysis in this chapter suggests, nevertheless, is that governments may not *need* to spend more than 1 percent of GDP annually over the next three decades as part of an aggressive and effective program to achieve net zero. In practice, actual spending is likely to be significantly higher than this because of the excessive use of subsidies to persuade households and businesses to do what is required. Even so, the additional spending may not exceed 2 percent of GDP.

In the analysis of overall spending pressures in the rest of this book, it therefore seems reasonable to assume that governments throughout the advanced world will before too long find themselves under powerful pressure to increase climate-related spending by at least 1 percent of GDP on average over the remainder of the period to the middle of the century.

Whatever the actual levels of future spending, it appears that even though climate change will constitute one important external pressure on government budgets, it will be of second order in comparison to pressures on health spending.

This might appear surprising, given that climate change presents such a grave challenge. There is, however, no direct relationship between the severity of a challenge facing humanity and the amounts of money governments should spend to address that challenge. Unlike, say, health or education, climate change is not a problem for which the main solution is the provision of government services. Achieving net zero requires changes in the way the economy operates, and these changes are not mainly to be achieved through government spending programs.

We should not drop cost-effectiveness criteria when considering spending proposals aimed at tackling global warming. For example, while significant expansions of public transport are unquestionably needed, it is important to avoid wasting large amounts of money on new or expanded services for which there is very little demand.[13] As grave and pressing as the problem of climate change is, there is absolutely no reason to take the view that any and all climate-related government spending is justified. Fighting global warming may indeed be the "moral equivalent of war." Choosing the best strategy is, however, crucial to winning any war, and indiscriminate spending is not a strategy.

Downplaying somewhat the budgetary implications of the fight against global warming may appear strange in the light of the huge price tags attached to Green New Deal packages currently being proposed in the United States and elsewhere. It is important, however, to remember that much of the spending proposed in these packages is not directed at climate change or even the environment more generally. Most GND-style packages are umbrella proposals for increased spending on a broad range of progressive causes – including, in the United States, a move to government-financed universal health coverage.

Paying for Climate Change Policies

Discussing climate change policies is not possible without briefly touching on the financing dimension. This is particularly true because carbon pricing would seem to offer the necessary financing for spending measures. If carbon pricing took the form of a carbon tax, then governments would raise quite a large amount of money so long as tax rates were set at appropriately high levels. (If, on the other hand, the "cap and trade" approach to carbon pricing were adopted, then – in theory at least – government would raise broadly similar levels of revenue if it auctioned, as opposed to giving away, emissions permits.) This would not constitute a permanent expansion of the revenue base, because carbon tax revenues will fall as we move to net zero. Nevertheless, large amounts of additional revenue would accrue over some decades.

Many proponents of carbon pricing assert, however, that the carbon tax should be "revenue neutral." This means that all the revenue governments raise from the tax would be paid back to citizens – in the form, perhaps, of "carbon dividend" checks. This is the stance adopted in the *Economists' Statement on Carbon Dividends* published by a group of leading economists in January 2019. The argument for a revenue-neutral carbon tax is purely political: it aims to make the carbon tax politically palatable to voters and, in the words of the *Statement,* "to avoid debates about the size of government."

The role of the carbon tax is widely misunderstood, with many people assuming that its effectiveness is contingent upon the revenue it generates being used to finance abatement measures. This is, however, not the case. The imposition of the tax itself is intended to change people's behavior – by changing "price signals" and thereby inducing large-scale abatement efforts – rather than the use of its receipts to pay for decarbonization measures (Gollier, 2019). Notwithstanding this, there is no economic principle that demands a carbon tax should be revenue neutral, and it is perfectly reasonable to favor the use of carbon tax revenues to finance climate-related government spending.

All of this may, however, turn out to have little practical relevance if, as suggested earlier, governments increasingly steer away from imposing or increasing carbon taxes for political reasons.

Some left-wing populists like to argue that there is no need to raise taxes to finance the large-scale government spending necessary to fight climate change (or indeed to finance other major new spending programs). Instead, they propose reliance on either or both borrowing and central bank money creation. The proposition that significantly increased government spending can be financed without raising taxes is discussed in detail in Chapter 8. The general position taken is that there is indeed a strong case for some use of borrowing to help fund the climate investment effort. To the extent that there is excess capacity in the economy, a case can even be made for limited and temporary use of central bank money creation. However, major limits remain on the scope for deficit spending. Running large budget deficits on a long-term basis is a sure road to ruin and it is therefore important to carefully limit the use of deficit funding.

Decoupling and the Future of Economic Growth

Global warming raises a more fundamental issue, which is the future of economic growth.

Many today take the view that it is impossible to halt global warming without radically shifting direction and moving to an economic model of *décroissance,* in which consumption is radically reduced and societies no longer pursue continual increases in living standards. More generally, the argument is that only by ceasing to pursue growth can mankind stop inflicting irreparable environmental damage on our planet.

Whether this turns out to be correct will depend in large measure on whether it proves possible to achieve net zero in coming decades while maintaining positive economic growth—whether economic growth can be decoupled from greenhouse gas emissions. Historically, carbon and other greenhouse gas emissions have risen with economic (and population) growth, and the challenge now is to sever that nexus.

On the surface, advanced countries have in recent years made progress in decoupling. Carbon dioxide emissions have in most advanced countries fallen even in the face of (generally modest) economic growth (Deutch, 2017; Aden, 2016). However, to an important extent, this has been the consequence of the transfer to developing countries of the production of many of the carbon-intensive goods consumed in advanced countries (Mir and Storm, 2016; Cohen et al, 2017). Although some genuine decarbonization has been happening, it has not been sufficient.

Inadequate progress in decoupling growth from greenhouse gas emissions is, however, hardly surprising given the inadequacy of the efforts to date to tackle the problem. The real question is whether with the right – aggressive – set of policies, the nexus between the two could be severed. The optimistic view that the answer is affirmative is based on the proposition that the technology to achieve decarbonization already largely exists and that technological gaps can be filled relatively rapidly with an appropriately aggressive research effort. Optimists consider that rising per capita living standards in advanced countries do not necessarily need to be associated either with increasing greenhouse gas emissions or, more generally, with increasing exploitation of non-renewable natural resources. To the contrary, future increases in living standards can and should be largely associated with increased consumption of services (such as better health services) and immaterial products. In the longer term, moreover, the shift to declining global populations will contribute to reducing the environmental impact of humanity. From this perspective, achieving radical decoupling is essentially a problem of making a sufficiently determined effort. It is, in other words, primarily a question of social and political will, rather than of fundamental technology or economics.

Based on this optimistic position, the analysis in this book assumes that per capita GDP will continue to grow in advanced countries in coming decades (even if quite probably at historically low rates). But this could all too easily turn out to be wrong.

Appendix 5.1: The Climate Investment Effort

This Appendix explains the basis for the claim in the main text that the extra government spending to finance that portion of the climate investment effort relating to government's own services and operations is unlikely to exceed 1 percent of GDP annually. This claim is based on available estimates of total (private sector plus government) abatement investment requirements, plus the assumptions that:

◆ Abatement investment pertaining to government's own services and operations would constitute only a small proportion of this total (i.e. not exceeding one-quarter)

◆ Adaptation investment by government will not exceed abatement investments pertaining to its own services and operations.

Abatement Investment Requirements

Most available estimates of the required abatement investment effort concern energy-related investments (supply-side and demand-side) and therefore exclude investments required (for example in agriculture) to reduce greenhouse gas emissions unrelated to the energy system. Energy-related investments are, however, likely to account for most of the total required abatement investments. Moreover, it is clear that little of the abatement investment unrelated to energy would pertain to government's own operations and services.

The European Commission (EC, 2018b: 16) estimates the additional energy-related investment required to achieve net zero at approximately 0.8 percent of European Union GDP annually over a period of two decades (raising prospective energy investment from 2.0 percent to 2.8 percent of GDP).

The International Energy Agency and International Renewable Energy Agency (IEA/IRENA, 2017) have estimated that additional energy-related investment to achieve the Paris COP21 objective of holding global warming to "well below 2°" at 0.3-0.4 percent of world GDP over the 30 years to 2050. This is a global estimate, not one for advanced countries specifically, although it seems reasonable to assume that the figure for advanced countries will not be dramatically larger. Nevertheless, the IEA/IRENA estimates imply a somewhat higher number than 0.3-0.4 percent for *net zero by 2050* because:

◆ Net zero translates into the tougher objective of holding warming to a maximum of 1.5°, which will require more abatement investment than the "well below 2°" target.

◆ The IEA/IRENA estimates do not count the cost of energy investments pursuant to the implementation of government policy commitments made *prior to* the COP21 Conference.

In the United States, a number of recent studies (generally less sophisticated than those of the EC and IEA/IRENA), as reviewed by Nersisyan and Wray (2019), estimate the total up-front spending required to achieve net zero in the key areas of energy, transport and buildings on average at the equivalent of approximately 1.5 percent of GDP per annum if spread over the 30 years.[14]

In the United Kingdom, the government's key advisory body on climate change has estimated the "net" annual cost of measures required to achieve net zero at 1-2 percent of 2050 GDP (Committee on Climate Change, 2019).[15] This estimate is more comprehensive than the others, because it includes the costs of actions in all areas including agriculture. However, it is not comparable with the others, because "net" cost deducts estimated savings (e.g. savings from reduced energy consumption) from the up-front gross investment expenditure.[16]

Placing too much reliance on any of these estimates would be inappropriate given that, as a technical advisory group to the UK Committee on Climate Change has observed, "both the costs and benefits of deep decarbonization are unknowable with any precision" (AGCB, 2019).

Nevertheless, it seems reasonable to interpret this body of estimates as indicating that additional total energy investments required to achieve net zero in advanced countries would not exceed 1 percent of GDP annually over the 30 years to 2050. If no more than one-quarter of this pertained to government's own services and operations, government abatement investment would not exceed 0.25 percent of GDP.

Adaptation Investment Requirements

Adaptation investment required to cope with global warming will undoubtedly be substantial (USGCRP, 2018: 1310-29; World Bank, 2011). Estimates of required adaptation investment in advanced countries are hard to find (there are more and better studies of probable costs in developing countries). The Stern Review (Stern, 2007) suggested that the annual cost of "making new infrastructure and buildings resilient to climate change in OECD countries" might be in the range of 0.05-0.5 percent of GDP annually. The huge range of this estimate, combined with an examination of the methodology used by the source on which it is based, suggests that it should be regarded as essentially a "back-of-the-envelope" calculation. A 2010 study commissioned by the European Union

(Oberghaus and Reif, 2010) estimated that the annual adaptation costs borne by budgets of EU governments would be €5.7 billion by 2050, which is a relatively modest amount.

It is difficult to believe that, for society as a whole, adaptation investments over coming decades – although very considerable – will need to be as large as abatement investments. If we therefore assume that government's adaptation investments do not exceed its abatement investments pertaining to its own services and operations, government investment in adaptation would also not exceed 0.25 percent of GDP.

An interesting point of reference for adaptation is that the Netherlands, much of which comprises reclaimed land below sea level, spends about 0.1 percent of GDP annually on its massive flood defense system.[17]

Adding adaptation and abatement investment requirements together, and then including additional government R&D spending (as noted earlier, a much lesser amount that on abatement), gives a total for additional government spending on the climate investment effort below 1 percent of GDP.

6. INFRASTRUCTURE DEFICITS

The state of infrastructure is a major preoccupation in many advanced countries today. Cracked and congested roads, structurally deficient bridges that have been closed to traffic, airports bulging at the seams and overburdened public transport are amongst the visible signs of the problem. Failing and inadequate infrastructure is not only a source of inconvenience for citizens as they go about their daily lives. It is also a threat to the development of national economies. Years of underinvestment and chronic neglect of maintenance are to blame.

During the 2016 US presidential election, the Democratic Party candidate declared that the United States faced a "national emergency" of failing infrastructure. Around the same time, the European Union's long-term investment bank warned that "increasing infrastructure gaps in almost all [European] countries" would "hurt the future competitiveness of the European Union" (EIB, 2017). In the EU's biggest member nation, an expert commission appointed by the government declared that "Germany has been suffering from a massive [infrastructure] investment backlog for years" (Fratzscher et al, 2015: 13).

In Canada, the Chamber of Commerce has drawn public attention to an "enormous bulge of public infrastructure requirements." And "down under" on the other side of the world, Australia's main professional engineering organization has raised the alarm about what it sees as an "infrastructure gap created by almost a decade of underinvestment" (EA, 2018: 46). The issue looms so large in that country that "in the competition for national airtime, voices bemoaning our national 'infrastructure deficit' come second only to those deploring the budget deficit" (Terrill and Coates, 2016).

The "austerity" policies of recent decades are widely held responsible. This is particularly so in Europe, where many agree with the influential manifesto *Green New Deal for Europe* that austerity has "starved Europe of investment in… public infrastructure," leaving "crumbling infrastructure" across the continent (GNDE, 2019: 15, 29).

Calls for large increases in government infrastructure investment follow directly from this assessment. In the United States, Democratic Party senators announced a plan in 2018 for $1 trillion in federal investment to "modernize our crumbling infrastructure" (Senate Democrats, 2018).[1] Similar calls have been made across Europe, particularly – but not exclusively – by the left-of-center political parties.

The emergence of infrastructure spending as a major issue in recent national elections in a number of countries highlights the mounting pressure on governments. In the 2019 British general election, for example, the ruling Conservative Party felt constrained to ease its austerity policies and announced a major change in fiscal rules to permit a large increase in infrastructure spending. After his victory, Prime Minister Boris Johnson moved to go further in releasing the purse strings – to finance, among other things, a major new high-speed train link to the north of the country.

It may prove that the deep economic crisis triggered by the coronavirus pandemic further changes the mood on infrastructure spending. It seems likely that at least some governments will increase infrastructure spending (including that which is part of the climate investment effort) as a means of boosting their economies during the recovery phase following the peak of the crisis.

Will the need to address the infrastructure problem be one of the major pressure points on government expenditure across the advanced world in coming decades? Will governments find themselves under irresistible pressure to permanently raise their infrastructure spending, not only to address past neglect but also to meet the need for new infrastructure and properly maintain existing assets?

This chapter suggests that the answer to this question is "yes and no." Yes, because in many advanced countries, including the United States, Italy, Germany, the UK and France, there is already a major problem and pressure is growing on governments to act. Sooner or later, governments in these countries will have little choice but to significantly increase infrastructure spending. But also no, to the extent that this is not the case everywhere. In some advanced countries, there is no good basis for believing that current levels of government infrastructure expenditure are inadequate, and any talk of infrastructure crises is either unjustified or grossly exaggerated. Japan, Switzerland, Australia and Norway are among the countries in this category.

Where do the majority of advanced countries sit on the spectrum between these two groups? It is difficult to make definitive judgments about the magnitudes of infrastructure deficits across advanced countries as a whole (at least without much more detailed country-by-country research than is possible in a book like this). There is nevertheless reason to believe that a *majority* of advanced countries have been underinvesting, and will feel, to varying degrees, pressure to increase spending.

When discussing here the issue of spending pressure, we explicitly put aside the separate question of the additional government infrastructure spending required as part of the climate investment effort. As discussed in Chapter 5, all advanced countries will need to undertake significant investment in abatement and adaptation measures, including with respect to public infrastructure.[2] This is on top of the spending discussed in this chapter.

Infrastructure and Government Expenditure Pressure

Estimates of the total investment required to close infrastructure deficits appear to suggest that governments in some countries will find themselves under pressure to spend truly astronomic amounts. In the United States, the American Society of Civil Engineers estimated in 2016 that more than $5 trillion in additional infrastructure spending will be needed over the period to 2040 (ASCE, 2016: 10). In Australia, the main professional engineers' association, Engineers Australia, some years back put a figure of

A\$700 billion on Australia's infrastructure deficit – an amount equivalent to more than half of the country's GDP.

There are, however, two points to be borne in mind in respect to such estimates.

The first is that estimates prepared by professional associations should be treated with a measure of caution because these associations are not disinterested. They are lobby groups, and many of their members depend upon infrastructure investment spending for their livelihoods.

The second and more important point is that these estimates do not purport to indicate required *government* expenditure on infrastructure. They are, rather, estimates of the magnitude of infrastructure investment required *from all sources*. Most infrastructure is not paid for by taxpayers. It is paid for by customers – i.e. by the individuals and businesses that use the infrastructure concerned – via *user charges*. It is, for example, electricity customers who pay, through their electricity bills, for the costs of the power grid and other electricity infrastructure. They do so irrespective of whether the electricity grid is owned and operated by private interests or by public enterprises.

The need to accelerate the development of "smart infrastructure" is a major preoccupation in many advanced countries and everyone agrees that government has a crucial role. This does not, however, mean government *paying* for smart infrastructure. Government's role in this area is primarily framework-setting and leadership, with regulation as its main policy instrument. Governments are increasingly playing this role in, for example, the development of smart electricity grids – grids that use digital technology to deliver two-way communication between supplier and customer and to manage the electricity system based on this information flow. Governments are encouraging and facilitating the development of smart grids, but they do not generally use taxes to pay for their development.

The same is essentially true for the development of broadband networks, the development of which has also been largely self-financed through customer charges. This is subject only to the qualification that many governments make strictly limited contributions to promote equity of access (see Box 6.1).

Box 6.1 Government Funding of Broadband

If provision of broadband infrastructure is left entirely to the market, rural and remote areas are likely to go unconnected. The costs of constructing the network extensions to provide connectivity to such areas are simply too high for the small number of customers involved. For this reason, governments in some advanced countries subsidize the network extensions required to serve these areas – funding this either through general tax funds or through earmarked taxes (e.g. on phone companies or customers). The sums of money involved are, however, small relative to government budgets. The British government, for example, has allocated £200 million (out of a total government budget of over £800 billion) to its *Rural Gigabit Connectivity Program* designed to connect to the "hardest-to-reach" 20 percent of UK households. This is broadly similar to the funding provided in the US by the Federal Communications Commission for rural and remote connections through its *Connect America Fund.* Even if the levels of funding for this intervention were increased many times over, it would make little difference to overall levels of government expenditure.[3]

Airports are something of an intermediate case. In most advanced countries, major airports are very largely self-financing. In other words, they fund their operations entirely, or very largely, through charges levied on passengers and airlines, together with other commercial revenues (e.g. from retail leases). This is true irrespective of whether the airports are privately or publicly owned, and irrespective of whether they are privately or publicly managed. (The United States, where many major airports are quite appalling, is an anomaly in this respect.[4]) Smaller regional airports tend to get significantly larger government subsidies, but the expenditure involved is not large.

Because this book is concerned with the future of government expenditure, we need here to put aside infrastructure investment funded from user charges and narrow our focus specifically to government-funded infrastructure.

One crucial issue is what is meant by the term "infrastructure." The

term's core meaning – that is, what everyone would agree that it covers
– is the key networks required for vital flows of goods, services, people
and information. This includes the road network, the electricity grid, the
rail network, the air traffic network (airports, air traffic control systems,
etc.), water and sewage services, telecommunications networks and mass
transit systems.

The term is, however, used by some in a much broader sense, so as to
include assets such as public buildings, public housing, schools and prisons.[5] The US Senate Democrats' $1 trillion "infrastructure" plan, referred
to above, uses the term in this broad way. The problem is that this approach
dissolves the distinction between government infrastructure investment
and government investment as a whole. All, or almost all, government
capital expenditure ends up being treated as "infrastructure" investment.

Here, we will stick to the narrower notion of what constitutes infrastructure. One reason is that when the key networks such as transport
networks, water supply and electricity supply fail in part or in whole, the
pressure on governments to act tends to be particularly intense. By contrast, voters tend to react much less if prisons and public housing become
dilapidated, overcrowded and inadequate. This is somewhat less true for
public school buildings, but only to a degree.

Transport Infrastructure Deficits

When we focus our attention on *government* infrastructure investment,
we are in most countries talking mainly about tax-funded transport infrastructure, particularly on roads, rail and mass transit. Across advanced
countries, transport is by far the largest area of tax-funded infrastructure
spending. The taxpayer contribution to transport infrastructure is large,
notwithstanding the role played by user charges. For example, passenger
fares typically cover significantly less than half of the costs of public transport. Road tolls are levied only on major highways – and then not for all
vehicles in all countries – which means that a large part of the cost of the
road network and associated infrastructure (e.g. bridges and tunnels) is
everywhere covered by government. The same is generally true for internal
waterways in countries where they play a significant role as transport routes.

No other area of public infrastructure receives anything like such significant levels of government funding. True, some governments contribute financially to help in disadvantaged and remote areas (as in the case of broadband). In the US, for example, the federal and state governments provide soft loans for water and sewage infrastructure. The sums involved are, however, tiny relative to what is spent on transport infrastructure. It therefore makes sense to focus particularly on tax-financed transport infrastructure when thinking about future pressures on government.

Is there a large deficit of such transport infrastructure across advanced countries?

Strong engineering evidence says "yes" for a number of countries. In the United States, the American Society of Civil Engineers has assigned ratings to the country's transport and other infrastructure, basing itself largely on official government engineering assessments. It gives the country's transit infrastructure (buses and commuter rail) an average rating of D-. Roads get a D and bridges a C+.[6] In the ASCE's judgment "America's roads are often crowded, frequently in poor condition, chronically underfunded, and are becoming more dangerous... One out of every 5 miles of highway pavement is in poor condition." With respect to transit systems, "symptoms of overdue maintenance and underinvestment have never been clearer." Again drawing on official data, the American Road and Transportation Builders Association reported that 47,052 (8 percent) of America's bridges were structurally deficient in 2018 (ARTBA, 2019).

In Germany, 12.4 percent of the country's bridges were, according to government figures, in poor condition.[7] A few have, so far, been closed after the discovery of serious cracks. Many roads – including some of the country's famous *autobahnen* – have developed cracks or are crumbling. In France, a Senate Commission reported in 2019 that 6 percent of the country's bridges were in poor structural condition, due to "chronic under-investment" (Sénat, 2019). Official measures of the state of the road network show a gradual degradation of the network, which has led to the "multiplication of temporary speed limits and other traffic restrictions" (Sénat, 2017a). In Italy, the problems of the aging and poorly maintained road network were graphically highlighted by the 2018 collapse of Genoa's Morandi Bridge, killing 43 people.

Increasing road congestion is frequently cited as evidence of serious transport infrastructure deficits. The ASCE, for example, views the dramatic increase in congestion delays in top US metropolitan areas as the direct consequence of underinvestment in roads and highways (ASCE, 2016: 13).

On rail, it is not hard to identify advanced countries with infrastructure problems. In the United Kingdom, commuter trains and urban metro systems in London and elsewhere tend to be unreliable, dirty and dilapidated. The United States is notorious for generally poor levels of public transport. In France – notwithstanding that the country is a world leader in the provision of efficient, high-quality rapid train services (the TGVs) – much of the rest of the rail network is in a regrettable condition. A series of technical audits have highlighted the "disturbing aging of the entire network" (Sénat, 2012; Putallaz and Tzieropoulous, 2012; Putallaz et al, 2018) and the presence of widespread unrepaired faults capable of causing serious accidents (such as one which occurred in Brétigny in 2013, killing seven people)[8].

These examples could readily be supplemented with similar stories from other countries.

Serious as these problems are, it does not necessarily follow that they are due to inadequate total spending on transport infrastructure. Other possible causes include incompetence, which played a major role in the Genoa bridge catastrophe (where repeated warnings from engineers were ignored by the authorities for years). Another possible factor is misallocation of resources *within* the total transport budget. Deliberate decisions to orient funding primarily to roads rather than public transport are, for example, a major reason for the inadequacy of public transport in some countries. Misallocation *within* the rail infrastructure budget has been a problem in France, in that one of the key reasons for the underinvestment in regional trains has been that successive governments have directed most of the available resources to the expansion of the rapid train network (Sénat, 2012: 6). For entirely political reasons, the TGV network has been extended at exorbitant cost to minor cities where the service is unwarranted on either economic or social grounds, thereby greatly reducing the resources available to the regional network.

When considering the role inadequate total spending may have played, it is useful to look at expenditure trends. Detailed data are available on investment in "inland transport" infrastructure – basically roads and rail – from the mid-1990s to the present (see statistical annex, Figures S6.1, S6.2, and S6.3). These data do not distinguish between public and private investment, but that does not matter when our focus is on infrastructure adequacy.

The data make it clear that in many of the countries where the state of infrastructure has become a major issue, spending has indeed been cut substantially. Spain, Canada and Germany experienced particularly large falls in total inland transport investment/GDP over the period 1995-2017, followed by France and Italy.[9]

Nevertheless, the spending cuts of the past two decades do not seem to have been the biggest problem. It is striking that transport infrastructure in the United States has become increasingly decrepit, despite the fact that there has in that country been no squeeze in transport infrastructure investment. US investment spending on inland transport infrastructure has been essentially stable as a percentage of GDP over the past two or three decades.[10] In France, the problems of the railway network have grown despite the fact that rail investment/GDP has in fact increased substantially over the 1995-2017 timeframe.

It seems clear that, in those advanced countries faced with serious transport infrastructure deficits, underspending started well before the spending cuts of the past two decades. In France, for example, experts trace the problems of the French railways back to a "collapse of investment from the beginning of the 1980s" (Sénat, 2012: 6). And in the US, the expenditure data suggest the country has been underinvesting in transport infrastructure since at least the 1980s.[11]

An important dimension of today's problems is that many countries are now facing the challenge that part of their transport infrastructure has reached, or is nearing, the end of its practical lifespan and requires replacement. This is particularly true for bridges and other structures built using reinforced concrete, many of which are seriously affected by the unanticipated problem of so-called "concrete cancer." Today's historically low levels of transport infrastructure investment/GDP are in many countries insufficient to cover the cost of replacing such assets.

How Much Additional Government Spending?

How much more will governments be under pressure to spend in coming decades in those countries facing serious infrastructure deficits? Some countries have produced ballpark estimates that are worth examining.

In the United States, the ASCE in 2016 estimated the required additional annual investment and maintenance expenditure on surface transport infrastructure (roads, bridges, rail and transit) at an amount equivalent to about 0.4 percent of GDP (ASCE, 2016: 12).[12] While this estimate did not pertain specifically to government infrastructure expenditure, it is clear that much of it would – at least given existing financing practices in the United States – need to be tax-financed. To this amount one would need to add additional, but smaller, government funding to address major problems in other areas, such as water and service systems and, at least under the current dysfunctional funding arrangements, airports.

In Europe, the European Investment Bank has suggested that transport infrastructure investment alone would need to rise by up to 0.5 percent of GDP per year to close the infrastructure deficit (EIB, 2016: 30). This estimate does not include necessary increases in maintenance expenditure. It includes, however, not only the areas of transport infrastructure that tend to have heavy government financing, but also other areas such as aviation and ports, which are essentially self-financing. The share which would require tax financing is unclear.

These types of estimates should be treated with great caution. The methodology underpinning the EIB estimate is, for example, very crude. It consists of nothing more than calculating the additional spending required to restore transport infrastructure spending to the same level as in 2008. If it is correct that transport infrastructure has been in many countries seriously underfunded for much longer than the past decade, the estimate would be conservative.

The ASCE estimate needs to be treated with caution for the opposite reason – it may be too high. As pointed out in a recent RAND Corporation study of US transport and water infrastructure – significantly entitled *Not Everything Is Broken* – estimates of required additional infrastructure spending prepared by US government experts tend to be significantly lower than those factored into estimates made by the ASCE and other infrastructure construction professionals. RAND notes that the concept of infrastructure investment "needs" is inherently subjective, and that although "experts familiar with transportation infrastructure are most qualified to assess needs, yet experts also are likely to be advocates for improved infrastructure" (Knopman et al, 2017: 53-67).

Spending needs also depend upon policies about user charging. One area where future policy changes could substantially reduce the pressure of transport infrastructure investment on government budgets is road charging (see Box 6.2).

Box 6.2 Road Charging and Future Tax-Financed Road Investment Requirements

Some of the countries with substantial transport infrastructure deficits are those where most highways are free for passenger vehicles. In Germany, for example, the federal government has for more than a decade resisted the imposition of any tolls on the passenger vehicle use of the *autobahn* network (other than for foreigners passing through). In the United States, the interstate highway system is, by design, largely toll-free (the original idea was to fund it wholly through the tax on gasoline). This contrasts with countries such as France, where tolls are charged for the use of the entirety of the national highway network. If countries such as Germany and the United States were to move more in that direction, the burden on tax financing would fall.

Another potential future direction is the increasing use of charging for urban road use. Only a handful of cities in major advanced countries (such as London, Stockholm and Milan) operate urban road charging systems at present. The attraction of systems such as that which Singapore operates – which not only employs

electronic toll charging but which uses variable pricing to deal with
the congestion problem – are very considerable. In such "congestion charging" systems, the charge per kilometer levied on vehicles
depends on the degree of congestion on the roads, so that it costs
more to drive one's car in peak hour than, say, on a Sunday. It is likely
that such systems will be increasingly introduced in major metropolises around the world (as will happen in Manhattan from 2021).
This will reduce somewhat the pressure on government expenditure.

As noted above, those who are most vocal about transport
infrastructure deficits cite growing road congestion as proof that
we need more road investment. But this is only partly true. In the
fast-growing metropolitan regions, congestion is primarily the
consequence of population pressure combined with the failure to
charge properly for the use of roads.[13] The growing number of vehicles on the roads cannot therefore be treated as a "need" that must,
come what may, be satisfied, which is essentially what most needs
analyses do.

Setting aside quantitative estimates such as those made by the ASCE and
EIB, there are two general arguments employed to suggest that very large
increases in government expenditure on transport (and other) infrastructure may be required in many advanced countries.

The first is based on comparisons between the spending levels of
recent years and those that prevailed in the decades after World War II.
In the United States, for example, public sector transport infrastructure
spending stood, at its peak at the end of the 1950s, at around 2 percent
of GDP – approximately twice what it is today. Spending levels then fell
progressively to the early 1980s, after that transitioning to the broadly
stable pattern of recent decades (Figure S6.4, statistical annex). In Western
Europe as a whole, inland transport investment/GDP (public and private
combined) stood at 1.5 percent of GDP in 1975. It subsequently declined
to 1.2 percent in 1980 and then to 0.9 percent in 1995 – also essentially
stabilizing after that point (ITF, 2017).

The fact that investment is so much lower today than in the post-
war decades is frequently claimed to be indicative of the scale of today's
underinvestment. If this were true, it would imply that we need to increase

spending to the level of the past – which would mean increasing it by something in the range of 50-100 percent.

This is, however, a dubious line of argument. The fact that transport infrastructure investment has been significantly lower than it was 40 or more years ago tells us precisely nothing about the magnitude of investment needed today. Following World War II, most advanced countries undertook massive investments to create modern highway networks. During this period, most countries (particularly Japan and the advanced European nations) also undertook the major investment required to electrify their railway networks, introduce automatic signaling and modernize rail more generally (including repairing considerable wartime damage in some countries).[14] Levels of transport infrastructure investment would be expected to fall substantially after the completion of these massive efforts to extend and enhance transport networks.

The second specious argument frequently advanced as proof that advanced countries need to *massively* increase their infrastructure spending, and in particular their spending on transport infrastructure, is the fact that countries like China and India are today spending much larger percentages of their national income on transport and other infrastructure. But given the vast gaps in infrastructure in these countries, heavy infrastructure investment is exactly what they need at this stage of their economic development.[15]

In summary, we know that many advanced countries face infrastructure deficits of various magnitudes. The amount of additional spending required on a continuing basis to address the problem cannot, however, be gauged by looking either at historic expenditure levels or at what is being spent today by countries that are trying to leap-frog to developed status.

On the Other Hand...

The discussion so far has focused on advanced countries with serious transport infrastructure deficits. But not all advanced countries find themselves in this position. There are quite a few – such as Japan, Switzerland and Norway – which are recognized internationally as having particularly high-quality transport and other infrastructure

The perception that transport and other infrastructure spending has been squeezed right across the advanced world does not correspond to reality. Inland transport infrastructure investment/GDP has, over the past two decades, actually increased in approximately half of the advanced countries for which data are available. The increases have, in some cases, been quite large. Significant increases in spending have even occurred in several eurozone countries.

Within total inland transport investment, investment devoted specifically to rail infrastructure has increased – in many cases very substantially – in two-thirds of the countries for which data are available. Road investment has fallen in some countries, but in many others it has not. There is, in short, no universal pattern and nothing like an across-the-board squeeze in transport infrastructure investment.

The data also illustrate the gap between rhetoric and reality in the public debate on infrastructure in certain countries. In the case of Australia, for example, the widespread belief that there has been a chronic squeeze on infrastructure investment is completely at odds with reality. Australia's inland transport infrastructure investment/GDP grew by 37 percent in the period 1995-2017. Within that aggregate, investment grew 54 percent for rail and 33 percent four roads. Levels of investment in Australia have, moreover, been high by international standards – much higher, for example, than in the United States – throughout the entire period 1995-2017. This is not to suggest that all government infrastructure in Australia is high quality. Governments have not always got their priorities right and public transport has been neglected in parts of the country. But overall spending has not obviously been inadequate.

Japan is an anomalous case. There, inland transport investment fell over 1995-2017 by 51 percent, which is more than in any other advanced country. But this has to be seen in context. In 1995, Japan was in the middle of a huge fiscal stimulus as the government fought the consequences of the asset price collapse of 1991 (Mühleisen, 2000). This fiscal stimulus took the form primarily of a massive surge in investment in roads, highways and bridges. Japan actually heavily *over*-invested in transport infrastructure, leading, for example, to the construction of many a "bridge to nowhere" (such as a bridge in northern Hokkaido Island that sees 10 cars a day). The fact that transport infrastructure investment has subsequently subsided is not evidence of underinvestment and does not presage a future infrastructure deficit.

At the impressionistic level, anyone who has made much use of European public transport systems knows that many of these systems are quite good. This shows up objectively in consumer satisfaction indicators for rail and urban transport reported by the European Commission's EU Transport Scoreboard. Austria and Finland are among the countries scoring particularly well.[16]

Broader Public Sector Underinvestment?

Governments not only invest in infrastructure, they also invest in major non-infrastructure assets such as schools, hospitals, public housing, other public buildings and defense systems. Total public investment/GDP (infrastructure and non-infrastructure) varies in advanced countries from a little under 2 percent (Ireland) up to around 5 percent (South Korea and Norway).[17]

There is great concern today that governments in many advanced countries are investing too little, and often also spending far too little on maintenance. Unfortunately, however, the issue of the adequacy of total government investment is not always clearly distinguished from that of the adequacy of government infrastructure investment.

Has there been a broad tendency across advanced countries for public investment – infrastructure *plus* non-infrastructure investment – to be reduced over recent decades? Even though everyone seems to "know" that this is the case, the answer is, in fact, *no*. Over the period since 1995, approximately as many advanced countries have increased government investment/GDP as have reduced it (see Figure S6.5, statistical annex). Investment levels are, moreover, higher today in a majority of advanced countries than they were prior to the global financial crisis (Figure S6.6, statistical annex).[18]

It is true, once again, that in most advanced countries total government investment levels are significantly lower today than they were in the three decades after World War II. (Figures S6.7 and S6.8 in the statistical annex illustrate this with the examples of Australia and the United States.) However, it is yet again the case that a large decline in investment spending is only to have been expected after the massive effort of the post-war period, not just for transport but also for investment in many other types of public asset. Take the example of schools: the post-war baby boom created a need for a large-scale school construction program, which faded once fertility rates declined.

A reduced need for infrastructure investment in countries already well-endowed with basic infrastructure is not the only factor at work here. Economic development typically brings with it a stronger private sector and better-developed financial markets. As a result, "the role of the private sector in the provision of infrastructure can be expected to increase" (IMF, 2004: 9). It is therefore impossible to draw conclusions about the extent of government underinvestment today merely from comparisons with levels half a century ago.

Box 6.3 The South Korean Exception

South Korea provides a counter example to the dominant pattern of government investment declining from post-war peaks through to the 1980s. In that country, there was no trend decline in government investment prior to the early 2000s (Figure S6.9, statistical annex). That government investment remained high for longer in South Korea makes perfect sense. It was only in the 1960s that the country started its transition from 'Third World' to advanced country status. The massive government investment effort needed to build the public infrastructure and other public assets required by an advanced modern society and economy started much later than elsewhere and consequently continued until much more recently.

Trends in total government investment over the past two decades (Figure S6.10 and Figure S6.11, statistical annex) have differed greatly between countries. At the low end of the spectrum, unsurprisingly, are countries such as Ireland, Spain, Italy and Germany, where the impact of austerity policies has been particularly marked. At the other end of the spectrum, with much higher levels, are countries such as Sweden and Norway.

The United States looks, superficially, to be about average among advanced countries with respect to its ratio of government investment/ GDP. This is a point to which some conservative commentators have drawn attention to rebut suggestions that American governments invest too little (Gregory, 2013, 2016). However, the picture changes if one excludes defense-related investment: US *non-defense* public investment is well below average. The US spends much more on defense-related investment than any other advanced country and this substantially boosts its level of total public investment.

The overall picture is, then, that there are quite a few advanced countries that have been neglecting investment not only in infrastructure but in non-infrastructure social assets. But this has not been the case everywhere.

Calls for a significant boost in total public investment expenditure are today being heard across the advanced world. These calls are, however, not always motivated by the desire to remedy past underinvestment. Often, they are driven by two other motivations. One is a desire, particularly in Europe, to deploy increased public investment as a means of stimulating economies that have not fully recovered from the 2007-2008 GFC and, since 2020, to counteract the pandemic-induced recession. The other is recognition of the role that public investment must play in the broad climate investment effort.

As discussed in Chapter 5, all advanced countries will need to spend significantly on upgrading non-infrastructure public assets such as schools, public buildings and public housing as part of the climate investment effort. In addition, those countries that have significantly underinvested in non-infrastructure assets for decades will no doubt experience additional spending pressure.

How Much Are We Talking About?

Just how much money is likely to be involved, and how powerful the pressure on government budgets will be, is not easy to say. It is exceedingly difficult to numerically estimate the additional spending on infrastructure that governments may feel obliged to undertake to address past neglect. The amounts required will be substantial, although they are clearly not going to be of the same order as future health spending increases.

The story is somewhat different with respect to non-infrastructure public investment. Here also, many advanced countries have neglected assets such as public buildings, public housing, prisons and even schools. It may, nevertheless, be that the greatest pressure for additional spending on these assets will be that created by the climate crisis. Governments may, in other words, feel under more pressure to spend on upgrading these assets to reduce their carbon footprint than they do to improve the quality of service they offer to, say, public tenants and prisoners.

Setting the climate investment effort aside, not every advanced country government will find itself under pressure to spend substantially more on infrastructure over the coming decades. In a number of advanced countries, there is no public infrastructure crisis. In this sense, spending pressures arising from accumulated infrastructure deficits are somewhat different from the spending pressures in the areas of health, long-term care and climate change, which will be felt everywhere.

7. INCOME SUPPORT IN THE NEW ECONOMY

A further area of potential government spending pressure is income support. Income support and other social protection expenditure on the elderly were discussed in Chapter 4. However, governments also spend large amounts of money on income support for working-age adults and children. This spending takes many forms, including unemployment benefits, income supplements and tax credits paid to the working poor, child benefits, and assistance to the sick and disabled.

Will income support for the working-age population and children be one of the areas of acute pressure on government budgets in coming decades? An influential strand of opinion argues that the answer is "yes." It considers that powerful forces are at work that will massively increase poverty in advanced countries over coming decades unless governments respond vigorously by, among other things, greatly increasing income support expenditure.

The reasoning is that the technological revolution now under way – the so-called Fourth Industrial Revolution – is pushing us toward a grim future in which demand for human labor, other than that of a small minority with special skills, will progressively diminish. The economy will as a consequence move toward "a tipping point where job creation will fall consistently short of what is required to fully employ the work-force" (Ford, 2015). Rapidly increasing poverty and inequality will be the result. The ranks of the poor will be swelled by a growing underclass cast aside from the labor market. Those still employed will for the most part have little bargaining power in a buyers' job market and will be forced to accept whatever terms they are offered. The overall result will be "dramatic increases in the numbers of people having to scrape by, doing precarious jobs that pay miserable wages" (van Parijs and Vanderborght: 2017).

This process of impoverishment will supposedly be facilitated by neo-liberal policies put in place over recent decades that have weakened job protection and undermined worker bargaining power. Globalization will be a further ingredient in this toxic brew. The growth of digital platforms will, in particular, lead to a new wave of offshoring, with further transfers of jobs to low-wage countries.

Faced with this prospect, the minimum response necessary to avoid a spectacular rise in poverty will be a large expansion of income support targeted both at the working poor and at those excluded from the labor market. The best and most comprehensive response to the problem would, however, be the introduction of an unconditional *basic income* system, under which everyone would receive a substantial regular income paid by the government.

So, at least, the widely held narrative goes.

But how far is this true? Is it really the case that government spending on income support must increase greatly over the coming decades if we are to prevent a massive expansion of the underclass of society? This is a question that must be answered as part of any satisfactory analysis of the long-term directions of government expenditure.

A Question of the Future of Poverty

The question at stake is fundamentally that of the future of poverty. The primary function of income support is to reduce poverty – to support people who, for one reason or another, have insufficient resources to enjoy an acceptable standard of living. Such support is the central component of the welfare state, the construction of which was one of the most important achievements of the late 19th and the 20th centuries.

More precisely, the question is what the future holds for *underlying* poverty in the working-age population. By "underlying" poverty, we mean the level of poverty that would exist in the absence of government income support and other redistribution via the tax system.[1] If government policies on eligibility for, and levels of, benefits were to remain unchanged, it would be changes in the rate of underlying poverty that would largely determine the evolution of total expenditure on income support.

We are not talking here about temporary increases in poverty during economic crises such as the global financial crisis or the pandemic-induced crisis which started in 2020. Underlying poverty always increases substantially during such periods, triggering big increases in government income support expenditure. This was particularly true in the immediate wake of the pandemic, when governments made large discretionary income support payments in addition to the usual unemployment and other welfare benefit entitlements. But this is by definition a temporary phenomenon. Economies eventually recover, underlying poverty rates subside, and income support spending falls back to more normal levels. Here, our focus is on long-term trends in underlying poverty, not short and medium-term fluctuations.

Great variations exist between advanced countries in the extent of government spending on poverty reduction. The United States, for example, spends much less of its national income on poverty alleviation than most other advanced countries. But the question of whether specific countries should adopt a more generous – or more restrictive – approach to income support is not the focus of our analysis. The main question addressed is, rather, the following: *if governments maintain their present degree of willingness to alleviate poverty, will growing underlying poverty put them under pressure to greatly increase income support expenditure for the working-age population and children over coming decades?*

Box 7.1 Absolute and Relative Poverty

The principal purpose of income support is to provide a social safety net to protect people against involuntary poverty. At the very minimum, this means – or should mean – providing protection against *absolute poverty.*

Absolute poverty describes the situation of households unable to afford the basic minimum requirements of food, clothing, accommodation and other services necessary to ensure physical health.

In the United States, the role of government in income support has historically been conceived mainly as addressing absolute poverty. To varying degrees, governments in advanced countries go beyond this in seeking also to reduce what is known as *relative poverty*. Relative poverty defines poverty relative to the overall standard of living (specifically, as a percentage of median household income).[2] This means that the threshold of relative poverty is – unlike that of absolute poverty – higher the more affluent the country. Although households in relative poverty are significantly poorer than the community as a whole, they may have a standard of living well above the threshold of absolute poverty.

The Lessons of Recent History

Predictions of imminent mass impoverishment in advanced countries are not new. A quarter of a century ago, Jeremy Rifkin (1995) warned of impoverishment as a result of the arrival in the (then) near future of worldwide mass technological unemployment. Automation resulting from the adoption of new information and communications technology (ICT) would be to blame. "More than 75 percent of the labor force in most industrial nations," he asserted, "engage in work that is little more than simple repetitive tasks. Automated machinery, robots and increasingly sophisticated computers can perform many if not most of these jobs."

At the same time, the Canadian social scientist David F. Noble wrote that "for a growing number of people, the ultimate guaranteed technologically delivered destination is the dole" (Noble, 1995). Noble was convinced that automation was already leading to "growing structural (that is permanent) unemployment and the attendant emergence of a nomadic army of temporary and part-time workers ... and a swelling of the ranks of the perpetually impoverished."

As it turned out, there was in fact no general impoverishment of the workforce. There are, nevertheless, many today who think the doomsayers' predictions proved partially correct. Many people who follow current affairs believe that technology and globalization have, as the sociologist Arne Kalleberg (2011) puts it, generated "pervasive job insecurity," greatly magnifying poverty. Many would, similarly, accept as factual

Johannessen's (2019: 15) claim that over recent decades poverty has been "spreading like an epidemic ... in the heart of the rich industrial nations," with "robotization" and other advanced technology largely responsible.

To understand the future, it is important to properly understand the past. Before examining future trends, we should therefore consider whether it is actually true that technology and globalization have already, over recent decades, had a major net adverse impact on employment and remuneration for the working-age population. The question here is not whether there have been losers from the economic shifts that have occurred in recent decades. Capitalist economies are in constant flux and there are always winners and losers. The relevant issue is whether the losers have been increasingly outnumbering the winners, so that a growing portion of the working-age population has found itself excluded, downtrodden and impoverished.

Let's be precise about the forces in question. With respect to technology, what generated great fear several decades ago was the arrival of ICT in offices and factories and the expectation of consequent job losses resulting from automation. Although the ICT investment surge began in the 1980s, it was from the 1990s that its full force was felt across the advanced world. The upward trend in ICT investment spending has continued, notwithstanding a temporary drop in the immediate wake of the 2001 dot.com crash. The impact on industry of this ICT investment surge is sometimes referred to as the "Third" Industrial Revolution.[3]

As for globalization, what provoked alarm was the sharp rise of manufacturing import penetration from low-wage countries – China, India and others – that was particularly concentrated in the period from the 1990s up to the 2007-2008 global financial crisis. Although the upward trend in low-wage imports started earlier, import penetration became supercharged in the 1990s with the rapid expansion of global value chains, in which low-wage countries played a key role in the labor-intensive stages of the production of manufactured goods (Hanson, 2012). One manifestation was the so-called "China Shock" – the very rapid growth of Chinese manufacturing exports – that hit US manufacturing particularly hard in the 2000s.

The acceleration of international economic integration in the period from the 1990s up to the global financial crisis is often referred to as the "second wave" of globalization (the first wave preceded World War I). The expansion of low-wage imports was only one of its constituent elements (increased financial market integration was another). One writer has memorably labelled this the era of "hyper-globalization" (Rodrik, 2012).

What we want to know, then, is whether underlying poverty has increased since the 1990s and, if so, whether this can be attributed to a deterioration of labor market conditions due to the impact of the ICT investment surge and globalization. In asking this question we need, of course, to put aside temporary increases in poverty due to economic crises such as that induced by the coronavirus pandemic.

The starting point of our analysis of the trends is important, because it would be misleading to focus on comparisons of poverty and labor market conditions with an earlier epoch. The 1970s and 1980s were a period of deep macroeconomic crisis, with two recessions. The oil shock and the harsh monetarist medicine inflicted on the economy to cure inflation were the main forces at work. Long-term unemployment, poverty and job insecurity all increased and remained permanently worse than they had been during the three halcyon post-war decades. But this cannot be attributed to the impact of technology, nor to globalization.[4]

What Has Happened to Poverty?

Although it is not easy to find statistics on trends in all advanced countries, data are available for a sufficient number to make it clear *there was in fact no general trend for underlying working-age poverty to increase between the 1990s and the pandemic-induced crisis of 2020* (see Box 7.2). In a substantial number of countries, underlying working-age poverty actually fell.

Box 7.2 Trends in Underlying Relative Poverty

Most official statistics provide data for poverty after transfers and taxes. Statistics on underlying poverty (before transfers and taxes) are more limited. Such statistics do, however, exist for Europe for the period 1995-2017. These indicate that, of the 11 advanced European countries for which data are available, five saw *falls* in the rate of underlying working-age relative poverty and only four (Finland, Italy, Germany and Spain) experienced significant increases.[5,6]

In the case of Canada, statistics exist on trends from 1980 in underlying poverty for the total population (i.e. including elderly households). These suggest, however, that there has been no long-term trend of increasing underlying working-age relative poverty.[7]

The United States reports statistics on underlying working-age poverty, but poverty is not measured there on the same relative basis as elsewhere. These data nevertheless imply a long-term trend of increases (dating from 1967) in underlying working-age poverty if measured on the relative basis used elsewhere.[8] (Note, however, that this trend significantly pre-dated the 1990s and has been widely linked to factors other than technology and globalization.[9])

Undoubtedly, underlying working-age poverty will have increased during the period concerned in a few other advanced countries. Japan is almost certain to be one, although relevant statistics are difficult to find. Summing up, the overall story of underlying working-age poverty in the advanced world is a mixed one, with no general trend.

Some might wonder whether data on underlying poverty may be misleading because of so-called "wage stagnation." Wage stagnation is what happens when real wages – more specifically, the wages of the *median* worker – fail to increase even though productivity is rising. Wage stagnation has the effect of holding down the threshold used to measure relative poverty, thereby in a sense artificially reducing measured relative poverty. (It does so because the threshold used to define relative poverty is, as mentioned, defined as a percentage of median household income, which is significantly influenced by median wages.)

Wage stagnation is today a much-discussed issue, essentially because it describes the experience over many decades of workers in the United States. However, contrary to what is widely believed, wage stagnation has not been a general phenomenon across the advanced world. The US experience has, in fact, been quite unrepresentative (shared by only two other advanced countries – Japan and Canada). Any suggestion that poverty statistics are misleading because of wage stagnation may therefore be disregarded. (Appendix 7.1 provides more detail.)

Mention of wage stagnation raises the broader issue of rising inequality, which is for good reason the focus of much attention these days. Inequality has been increasing throughout the advanced capitalist world, in a long-term trend that started well before the 1990s but which many consider to have been aggravated by ICT.

However, although inequality has been on the rise, we are concerned here with government income support expenditure, and the key driver of income support expenditure is poverty, not inequality. The two are not the same. Inequality can increase – and indeed has increased – in ways that do not increase poverty. Moreover, as discussed later, income transfers from government are not the main, or even necessarily an appropriate, instrument for fighting rising inequality.

Although the poverty statistics seem clear, we need to be sure that they are not missing something. It is therefore important also to look directly at labor market developments to see if they have undergone, at least to some extent, the deterioration predicted by Rifkin, Noble and others. This means checking whether there has indeed been a long-term increase in unemployment and exclusion from the labor market, and whether pay and employment conditions for those in work have eroded in a way that has swelled the ranks of the working poor.

Unemployment and Exclusion from the Labor Market

Starting with unemployment, the best test of the doomsayers' predictions is trends in *long-term* unemployment.[10] Here the statistics are clear. There has been *no* ongoing general trend in recent decades for rising rates of long-term unemployment in advanced countries. Indeed, long-term unemployment in 2017 was generally a little lower than it was several decades ago.[11] (Just like underlying poverty, unemployment is highly cyclical, meaning that it increases substantially during economic crises and then gradually falls once economies recover. However, it is long-term trends, rather than cyclical ups-and-downs, which are relevant here.)

But maybe the long-term unemployment statistics are misleading. Perhaps more working-age people have become so discouraged by the difficulty of finding work that they have dropped out of the labor market, becoming what is technically known as "inactive" and, as a consequence, no longer being counted in the official statistics as unemployed. This has indeed been a big problem in the United States. More precisely, it has been a big problem with working-age *males* in that country, where the prime-age male "inactivity rate" increased by 5.2 percent (from 15.8 percent to 21.0 percent) over the past two decades (Black et al, 2016). But US experience is unrepresentative of advanced countries in general, most of which have experienced either falling or stable male inactivity rates.[12] (The US trend, moreover, started in the 1960s and – like increasing underlying poverty in that country – cannot easily be attributed to economic forces that came into play only in the 1990s.)

There has been a major expansion of *female* participation in the workforce in advanced countries. The overall result has been, almost everywhere, a large long-term increase in the labor market participation rate of working-age adults as a whole (males plus females). Claims that an increasing portion of the working-age population has been excluded from the labor market simply do not hold water.

In-Work Poverty

Even without an increase in the ranks of the unemployed and inactive, poverty could still have increased over the long term if there had been an increase in the numbers of the working poor – that is, in the numbers of working-age adults who are employed but whose households are below the poverty line. Has this been the case?

It is difficult, unfortunately, to judge whether there has been a trend increase since the 1990s in the rate of underlying in-work poverty, because statistics on the rates of poverty *before benefits and taxes* of working households are not easy to find.[13] (Increases in rates of in-work poverty *after benefits* in certain countries – such as the UK – are a different matter, and must be seen in the context of government cuts to welfare benefits.[14])

Perhaps, however, there are indirect indicators of what has happened.

One possible indirect indicator is *low pay*,[15] popularly considered to be a leading cause of in-work poverty. If the proportion of the workforce subject to low pay had been increasing – as some suggest – it might perhaps be inferred that there must have been a rise in underlying in-work poverty, irrespective of what the poverty statistics seem to say.

Plausible as this might seem, across advanced countries as a whole there is in fact no credible basis for the proposition that there has been a general long-term increase in in-work poverty due to low pay. OECD statistics suggest there has been no general trend increase in the prevalence of low pay – indeed, it seems to have fallen in more countries than it has risen.[16] But more importantly, the relationship between low pay and in-work poverty is, in reality, not a strong one. Poverty is a characteristic of households rather than individuals, and many low-paid workers are members of households that are not poor because other adult members of the household (in particular, their partners) are significantly better paid. This is why the statistical correlation between low pay and in-work poverty is weak in advanced countries generally, including the United States (Gautié and Ponthieux, 2016; Henning, 2018). A 2012 study estimated that only 13 percent of low-paid workers in the EU were poor (Maître, Nolan and Whelan, 2012).

Underemployment is another conceivable indicator of trends in the numbers of the working poor, because in most advanced countries it is a more important cause of in-work poverty than low pay (Halleröd, Ekbrand and Bengtsson, 2015). Underemployment may lead to chronic underlying poverty, as in the case of a single person searching for a full-time job who has only been able to find part-time work for 10 hours a week. More often, perhaps, it leads to intermittent poverty, particularly for people who have repeated spells of unemployment between short-duration full-time jobs.

Box 7.3 Underemployment

The underemployed are those who work on average less than the equivalent of continuous full-time employment but who want to work more. Underemployment therefore does not describe the position of those who are unemployed or labor-market inactive. Statistics on low pay do not measure underemployment because low pay is defined with respect to *hourly* pay rates, rather than to weekly earnings.

The underemployed working poor have unquestionably long been a significant part of the poverty problem. But the relevant question here is whether there has been a general trend for this group to increase as a percentage of the working-age population. Statistical evidence suggests there has probably been *no* such trend in the United States,[17] but that there may well have been in the United Kingdom (Blundell at al, 2018).[18] For other countries, there doesn't seem to be much direct data available.

Although the rate of underemployment has grown over the long term in most advanced countries, it would be quite wrong to draw from this the conclusion that the prevalence of in-work poverty due to underemployment must also have increased. While it is true that there are many people who are poor because they are underemployed, it is equally true that many of the underemployed are not poor (see Box 7.4).

Box 7.4 Trends in Underemployment and In-Work Poverty

Underemployment has grown over the long term. International Labor Organization statistics for 14 advanced countries with data going back a decade or more prior to 2017 show significant increases in underemployment in 10 of them.[19] However, it is impossible to conclude from this that there has been a corresponding long-term growth in in-work poverty arising from underemployment. A large, and probably growing, percentage of underemployed persons are not poor. In the first place, they may be part of households that collectively have incomes well above the poverty threshold. (With the rise of female part-time employment, there may well have been an increase in the number of women who would like to increase their hours of employment but whose households are not poor.) In the second place, some of the underemployed are – notwithstanding that they are working less than full-time and would like to earn more – already earning enough in their own right to put their households above the poverty threshold.

Underemployment, "Precarious Work" and Poverty

It is often suggested that the ranks of the underemployed working poor have been continuously increasing because of the sustained long-term growth in the percentage of the workforce engaged in "irregular" work. Irregular work – also known as "non-standard" or "atypical" work – refers to work arrangements that do not involve a continuing (i.e. open-ended) full-time equivalent contract with a single employer. It includes part-time work, temporary work, agency work and self-employment.

Those most convinced that the growth of irregular work has led to a large increase in the ranks of the underemployed working poor are the *precarity theorists*, whose diagnosis of the ills of the modern labor market revolves around the notion of "precarious work." Precarity theorists tend to take it for granted that irregular work is precarious work. This leads them to infer from the growth of irregular work that a large and continuously growing portion of the contemporary workforce are precarious workers. The most prominent precarity theorist, Guy Standing (2014), claims that at least one-quarter of the workforce of advanced countries are precarious workers.

There is no clear and generally agreed definition of precarious work.[20] It is a slippery notion, frequently abused for ideological reasons. To avoid confusion when discussing the views of the precarity theorists, it is better to focus on what we might call *earnings precarity* – which we can define as exposure to a high risk of the loss, or drastic reduction, of labor income as a consequence of the loss of one's job or of an unanticipated and involuntary reduction in hours of work. Whatever other varying senses precarity theorists may give to the notion of "precarious work," earnings precarity defined in this manner is usually part of what they have in mind.

To assess the claims made by the precarity theorists, we can therefore focus on one clear question: *Is it true that the growth of irregular work has led to a long-term increase in the level of earnings precarity across the workforce as a whole, such as to significantly increase underemployment and poverty?*

Relevant trends in irregular work are considered in detail in Appendix

7.2. The analysis shows no persuasive basis to believe that the increased role of irregular work has over the long term led to a continuing increase in the level of earnings precarity in advanced countries generally.

By far the largest growth in irregular work has been in part-time work. A substantial majority of those who work part-time do so, in most advanced countries, as a matter of choice[21] and do not wish to increase their working hours.[22,23] Not only are most of them not poor, but the growth of part-time work has been a force *reducing* poverty because it often helps to diminish household reliance on the earnings of a single breadwinner.

At the same time, those forms of irregular work with the least *formal* job security – and which may therefore entail greater *potential* exposure to underemployment and in-work poverty – have either not grown across advanced countries as a whole (temporary work, self-employment) or account for only a quite small percentage of the workforce (agency work, on-call part-time work).

The fact that someone may be employed in a job with little or no formal job security does not necessarily mean that in practice they face a high degree of risk of losing their job or having their hours drastically cut. Lack of formal job security does not, in other words, automatically mean earnings precarity. So rather than simply basing their claims on the fact that irregular work has become more common, what the precarity theorist should do is offer evidence of how the *actual* degree of earnings precarity faced by the average worker has changed. An obvious way is to measure the extent to which members of the workforce actually experience drastic involuntary reductions of labor income. Key exponents of precarity theory like Standing have not, however, bothered to undertake this type of analysis.

Box 7.5 Income Precarity in the United States

In the United States, Jacob Hacker attracted considerable attention with his 2006 book *The Great Risk Shift*, in which he presented statistics that purportedly demonstrated a large long-term trend increase in labor income volatility in the United States, as measured by the proportion of working-age adults who in any given year experienced a decline of 25 percent or more in inflation-adjusted household income relative to the preceding year.[24] (Although this is not the same as our concept of earnings precarity, it bears some relationship to it.[25]) Hacker's interpretation of the data was, however, subsequently comprehensively debunked as statistically misleading by Scott Winship (2012). Winship re-analyzed the data and found that they showed there had been only a small increase in this measure of income volatility over the decades preceding the GFC.[26] (Income volatility always rises temporarily during recessions, so the increase during the GFC that followed was to be expected and is not necessarily indicative of any long-term trend.) Winship concluded that "claims of dramatically increased volatility simply don't stand up." In the second edition of his book, Hacker (2019: 11) updates his volatility indicators to 2014 and repeats the same claims he made earlier. However, his updated measures do not show any clear trend since the 1980s.[27]

Some light on actual earnings precarity is shed by OECD analysis looking at what has happened to what it calls – with its talent for catchy terminology – "job-to-nonemployment transitions" rates. This measure reports the percentage of people who, after their employment in a job terminates (for whatever reason), find themselves out of a job (i.e. are unemployed or labor-market inactive), rather than in another job. It measures, in other words, the proportion of people who find themselves without any employment earnings after their jobs terminate. The OECD's analysis reveals that over the period 2006-2017, out of 14 major advanced OECD countries, the rate of job-to-nonemployment transition increased significantly in only two countries (OECD, 2019c: 99). It *fell* significantly in seven and was essentially stable in five.[28] This indicates that the degree of earnings precarity – at least that part pertaining to the risk of losing one's job entirely – has been falling.

More than a decade ago, in response to the precarity theorists' claims, Kevin Doogan (2009) examined trends in job tenure in the United States and Europe. He did so because precarity theory suggested that average job tenure was becoming shorter as a consequence of employers being increasingly willing to show their employees the door. What he found was that, to the contrary, average job tenure had been increasing. His conclusion was that on the whole employers, rather than wishing to play fast and loose with their employees, were *increasingly* keen to maintain longer-term employment relationships. Doogan found the precarity theorists guilty of "systematic exaggeration," and suggested that increased precarity was more a matter of subjective feeling than reality.[29]

To reject the claims of the precarity theorists is not to deny that there are, in all advanced countries, people at the margins of the workforce – in particular, the poorly educated – who experience high levels of earnings precarity. Nor is it to refuse to acknowledge that there are some industries where easy hiring and firing is commonplace and earnings precarity is correspondingly high. The key point is that the percentage of the workforce affected is *much* smaller than the precarity theorists suggest. Claims that the rise of irregular work has produced a growing army of underemployed working poor are, thus, without foundation.

Box 7.6 Temporary Work and the Young in Dual Labor Markets

One widely discussed form of precarity is the difficulty young people generally face in some countries – France, Spain, Italy and Japan being good examples – in finding continuous full-time employment. In these countries, a large portion of young people, even those with university degrees, are obliged to take a succession of temporary contracts at the start of their working lives.

This is a problem heavily concentrated in countries that have granted so much job security to permanent employees as to give enterprises little flexibility to adjust the numbers or working hours of such employees in the face of fluctuations in demand for their products. Because this sort of inflexibility destroys employment (by making enterprises very cautious about hiring on permanent contracts), it became clear decades ago that the means would need to be found to give enterprises somewhat greater employment flexibility. Governments in these countries were, however, generally reluctant and slow for political reasons to deal directly with the problem by reducing the excessive protection granted to permanent employees. They therefore took the path of least resistance by greatly extending the opportunity for enterprises to hire part of their workforces on temporary contracts – while leaving largely untouched the privileged position of permanent employees. Those employed with the "second-class citizen" status of temporary contracts are, by definition, those who firms are able to dispense with more easily. Their position is exactly the inverse of permanent employees: they have too little formal job security. Young people, as new entrants to the labor market, are particularly likely to be hired on this basis. But they are not the only victims – some categories of older workers are also affected.

The result has been dual labor markets in which insecurity, and earnings precarity, is disproportionately concentrated on those with temporary contracts, including young people. The problem is much less prevalent in countries without such excessive levels of security for permanent employees. In most English-speaking countries, for example, youth employment difficulties are concentrated mainly on those who are poorly educated and have limited skills (although there is increasing abuse of unpaid internships).

Another dimension of this problem precarity theorists rarely acknowledge is that in countries such as France, the education and training system has for a long time done a poor job of equipping young people generally with the right skills. In France, much tertiary education is largely irrelevant to work. The country lacks a good system of technical apprenticeship and the school system delivers unsatisfactory results on basics such as literacy and numeracy. These are problems that the Macron government explicitly recognized and worked vigorously to address.

The extent of the problem facing young people in these countries is, nevertheless, sometimes exaggerated. In Japan, for example, it appears that – notwithstanding the common experience of temporary contracts at the start of their career – the great majority of young men (perhaps around 80 percent) find continuing jobs by the time they reach their early thirties (Gordon, 2017). (Finding continuing jobs is, and always has been, more difficult for young women in Japan, but this is essentially for reasons of gender-based discrimination.)

Underemployment is not the only way in which precarious work has, according to the precarity theorists, increased in-work poverty. They claim that it has also done so by aggravating the problem of low pay. We have already noted that there is a relatively weak correlation between low pay and in-work poverty. But setting this aside, has the rise of irregular work increased the numbers of low-paid workers? There is no clear evidence of this. In countries with dual labor markets, such as Japan, irregular workers are on average paid less well than equivalent permanent corporate employees (Aizawa, Dekle and Helble, 2017). But this is not the result of irresistible economic forces – it is the consequence, rather, of misconceived government regulation and labor market traditions (see above). The more pertinent question is whether, in countries *without* perverse dual labor markets, irregular work has pushed remuneration down and, more par-ticularly, whether it has forced large numbers of workers into the ranks of the low paid. Evidence in Australia, at least, suggests that this is not the case. In that country – once worker characteristics such as education and experience are taken into account – irregular workers are not paid less on an hourly basis than regular workers (Laß and Wooden, 2019; Booth and Wood, 2008).[30]

One specific form of irregular work – pseudo-independent contracts with workers who are de facto employees – has been used in *some* coun-tries to drive down remuneration, thereby contributing to low pay. But pseudo-independent contractors are generally not a large part of the irreg-ular workforce, even in countries that have been most permissive about this particular abusive practice (see Appendix 7.2).

Self-employment more generally should not be equated with low pay. A recent international survey conducted by McKinsey, for example, reports a substantial majority of those who are genuinely self-employed (i.e. excluding pseudo-independent contractors) consider themselves to be well remunerated relative to what they would earn as company employees.

In summary, unsubstantiated claims by precarity theorists to the effect that irregular workers are generally underpaid (e.g. Johannessen, 2019: 5) should be discounted.

One final point on the impact of so-called "precarious work" on poverty concerns the trade-off between precarity and unemployment. Countries that precarity theorists point to as having the highest numbers of precarious workers – such as the UK, Germany, Japan and the United States – tend to have the lowest rates of unemployment. This is, in part, because many people employed in these countries in jobs with low levels of formal security would otherwise be unemployed. These include people who are poorly educated and have limited job-relevant skills, including many migrants from underdeveloped countries. If for such people the alternative to insecure work is unemployment, then whatever earnings precarity they may experience clearly cannot be said to increase the overall rate of underlying poverty.

Box 7.7 Poverty and Irregular Employment in Germany

Germany is well known for the growth of irregular employment, dating particularly from the Hartz labor market reforms (implemented in several stages starting in 2003). These reforms put considerable pressure on the unemployed to accept irregular work – in particular, so-called "mini-jobs" – both because of reductions in the duration and level of unemployment benefits and because of requirements that beneficiaries accept almost any job offered to them. Mini-jobs unquestionably entail a significantly elevated level of earnings precarity. Even so, it is not obvious that the Hartz reforms have increased poverty. On the one hand, many of those doing mini-jobs would otherwise have been completely unemployed. On the other hand, access to mini-jobs has helped reduce structural unemployment due to what economists call "hysteresis" – that is, to the fact that the longer someone is outside the workforce, the less likely it is that any employer will give them a job. The relatively low level of unemployment in Germany is clearly not primarily due to these reforms, but they have helped.

Many critics of the Hartz reforms assert they have been in large measure responsible for the significant long-term increase in the rate of poverty in Germany. However, careful analysis by German labor economists reveals that the rise in poverty rates since the 1990s is "mainly the result of the higher proportion of migrants" (Grabka and Goebel, 2018). In other words, the large inflows of relatively poorly educated and trained immigrants into the country have significantly increased the poverty rate above what it would otherwise have been.

A good case can be made that aspects of the Hartz reforms were unduly harsh. A particular problem was the absence in Germany, prior to 2015, of a legal minimum wage. However, the basic idea of creating strong incentives for the unemployed to engage in work or training – rather than remain passively on unemployment benefits – is clearly correct (and has been applied in a less harsh form in countries like Denmark).

The Doomsayers Were Wrong

The verdict, then, is quite clear. Those who predicted, several decades ago, that a large portion of the workforce would be tossed out of the labor market by the impact of ICT and globalization, and that many of those remaining in employment would join the ranks of the working poor, were *entirely* wrong. Advanced capitalist countries have not experienced a broad increase in underlying poverty in the working-age population. The ranks of the working poor and those excluded from the labor market have not generally swelled. Some of these things have happened in some countries – including, most notably, the United States. But most advanced countries have not witnessed such trends.

Even in the United States, it is not plausible to attribute the long-term growth in relative poverty to ICT and globalization. The timing is all wrong, because the trend started well before the 1990s – it dates back to the 1960s. Explanations that focus on other factors, including the weakening of worker protection and the poor quality of much public education, are more persuasive. There is, in any event, a tendency in international policy debate to give disproportionate attention to US developments. Too many commentators simply assume phenomena that have attracted a lot of attention in the US – such as wage stagnation and growing labor market inactivity rates – are representative of advanced capitalism generally, when this is often not the case.

None of the above is intended to suggest that everything is wonderful in contemporary labor markets. Far from it. Things are difficult for specific groups, including the poorly educated.[31] Inadequate labor legislation and the decline of labor unions have, in some countries, left workers with too little formal job security. But these are different issues.

Why Didn't ICT Devastate Employment and Wages?

Why is it that, although the ICT investment surge led to considerable automation of tasks previously performed by humans, there has been no general trend of growing poverty in the working-age population? Why is it that we have not seen anything like the growth in labor market exclusion and in-work poverty predicted by the doomsayers?

In answering these questions, it is important to put the technological advances of recent decades in context. Automation is nothing new. The replacement of human labor by machinery has been an ongoing feature of capitalism throughout its 400-odd year history. It is the main reason why productivity and living standards have progressively risen. The impact of the automation triggered by the ICT investment surge has, so far, not even been particularly impressive by historical standards. Although the ICT investment surge led to considerable automation in some parts of the economy, its impact was not sufficient to accelerate productivity growth across advanced economies as a whole. To the contrary, recent decades witnessed a *productivity slowdown* – exactly the opposite of what would have happened if the dramatic effects predicted by the doomsayers in the 1990s had come to pass (Gordon, 2016). This underlines the considerable time lags in implementing and realizing the productivity benefits of major new technologies (van Ark, 2016; Goldin et al, 2018; Brynjolfsson, Rock and Syverson, 2017). Technological revolutions do not occur overnight.

But irrespective of the magnitude of the impact of the ICT investment wave, it is a mistake to view automation – or technological innovation more generally – as intrinsically job-destroying. The reasons why have been repeatedly explained by leading economists.

The first key point is that, when considering the impact of automation, it is misleading to focus only on direct job losses. While it is obvious that the *direct* impact of automation is to reduce the demand for labor – as happens, for example, when industrial robots rather than human workers weld car panels[32] – automation also works *indirectly* in two important ways (see Box 7.8) to increase the demand for labor (Autor and Salomons, 2018). Specifically:

◆ By boosting aggregate demand for goods and services. This works via the "income effect." Automation increases productivity – because it augments the productivity of workers performing production tasks that have not been automated – and thereby increases incomes. Those whose incomes increase spend more, creating jobs. The more labor-intensive are the goods and services people wish to buy with their increased incomes, the stronger is the increase in the demand for labor resulting from the income effect.[33]

◆ By stimulating the growth of downstream (customer) industries through lower input prices. Increased automation in "upstream" industries (industries supplying goods or services to other industries) typically stimulates connected downstream industries.

Box 7.8 Estimates of the Employment Impact of ICT-Driven Automation

A number of studies have sought to estimate the impact – direct and indirect – of ICT-driven automation on employment. Gregory, Salomons and Zierahn (2016), for example, examined the impact of what they call "routine-replacing technological change" across the European Union in the period 1999-2010. They estimated that although the direct impact of automation was to reduce labor demand by 9.6 million jobs, this was more than compensated by the indirect effects that created 23 million jobs. Focusing more narrowly on the impact of automation due to the introduction of industrial robots in 17 advanced countries – including the United States, South Korea and a number of European countries – over the period 1993-2007, Graetz and Michaels (2015) estimated that there had been no significant net loss of employment (but some positive effect on wages). Dauth et al (2017) obtained broadly similar results with respect to the impact of robots in Germany over the period 1994-2014.

The second key point is that to look at the impact of technological innovation only in terms of automation is too narrow. Technological advances lead to the development of new types of goods and services for which there are ready markets. People need to be employed to produce these new products, increasing the demand for labor.

Again, the more labor-intensive these new products are, the stronger the positive impact on the demand for labor. An historical example is the way in which the arrival of a host of new manufactured products (cars, domestic appliances and many others) led to the creation of manufacturing jobs that offset the massive automation-driven reduction of agricultural employment over the course of the 20th century. So when we think about the impact of technological innovation, we need to consider the impact of technologically driven *product innovation*, and not limit ourselves to thinking about the way in which technology changes how preexisting goods and services are produced (*process innovation*).

These mechanisms have worked to boost the demand for labor over recent decades in many ways, thereby countering the direct effects of ICT-driven automation. The income effect has come into play, for example, when people have spent a growing share of their increased incomes on labor-intensive services such as education, restaurants and tourism. The impact of technology-driven product innovation is manifest – as discussed in Chapter 2 – in how the continual development of new and better health treatments has driven the growth of the health sector and of health-sector employment. These examples illustrate the powerful job-creating impact of the rise of relatively labor-intensive service industries, which has been a key long-term trend in advanced capitalist nations (Autor and Salomons, 2017).

Focusing exclusively on the direct job losses from automation is the basic miscalculation made by technology alarmists in the Rifkin tradition. This error is the origin of misconceived predictions of the impact of technological advances on employment based on the percentage of currently existing jobs or work tasks that are under threat of automation. The same exercise, carried out a century ago, would have predicted that the coming automation of agriculture would result in most of the workforce being permanently unemployed.

Capitalism is by its very nature dynamic. Technology, industry structure and the types and location of jobs are constantly changing. Industries rise and fall, as do towns and regions. Job are constantly being destroyed but, at the same time, the capacity of the system to generate new jobs has been, over the long haul, quite extraordinary.

Notwithstanding these points, there is no economic law saying that, in any given period, things will *necessarily* work out to the advantage of workers. As history demonstrates (Frey, 2019), under specific circumstances, technological change may have a substantial net negative effect on the demand for labor. In other words, it is possible the increased labor demand arising from the income effect, stimulus to customer industries and technologically driven product innovation may be insufficient to offset the direct impact of automation. (What actually happens to the labor market depends, moreover, not only on changes in the demand for labor but also on what happens to labor supply – e.g. on changes such as increased female labor market participation, or the level of education and training).

In practice, however, things have worked out well on the employment front in recent decades – setting aside recessions – as has been true during most of the history of capitalism. Notwithstanding extensive ICT-driven automation since the 1970s, employment growth has been sufficient to absorb the growing workforce – clear testimony to the strength of the forces increasing the demand for labor over recent decades.[34]

But before we wrap up our discussion of the impact of technology on the labor market, we need to consider the question of its impact on wages. A deficiency of demand for labor relative to supply need not necessarily result in increased unemployment. It could instead result in lower real wages. This raises the possibility that technological change did perhaps weaken the demand for labor after all, but that the result was the erosion of real wages rather than increased unemployment.

Some economists – particularly in the United States – say this is indeed what has happened. Specifically, they assert that US wage stagnation has in significant measure been the consequence of technology weakening the demand for labor. Many other economists, however, firmly reject this point of view. The latter consider technology to be a "red herring" in the debate about the causes of wage stagnation. They point out that wages started to stagnate in the US decades before the ICT wave got under way, demonstrating that factors other than technology must have been responsible. For them, the most important cause of wage stagnation has been the long-term weakening of worker protection and bargaining power in the

United States as a result of de-unionization and the large decline of the legal minimum wage (Bivens et al, 2014; Mishel and Bivens, 2017; Card and DiNardo, 2002; Krugman, 2019).

From a broader international perspective, further doubt is cast on the supposed role of technology in driving down wages because wage stagnation has, as noted earlier, been the exception rather than the rule among advanced countries.

The Impact of Globalization

What about globalization? Why didn't the "second wave" of globalization produce lingering mass unemployment and poverty across the advanced world? Because our focus is on lessons of relevance to the future, the answer to this question may not matter much. The second wave of globalization appears now to be over. The expansion of global value chains, in which many steps in the production process of integrated products were transferred to low-wage countries, has faltered. Global value chains are now being at least partially unwound, and the process has been given added impetus by the market vulnerabilities exposed by the coronavirus pandemic (Farrell and Newman, 2020). Any threat posed by globalization to employment in advanced countries in coming decades is likely to be a different one – namely, off-shoring of professional tasks via digital platforms (although the extent of that threat is exaggerated – see Appendix 7.3).

In some countries, the workforce as a whole benefited from the second wave of globalization. Germany is the clearest example, having derived a large net benefit primarily as a result of its increased exports of industrial machinery (Marin, 2017). On the whole, however, the impact on labor markets in advanced countries seems not to have been a positive one. Manufacturing was particularly adversely affected. This was especially true in the United States, where the "China shock" in the 2000s was relatively severe. Leading labor economists have estimated that low-wage imports led to a net loss of something like 2.4 million jobs in the United States between 1999 and 2013, both directly in manufacturing and as an indirect consequence of the damage to manufacturing (Acemoglu et al, 2016; Autor, Dorn and Gordon, 2016; see also Kemeny, Rigby and Cooke,

2014, and Klein, 2016). By contrast with automation, there seems in the US to have been relatively little indirect job-creation impact from trade globalization during that period (Autor, Dorn and Gordon, 2013b, 2013c, 2016; Pierce and Schott, 2016).

What happened was essentially that job losses resulting from the surge in low-wage imports were more than offset by large job creation elsewhere in the economy, particularly in services, health care and public sector employment (Spence, 2011). Where lingering damage was done was typically in specific regions, particularly manufacturing towns. But this tended to generate local pockets of long-term unemployment rather than weakening national labor markets as a whole.

Will the Future Bring Mass Technological Unemployment?

The doomsayers were proven wrong about the past. But perhaps the future will be different. Perhaps now, finally, we are moving toward a dystopian world of mass technological unemployment. Those who think so base their view on the belief that in the coming decades digital machines – in particular, advanced computing and robotic ("cyber-physical") systems – will be able to do so many things as well or better than humans that labor market opportunities for human workers will shrink rapidly, leaving much of the workforce stranded.

If this were to turn out to be true, the implications for government spending would indeed be enormous. With the link between production and employment broken, only government action would be able to prevent mass poverty and suffering. Only government could carry out the massive redistribution required, from those who own the means of production to the population as a whole. Only government would be able, alternatively, to take the means of production into public ownership so as to assert direct control over the distribution of national income.

A basic income would under these circumstances be essential. Indeed, for a fair society, much more than the mere provision of a "basic" income would be required. It would be necessary to provide the mass of the population with more than the equivalent of the dole to ensure a reasonably fair distribution of the large machine-generated output of the economy. In the context of an increasingly jobless economy, such extensive redistributive action would also be necessary to prevent the emergence of chronic demand deficiency – so-called *secular stagnation* (see Chapter 8) – on a massive scale. Redistribution would, in other words, be essential to ensure that there are sufficient consumers to purchase the economy's output.

The Impact of Artificial Intelligence

One version of the narrative of mass technological unemployment predicts the imminent arrival of artificial general intelligence (AGI). AGI means that machines will be able to do *literally everything* as well or better than humans. If and when this point is reached, human workers will start to become expendable. Machines will be able to do anything that involves higher-level cognitive skills – so say goodbye to the skilled professionals. They will also be able to do anything involving so-called social intelligence: advanced social robots will do an astonishingly good job of deftly responding to social signals and of providing a convincing display of empathy. None of the other capabilities that are today uniquely human would remain so. The human worker would become essentially redundant – going the way of the horse, more than a century ago, as a mode of transport.

AGI is, however, nowhere near becoming a reality. What we have is "narrow" AI – also referred to, with good reason, as "weak" AI. This describes artificial intelligence systems that can undertake only quite narrowly defined tasks – such as pattern recognition – even if in many cases extremely well. Whereas the advent of AGI would mean machines with broad and flexible intellectual capabilities (like humans), narrow AI is more like an "idiot savant" – that is, like the autistic genius who can do amazing feats in some very limited field such as mental arithmetic but is essentially incapable of much else.

In this context, some pessimists base their expectation of the imminent arrival of mass technological unemployment not on the assumption that AGI is around the corner, but rather on the expectation that narrow AI will advance so rapidly, and on so many fronts, that the impact on the demand for human labor will be devastating. Once again, they see this as adversely affecting most types of workers. In this view, for example, AI will be soon in a position to take over most of the work carried out by professionals. Even if, in this view, machines will not be able to do absolutely *everything* better than humans, there will be so many things that they can do better that an increasing portion of the workforce will find itself permanently out of a job.

Whether founded on the expectation of the imminent development of AGI, or on the expectation of the rapid development of narrow AI across many fronts, the basic story advanced by the pessimists is that technology is developing at such an "exponential" rate that its impact on the labor market will be felt like a tsunami over the coming decades.

This story, however, should be doubted for three compelling reasons. The first is the sheer immensity of the gap between today's technology and what would be needed to develop machines with a capacity to do everything, or even most of the things, that humans can do. The second is the questionable nature of the supposedly exponential rate of technological development. The third is the relative slowness, in the real world, of the implementation of new "general purpose" technologies: that is, the considerable time lag between the development of fundamental new technological capabilities and their widespread adoption across the economy is typically measured in decades at a minimum.

The proposition that the arrival of AGI is imminent looks particularly fanciful. Ray Kurzweil famously predicted in 2005 that AGI would arrive by 2029, and that it would be followed shortly after by the so-called "singularity" (a hypothetical point at which autonomous, self-improving AI will rapidly surpass human beings). This prediction looked far-fetched even when it was made. Other experts in the field, such as Margaret Boden (2018), believe that "the prospects for human-level AGI look dim." Notwithstanding the impressive feats of AI systems – whether in diagnosing skin cancers or beating grandmasters at chess – AI is, according to Boden, "less promising than many people assume" because it faces a range of formidable obstacles (such as grappling with "relevance" and with the unexpected). It would be naïve to expect that the two main limitations of current AI systems (i.e. their inability to do many things that are simple for human beings – including applying common sense – and the so-called "brittle" nature of narrow AI systems) will be rapidly overcome.

Even experts who are more optimistic than Boden about the development of AGI, like Yann Lecun,[35] consider that the obstacles are so great it could easily take 50 or 100 years. As for the singularity, this looks even more "highly improbable" (Ganascia, 2017).

Those with the most optimistic expectations of future technological development systematically underestimate the extraordinary complexity and sophistication of the human brain, which is light years ahead of anything that machines either can do now or are likely to do in the foreseeable future. As Daniela Rus[36] of MIT says, "the gap between [existing AI] and human-level intelligence is extraordinary, and it will take us a long time to get there". One aspect of the problem is that, as Judea Pearl (2019) of UCLA puts it:

> Current machine-learning systems operate almost exclusively in a statistical, or model-blind, mode… To achieve human-level intelligence, learning machines need the guidance of a blueprint of reality, a model… My general conclusion is that human-level AI cannot emerge solely from model-blind learning machines; it requires the symbiotic collaboration of data and models.

In the same vein, the Microsoft founder Paul Allen (2014) has convincingly argued that progress toward the development of AGI will continue to be slow, constrained most fundamentally by what he calls the "complexity brake" – the great complexity of the mechanisms of human cognition and the sheer enormity of the gaps in our current scientific understanding of those mechanisms.

Suggestions computers are about to take over everything have consistently proven to be wrong. A memorable example is the often-quoted prediction made by the eminent cybernetics theorist Herbert Simon in 1965 that "machines will be capable, within 20 years, of doing any work that a man can do." As cynics have observed, predictions of the coming technological employment apocalypse have usually situated the event 20 or 30 years into the future.

The claim that the rate of technological progress is increasing expo-nentially has superficial plausibility, because so often we look at the news and find what appear to be impressive technological breakthroughs. However, progress in the development of AI has in fact proven to be slower than expected by many scientists. To quote Rus once again, "we have been working on AI problems for over sixty years, and if the founders of the field were able to see what we tout as great advances today, they would be very disappointed because it appears we have not made much progress."

Of course, it is true that the rate of increase in the processing (num-ber-crunching) power of computers has been more or less exponential. However, processing power alone does not create powerful AI and will cer-tainly not enable machines to match humans across the board. Processing power is only as good as the software available, and we are nowhere near developing the complex software needed to match the extraordinary capa-bilities of the human brain.

Moreover, whatever the rate at which the frontiers of technological innovation advance, the *implementation* of new technologies across the economy is a considerably slower process. The unambiguous lesson of eco-nomic history – whether it is the ICT wave of recent decades, or previous periods of major technological change – is that the adoption of new "gen-eral-purpose" technologies takes many decades. Even if, contrary to sober expectations, AGI were to be developed in the laboratory within 30 years, the application of the new human-level machines across the economy would take considerably longer.

The Alternative, More Optimistic Scenario

One can imagine an alternative, more optimistic scenario for the coming decades. In this scenario, notwithstanding continuing important advances in narrow AI, there will remain many types of work (more precisely, tasks) that only humans can do, or can do much better than machines. This will include both many tasks requiring high-level cognitive skills (AI being able to do only some of these), as well as many requiring social intelligence, common sense and the ability to cope with changing and uncertain environments. As part of this, "any activity that involves

judgment independently of data-processing will remain in human hands"
(Pissarides, 2019).

In the optimistic scenario, advanced computing and robotics will
in considerable measure complement human workers, augmenting their
productivity, rather than just replacing them. Machines will, in Kurzweil's
memorable phrase, serve widely as "brain extenders" for human workers
– in broadly the same way that so much digital technology has done over
recent decades. In this context, there will be ongoing extensive growth in
employment opportunities for people with the right training and skills to
work *with* the machines, as well as in designing, producing and servicing
machines. This does not mean more job opportunities only for people with
PhDs. Rather, it will mean many more middle-skill jobs requiring serious
technical training, underpinned by sound school education. Although
technological progress will continue to automate routine jobs, the expansion of middle- and high-skilled *non-routine* jobs will more than offset
this. In this scenario, the process of "hollowing out" – which, as discussed
earlier, has in the past seen a reduction in the availability of middle-skill
jobs and a polarization of the labor market – will be reversed.

Moreover, substantial growth will take place in sectors of the economy
in which human capabilities remain particularly important, and this will
bring with it substantially increased employment opportunities. This
growth, as in the past, will be driven by both the income effect and product
innovation. The health sector, in particular, will continue to expand and
will – notwithstanding the increased use of sophisticated technology,
including artificial intelligence – bring with it major growth in the health
services workforce. Employment growth in health will be seen across the
skill spectrum – from medical specialists, through to nurses and technol-
ogists, and to less-skilled staff.

Extensive growth will also occur in "craft worker" employment opportunities – meaning jobs in the production of highly customized goods and
services, whether for consumers or for other industries (Nübler, 2018).
Growing demand for such goods and services, which will in general
require a significantly larger skilled labor input than mass-produced man-
ufactures, will arise both from increased demand for artisanal products

(driven by the income effect) and from the increased scope for customized products created by flexible production technologies (e.g. 3D printing).

Although the economy of the future will, even more than today, be an economy of services, manufacturing job opportunities may in advanced countries receive a boost from the process of "in-sourcing" – the return of more manufacturing jobs to locations near the customer – facilitated by technology that reduces the importance of labor cost differentials in locational decisions (Nübler, 2018). Powerfully reinforcing this will be the rapid growth of "green" jobs, particularly those required to give effect to the energy transition away from fossil fuels. Job opportunities will increasingly open up in areas including energy-efficient construction and retrofitting and renewable energies (High-Level Commission on Carbon Prices, 2017: 49).

The quality of much of the work that humans do will also be improved. In the health sector, the time savings accruing to doctors – as a result of technology further automating and augmenting certain of their work tasks – will hopefully make it possible to enhance medical care by allowing doctors to spend a little more time interacting with patients and each other. Another example of this quality effect can be seen in legal practice during the research and "discovery" process, when relevant information to inform proceedings is gathered and shared. With this process becoming increasingly automated, a much more systematic and comprehensive gathering of relevant documentary information now takes place than was the case decades ago when all such work had to be done manually. As a result of having to spend less time searching for relevant material, lawyers are now able to allocate more time to analysis and strategy formulation.

In summary, although the *direct* impact of automation will continue to be to reduce labor demand, this will be offset by job creation. What is true, say, for the health sector, will be true for the economy as a whole – sufficient work will remain for both highly skilled and lesser-skilled workers. For lesser-skilled workers, job opportunities will include many tasks for which human interaction will remain extremely important – such as long-term care – but will be by no means confined to these areas.

In this optimistic scenario, far from being a source of mass unemployment, advanced computing and cyber-physical systems will be part of the solution to the labor-supply challenge posed by gradual population decline during the second half of the century. At the same time, higher productivity will pave the way for further reductions in working hours – thereby continuing the long-run trend to greater leisure and improved work/life balance. Technology will aid the transformation of advanced economies into systems where most people – including, but not limited to, those with child-raising responsibilities – work part-time. (The Netherlands is almost there already, having been described as the world's first part-time economy.)

In this scenario, the progress in the development and implementation of narrow AI systems will be progressive. Rather than resembling a tsunami hitting the labor market, it will proceed at a pace that will allow significant time for necessary adjustments. The standard prescriptions of economists – appropriate education and training, combined with active labor market programs to help workers shift to take up emerging job opportunities – will have sufficient time to do their work, keeping the transitional pain to a manageable level.

The essence of the optimistic scenario is, then, to deny the likelihood of emerging technological unemployment. (This does not necessarily mean that income distribution will not be adversely affected – an issue further discussed below.)

Who Is Right?

The future is uncertain. Although the optimistic scenario looks more realistic than the dystopian scenario, it is possible that the optimists will be proven to be somewhat too optimistic. Maybe what eventuates will be something in between the two scenarios. It is, for example, not entirely impossible that the rate of technological progress will speed up so much that – even if the economy does over time generate new jobs for displaced workers – the transitional pain will be large, in the way that the pain of the "China shock" was felt in the US economy in the 2000s. Only time will tell.

But even if one cannot completely dismiss the pessimists' gloomy predictions, it remains the case that at present it is not credible to predict the imminent arrival of mass technological unemployment. It is not even reasonable to claim that there is such a high risk this will happen that we should, based on some version of the "precautionary principle," act now to prepare ourselves for the eventuality. Basing public policy on the expectation of mass technological unemployment would therefore right now be reckless. If it turns out later that the optimists are wrong, we will have plenty of advance warning. Then – and only then – will it be appropriate to redesign income support and other social systems to cope with the severing of the link between employment and income.

More Working Poor?

Less implausible than the story of machines rendering human labor obsolete is the claim that technological change will swell the ranks of the working poor. The argument here is that technology will significantly reduce the demand for workers who are poorly educated and have limited skills. This will reduce the "equilibrium wage" for such workers – i.e. the wage levels at which they can find employment. With increasing numbers earning wages below the poverty line, government income support spending on the working poor would need to increase substantially.

What are we to make of this view? It is easy to agree that technological change will progressively reduce demand for poorly educated/low-skilled workers. This is precisely what technology has been doing for a long time – it is a large part of what is meant by the economists' notion of "skill-biased" technological change. However, it does not inevitably follow that the result will be starvation wages for such workers and a massive increase in the ranks of the working poor. What it means is simply that government needs to act decisively to make sure there are fewer poorly educated, low-skilled workers, by improving education systems and working with business to greatly improve industrial training. The model for this is already in place in countries such as Germany, Switzerland and Denmark. It centers not so much on increasing the amount of education and training (although that is certainly necessary in some countries) but on making education and training more industry- and jobs-relevant. And it also requires that public education systems do a good job of imparting basic education – including literacy and numeracy – to all students.

In short, the main solution is a very familiar one: to make sure that rising levels of skills and education match the demands of an increasingly high-tech economy.

Of course, no matter how good the education and training systems are, there will always be a portion of the workforce with low skills and limited educational attainment. Even putting to one side the impact of social disadvantage, there is the fact that there are, by definition, always individuals who are on the lower end of the intelligence distribution. This would be a problem if almost all job opportunities for those with limited skills and low educational attainment were to disappear. But there is no reason to expect this will happen. The realistic expectation is that, even with the availability of such job opportunities progressively declining, there will remain many tasks that minimum-wage workers can do that machines are unable to do. As long as the general level of skills and education of the workforce is rising, the position of the (diminishing) part of the workforce with few skills may – if bolstered by appropriate protection including adequate minimum wage laws – turn out to be fine.

So, in this more optimistic narrative, there is nothing inevitable about rising in-work poverty. Rather, it can and should be avoided through appropriate action by government and business. If governments do find themselves faced with a need to spend increasing amounts on income support for the working poor, it will be a reflection of their failure to have provided those at the lower end of the labor market with the right type of support and assistance in the face of the requirements of the new economy.

Whether the problem of in-work poverty will worsen – forcing governments to increase income support spending – is a significantly narrower question than whether inequality will continue to increase. Inequality may quite possibly increase further in coming decades in ways that do not increase the ranks of the working poor. For example, a widely discussed scenario is that technology will soon significantly reduce job opportunities for highly skilled, high-paid "knowledge workers." This is seen as the likely consequence of a new wave of offshoring – this time of professional services via digital platforms exploiting the full possibilities of sophisticated new communications technologies (Baldwin, 2019). Assuming the position of the top 1 percent is unaffected, this would by definition increase the level of inequality (as measured, for example, by the widely used "Gini" index).

There are reasons to be skeptical about the story of declining high-skill employment opportunities, even if some professions are adversely impacted. These are outlined in Appendix 7.3.

The focus of our analysis is future trends in government expenditure. Most of the potential policy responses to growing inequality do not involve increased government spending at all – the most obvious example being tax increases on those at the top of the wealth and income distribution. The same is true for action to prevent top corporate managers from abusing their power to pay themselves stratospheric levels of remuneration, as well as for measures to attack the monopoly "rents" that, according to Stiglitz (2015) and others, are a major factor behind the disproportionate income and wealth of the top 1 percent. These points underline, yet again, the importance of clearly distinguishing between the problems of poverty and of inequality more generally.

Freelance Work and Precarity

Another popular narrative about the imminent immiseration of much of the workforce does not depend – at least explicitly – on the assumption that technology will bring about chronically deficient demand for human labor. This suggests technology is destroying stable, continuing jobs and that in future most workers will be hired only for specific and temporary tasks or projects. This alleged "megatrend" supposedly means that the future workforce will be comprised overwhelmingly of *freelancers* – people who do not expect that their relationship with their client/employer will continue beyond the completion of the specific task or project for which they are currently engaged.[37]

This is the idea captured by the fashionable term "gig economy." But it involves much more than people using new digital platforms such as Uber and Task Rabbit as intermediaries in carrying out tasks for individual "retail" clients. What is being suggested is that enterprises will hire almost all the human labor they need on a task or project basis, largely dispensing with traditional employees who are engaged on a continuing basis and who carry out whatever series of tasks or projects management directs them to undertake. Traditional corporations with many continuing employees will, according to this narrative, become "vestigial rather than central pillars of the economy" and will be replaced by "virtual corporations" with very few continuing employees (Davis, 2016).

The pessimistic version of the freelancer vision of the future labor market asserts that it will lead to a large increase in precarity, because many freelancers will experience significant periods without work between engagements. This is a story with natural appeal to precarity theorists.

This supposed transition to a freelance labor market is seen as the inevitable consequence of the rise of digital platforms and their progressive broadening into the basis of a broader "marketplace of skills" companies will mainly use to hire skilled and professional labor (Giger and Minster, 2015: 17-19).[38] Hence the prediction that "left undisturbed, our current trajectory points towards Uberization" of the entire workforce (Davis, 2016: 178).

For those who are deeply worried about the freelance future, increased earnings precarity is not the only problem. They also see freelancing as aggravating the problem of low pay because of the way it forces people to bid against each other for work on digital platforms. They believe that, if this trend is allowed to continue, the imperative of undercutting other freelancers will supplant the traditional collective solidarity of employees in determining remuneration.

Although superficially plausible, the idea that employers will generally prefer to hire people on a temporary tasks/project basis – and to part readily with them all once their tasks/projects are completed – is inconsistent with everything that common sense and economics tell us about the motives guiding enterprise hiring decisions. There are powerful incentives for enterprises to generally prefer continuing employment relations with people who are able to competently carry out the work enterprises need on an ongoing basis. Continuing employment increases workforce loyalty, strengthens job-specific competences, creates stronger performance incentives, ensures the immediate availability of human resources and saves on the cost of finding suitable staff.

The fact that there are some industries, and some types of jobs, where easy-come-easy-go is the rule does not mean this approach to hiring will dominate the economy as a whole.

Hiring on a tasks/project basis is most appropriate when it is easy to clearly specify tasks or project deliverables in advance or when the tasks/project call for skills the enterprise only needs occasionally. Most of the work that the typical enterprise relies on its employees to perform does not fit either of these descriptions.

Box 7.9 Employment and the Online Digital Economy

People who find work via the new digital platforms – i.e. the so-called "online gig economy" (Harris and Krueger, 2015) – are only one part of the freelance workforce. Exponents of the freelancer vision tend nevertheless to focus primarily on the role of these platforms and to overestimate the extent to which enterprises are likely to use them for hiring. Businesses already have well-established and effective mechanisms to identify pools of job candidates. Digital technology has enhanced these somewhat, helping to reduce search costs, but has not radically transformed the search process. Completely different is how the new platforms have transformed the process by which individual consumers find freelancers willing to undertake specific tasks such as babysitting their pets or putting together IKEA furniture – a search process that was previously quite difficult.

Nevertheless, for the majority of jobs it will remain important for enterprises to continue to undertake their own search and selection processes (with or without the aid of recruitment agencies or platforms).

The contribution of new digital platforms – the online gig economy – to creating employment has sometimes been inflated. In the US, recent estimates suggest they contribute no more than 0.4-1 percent of employment, with Uber alone accounting for at least half of that (Mishel, 2018; McKinsey, 2016: 36). Many of those undertaking gig work do so, moreover, to supplement income from their main employment.

None of this is to deny that there has been some long-term growth in freelance work across advanced countries as a whole. Digital technology has indeed reduced search costs and has thereby facilitated outsourcing, including freelancing. Measuring the magnitude of, and trends in, freelance work is difficult because freelance work does not correspond to any of the usual categories of irregular work measured in official statistics.[39] Some data, however, do indicate an increased role for freelancers.[40] Nothing, however, gives any reason to believe that the traditional job – in whatever form it comes – is under threat as the predominant form of employment. Nor does the possibility of a future further expansion of freelance work necessarily imply an increase in earnings precarity for the workforce as a whole. There is, after all, an ongoing long-term decline in self-employment (e.g. small shopkeepers) working in the opposite direction, significantly reducing earnings precarity.

We have heard the story about the end of the job and the arrival of the virtual corporation before. Two decades ago, it was in vogue among a certain school of management gurus. According to William Bridges (1994a, 1994b), for example, the traditional job was in the process of "going the way of the dinosaur" and the new "post-job worker" would "be far more likely to be hired for a project or a fixed length of time than a job-holder is today." Corporations, Bridges opined, were "well along the path to being 'de-jobbed'." Experience proved this to be entirely wrong – as it will again be proven to be entirely wrong in the decades to come.

Directions for Future Income Support Spending

Scaremongering about future mass technological unemployment, and the danger posed by robots and AI, is a proven strategy for selling books. However, a dispassionate look at future trends, and at lessons of the past, tells us there is no good reason to believe it is probable – let alone certain – that mankind faces such a future in the coming three decades or anytime soon after that. The temptation to exaggerate the capabilities, and speed of implementation, of new technologies needs to be firmly resisted.

Assuming that governments in advanced economies will find themselves faced with a growing problem of mass impoverishment that demands a large increase in income support expenditure is therefore inappropriate. Risks, of course, exist. If governments do too little to help workers adjust, and to ensure that the workforce is appropriately trained and educated, there could well be a growing problem of people at the bottom end of the labor market marooned in the face of technological and structural change in the economy. Insufficient effort to help the workforce adapt would mean more people stuck on welfare benefits. But this risk can be avoided with the right combination of policies and supportive action from business.

This conclusion has nothing to do with the question of whether, on moral and other grounds, governments should provide more generous income support for the poor. To read recent reports on poverty in the United Kingdom and the United States, prepared by the United Nations special rapporteur on extreme poverty and human rights, is to be shocked at the gaps in current government support. Addressing poverty in a more compassionate way would, in some advanced countries, require significant increases in government expenditure. But this is not an issue that is relevant to the subject matter of this book.

Is a Basic Income the Answer?

There are those who are so convinced that we are treading down the path to mass technological unemployment that they demand the immediate introduction of the *basic income* – a regular income that government would pay to everyone, unconditionally. To be capable of ensuring social justice if and when mass unemployment arrives, a basic income would need to provide everyone with an income sufficient by itself to ensure a decent standard of living. This means an income at or above the relative poverty threshold. Unconditional payments set at such a level would constitute what we might call a *generous basic income.*

It has been repeatedly demonstrated that a generous basic income would be extremely costly. This is even assuming that the basic income replaced most existing welfare benefits and that it was taxable.

This simple reality has meant that many basic income proposals call instead for a level of payments well below the relative poverty line. These are proposals for what might be called an *austere basic income*. A leading austere basic income option involves paying benefits at broadly the same level as what is known as the "guaranteed minimum income." This is a technical term referring to the level of benefits paid under existing welfare systems to the long-term unemployed. The guaranteed minimum income differs from one country to another but is invariably well below the relative poverty line. In the United States, it is particularly low. The OECD (2017b) has closely examined introduction of an austere basic income, and its analysis highlights two points. The first is that even at this low level a basic income would remain very expensive (again, even assuming it replaced most welfare benefits and was taxable). The second is that many of the poor would actually lose out under such a system. This is because existing welfare benefits are, for important segments of the poor such as lone-parent households, higher than the guaranteed minimum income. The incidence of poverty would, as a consequence, actually increase in many countries if an austere basic income were implemented.

Whether generous or austere, the overall redistributive effect of a basic income would be negative because, on the whole, it would advantage middle-income households relative to low-income households. This should not be surprising, because what a basic income does is to replace most *targeted* welfare benefits (i.e. benefits designed to reach those who need them most) with *untargeted* payments (paid irrespective of need).

The main argument to justify the untargeted nature of the basic income is the proposition that, with the rise of irregular work, the targeted approach of traditional social security systems is letting increasing numbers of people slip through the gaps. Whether this is actually true is debatable, given that in the past there were considerably more self-employed people (e.g. small shop owners), many of whom constantly flirted with poverty and who had limited access to welfare benefits. But the fact that there are significant gaps in existing targeted welfare systems is an argument for improved targeting to fill those gaps, rather than for indiscriminately dispensing large amounts of money to people who do not need it.

To massively ramp up income support spending now through the introduction of a substantial basic income – whether set at generous or austere levels – would significantly aggravate the fiscal pressure on governments and compromise their ability to respond to the real and demonstrated need for increased spending in other areas of manifest need, such as health and climate change. Fundamentally, the issue here is one of spending priorities. There is no free lunch. If you spend a lot of money providing a basic income, you have to spend less on other social needs and priorities.

A third, widely advocated model, is the *basic income lite*. The basic income lite proposal is that everyone should receive only "a modest monthly payment" (Standing, 2014; van Parij and Vanderborght, 2017). This would be a payment well below the guaranteed minimum income, set at levels at which no one could survive. It would apparently serve more as a type of "social dividend," the purpose of which would be to reduce inequality and "spread the wealth." By definition, a basic income lite would be much less costly. This version of the idea is nevertheless particularly unconvincing, as it would neither provide financial security nor serve as an efficient way of reducing inequality. Clearly it would not deal with the poverty generated by mass technological unemployment.

Setting the basic income lite aside, one of the much-debated issues surrounding a basic income is its impact on work incentives. Paying an unconditional income at a level sufficient to survive could swell the ranks of the labor-market "inactive." This would be regrettable. Unless one believes that such people are doomed by technological advances to remain outside the labor market, it is surely preferable to take every possible step to integrate them better into the workforce.

Proponents of a basic income seized upon the 2020 pandemic-induced economic crisis as a vindication of their position. The crisis, they urged, was precisely the time to introduce a basic income so as both to provide comprehensive income support quickly and bolster aggregate demand. This position was not totally implausible. Under particularly grave circumstances, unconditional handouts may make good sense – as recognized by a number of governments which sent out one-off checks to all their citizens. However, no argument which might be made for a basic income as an instrument for fighting an economic crisis as extraordinary and exceptional as that triggered by the coronavirus pandemic could possibly justify its introduction as a permanent feature of the modern welfare state. When faced with a burning building, firefighters turn on their high-pressure hoses, but they turn them off afterwards.

◆ ◆ ◆

Over the horizon to the middle of this century, governments face many serious expenditure pressures. There is, however, no good reason to expect that external forces will oblige them to greatly expand spending on income support to the working age population and children. The fact that income support expenditure increases temporarily during economic crises tells us precisely nothing about long-term trends. Indeed, when we look at the longer-term, what appears more likely is that government spending will be reduced by deliberate policy decisions to shave, or even substantially cut, welfare spending as one of the means of coping with acute fiscal pressure. We will return to this possibility in the final chapter.

Appendix 7.1: Wage Stagnation, Decoupling and Poverty

When looking at trends in poverty, the question arises as to whether there may be a statistical illusion at work, arising from how relative poverty is defined. As mentioned in the main text, the threshold used to define relative poverty is based on the income of the *median* household (the most common threshold being 60 percent of median household income). Median household income is significantly influenced by the level of median earnings (how much the median worker earns). If median wages stagnate – that is, fail to increase even though productivity and per capita national income are increasing – then, other things remaining equal, the threshold used to measure poverty will also fail to rise. The poverty threshold will, as a result, become progressively less appropriate as a measure of the relative living standards of people at the bottom end of the income distribution in relation to the *average* household – and will therefore in a certain sense understate the true rate of relative poverty.

It follows that if the US experience of wage stagnation had been replicated across the advanced world in general, statistics that show underlying poverty stable or falling in many countries would need to be treated with suspicion. However, this appears not to have been the case. Recent OECD statistics covering the period 1995-2013 (OECD, 2018b: 56) indicate that wage stagnation occurred in only three of 20 advanced OECD countries.

This interpretation of the OECD statistics is based on a definition of wage stagnation[41] as an annual rate of growth of median real wages that is both (i) equal to or less than 0.5 percent and (ii) significantly below the rate of growth of labor productivity. By this definition, the three countries experiencing wage stagnation over the relevant time period were the United States (0.5 percent annual median real wage growth), Canada (0.2 percent) and Japan (0.2 percent). There are two other countries that experienced growth in median wages equal to or less than 0.5 percent – Germany (0.5 percent) and Italy (0.2 percent) – but they do not meet the definition of wage stagnation used here because in each case their low rate of growth of median wages was above or only slightly below the rate of growth of labor productivity growth (which was 0.7 percent in Germany and -0.3 percent in Italy).

The same OECD statistics also provide information on trends with respect to the broader phenomenon of "decoupling" of wages from labor productivity. Decoupling refers to the situation where median wages do not necessarily stagnate but grow at a rate significantly below the average annual increase in labor productivity. Even here, no general trend emerges. Significant decoupling – defined analogously to the way in which wage stagnation is defined above – has occurred in nine of the 20 countries.[42] In eight others – including the United

Kingdom and France[43] – median wages have risen at a rate equal to or exceeding that of productivity growth, while in the remaining three[44] they increased at a rate only marginally below productivity.

Appendix 7.2: Irregular Work and Precarity

When analyzing the implications of so-called precarious work for future income support expenditure, it is best, as noted, to focus on the precise concept of "earnings precarity" rather than on the ill-defined notion of "precarious work." As a working definition, we can say that a member of the workforce is in a state of earnings precarity if they are at high risk of experiencing involuntary major reductions in their labor earnings to a level well below the median wage due to loss of employment or reduction in hours of employment. Thus defined, the degree of earnings precarity in the labor market as a whole is capable of being measured *ex post* by the percentage of the workforce who, during a given year, experience such involuntary major reductions in earnings.

Earnings precarity defined in this way depends not only on the risk that individuals face of losing their existing job, but also on the ease with which they are able to find a replacement job. If a person is justifiably confident that, even if they lost their existing job, they could readily find another similar job, they would not be said to be in a situation of earnings precarity.

Defining earnings precarity in this way – with reference to the actual risk of major earnings loss – points to a difficulty with how the notion of "precarious work" is usually used, which is to deem as a precarious worker any individual who does not have a legal guarantee, or commitment from their employer, to continuing employment. The focus is, in other words, on the level of *formal job security*. However, many workers who have no such guarantees or commitments – little or no formal job security – are nevertheless, *de facto*, relatively secure in the sense that they face low levels of risk of being fired or of having their hours suddenly cut. (If one equates precarious work with limited formal job security, a large majority of workers in the United States, where formal job security tends to be quite limited, would be considered to be in precarious work.)

A concept of precarious work focused on formal security rather than the actual level of earnings risk also means that any reduction in the legal barriers to dismissing workers – which may be highly desirable in excessively rigid labor markets – will immediately be read as increasing precarity, even if in practice there is little or no increase in the overall level of risk of involuntary major reductions in earnings faced by the average worker.

Official labor market statistics do not, unfortunately, measure earnings precarity as defined here (even though the data reported by the OECD – see main text – sheds some light on the matter). Official statistics report the total number of people engaged in irregular (a.k.a. "non-standard") employment and decompose this total into specific forms of irregular work (e.g. temporary work, agency work). The most that these statistics can do is to shed some light on the level of formal security of workers, as opposed to the degree of actual earnings precarity. Certain forms of irregular work tend by definition to have a lower level of formal security – i.e. it is much easier for an employer to discontinue the workers' employment or reduce their hours. This means that, even if our interest is in the level of actual earnings precarity, there is some value in looking at international trends in those categories of irregular work that tend to have lower levels of formal security.

Available official statistics indicate there is no ongoing long-term increase across advanced countries as a whole in the prevalence of forms of irregular work with the lowest levels of formal security. National experience and trends differ significantly, but in ways more reflective of national legal frameworks and other country-specific factors than of the impact of broad economic forces such as technology and globalization.

Temporary Work

Although it is often asserted that the temporary workforce has been constantly growing across the advanced world, this seems not to be the case. National statistics surveyed in a report by the ILO (2016), and which depending on the country cover periods of between one and two decades up to 2014, indicate that there are only six advanced countries that experienced large increases in the temporary workforce (Ireland, Japan, South Korea, Italy, France and the Netherlands). All others have seen either stable levels of temporary employment, only marginal increases or (in one case) falls.[45]

More recent data on Ireland – a country particularly hard hit by the global financial crisis – indicate that in 2016 temporary work accounted for 7.7 percent of the workforce, down from 9.2 percent in 1998 (Bobek, Wickham and Pembroke, 2017).

In Europe, Eurostat (2018) has reported that the percentage of EU workers working under contracts not exceeding three months' duration – which is, of course, a narrower measure than temporary work – was 2.3 percent in 2016, and that this figure had remained "relatively stable" over the preceding decade.

In the United States, the "employment at will" philosophy means that the distinction between temporary and permanent labor contracts used elsewhere is not very useful – there is no need, on the whole, for employers to use explicitly temporary contracts. However, the Bureau of Labor Statistics (BLS) measures the numbers of what it calls "contingent workers," defined as persons who do not expect their jobs to last or who report that their jobs are temporary. Its May 2017 report put the percentage of workers holding contingent jobs at 3.8 percent, slightly lower than it was when previously measured in 2005 (BLS, 2018).

Self-Employment

Self-employment is the other major category of irregular work that has, by definition, low levels of formal security. The percentage of the workforce in self-employment in the vast majority of advanced countries has continued to fall over the long term.[46]

In the United States, the BLS has reported that the percentage of the workforce who are independent contractors (defined to include independent consultants and freelance workers) was lower (at 6.9 percent of total employment) in 2017 than it was in 2005 (7.4 percent).[47]

Within the category of self-employment, a particular area of concern is pseudo-independent employment – that is, artificial arrangements that transform employment relationships into fake independent contractor arrangements. These have been used in certain countries (particularly Anglophone countries and South Korea) as a means of undermining employee wages and conditions. However, for all the heated discussion this type of abuse has – quite appropriately – generated, it appears that pseudo-independent employment accounts for quite a small percentage of the workforce in most advanced countries. Even in Anglophone countries, the percentage of the total workforce affected is quite low and these types of worker are mainly concentrated in specific industries (e.g. construction). For example, the ILO estimates that approximately 1.7 percent of the workforce fell into this category in Australia in 2013 (ILO, 2016: 100).

On-Call Employment

"On-call" contracts are employment arrangements under which the employer has discretion to vary the number of hours of part-time work at will and without notice. They are the form of part-time employment most open to involuntary fluctuations in hours worked, and therefore potentially to earnings precarity.

It appears that in most advanced countries, workers with on-call contracts account for a very small percentage of the workforce. In the United States, for example, the BLS (2018) estimates that they represent 1.7 percent of total employment.[48]

South Korea is one of the countries with the highest rate of on-call employment, at a little less than 5 percent of the workforce in 2013 (ILO, 2016: 87). This rate appears not, however, to have changed much over the past decade (after having increased significantly in the early 2000s in the wake of the Asian financial crisis) (ILO, 2016: 86).

Zero-hours on-call contracts – on-call contracts under which there is no guarantee of any minimum hours of work – appear not to be extensively used in the majority of countries. In Europe, the countries making most use of such contracts are the UK, the Netherlands and Austria (European Parliament, 2016: 11). Their use is, again, heavily concentrated in specific sectors such as retail and hospitality. Official UK statistics (ONS, 2018) indicate that they covered approximately 6 percent of employees in 2018, which is similar to the level in Austria (European Parliament, 2016: 14). Although the British figure has grown rapidly since 2012, the ILO (2016: 86) warns this may be partly a statistical artifact.

Agency Work

Another type of irregular work with a low level of formal security, and which has grown almost everywhere, is agency work. However, this is once again a form of employment that accounts for only a small proportion of the workforce in advanced countries (ILO, 2016: 87-92). In the United States, 0.9 percent of the workforce fell into this category in 2017 (BLS, 2018). A report for the European Parliament estimates the figure at 1.5 percent on average for the EU (European Parliament, 2016: 13).

Trends in Aggregate Measures

In the United States, the BLS produces a measure of workers operating under "alternative work arrangements," essentially irregular workers excluding most part-timers (but including part-timers employed under on-call arrangements). It reports that 10.1 percent of the workforce fell under this heading in May 2017, down slightly from previous survey results in 2005.[49]

In Australia, statistical analysis by Laß and Wooden (2019) finds that the share of irregular workers in the total workforce had "not increased much since the turn of the millennium". (There was, however, a rise in irregular *employment* – i.e. irregular workers excluding the self-employed – which was largely offset by the continuing decline in self-employment.)

Most of the above statistics assess trends by comparing the pre-pandemic prevalence of various types of irregular work with that prior to the GFC. In an approximate type of way, this adjusts for the obviously cyclical nature of the prevalence of forms of irregular employment with low job security. It is equally obvious that earnings precarity is heavily cyclical – i.e. the fact that the risk of being made redundant or having one's working hours drastically reduced increases significantly during recessions and then falls after. Precarity theorists understandably made much of the rise in precarity in the wake of the GFC. They will undoubtedly do the same in the wake of the pandemic-induced economic crisis. However, what is relevant here is not cyclical changes in the degree of earnings precarity, but long-term trends – in particular, the trends in earnings precarity since the 1990s.

It may be the case that compared with the halcyon era of the three post-war decades (1945-1975), formal job security has in recent times been lower and earnings precarity greater. But even if correct, this does not mean the continuing trend is for earnings precarity to increase.

Appendix 7.3: Is High-Skilled Employment in the Firing Line?

Some analysts think opportunities for high-skilled, well-paid employment will fall substantially over the coming decades as a consequence of the next phase of globalization, in which professional employment in advanced countries will decline massively as a consequence of the offshoring of many forms of professional work (e.g. Baldwin, 2019). This line of argument overlooks, however, the likely continued growth in high-skilled employment linked to the demands of sophisticated technology (e.g. in the capital goods industries, which will design and produce robots, AI systems etc., as well as in user industries and associated technical support services). It may also considerably exaggerate the extent to which professional work can be efficiently offshored. Many factors – such as detailed knowledge of local laws/regulations and customs, language and the value of physical contact with the client or job – limit the scope for such offshoring. At the same time, well-paid local employment opportunities will continue to grow for professionals in major developing countries such as India, significantly reducing the remuneration differentials that provide the basic rationale for offshoring. This is not to deny that there will be a significant increase in the offshoring of *some* professional tasks in the decades to come. Overall, however, what appears most likely is that there will be a net growth in high-skilled, well-paid employment opportunities, although with a major shift in the composition of those opportunities.

The literature on the supposedly coming era of mass technological unemployment is rife with exaggerated claims about the threat faced by knowledge workers of all types. An example is Martin Ford's (2009: 70) curious suggestion, a decade ago, that computers may be able to take over the task of formulating legal strategies by using the "brute force" technique of reviewing "every known legal argument since the days when Cicero held forth in the Roman forum" in order to identify the winning strategy – in the same way that a sufficiently powerful computer might evaluate every possible sequence of moves in an evolving chess game. Far from this being the case, developing a winning strategy in a complex legal case demands precisely the types of capacities which AI does not possess and is having great difficulty developing – including a sense of relevance, common sense and social intelligence.

8. BORROWING AND THE PRINTING PRESS?

Governments have spent aggressively in response to the economic crisis induced by the coronavirus pandemic. Income support expenditure has increased dramatically, with many governments making substantial discretionary payments (such as the $1,200 relief checks sent out by the US federal government) on top of standard unemployment and other welfare benefits. Extensive financial assistance has been provided to businesses, some in the form of grants and some in the form of loans, many of which will never be repaid. This money has gone not just to big banks and giant corporations, but also to small and medium enterprises. For hard-pressed health systems, there has been an open checkbook.

Government budgets are now sailing in a sea of red ink, with massive deficits reflecting not only the additional temporary spending, but also a slump in tax revenue. Central banks have kept the ship as stable as possible by standing ready to purchase increased volumes of government bonds – so much so that even the Italian government has been able to run up more debt without having to fear the reaction of the financial markets. Certain influential economists have called upon the central banks to go even further, through distribution of so-called "helicopter money" (Buiter, 2014) – shorthand for central banks "printing" money and giving it directly to citizens.

All of the conventional taboos against spending financed by deficits and money creation seem to have been set aside. This has, however, happened in response to a crisis from which the world economy will eventually recover. What about the longer term? Does the abandonment of orthodoxy create a precedent for the future?

The analysis in this book makes this question highly pertinent because it points to large increases in expenditure that will take place in all advanced countries over the next 30 years. Our analysis suggests that health, climate change and long-term care can together be expected to push government expenditure/GDP up by at least 6 percent of GDP in all countries over that time horizon. In addition, many governments will spend more on pensions in 2050 than they do today, assuming policies remain unchanged. Taking all this into account indicates that a majority of advanced nations, including the United States, can expect to see total government expenditure/GDP increase by at least 7 percent of GDP between now and the middle of the century. This is without taking into account spending to address infrastructure deficits, which would be additional.

We are talking, moreover, about a permanent rise in government expenditure, which will endure beyond the mid-century point. This is because health expenditure can be expected to keep on rising after that point, offsetting subsequent declines in pension spending and climate-related investment.

Common sense suggests that, in the face of such very large long-term expenditure increases, one of two things will be necessary: raising taxes substantially, or making large offsetting cuts in the range of services and benefits provided by government. Otherwise, the result will be huge, unsustainable budget deficits, with disastrous economic consequences. But what if common sense is wrong? What if we were to continue even after the current crisis to ignore the orthodox taboos? Might it not be possible to continue to fund all, or much, of the additional spending by borrowing? Perhaps – even better – central banks might be able to safely print money on the required scale and provide it to governments, thereby avoiding even the need to borrow.

There are vocal participants in the contemporary policy debate who have for some time been arguing that it is indeed possible to finance very large increases in government spending without major increases in taxation. These include certain proponents of so-called "modern monetary theory," together with advocates of "people's quantitative easing." Has the time perhaps come to put their thinking into practice?

This chapter sets out to answer these questions. It offers two principal conclusions.

The first is that the short term "whatever it costs" approach to government expenditure does not offer a precedent for the longer term. Over the 30-year time horizon, neither money creation nor borrowing can be used to fund additional spending of the magnitude identified in this book. The monetary route would overheat the economy and trigger accelerating inflation and currency depreciation, ultimately inflicting severe damage on economic activity and living standards. Relying on borrowings to finance all or most of the increased spending would undermine fiscal sustainability and eventually provoke debt crises. It is therefore an illusion to think that, in the face of the large prospective spending pressures, there is an alternative to substantial tax increases and/or drastic offsetting spending reductions.

The second conclusion is that the pandemic-induced surge in government spending will not change the nature of the longer-term budgetary challenge facing governments. Even if there is a big increase in spending on public infrastructure and the climate investment effort, this will not greatly change the spending pressures which governments face over the longer term.

Government Expenditure and the Pandemic-Induced Economic Crisis

Fiscal policy is the most powerful instrument available to respond to an economic crisis as grave as that which hit the world economy in 2020. Only government spending can under such circumstances limit the collapse in aggregate demand that would otherwise magnify the crisis tenfold by sucking oxygen out of the economy. Government is also the only actor able to provide a lifeline of support to businesses and thereby limit the extent of the economic wreckage that would result from widespread bankruptcies.

Monetary policy – cuts in interest rates and associated measures – has a more limited role. At the time the pandemic hit, interest rates were already very low and central banks had already made maximum use of almost everything in their bag of tricks (especially quantitative easing). In such a context, the role of central banks becomes essentially a secondary one: to ensure that governments can run whatever deficits are required, while at the same time doing whatever is needed to prevent the financial markets from seizing up (Buiter, 2020).

Given the severity of the pandemic-induced recession, it has been essential not only that fiscal stimulus is aggressive, but also that it is not withdrawn too quickly. Advanced nations need to learn in this respect from the mistakes made in response to the 2007-2008 global financial crisis, when the fiscal response was too timid and too short-lived. But even with a strong government response, the crisis will not be over quickly. It could easily take five years or more for advanced economies to fully recover.

One important element in the response to the crisis should be a substantial increase in government expenditure on infrastructure, including on the climate investment effort. However, this is not spending that can be initiated rapidly, because infrastructure projects take time to get under way. But even if it takes several years to fully ramp up spending on new projects, infrastructure should play an important part in the recovery phase.

To the extent that this brings forward some portion of the climate-related and other infrastructure spending that would otherwise have been undertaken in later years, it will reduce the longer-term expenditure pressure on governments. But not by much. It will leave completely unchanged the future trajectory of expenditure on health and long-term care. Climate-related spending accounts, moreover, for only 1 percent of GDP of the future expenditure increases projected in this book, and other infrastructure spending is not factored into the numerical estimate at all.

It should also be noted that governments will come out of this crisis with appreciably higher levels of debt, reducing their longer-term budgetary room to maneuver (see below).

As mentioned above, the severity of this crisis is such that it could take a full five years for economies to recover. Post-recovery, what role might deficits and money creation play in helping to finance big projected increases in government expenditure? This is the question the remainder of this chapter addresses.

The Real Resources Perspective

In discussing the potential for financing additional government expenditure over the longer-term without recourse to higher taxes, the basic principle to bear in mind is that additional government spending means less private spending.

There is one and only one exception to this principle: if there is *excess capacity* in the economy, government spending may be increased without any reduction in private spending. Excess capacity means that there is unused production capacity – that the economy is not producing as much as it is capable of producing, and that there are competent workers and machines that are involuntarily idle. Under these circumstances, government spending can be increased by making use of this excess production capacity, avoiding the need to reduce private spending. Additional government spending does this by filling the *demand* gap, which refers to a shortfall in aggregate demand. This is precisely the situation in which the world finds itself in the wake of the coronavirus pandemic (combined with a substantial *supply* shock, where output has been reduced because of pandemic-induced shutdowns).

Taking this qualification into account, the basic principle may be reformulated in the following way: *additional government spending must mean less private spending unless there is a demand gap.*

Demand gaps aside, governments must act to reduce private spending if they wish to increase government spending. Taxes are the main way that they do this because, when taxes are increased, people are left with less disposable income and are therefore obliged to reduce their spending.

Monetary Financing of Deficits

What then is the scope for governments to finance longer-term increases in expenditure by printing money? "Printing money" is a figure of speech. The main way in which central banks create money is not by printing banknotes, but by simply electronically crediting bank accounts. The most direct form of monetary financing of the deficit would be for the central bank to credit the government's bank account at the central bank with a substantial amount of additional money, without stipulating any obligation that this additional money be at some stage repaid by the government. Such direct monetary financing of government is frowned upon or contrary to the law in most advanced countries. But essentially the same effect is achieved by the indirect means of government issuing bonds to finance extra spending, with those bonds then being purchased – directly or on the secondary markets – by the central bank. The difference between direct and indirect monetary financing is not important here.

Such largess on the part of the central bank would give the government additional spending power without impinging on private spending power. When the additional funds were spent by government, aggregate demand would increase because government spending would rise without any offsetting reduction in private spending.

This may be unproblematic to the extent that, as in the current crisis, the additional government spending filled a demand gap – in other words, to the extent that there was excess capacity in the economy. However, once economic recovery has proceeded far enough for demand gaps to disappear, there would be a problem. If demand is already sufficient to purchase all of the goods and services the economy is capable of producing, the addition of extra government spending will create *excess demand*. This means that spending exceeds the productive capacity of the economy. Too many buyers chase limited production, which leads suppliers to raise their prices. If monetary financing is used on a *continuing* basis to fund *large* deficits, the excess demand will be correspondingly large and continuing. This will trigger a massive boom, in which the economy rapidly overheats. Inflation will accelerate, and ultimately there will be a crisis and a severe recession. This is a process seen repeatedly throughout history, including in recent times in Venezuela, Argentina and Zimbabwe.

The fact that excess demand brings about overheating and inflation has led some economists to coin the term *inflation barrier* to refer to the point at which aggregate demand is just sufficient, and there is neither a demand gap nor excess demand.

The temporary deployment of a joint fiscal-monetary stimulus during crisis conditions is, then, something quite different from any attempt to use monetary financing to fund massive *permanent* increases in government expenditure. There can be no justification, under normal economic circumstances, for "printing" every year the huge amount of additional money required to finance very large permanent increases in spending.

Debt Financing and the Real Resource Constraint

What about using debt to finance the deficits concerned? Separating government borrowing from monetary policy is a somewhat complicated business, and no useful purpose would be served by becoming unnecessarily technical here on the interaction of fiscal and monetary policy. The fundamental point is simply that the use of debt does not in any way change the real resource constraint. It remains the case that, unless the economy has excess capacity, additional government spending will create excess demand *unless* there is a corresponding reduction in private spending. If debt financing is used instead of taxes, the necessary reduction in private spending must be delivered by the impact of higher interest rates.[1] Higher rates operate by reducing interest-sensitive private spending (business investment, housing construction or purchases of cars or consumer goods commonly made using credit). This is a form of what is referred to as the "crowding out" of private spending.

When the government borrows, the central bank needs to act to avoid the emergence of excess demand by ensuring that interest rates rise to the extent necessary to achieve the required reduction in private spending. A simple way of thinking about this – although it is not quite the way things actually work – is that when the government increases the amount it borrows from the public, it needs to offer a higher interest rate to obtain the funds it required.

There is nothing inherently wrong with using borrowing to displace some private spending with government spending. Governments routinely use debt to finance infrastructure spending, much of which yields great social and/or economic benefits. To the extent that the benefits generated by debt-financed government infrastructure spending exceed the benefits of the private investment and other expenditure that has been "crowded out," such displacement is highly desirable.

The problem is the size of the government's ongoing borrowing requirement. In the absence of excess demand, the larger the amount government needs to borrow, the higher the interest rate will need to be. If the government wishes to fund a very large ongoing increase in its spending by borrowing, it will need to displace a correspondingly large amount of private spending and interest rates will need to go up very considerably.

Unfortunately, it is almost impossible to use high interest rates in this manner to displace sufficient private spending to make enough room for a large permanent increase in government spending without triggering a severe economy-wide recession. The magnitude and timing of the impact of higher interest rates on private sector economic activity is somewhat unpredictable. Raising rates significantly runs a major risk of overshooting and squeezing interest-sensitive private spending more than is intended, with spillover effects that depress the economy as a whole.[2] (The only way of avoiding this danger is to borrow on a large and continuing basis from abroad, which can lead to a dangerous accumulation of external debt and potentially to a major fiscal sustainability problem.)

It might be objected that the central bank can easily prevent interest rates from rising to damagingly high levels by injecting more money into the economy.[3] While this is true, once the central bank does this, private spending will no longer be displaced on the scale necessary to make room for the desired large increase in government spending. Such action by the central bank would effectively constitute a reversion to the pure monetary financing scenario discussed above, with the same consequences of excessive demand, overheating, accelerating inflation and ultimate crisis.

When, during an economic crisis, a substantial demand gap emerges, the problem just described does not arise. Under these circumstances, additional debt financing can be used without any increase in interest rates, and therefore without any reduction in private spending. The economy copes with the extra government spending by drawing on its excess capacity. Far from being displaced, private spending increases, because the economy as a whole receives a valuable stimulus. But *only* to the extent that there is a demand gap. Here again, we need to distinguish clearly between the circumstances of the current pandemic-induced economic crisis, and those which will prevail in the longer term once the world economy has recovered.

Fiscal Sustainability and Debt

Deficits funded by borrowing raise the issue of *fiscal sustainability*. This refers to the possibility that the debt burden borne by governments may reach such high levels that lenders fear government will default on its debt. Such fear makes lenders increasingly reluctant to finance government deficits. Initially, this reluctance manifests itself in a willingness to lend only at ever-increasing interest rates (i.e. interest rates that offset the perceived higher risk of default). Rising interest rates worsen the government's budget deficit, pushing debt even higher (see below) and further increasing the perceived default risk. If this game were played out to its endpoint, government would find itself ultimately unable to borrow to finance its deficit at any interest rate. In practice, however, governments typically default on their debt well before this point is reached.

It is not the mere fact of running a budget deficit that creates a threat to fiscal sustainability. It is obvious that if the government runs continual budget deficits, public debt must continually increase. However, rising public debt is not necessarily a problem. When the economy is growing, and the government's tax base with it, the government is able to support increasing amounts of debt. It is for this reason that the debt burden is typically measured not by the quantum of debt, but rather by the ratio of debt/GDP. (Similarly, the burden of interest payments on the budget is measured by interest/GDP.) The fiscal sustainability problem arises when the debt/GDP and interest/GDP ratios get too high, and this is what puts constraints on the size of the deficit.

Debt/GDP was already at historically high levels in many advanced countries prior to the current crisis. In the United States, for example, gross debt/GDP stood at 107 percent in 2018 (and net financial worth, an alternative debt measure, at minus 83 percent). In France, the figures were 122 percent for gross debt/GDP and minus 77 percent for net financial worth, while in Italy they were 148 percent and minus 120 percent, and in Japan, 222 percent and minus 124 percent. Debt levels had already jumped considerably in most countries as a consequence of the global financial crisis (see Figure 8.1).

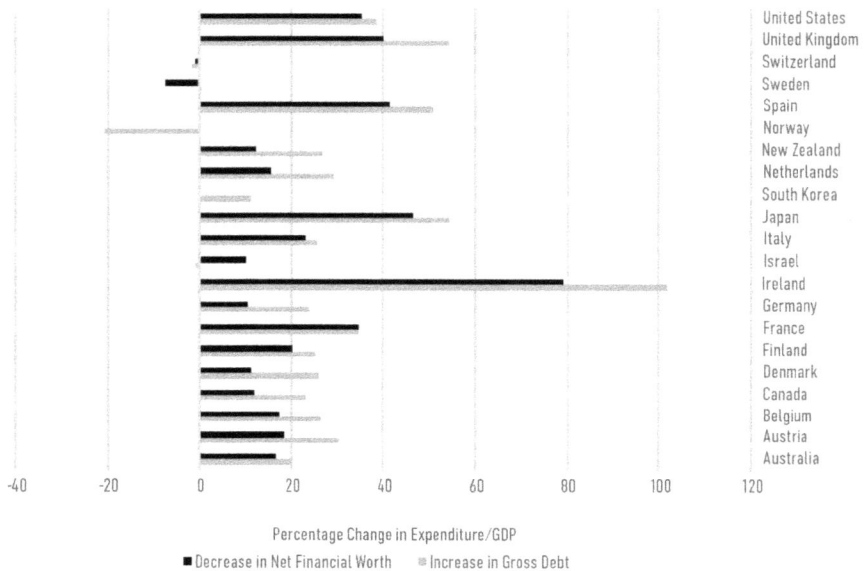

Percentage Change in Expenditure/GDP
■ Decrease in Net Financial Worth   ▩ Increase in Gross Debt

Figure 8.1
Increases in Government Debt Induced by Global Financial Crisis (2007-2012)
Percentage Changes in Gross Debt/GDP and in Net Financial Worth/GDP

Every advanced country will almost certainly experience further large increases in government debt as a consequence of the current pandemic-induced crisis, which is considerably more serious than the global financial crisis. A conservative assumption would be that debt/GDP will increase everywhere by at least 20 percent. This is the context that we must consider when we look beyond the current crisis and ask about the capacity of advanced countries to run continuing budget deficits in the longer term.

When asked about the "safe" level of budget deficits, economists have traditionally responded that deficits should not be so large as to cause a *debt snowball* – meaning a situation in which debt/GDP continues to rise without any upper limit. The risk of a debt snowball depends on the pre-existing level of debt and upon the extent to which government borrows to pay interest, rather than paying at least some of its interest obligations from tax revenue. In the usual analysis, if the government continually finances *all* its interest payments by new borrowings, debt/GDP will snowball (see Box 8.1), eventually causing a crisis.

Box 8.1 A Debt Snowball

Running a deficit is equivalent to borrowing to pay for some of the government's interest obligations, rather than paying all interest from revenue. To see what may happen when the government borrows to pay *all* its interest obligations, take the example of a government that starts off in 2017 with a debt of $1 trillion, an amount that happens to be equivalent to 100 percent of GDP (i.e. GDP is also $1 trillion). Suppose that the interest rate on government debt is 6 percent, and that GDP is growing at 3 percent annually.[4] If the government runs a deficit equal to its interest payments – meaning that it pays none of the interest from revenue – then the next year (2018) its debt will be $1.06 trillion. GDP, on the other hand, will have grown to $1.03 trillion. Debt/GDP will therefore then stand at 103 percent (1.06/1.03). If government continues year after year not to pay any of its interest from revenue, debt/GDP will continue to increase in this manner. After 10 years, it will reach 133 percent. After 20 years it will be 178 percent of GDP, and so on without end. In this type of scenario, there are no limits to the increase in debt/GDP that will result. The debt burden increases exponentially over time, which is unsustainable.

But this understates the problem. As mentioned, the fact that debt is on an unsustainable upward trajectory would at some point lead financial markets to fear that the government will eventually default on its debt. The perceived increased default risk would lead to a vicious cycle of increasing interest rates and accelerating increases in debt/GDP, hastening the day of reckoning.

This seems to imply that, to avoid a debt snowball, government must pay off at least some of its interest obligations from revenue. Economists formulate this point in terms of what they call the *primary* budget balance.

The primary balance is the difference between revenue and *non-interest* expenditure (whereas the overall budget balance is the difference between revenue and *all* expenditure, including interest). The requirement that at least some of the government's interest obligations are paid from revenue rather than new borrowings is equivalent to a requirement that there be a primary *surplus* (i.e. that revenue exceed non-interest expenditure, leaving something over to go toward paying interest).

In the type of scenario just outlined, for any given level of public debt, a primary surplus of a particular size is necessary to stabilize the level of debt and avoid it snowballing. If we take the example in the box above, a primary surplus of approximately 3 percent of GDP is required to ensure that debt/GDP remains at 100 percent, rather than growing without limits. This primary surplus requirement sets a limit on the size of the overall budget deficit (the deficit including interest payments) that is fiscally sustainable. (In this example, the overall budget deficit would be limited to about 3 percent of GDP, once one subtracts interest payments from the required primary surplus.)

From this perspective, the future prospects of advanced countries look alarming. In the recent period "between the two crises" – i.e. between the global financial crisis and the present crisis – more than half have actually run primary *deficits* (meaning they have been borrowing not only to pay all of their interest obligations, but also to pay a little of their non-interest expenditure). Primary surpluses, in those countries which have run them, have mostly been quite small (see Appendix 8.1).[5] If we think of this as a post-recovery starting point, the large increases in government spending over the next three decades foreshadowed in this book would push every advanced country progressively toward large permanent primary deficits. Rough calculations suggest that the primary deficit would exceed 7 percent of GDP in approximately half of advanced countries, and would nowhere be less than 4 percent.[6]

This seems terrifying. There is, however, a problem with this conventional story. The problem is that the debt snowball effect arises *only* if the interest rate is greater than the GDP growth rate. If, as is generally the case at present in advanced countries, interest rates on government debt are less than the rate of growth, then the story is different. Under these circumstances, even if the government fails to pay *any* of its interest obligations from revenue, debt/GDP will fall rather than rise. There will be what might be called a "melting snowball" effect (see Box 8.2).

Box 8.2 Melting Snowballs

Take the hypothetical example in the box above (initial debt of $1 trillion and an initial debt/GDP ratio in 2017 of 100 percent) but assume now that the interest rate is 1.5 percent (rather than 6 percent), while the growth rate remains at 3 percent. Now, if government does not pay any interest from revenue, debt will grow to $1.015 trillion in 2018. GDP will still have grown to $1.03 trillion. Debt/GDP will then have fallen from 100 percent to 98.5 percent (1.015/1.03). It will keep on falling in subsequent years (still assuming the primary deficit remains constant). This "melting snowball" effect is the direct consequence of interest rates below the GDP growth rate.

The implications are quite far-reaching. No longer is it necessary to run a primary surplus. Even if government borrows not only to pay its interest bill, but to fund some of its non-interest expenditure, there will be no *unlimited* increase in the debt burden. Debt/GDP may increase, but not beyond a certain limit. Moreover, with low interest rates, the interest burden may remain low.

This may be illustrated by taking the example in the ("melting snowballs") box immediately above, with the single modification that the government now continuously runs a primary deficit of 2 percent of GDP. This means that borrowings are being used not only to meet all interest payments, but also to pay for non-interest spending equivalent to 2 percent of GDP. With a continuing primary deficit of this size, debt would gradually increase but would never exceed 137 percent of GDP. It can be shown that with a slightly smaller continuing primary deficit (1.46 percent of GDP), debt/GDP would never increase at all, but would remain at 100 percent.

Box 8.3 How Can Debt/GDP Increase Continually While Being Limited?

The fact that when the interest rate is less than the growth rate, increases in debt/GDP are limited in the manner described above may not make sense intuitively. But it is rather like the story of the frog that starts off on a lily pad in the center of a pond. He initially jumps half the distance to the edge of the pond. In his next jump, he jumps half the distance of his first jump (i.e. one-quarter of the total distance). In the third move, he once again jumps half the distance of his previous (second) jump (one-eighth of the total distance), and so on for subsequent jumps. The cumulative distance jumped by the frog continually increases, but never exceeds the total distance from the center to the edge of the pond, because he never quite gets there. If the primary deficit/GDP is constant, then even though debt/GDP increases each year, the cumulative increase will be limited in broadly the same way.

It is a mathematical fact that, when the interest rate on government debt is less than the growth rate and the primary deficit is constant (i.e. always 2 percent, 3 percent, 10 percent or any other number), then *no matter how high the ongoing primary deficit is*, debt/GDP will always be limited in this manner. There can never be a debt snowball. However, as discussed below, this does not necessarily mean that the levels the debt/GDP ratio would reach would be sustainable in practice. The "limit" may be very high indeed.

This seems to put a better light on the budgetary position of advanced countries. In the period between the two crises, only four countries ran primary deficits averaging in excess of 2 percent of GDP (Japan, the United Kingdom, the United States and Norway).[7] The relatively high pre-crisis debt/GDP ratios of many advanced countries were, moreover, essentially painless, given low interest rates (significantly lower in some countries than the 1.5 percent assumed in the example).

It might be thought that this is an aberration. Surely it is only the exceptionally low level of interest rates of recent years that has produced the situation in which interest rates are below the growth rate of the economy?[8] Can't we therefore expect to get back to the "normal" relationship of the two variables sometime in the future?

Many economists think the answer is "no" – and thought so well before the coronavirus pandemic knocked the world economy flat. They assert that low interest rates are due to structural forces that will continue to operate for at least several decades to come (Bean et al, 2015).[9] Moreover, close examination of the historical record indicates it is relatively normal in most advanced countries for interest rates on government debt to be lower than the GDP growth rate (Arestis and Sawyer, 2003; Mauro et al, 2015; Blanchard, 2019a, 2019b).[10]

There is no question that interest rates will be kept at rock-bottom levels for the entire duration of the current crisis. But it seems probable that interest rates on government debt will remain lower than the average growth rate for quite some time after the world economy recovers. If this is the case, does it mean that the need to maintain fiscal sustainability no longer limits the deficits governments can run in the long term? Does it mean that there is no problem with government using debt to fund long-term large primary deficits – possibly even as high as 7 percent of GDP, or more?

The answer to these questions is unambiguously "no."

One reason why the answer is "no" is the impact *very* large primary deficits would have on both debt levels and the interest rate/growth rate relationship. If ongoing debt-financed deficits were very large, debt/GDP would reach very high levels even if the gap between interest rates and the growth rate were to remain unchanged for many decades to come. This is true notwithstanding the fact that, as mentioned above, there will be a limit the debt/GDP ratio will not exceed.

Instead of illustrating this with hypothetical examples, as in the boxes above, let's take the concrete case of the United States. The US government has for some time run primary deficits, and the spending pressures outlined in this book would probably increase that deficit to something in excess of 9 percent of GDP. Based on the pre-crisis levels of government debt, interest rates and GDP growth rates,[11] continuous primary deficits this large would result in debt/GDP gradually increasing toward a "limit" somewhat above 450 percent of GDP. This would be an extremely high level. It is, for example, more than four times the historic peak level of government debt at the end of World War II.

Such mechanical projections of debt trends understate the problem because, in practice, the relation between the interest rate and growth rate would not remain unchanged in the face of such huge primary deficits. With very large increases in spending, any pre-existing demand gap could be expected to close rapidly. Once this was the case, large continuing primary deficits would require large increases in interest rates to achieve the necessary displacement of private spending. Even if this merely *compressed* the gap between interest rates and the growth rate, with interest rates still remaining below the growth rate, it would have major consequences. Continuing with the US example, an increase of 1 percent in interest rates on government debt would raise the "limit" to which debt/GDP would trend to a number above 900 percent of GDP. This would be despite the interest rate remaining well below the GDP growth rate.

Let's take another example: Italy. Italy has for some time had, thanks to the European Central Bank, the advantage of low interest rates on government debt (around 0.9 percent immediately prior to the pandemic). During the period "between the two crises," it had the additional advantage of running the highest primary *surplus* of all advanced countries (around 4 percent of GDP). Assuming this starting point, the spending pressures outlined in this book would in Italy's case push it toward a permanent primary deficit of something around 4 percent of GDP. In this respect at least, it would be better off than everybody else, and much better off than the United States. Unfortunately, however, Italy has had the major disadvantages of chronically low GDP growth rates[12] and a relatively high level of government debt/GDP (121 percent in 2018). Overall, these circumstances mean – on the assumption of growth and interest rates at pre-crisis levels – that an increase in the primary deficit to 4 percent would push Italy towards a debt "limit" of over 800 percent of GDP. If, however, the stimulus to the economy led to interest rates on Italian government debt rising even as little as 0.4 percent (at which point they would still remain slightly below recent GDP growth rates), the "limit" to which debt/GDP would trend would be a number in excess of 4,000 percent!

In practice, debt/GDP would in no country reach levels of 400 percent, let alone 800 percent or 4,000 percent of GDP. Well before debt reached such stratospheric levels, large primary deficits would produce a growing – and entirely justified – fear of default. Lenders are not stupid and they can work out the mathematics. In response to the growing default risk, they would demand higher interest rates, further compressing the interest rate/growth rate difference and aggravating the situation. At some point, interest rates could be expected to push above the growth rate, triggering a debt snowball (Alcidi and Gros, 2019). Crisis would be inevitable unless government implemented severe fiscal consolidation measures (dramatic spending cuts and/or large tax rises).

The danger of such a debt crisis will only be increased by the substantial increase in debt levels which will, as mentioned above, occur as a result of the current recession and government efforts to support the economy.

Two further considerations need to be borne in mind. The first is uncertainty about the long-term future of low interest rates. One cannot dismiss the possibility that some measure of normalization of interest rates, unrelated to the pressure of large deficits, will compress the gap between interest rates and the growth rate over the longer term.[13] As Blanchard and Summers (2019) put it, "because of our limited understanding of the relative role of the factors that lie behind the low safe rate [i.e. the interest rate on government bonds]… one cannot be sure that the inequality [between interest rates and the growth rate] will not reverse at some point in the future."

The second consideration is that whether interest rates will remain well below the rate of growth depends not only on the continuation of low interest rates, but also on future GDP growth. Yet – setting to one side the temporary damage of the recession induced by the coronavirus pandemic – it is by no means certain that GDP growth will remain at the levels of recent years (or higher) over the longer term. The challenges of global warming alone suffice to create real doubt. As mentioned in Chapter 5, it is not clear to what extent the world will succeed in decoupling GDP growth from greenhouse gas emissions so as to maintain solid growth while achieving the necessary degree of decarbonization. At the same time, there is the high probability that the failure to decarbonize sufficiently to rein in global warming will *severely* undermine economic activity because of major climatic disruption.

Secular Stagnation and Long-Term Deficits

In the picture painted above, the size of the deficit the government can run at any point in time depends in significant measure on the extent of any demand gap the economy may be experiencing. This makes the magnitude and duration of demand gaps an important determinant of the size of acceptable budget deficits.

Demand gaps are usually thought of as short-term phenomena that arise only in recessions, disappearing when the economy recovers. This makes them a justification only for *temporarily* higher deficits. There is, however, a school of thought that many advanced countries have in recent times suffered from *chronic* demand gaps. This is the doctrine of *secular stagnation*. Roughly speaking, the secular stagnation proposition is that, even after recovery from recession, aggregate demand is inadequate to keep the economy operating at full capacity *unless* government itself fills the chronic demand gap. Continuous fiscal stimulus – government deficit spending to create additional demand – is, in this view, required because the conventional tools of monetary policy (low interest rates) are insufficient to do the job. This makes demand gaps a longer-term phenomenon, justifying larger ongoing budget deficits.

Secular stagnation is considered briefly in Appendix 8.2. The key point made there is that, even if this doctrine is valid, it cannot provide a justification for ongoing truly massive primary deficits on the scale implied by the expenditure trends identified in this book.

◆ ◆ ◆

With reference to long-term post-recovery fiscal policy, the very most that can be plausibly argued is that it may be reasonable for some advanced countries to run small ongoing primary deficits for a time (the exact magnitude and duration of such deficits varying from country to country). And even this depends on accepting theories concerning the future interest rates/growth rate relationship – and perhaps also about secular stagnation

– which remain open for debate. This reality is in no way changed by the appropriateness of large *temporary* deficits in times of grave economic crisis such as that triggered by the coronavirus pandemic.

The commonsense view that any large *permanent* increase in government spending must be paid for mainly by increased taxation is, then, correct. The only way of avoiding this would be to make large offsetting reductions in government spending. We look at one aspect of this – the scope for making savings by eliminating waste – in the next chapter.

As mentioned at the outset, some exponents of "modern monetary theory" and "people's quantitative easing" appear to disagree with this conclusion and to believe that very large long-term increases in government spending can be financed without major increases in taxation. Their views are discussed in Appendix 8.3.

Appendix 8.1: Primary Budget Balances

As discussed in the text, the impact of the large prospective increases in government expenditure discussed in this book on debt levels and fiscal sustainability in individual countries depends in part on the size of the primary deficits they start with. The following table provides information on the primary deficits that advanced countries ran during the period "between the two crises," which is used as the basis for certain of the calculations in the main text. "Structural" refers here to the adjustment of measured primary balances to remove the effects of the economy being either in recession or in boom conditions.

General Government Structural Primary Balances (as percentage of potential GDP)

	2018	Average (2007–2018)
Australia	-0.05	-1.23
Austria	1.37	0.72
Belgium	0.52	0.89
Canada	-0.77	-0.19
Denmark	-0.32	0.52
Finland	-0.89	-0.18
France	-0.01	-1.23
Germany	0.00	1.10
Ireland	1.14	-2.16
Israel	-0.27	0.00
Italy	3.2	2.75
Japan	-4.6	-5.49
South Korea	2.33	1.19
Netherlands	1.64	-0.41
New Zealand	0.74	0.51
Norway	-2.77	-2.32
Spain	0.8	-0.55
Sweden	-0.2	0.81
Switzerland	1.22	1.09
United Kingdom	-1.24	-3.49
United States	-2.14	-3.25

(Negative numbers represent primary deficits, positive are primary surpluses)
Source: OECD.Stat (extracted 10 August 2019)

Appendix 8.2: Secular Stagnation

The proposition that the economy suffers from a *chronic* demand gap is an old idea in economics that has resurfaced as a result of its adoption by prominent economists including Lawrence Summers (2014a, 2014b). The idea is, as Summers puts it, "that the private economy – unless stimulated by extraordinary public actions especially monetary and fiscal policies and, or, unsustainable private sector borrowing – will be prone to sluggish growth caused by insufficient demand" (Summers, 2018).

The implication of the secular stagnation thesis is that fiscal stimulus may be appropriate not only temporarily during recessions, but also on a longer-term basis in order to ensure that the economy is operating at full capacity. If the thesis is valid, it provides further support for the idea that governments can run longer-term primary deficits. It also implies that these ongoing deficits can safely be larger than if there were no chronic demand gap.

A number of reasons have been offered as to why certain advanced economies may have been suffering in recent times from chronic demand gaps. These include "balance sheet repair" after financial bubbles, population aging and income inequality, all of which depress consumption expenditure and/or business investment.

The secular stagnation doctrine is controversial. Its prominent critics include Joseph Stiglitz (2018) and John Taylor (2014).

Of relevance to this book is the question of whether the existence of chronic demand gaps might make it feasible to use borrowing – or, for that matter, monetary financing – to finance all or most of the large prospective increases in government spending identified in the preceding chapters. The answer to this question clearly depends on both the magnitude and the anticipated duration of any chronic demand gap.

With respect to the *magnitude* of the gap, secular stagnation could clearly only provide a justification for very large long-term deficits if the chronic demand gap was equivalently large.

The advanced country where it might be argued that the demand gap arising from secular stagnation has been largest is Japan. The Japanese government has run large structural primary deficits for years (averaging 5.5 percent of GDP over the period 2007-2018)[14] and debt/GDP has risen considerably. From the outset, critics have condemned these fiscal policies as unsustainable and predicted a debt crisis. There has, however, been no such crisis. Interest rates have remained low.

It has been persuasively argued that, given the magnitude of the chronic demand gap in Japan, it has been not only appropriate, but essential, for the

Japanese government to run large primary deficits. Richard Koo, for example, asserts that the chronic demand gap has been particularly pronounced in Japan because of the prolonged process of balance sheet repair after the collapse of its spectacular financial bubble in 1990 (Koo, 2009; 2015). Also relevant is the fact that Japan has experienced much more accelerated and extreme population aging than almost all other advanced countries.

Critics of Japanese policies habitually refer to the Japanese government's *gross* debt, which stood at 238 of GDP in 2017. However, this exaggerates the problem, because *net* public debt (124 percent in 2017) is more meaningful for international comparisons.[15] In addition – and this is a point upon which every-one agrees – Japan is helped by borrowing essentially from Japanese rather than external lenders, so that the government does not have to worry about a crisis of confidence of foreign creditors.

What does this mean for the rest of the advanced world? There is broad agreement that Japan's case is extreme. Nobody argues, or at least offers evidence, that other advanced countries have experienced secular stagnation on the scale of Japan. (If they did, they would either have been much more depressed than they are or, alternatively, their primary deficits would have been much larger.) Even those who are most supportive of the fiscal policies of Japanese governments generally agree that it would be risky for the Japanese debt/GDP ratio to rise *greatly* beyond its current levels. With current low interest rates, the rate at which debt rises is quite slow. The fact that little of the country's government debt is held by foreigners also greatly mitigates the risk of rates suddenly being pushed up as a result of perceived default risk (as happened, for example, a few years ago to Italy). Japan therefore has considerable time to reduce its primary deficit. The deficit is, nevertheless, clearly unsustainable in the long run.

This suggests that, even if the secular stagnation theory is valid with respect to some advanced countries, it does not provide a justification for running long-term primary deficits at or above Japanese levels in advanced countries generally. By extension, it certainly cannot justify permanent primary deficits of 7 percent or more of GDP.

With respect to the *duration* of any chronic demand gap, the secular stag-nation thesis does not suggest that any gap is necessarily permanent. To the extent that any gap is, for example, due to population aging, one would expect it to largely disappear once the period of accelerating aging associated with the "baby boomer" generation is over (approximately speaking, and depending on the country, within the next two decades). To the extent, on the other hand, that it is due to Japanese-style balance sheet repair, it could be expected to end once businesses and households have reduced debt levels and rebuilt positive net asset positions. The doctrine would not therefore normally justify *permanently* higher budget deficits.

This leads to a further point. Even if there is a chronic demand gap, it does not follow that policymakers should rely entirely, or even mainly, on fiscal stimulus and deficits to address the problem. Given that it is dangerous to let debt levels reach extremely high levels, it makes sense to work to directly tackle, as far as possible, the sources of chronic demand gaps. For example, to the extent that secular stagnation might be due to debt overhang after a financial bubble, aggressive government measures to help households and businesses repair their balance sheets more rapidly will significantly shorten the period during which the economy suffers from underlying demand deficiency. (An example is action to permit households to more easily write off excessive mortgage debt after the collapse of a real estate bubble.) Similarly, if rising inequality is holding consumption expenditure down, it makes sense to redistribute income. The idea that improving the distribution of income is desirable not only on equity grounds, but also to boost demand, has a long lineage in economics.

Secular stagnation, then, does not change the fact that there are significant limits to the extent to which increased government spending can over the long term be financed by debt.

Appendix 8.3: Modern Monetary Theory and People's Quantitative Easing

Modern Monetary Theory

Leading exponents of modern monetary theory (MMT) include the Australian economist William Mitchell and, in the United States, Stephanie Kelton, L. Randall Wray, and Pavlina Tcherneva. MMT explicitly accepts there are *in principle* limits on the size of government deficits (Wray, 2015; Mitchell and Fazi, 2017),[16] based on the availability of real resources. Nevertheless, many MMT economists seem to deny that these limits apply *in practice*. Wray, for example, has argued that there is no need for taxation to finance a massive Green New Deal spending program in the United States (Nersisyan and Wray, 2019). Mitchell asserts that the British government can and should run a "persistent and substantial fiscal deficit" (Fazi and Mitchell, 2019). Overall, the main MMT message on budget matters seems to be that people should "stop worrying about fiscal deficits altogether" (Mitchell and Fazi, 2017: 262).

MMT economists tend to systematically downplay the risk of triggering excess demand and inflation through large spending increases that are not tax-financed. Sometimes they do so on the grounds that there is (supposedly) vast excess capacity in the economy (Nersisyan and Wray, 2019), and sometimes based on vague reasoning such as the proposition that "if the net government spending is purchasing real goods and services that are available for sale, then such spending is unlikely to trigger inflation" (Fazi and Mitchell, 2019). They also tend to deny or minimize the contribution of irresponsible fiscal and monetary policies to hyper-inflationary episodes such as those experienced in Zimbabwe (Wray, 2015).

Many MMT economists also deny it is possible for debt to get so high as to cause serious problems. In defense of this position, they point out, correctly, a country that issues its own currency can always repay its debt (by simply "printing" more money). They also note that the central bank can always prevent interest rates from rising through its monetary policy operations, and claim that on this basis there need never be a problem of interest rates exceeding the growth rate (Kelton, 2019; Wray, 2015). A debt snowball will, in this view, never occur unless the central bank for some inexplicable reason allows it to occur. Therefore, there is no reason for lenders to fear default and no reason for them to demand higher interest rates or refuse to lend to government, even if debt levels reach very high levels.

However, as discussed in the main text, if government is running continuous, large primary deficits well in excess of what might be justified by any demand gap, interest rates *must* rise substantially or the economy will seriously overheat. The threat of interest rates exceeding the growth rate and the development of a debt snowball is therefore a very real one. If a debt snowball does develop, then even a government that controls its own currency has incentives to default. Lender fears of default are thus well-founded. There are very good reasons why at some point lenders would begin to demand higher and higher interest rates and ultimately refuse to finance government deficits. Faced with such lender resistance, the authorities' only alternative would be to monetize the deficit, which would inevitably lead to massive excess demand and hyperinflation.

People's Quantitative Easing

An alternative position is that so-called "people's quantitative easing" (PQE) can be used to finance a large ongoing increase in government spending (Coppola, 2019). PQE has enjoyed great popularity on the political left in a number of advanced countries. In the United Kingdom, it was proposed by the former Labour Party leader Jeremy Corbyn. Green politicians in the UK,

France and other countries have advocated a variant of it in the form of "green quantitative easing."[17]

Quantitative easing (QE) – that is, *conventional* QE – is the process by which many advanced country central banks have, particularly since the GFC, undertaken large-scale purchases of financial assets on the open market. This includes purchases of longer-term government bonds held by the public, private sector debt instruments (e.g. mortgage-backed securities) and (in the case of Japan) shares. The central banks have financed these purchases by creating money, so that it is through these asset purchases that this money has been injected into the economy.

The value of these asset purchases, and of money creation to finance them, has been very large. In the United States, the Federal Reserve purchased around $4.5 trillion in assets under its QE program between 2008 and 2014. In Europe, the European Central Bank spent over €1 trillion. The volume of asset purchases in Japan, which pioneered QE, dwarfs those in both the US and Europe: by 2018, Japan's central bank had total asset holdings valued in excess of the country's GDP (by comparison, the figures were approximately 20 percent in the US and 40 percent in the EU) (Takeo, 2018).

PQE, on the other hand, is the notion that central bank money creation should be used to fund government spending or to put money directly into citizens' pockets. A common version of the PQE narrative runs as follows. In undertaking quantitative easing, the central banks have created and spent a massive amount without triggering inflation. Why not use broadly the same process of money creation, but to finance government?[18] The additional government spending this would permit would have no greater inflationary impact than quantitative easing has had. Channeling the monetary stimulus through government rather than through the private financial markets would, moreover, be more socially useful and would provide a more effective stimulus to the economy. It would constitute quantitative easing for the people, as opposed to quantitative easing for the benefit of the financial markets. So, at least, the argument goes.

The problem with this reasoning – and indeed with the very term "people's quantitative easing" – is that it draws a completely misleading parallel between (real) quantitative easing and the use of money creation to finance government spending. These are, in reality, completely different things. Quantitative easing has not been an exercise in giving money to the private sector (households and businesses) for them to spend. To the contrary, private sector agents who receive the money created by central banks do so in return for selling financial assets. While quantitative easing has been intended to stimulate private spending, it does not purport to achieve this effect by *giving* households or businesses money. This makes it totally different from creating money and giving it to government for the express purpose of financing increased government expenditure. The use of the misleading term "quantitative easing" to describe the latter encourages the completely false notion that the magnitude of monetary financing of deficits could and should be similar to the magnitude of the quantitative easing operations undertaken over recent years.

As already indicated, the idea that money creation should be used to finance additional spending when the economy is depressed (and monetary policy is largely ineffective) is one which is today held by many economists. But this has nothing to do with the notion of applying quantitative easing principles to financing government.

There is much debate about the extent to which quantitative easing actually succeeds in stimulating private spending. Many economists are skeptical about its efficacy and concerned that its main impact has been to stoke new financial bubbles. Even more consider that fiscal stimulus financed by central banks would have been preferable to conventional QE.[19]

The most fundamental point is that, irrespective of the magnitude of the quantitative easing operations carried out in recent years by central banks, the scope for additional government spending financed by money creation remains constrained by the degree of excess capacity in the economy. It is therefore completely unrealistic to view PQE, in the way that Coppola (2019) and some others do, as the solution to all of the major long-term government spending pressures including climate change and (supposedly) technological unemployment.

9. TRIMMING THE FAT

Before we turn to the tough options of raising taxes or cutting services and benefits, there is one other important question which must be asked: *how much scope is there to ease the pressure on government budgets by improving efficiency*?

When government is under fiscal strain, it is essential to realize all possible savings which can help contain the increase in aggregate public expenditure. This will be truer than ever in coming decades, given the extent of the spending pressures on governments in all advanced nations. With this in mind, this chapter looks at the potential for reducing government expenditure through measures to deliver better value for money.

The main message of what follows is that although the continuing pursuit of efficiency savings is important, it cannot be expected to provide a solution to governments' budgetary problems. Even with the most vigorous efforts, it will not be possible to achieve through efficiency savings alone reductions in expenditure large enough to offset all or most of the big increases in spending identified in this book.

It is important to be clear about what we mean by efficiency savings, because discussions about the potential for "trimming the fat" are often bedeviled by a failure to distinguish between efficiency savings and *spending cuts*. A true efficiency saving arises when spending is reduced by delivering the same services, or achieving the same outcomes, at lower cost.[1] Reductions in expenditure achieved by winding back or eliminating government services and benefits are completely different – they represent spending cuts.

In this chapter, our focus is exclusively upon efficiency savings. We are therefore not concerned with the scope for reducing expenditure by eliminating programs that some consider to be low priority or to be pursuing the wrong policy objectives. Options such as terminating the unemployment benefits of people who fail drug tests or reducing military budgets to end foreign wars are irrelevant in this context.

The Scope for Efficiency Savings

In nearly all advanced countries, the biggest area of government expenditure is *social benefits*, such as pensions, family allowances and unemployment benefits.[2] Here, the scope for true efficiency savings is small relative both to total government expenditure and to GDP – at least if certain major nations can be taken as representative of advanced countries as a whole.

In line with the distinction made between savings and cuts, we need to be clear about what "efficiency savings" means with respect to benefit expenditure. It does *not* mean spending reductions achieved by changing policy on benefit levels and entitlements. What it means is, rather, spending less by stopping paying benefits to which the recipients are not legally entitled or by reducing overpayments of benefits due to error or fraud.

How big could such savings be? In the UK, net overpayments of social security were estimated in 2018 at £3 billion (DWP, 2019[3]) – an amount which, while large in absolute terms, was equivalent to only 1.6 percent of benefit payments and to 0.15 percent of GDP. In the US, careful estimates made by the Social Security Administration suggest an even lower rate of net overpayments, equivalent to 0.03 percent of GDP in 2018.[4] It may well be that there are other advanced countries where the rates of overpayments are higher,[5] but on the whole it seems reasonable to put social benefits expenditure aside when we think about the order of magnitude of potential efficiency savings across government expenditure as a whole.

The two areas of government spending where the biggest efficiency savings might potentially be made are *employee compensation* (wages and salaries paid to government workers) and *goods and services* (what government pays for computers, electricity, IT and other services provided to it by the private sector, pharmaceuticals, schoolbooks and all of the other goods and services it needs to carry out its operations).

Combined government expenditure on employee compensation and goods and services ranges in advanced countries from 9 percent to 24 percent of GDP (see Figure 9.1). This tells us that if it were possible to save, say, a full 10 percent of expenditure in these areas by efficiency measures, total government expenditure would be reduced, depending upon the country, by between 0.9 and 2.4 percent of GDP – a range which can be viewed against the pressures for additional spending of 7 percent or more of GDP in a majority of advanced countries discussed in this book.

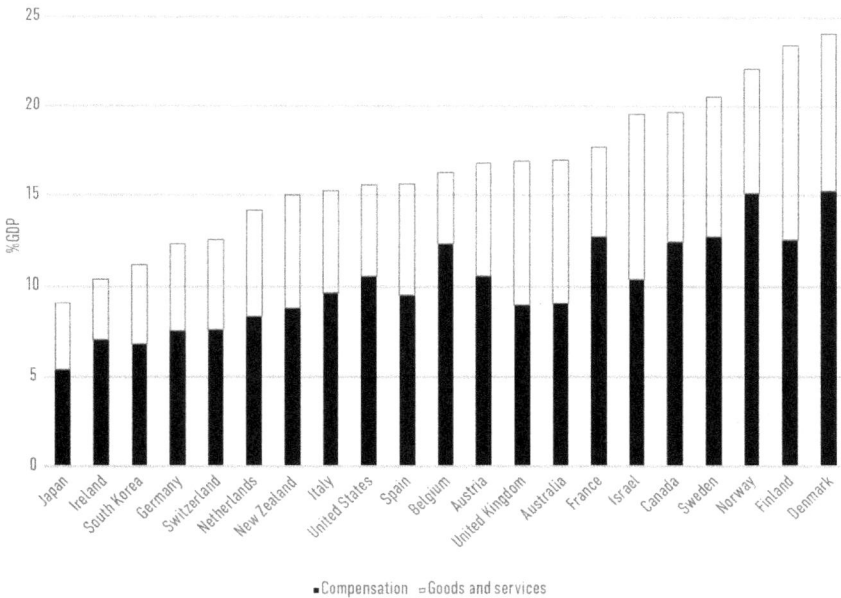

■Compensation □Goods and services

Source: OECD.Stat
Goods and Services is "intermediate consumption"

Figure 9.1
Government Expenditure on Compensation and Goods & Services (2017)

Another way of looking at it is that in the United States, for example, off-setting spending increases of 7 percent of GDP would require efficiency savings equal to at least 45 percent of government spending on compensation, goods and services. In the case of Italy, where projected spending increases are lower than elsewhere (at perhaps 4 percent of GDP) it would be necessary to save through efficiency measures at least 26 percent of this type of spending.

What can be said about the feasibility of savings of this magnitude? Is it realistic to think that efficiency savings in compensation and goods and services spending of the order of 45 percent, 26 percent or even 10 percent are potentially available in some or all advanced countries?

In attempting to answer these questions, we will start by considering the potential for efficiency savings that depend only upon doing things better, or differently, using current know-how. Following this, we turn to the question of the potential for savings from the exploitation of technologies likely to be available in coming decades.

The Magnitude of Potential Efficiency Savings

Many studies and reports are available that estimate the magnitude of potential efficiency savings. Most of them focus on assessing the opportunities for *input savings opportunities* in specific areas of government operations. An example might be a study of opportunities for savings in the procurement of computers. Such a study might point to certain government agencies, or private corporations, which manage to buy their computers for $950 a unit through good procurement practices, whereas the great majority of government agencies pay $1,000 or more for the same computers. From this it is inferred that there is a potential for savings of 5 percent across most of government through the adoption of good procurement practice, and that government as a whole might save, say, $5 million annually by doing this. In addition to studies such as this, that focus on opportunities for purchasing government supplies of goods and services more cheaply, there are similar studies looking for opportunities to save money by reducing the wage bill – by reducing overstaffing, adopting more efficient work practices or avoiding excessive remuneration.

These types of studies – useful as they are – are, unfortunately, of limited value in gauging the potential overall magnitude of efficiency savings across government as a whole. They are simply too narrow in focus, and too incomplete in their coverage, to be tacked together into an overall picture.

There are a handful of studies that take a quite different approach, seeking to estimate efficiency savings either for specific sectors of government operations (health, education, etc.) or for government as a whole. Because these types of studies tend to attract a lot of attention, it is important to understand their methodology and to determine whether the estimates of savings they provide are credible.

A prominent recent example of this type of study is a 2017 report from the McKinsey Global Institute (MGI, 2017). It claimed that governments around the world could make efficiency savings equivalent to a full 9 percent of government expenditure by emulating the world's most efficient governments. The figure of 9 percent does not pertain specifically to advanced economies. But for what it is worth, 9 percent of government expenditure in advanced countries is equivalent on average to around 3.5 percent of GDP (with a range of 2.4-5.1 percent of GDP, depending on the country). Savings this large would go a long way to offsetting prospective spending pressures.

How does McKinsey come up with this estimate? It does so by using a form of what might be called *outcomes cost benchmarking* – using this term to refer to studies that attempt to measure the potential scope for improving productivity by looking at differences in what it costs agencies, sectors or whole governments to achieve outcomes for the community. (Outcomes, by the way, are intended changes brought about by public interventions upon individuals, social structures or the physical environment. Examples are improved air quality, better educated young people, lower crime and improved public safety (Robinson, 2007).)

McKinsey purports to compare the costs of achieving outcomes across different countries. In simplified terms, using the example of health, its reasoning is as follows: The outcome governments are trying to achieve by delivering health services is a healthy population, and their success in achieving this outcome can be measured by "healthy life expectancy" (HLE) – the number of years of life a citizen can expect in good health. Suppose then that two countries – country X and country Y – spend the same amount annually per capita on health services. In country X – the efficient country – HLE is on average 75 years, whereas in country Y it is only 60 years. In McKinsey's reasoning, this gap in outcomes achieved for the same expenditure is a measure of the relative efficiency of the health systems in the two countries and represents what the consultancy calls a *productivity opportunity*. This means that if country Y were to improve the efficiency of its health system, it would be able to do one of two things. The first would be to increase its citizens' average HLE by 25 percent (from 60 to 75), without spending any more money. The second – which is relevant here – is that it could purportedly *reduce spending very substantially while maintaining HLE at its current levels*.

The same reasoning is applied by McKinsey to other areas of government, such as education, where the focus is on educational outcomes (what students learn) relative to education spending, and public safety, where the focus is on outcomes such as homicide rates in relation to spending on the police. It is from this analysis that the overall estimate of potential savings of 9 percent of government expenditure is derived.

There is no point being polite about this. McKinsey's reasoning is nonsense. It is absurd to take, as measures of relative efficiency, differences in the outcomes associated with any given level of public spending. It might be the case that in country Y people eat badly, get little exercise and drink far too much. There might also be in that country a particularly large portion of the population living in poverty and material deprivation, and therefore more prone to ill health. These factors alone might account for much, if not all, of the difference in HLE between the two countries. It could be that the amount and quality of health care delivered by the government is the same in the two countries, and that the difference in health outcomes is *solely* due to such factors outside the healthcare system. To the extent that difference in health outcomes achieved per dollar spent were due to such factors outside the healthcare system, it would make no sense to treat them as a "productivity opportunity."

The general point this highlights is that the outcomes achieved by government services – whether literacy, numeracy, reduced crime, better air quality or whatever – are almost always determined not only by what government does, but also by the impact of *external factors* outside the government's control (Robinson, 2007). Often, the impact of external factors on outcomes achieved is quite large.

McKinsey's disregard for the role of external factors[6] is amateurish and is sufficient to deprive its estimate of potential efficiency savings of any credibility.

Ignoring external factors is not a mistake commonly made in the outcomes cost benchmarking carried out by serious economists, much of which is based on a methodology called *data envelopment analysis* (DEA). Broadly speaking, the idea behind DEA is the same as that of the McKinsey study. However, in DEA analysis, external factors are typically explicitly recognized as an important influence on the outcomes government is able to achieve in areas such as community health, crime rates and education levels.

What does this type of analysis suggest about the magnitude of potential efficiency savings? DEA analysis in 2010 by OECD economists of the relative efficiency of health systems – in this case taking life expectancy at birth as the measure of outcomes – led the Paris-based organization to claim that "by improving the efficiency of the health system, public spending savings... [could be achieved of] almost 2 percent of 2017 GDP on average in the OECD" (OECD, 2010). Another OECD study around the same time looked at the relative efficiency of primary and secondary education in 28 OECD countries (Sutherland, Price and Gonand, 2009). Again, it compared educational outcomes (using, like McKinsey, PISA scores achieved by students in different countries) with expenditure. This latter study claimed that most of the countries concerned could make efficiency savings in the range of 0.2-0.4 percent of GDP by improving the efficiency of their school education systems. Of course, reducing expenditure was not the only option in either of these studies: the other option was to use the efficiency gaps to improve outcomes without increasing spending.

If one were to accept these findings on the potential magnitude of savings as credible, and to extrapolate them to the rest of government expenditure,[7] one might conclude that all or most of the big prospective increases in government expenditure discussed in this book could be offset by determined efforts to radically improve efficiency.

Unfortunately, these estimates of potential efficiency savings are not credible, not because the studies are technically flawed or because their results are uninformative, but because the methodology employed is unsuitable as a guide to the magnitude of potential efficiency savings.

In considering why this is the case, we can put aside – for the moment – the issue of external factors. We can also, again for argument's sake, ignore the fact that DEA analysis is full of short-cuts and approximations, which are unavoidable to make the mathematics work but mean that the precise numerical results should not be taken too seriously.

To see what the more fundamental problems with this type of analysis are, consider the OECD health study. In that study, Switzerland emerged as the country that achieved the best health outcomes per dollar – or, rather, Swiss franc – spent. Ireland was the country with the worst. The magnitude of the estimated efficiency gap between the two countries suggested, according to the study's reasoning about potential savings, that if Ireland changed its health system to make it as efficient as the Swiss system, it would be able to save more than 4 percent of GDP.

Let's take ourselves back to that time and assume that the Irish government knows precisely which concrete measures it could take to raise the efficiency of its health system to the Swiss level. The first big problem it would face is it may be impossible and/or unethical to use many of these measures to reduce expenditure. Imagine that Ireland established that one of the big reasons its health system was lagging behind Switzerland's was that its doctors were in too many cases treating patients using outdated, less effective treatment techniques. For example, although both countries spent the equivalent of €10,000 per patient to treat patients with non-ST segment elevation myocardial infarction – a type of heart attack – Irish doctors were using a treatment that was no longer recognized as best-practice, with the consequence that in Ireland the mortality rate was 40 percent whereas in Switzerland it was 20 percent. This difference in mortality rates would contribute to the measured efficiency gap because it would lower overall Irish life expectancy for any given level of health expenditure. This part of the measured efficiency gap could – and clearly should – be used to dramatically cut Ireland's post-heart attack mortality rate by ensuring that all of its doctors use the new treatment technique to treat all patients. But in the DEA story, this is not the only option. The other option would be to use the efficiency gap to cut spending. Concretely, Ireland could choose to treat 75 percent of patients using the new technique, while refusing treatment to the other 25 percent (all of whom would die as a consequence). If it were to do so, the overall mortality rate for patients suffering this type of heart attack would remain at 40 percent, but spending would be reduced by 25 percent. Same outcome, lower expenditure.

Clearly, no government – and no community of medical practitioners – would make such a choice.

The general point this example illustrates is that it is unreasonable to assume that any efficiency gaps identified by DEA analysis can necessarily be used *either* to reduce spending or to improve outcomes. In many cases, the only real option would be to exploit them to deliver better outcomes to the community. The choice would have to be better outcomes for the same money, rather than the same outcomes for less money.

A second problem is that in practice the Irish government would probably have only a partial and imperfect knowledge of the specific reform measures required to emulate Switzerland and thereby improve its efficiency by the equivalent of 4 percent of GDP. Just copying everything that Switzerland does would make no sense. Health systems are, moreover, so complicated that there is no clear "best practice" in all areas that Ireland could simply follow. There would be no point looking for answers to the DEA analysis. DEA identifies supposed efficiency gaps between countries or agencies but says absolutely nothing about the causes of those gaps. Thus, once Ireland had implemented all the reform measures it was confident were appropriate, there would probably be a substantial residual efficiency gap it would have no idea how to go about closing. Under such circumstances, the notion that the totality of any measured efficiency gap represents a "productivity opportunity" looks dubious. Any productivity gain you know exists but have no idea how to achieve is purely theoretical, with no practical importance. It is a mere will-o'-the-wisp.

Despite having set the issue aside, it must be noted that external factors also remain an issue. Because of the unavoidably crude way in which these are factored into DEA analysis, it not possible to be confident that their impact has been adequately recognized. Ireland could therefore never be entirely sure that at least some part of the supposed efficiency gap with Switzerland was not due to external factors outside the operations of the health system.[8, 9]

All of this means that we have no choice but to dismiss estimates of the magnitude of potential efficiency savings derived from outcomes cost benchmarking studies, even when these are careful DEA studies. The principal value of DEA analysis of this type is not to measure potential efficiency savings but to give a rough indication of the scope that *may* exist for governments to improve the outcomes achieved with given levels of spending. Even here, they need to be treated with great caution. Like the Wizard of Oz, DEA analysis looks superficially impressive, but when one pulls the screen away and sees how the methodology works, one is somewhat less awe-struck.

A possible alternative way of getting an indication of the true scope for efficiency savings is to look at savings achieved by governments via *spending review* processes. Spending reviews are systematic and deliberate searches for opportunities to reduce expenditure, and have been carried out by fiscally stressed governments in many advanced countries over recent decades (Robinson, 2013). Caution is required in interpreting the results achieved by spending reviews because most of them have not confined themselves to searching for efficiency savings but have also devoted much of their effort to identifying opportunities to make cuts by changing policy. One spending review exclusively focused on identifying efficiency savings was, however, that conducted in the United Kingdom in 2004, under the independent leadership of a prominent businessman (Gershon, 2004). It was a particularly thorough review, making the magnitude of the savings achieved of special interest.[10] According to the review itself, the measures it identified – and which the government agreed to implement – were capable of yielding efficiency savings of £21.5 billion annually. We have, however, a more objective estimate of the real value of the efficiency savings, because the British government requested the UK National Audit Office to carry out an *ex post* independent calculation of savings achieved. The NAO's conclusion was that the actual annual efficiency savings delivered were £10.2 billion (NAO, 2007). This is a lot of money, and made the efficiency review an outstanding success. The fact remains, however, that these savings amounted to "only" 0.6 percent of GDP.

Other spending reviews in other countries have, in some cases, yielded significantly larger reductions – of up to several percent of GDP. Examples include spending reviews in Ireland after the GFC and in the Netherlands in 2010 (Robinson, 2013). Without exception, however, spending reviews yielding such relatively large reductions in spending have not – unlike the British review – focused exclusively on identifying efficiency savings. While they have sought to deliver efficiency savings, most of the expenditure reductions they achieved were due to cuts made by eliminating or scaling back services and benefits. Indeed, a clear lesson from international experience with spending reviews is that if a government wishes to make quite large reductions in government expenditure, it has to be prepared to rely *primarily* on policy-driven cuts.

In considering the scope for efficiency savings, we also have to take into account the major efforts that governments in most advanced countries have already made over past decades to achieve such savings. Spending reviews have been part, but only part, of this effort. In many public hospital systems, for example, the efficiency gains achieved have been enormous.[11] The effort put into achieving such savings has been a direct consequence of the intense pressure to which government budgets in most countries have been subjected for decades (see Chapter 1). While it would be absurd to suggest that the efforts made over past decades mean that there are no further efficiency savings to be found in government, it is clear that in most countries a great deal of the fat has already been trimmed.

Claims by political leaders that major spending reductions can be achieved solely or mainly through improved efficiency have been revealed time and time again to be hollow. It is easy to understand why politicians tell this type of fairy story: it enables them to claim that they can cut taxes or finance new spending promises by making large savings which will not cause anyone pain. However soothing this may be, it is not the reality.

Some will say that past efforts to find efficiency savings were insufficiently vigorous, or that they were too constrained by politics. There is nothing as unshakable as the typical 'small government' conservative's belief that all government is grossly inefficient, and that all that is needed to make very large efficiency savings is willpower and the application of private sector know-how. This is, however, an ideological prejudice rather than a position based on evidence or experience. The UK efficiency review referred to above is not the only instance of a government appointing a businessman with a brief to root out inefficiency. Similar exercises have been conducted in many countries over the past century. Ronald Reagan and Margaret Thatcher commissioned such reviews, as did earlier governments in the wake of the Great Depression of the 1930s. The efficiency savings achieved, while sometimes substantial, were never earth-shattering.

Distinguishing between efficiency gains that are theoretically available and those that are practically realizable is also important. In the United States, pharmaceuticals and medical treatments are far more expensive than they should be and more expensive than in other advanced countries (IFHP, 2019). This costs government dearly. In theory, large efficiency savings for Medicare and Medicaid could be realized if decisive action were taken to cut excessive medical practitioners' incomes, force down drug prices and drastically reform the fragmented health system. In practice, however, realizing more than a fraction of savings would be very difficult, both politically and legally. Savings would also take a long time to realize and, in the short term, there would be transitional costs of implementing the reforms that might increase rather than reduce spending. The savings available in practice even to an actively reformist government would therefore be – other than in the quite long term – substantially smaller than suggested by international comparisons of drug and treatment prices.

All of this tells us that we need to be realistic about the scope for efficiency savings. It is indeed essential to vigorously pursue all practical opportunities for delivering government services, and achieving outcomes, at lower cost. It would, however, be a delusion to think that there is a huge "free lunch" of efficiency savings ready and waiting for any government sufficiently determined to sit down and eat it.

Savings Delivered by New Technology

What about the efficiency savings which might be achievable over coming decades through the aggressive use of new technologies? Is it possible that advances in artificial intelligence and other sophisticated information technology may change the whole story, opening the door to dramatic reductions in the cost of delivering government services?

Experience shows that excitement about the potential for savings through the use of new digital technologies by government is well justified. The principal area where such technologies are already being applied is customer transaction services – that is, services where citizens apply for benefits, pay taxes, seek licenses and make other applications capable of being lodged and (in significant measure) processed digitally. Many advanced countries have already made great strides in digitizing such services. Others are lagging. But even in the countries that lead in digital government, there is scope for increasing savings in the delivery of these types of services, both from more citizens choosing to use online services and as a result of the growing sophistication of computerized decision-support systems. Future advances in technology no doubt offer great possibilities for additional savings.

However, in thinking about the potential for technologically driven efficiency savings, it is essential to remember that many of the services delivered by government are intrinsically impossible or very difficult to automate. Take the example of school education, which represents a big part of government expenditure. At school and pre-school level, interaction with human teachers is central to effective learning and socialization. Teachers do not only impart knowledge. They also encourage and provide behavioral guidance. They react to often subtle clues from their students to gauge when they need to clarify and explain matters further. They rely on exclusively human skills to motivate their students. There is correspondingly little scope for automation.

The only possibility of this changing would be the future replacement of human teachers with robotic teachers, learning software or other advanced information technology. But this would be manifestly inappropriate for school-level education. Children and teenagers do not have, in general, sufficient capacity for self-directed learning to be taught exclusively or primarily by machines or software. As discussed in an earlier chapter, it is unrealistic to believe that social robots will be developed in coming decades that will replicate the high-level human interaction required of a successful teacher.

As in the case of long-term care, the role for information technology in school education will continue to be primarily one of helping to improve the quality of education, rather than to reduce its labor input. Concretely, this means teachers making increasing use of technology to support and enrich the learning process. In some areas, such as teaching foreign languages, the scope for the use of technology is larger than in others, but even in such areas it will remain critically important to maintain the hands-on supervision and direction of teachers. In general, the greatest scope for technology-driven efficiency savings in school education is not in the classroom but in school administration and support services, which account for only a small portion of costs.

The same is true of many other types of government services. Consider, for example, policing. Here, new technologies have considerable potential to support police officers in their daily work. Impressive software has, for example, become available to aid detectives in criminal investigations by using algorithms and data mining to identify potential suspects. It is, however, hard to see future developments in such technologies reducing the size of the police workforce. Human contact and an understanding of how human beings think and behave is essential to the job. The problem that police face is that they often have such large caseloads that they have far too little time for most of the individual cases on their desk. What technology can be expected to do is improve the effectiveness of policing – increasing the proportion of cases successfully resolved – rather than cut its human input.

This is true more generally of *human services* – i.e. of the many services government offers that provide individuals or families who face difficulties with counseling, guidance or direction. It is, for example, inconceivable that robots could supplant social workers in the work they do in monitoring, assisting and intervening in dysfunctional families to protect children.

Emerging technologies will nevertheless have an increasing role to play in human services. An indication of the possibilities is the way software is now being used by probation officers in many countries to measure the level of risk of re-offense of ex-prisoners on parole. The availability of a machine-based risk rating helps them make better decisions about whether to revoke parole or whether to relax parole conditions (e.g. by stretching the time between visits to the parole office to two weeks rather than one).[12] Again, the great potential of this type of software lies not in the possibility of replacing human parole officers with computers, but in helping overworked humans do a better job.

It would be wrong, however, to be too pessimistic about the potential for efficiency savings in general. Beyond the area of customer transaction services, exciting possibilities lie in other areas of government expenditure, such as tertiary education. Here, there would seem to be considerable potential for the future replacement of humans by the use of teaching software and other information technology. This has been demonstrated by so-called MOOCs (massive open online courses). In an ideal world, all tertiary students would get the type of individual guidance and personalized intellectual interaction offered by the tutor system that a handful of leading universities maintain.[13] In the real world, very few universities in advanced countries offer undergraduate students much in the way of individual contact with academics. Mass lectures and a few hours of large-group "tutorials" are the norm. Under these circumstances, students would in many cases gain through greater use of off-the-shelf online lectures by top international experts. Other possibilities may emerge for savings and quality improvements through the use of future technologies in the practical dimensions of training of, for example, science and medical students (e.g. virtual reality procedures partially replacing the use of cadavers in surgical training). In those many advanced countries where government pays a large part of the cost of tertiary education, the potential efficiency savings are considerable, despite resistance from some academics (Bowen, 2012).

Despite such possibilities, it would be unrealistic to expect that even the most aggressive implementation of future new technologies could have the effect of reducing government expenditure overall. The reason lies in the Baumol cost disease. As outlined in the chapters on health expenditure, the implication of Baumol's theory is, approximately speaking, that productivity gains in any given sector of the economy can only be expected to lower the cost of the services that sector produces if productivity increases more rapidly there than in the economy as a whole. If this is not the case, then productivity gains in the sector concerned are likely to be swallowed up entirely in wage increases.

Thus, the aggressive application of future technologies will only curb government spending if it leads to productivity increases that are more rapid than in the rest of the economy. The fact that so many government services are like school teaching and human services, in that they are difficult or impossible to automate, seems to make this impossible. These are precisely the types of services Baumol had in mind when he developed his cost disease theory.

It nevertheless remains very important that government actively exploit the new opportunities for automation that newly emerging technologies will offer. Government is, taken as a whole, a labor-intensive operation. The budgetary pressure on government as a result of the need to increase the wages and salaries of government workers in line with community-wide wage movements is enormous. Although automation cannot be expected to reduce government expenditure/GDP, it does offer a crucial means of offsetting, in part, this pressure.

In some advanced countries, governments have "dealt" with wage bill pressures in particularly labor-intensive areas partially by refusing to increase remuneration in line with economy-wide movements. In the United Kingdom and some other countries, for example, nurses' relative pay has fallen behind badly. In countries with government-run university systems, academic pay has in many cases fallen substantially in relative terms. Such squeezes on remuneration do not represent efficiency savings, and they are not a sustainable long-term strategy for dealing with budgetary pressure. Almost inevitably, they lead to pressure building up to the point where it boils over and substantial remuneration catch-ups are unavoidable – because, for example, it becomes increasingly difficult to recruit suitable staff in sufficient numbers.[14]

Concluding Reflections

Exaggerated claims about the scope for efficiency savings in government have been always with us. 'Small government' ideologues have been prominent offenders. So have consulting firms eager to win business through claims that they hold the magic key to unlock vast savings.

The pursuit of greater efficiency in government is a never-ending quest. The opportunities for efficiency savings are very real and are increasing as new technologies emerge. Vigorous efforts to minimize waste therefore can and should play a role in helping governments cope with the huge spending pressures they will face in coming decades. Expectations of what can be achieved should, nevertheless, be kept practical and realistic. No credence should be given to the notion that there are potential efficiency savings waiting to be exploited that are large enough to offset all or most of the big increases in expenditure on health, long-term care, climate change and infrastructure that will face governments over the coming decades.

10. BIGGER GOVERNMENT

After the massive tide of temporary government spending in response to the coronavirus pandemic recedes, it will become progressively clearer that governments in advanced nations face an enormous longer-term fiscal challenge. The large prospective increases in spending on health, long-term care, climate change and infrastructure outlined in this book will, other things unchanged, result in government getting much bigger. The only means of curbing a large part of this growth in expenditure will be large *compensatory spending cuts* – in other words, measures that reduce spending by scaling back or eliminating services and benefits the state provides. As noted in the last chapter, efficiency savings – although useful – are unlikely to be sufficiently large to make a big difference to the trend.

In this concluding chapter, we discuss the constraints governments will face in responding to this challenge. The analysis points to three overarching conclusions.

First, the longer-term pressure to make significant compensatory cuts will be very intense. Unless governments have recourse to large *permanent* budget deficits and money creation – with all the damage that would cause over the long term – the price to be paid for avoiding any compensatory spending cuts would be near-exclusive reliance on tax increases. This would be politically difficult, particularly in countries where tax levels are already high.

Second, it is extremely unlikely that compensatory spending cuts will, in any country, be of a sufficient magnitude to wholly offset the long-term upward spending pressures. There are simply too few options for making such cuts without inflicting severe damage and provoking massive political resistance. Government will therefore get bigger everywhere.

The third conclusion follows directly from this – one can forget smaller government. Downsizing the state is not a practical objective in advanced capitalist economies. The point here is not merely that a crisis such as that triggered by the coronavirus pandemic is no time to be rolling back the state. It is that in the longer term, even in the absence of economic crises, the forces pushing government spending up are so powerful as to make the goal of smaller government a pipe dream.

The Scope for Compensatory Expenditure Cuts

In most areas of government, the scope for substantial compensatory expenditure cuts is today limited, in the concrete sense that the imposition of large cuts would inflict great damage. Many governments have been vigorously pruning spending for years or even decades. They have been doing so principally to offset the huge pressure on their budgets of rising health expenditure and pension spending. In many areas, spending has already been cut to the bone. The chronic underfunding of infrastructure in many countries is a case in point.

Defense provides another illustration. Over the past two decades, military spending has been cut very considerably almost everywhere, as shown in Figure 10.1.[1]

Further defense cuts are, in most countries, virtually inconceivable given today's increasingly challenging security environment. In Germany, for example, the armed forces are in a parlous state. Much of their equipment, including transport aircraft and submarines, is out of action because of inadequate maintenance. Soldiers are poorly trained and many positions are vacant (Chazan, 2020; Deutscher Bundestag, 2019; Buck, 2018).

Anyone who thinks Germany is an unrepresentative case might like to consider France. The land of Voltaire spends the most on defense among all European Union members and is the only one that – since the departure of the United Kingdom – can be considered to be a serious military power. There is nevertheless an almost universal recognition in France

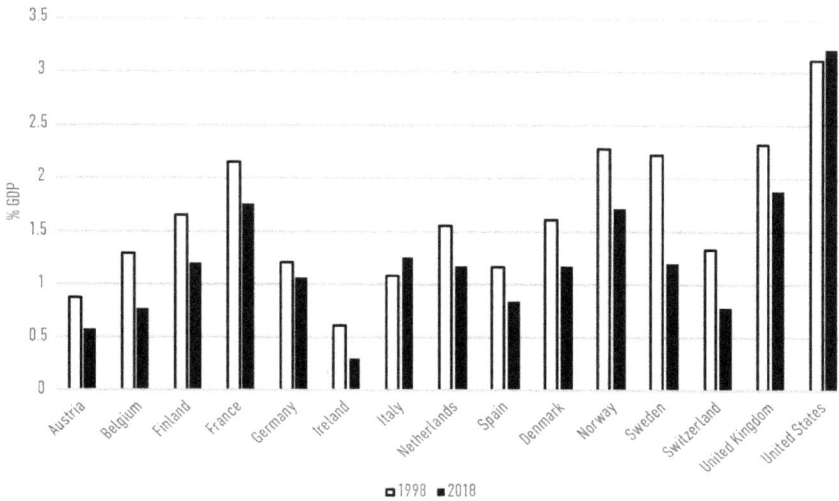

Source: IMF Data, GFS, Expenditure by Functions of Government

Figure 10.1
Defense Expenditure/GDP: Selected Advanced Countries (1998 vs 2018)

that current levels of military expenditure are seriously inadequate, particularly given the frequent domestic deployment of the military in the face of terrorist threats and the scale of engagements abroad (mainly in Africa). Pressure on the French military is so severe that it triggered a head-on confrontation in 2017 between the Armed Forces and the newly elected President, Emmanuel Macron, following the new government's imposition of further budget cuts. These cuts proved to be the straw that broke the camel's back. In an unprecedented reaction, the country's then military chief, General Pierre de Villiers, told parliamentarians that "I won't be screwed over like that" and bluntly set out the profound damage that had been inflicted over the years to the country's defense capability. The general was sacked (but the pressure on the defense budget has since eased a little).

This problem is in no sense confined to Europe. Japan[2] spends less on defense than Germany (0.9 percent of GPD in 2017). Yet the country faces a security environment even more challenging than that in Europe.

Education, an area where governments spend a lot more than on defense, also illustrates the pressure on public spending over recent decades. Despite the pivotal role of education in ensuring that citizens have the right skills to find a place in the new economy, a majority of advanced countries have reduced spending appreciably as a proportion of GDP over the past decades (Figure 10.2). In this labor-intensive sector, further large spending reductions would require measures such as cuts in teacher pay or increases in class sizes that would have a marked negative impact on the quality of public education. The poor quality of schools in the United States and Israel,[3] both of which pay teachers *much* less than other advanced countries (OECD, 2019d), highlights the risks.

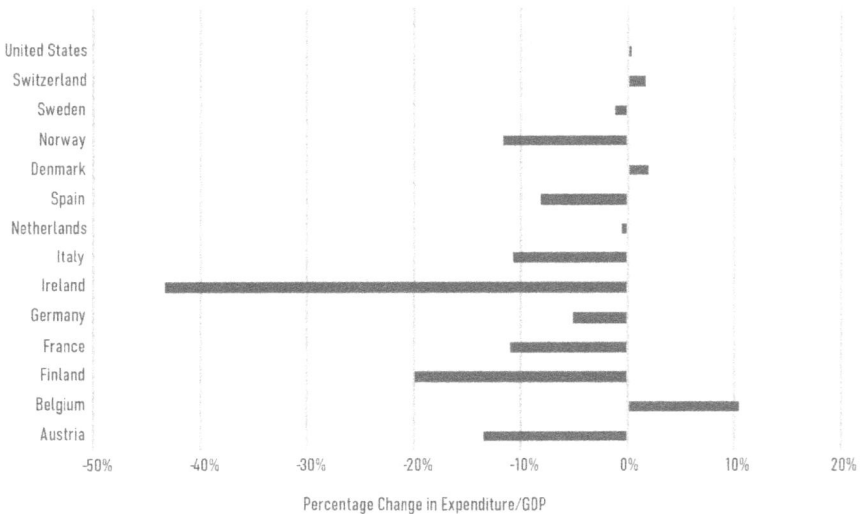

Figure 10.2
Change in Education Expenditure: Selected Advanced Countries (1995-2018)[4]
Percentage Change in Education Expenditure/GDP

At a time when the full force of the coronavirus pandemic is being felt, any notion of making cuts to health expenditure would seem particularly absurd. But setting aside temporary pandemic-related spending, a key message of this book is that large compensatory spending cuts could only be achieved by backing away from the principle of universal health coverage (or, in the American context, substantially reducing access to Medicare and Medicaid). It is wishful thinking to imagine there is some magic wand that might be waved to painlessly reduce spending – to believe, for example, former US Republican congressional leader Paul Ryan's claim that more "choice and competition" would do the job. The scope for compensatory health spending cuts is further constrained because public health systems have in many countries been under severe financial strain for years (the examples of France, Denmark and the United Kingdom were highlighted in Chapter 1). The fragile financial position of public hospitals is, as mentioned in Chapter 3, one of the reasons why many were so poorly equipped to respond to the coronavirus pandemic.

There are, in fact, only a very few areas of government spending outside health and social protection that have not experienced major cuts in most countries. One of these few is the *environment* (Figure S10.1, statistical annex), where the magnitude of the climate change crisis means that there is no possibility of making compensatory spending cuts. The other is *public order and safety* (Figure S10.2, statistical annex), which covers mainly policing, the courts, prisons, and fire and emergency services. Here the story is the same: given the scale of contemporary challenges such as climate-related natural disasters and terrorism, it is difficult to see how spending could be cut much. In any event, neither of these areas account, in most countries, for expenditure exceeding 1-2 percent of GDP.

The biggest question mark about the scope for future compensatory spending cuts lies in the area of social protection. As mentioned in Chapter 1, spending in this area has not escaped unscathed from the cuts of recent decades. In almost all advanced countries, eligibility conditions have been tightened and payments reduced for many welfare benefits. The only reason why there has been no general trend of decline in total social protection expenditure as a proportion of GDP has been the impact of demographic aging on pension spending. However, notwithstanding this history of retrenchment, it cannot be said that the scope for cuts to social protection expenditure has been exhausted across the advanced world as a whole. What happens in future in this sensitive area is likely to vary considerably between countries.

The United States

What is the scope for compensatory expenditure cuts in the United States? The political right in that country fervently believes that there is enormous

potential to slash "big government." This is, at least on the surface, remarkable given that American government spends and taxes considerably less
than in most other advanced nations (see Figure 10.3 and Chapter 1).
There is, however, no mystery about where the potential for big cuts supposedly lies: right-wing politicians and pundits are very clear in
nominating welfare as the target.

The American left is, by its very nature, not focused on cutting public
expenditure. Nevertheless, it also firmly believes that there is scope for
big cuts to government expenditure – specifically, to defense spending.
Examining the potential for cuts to welfare and defense is therefore a good
way to assess the true scope for using compensatory expenditure cuts in
the United States to offset the long-term expenditure pressures identified
in this book.

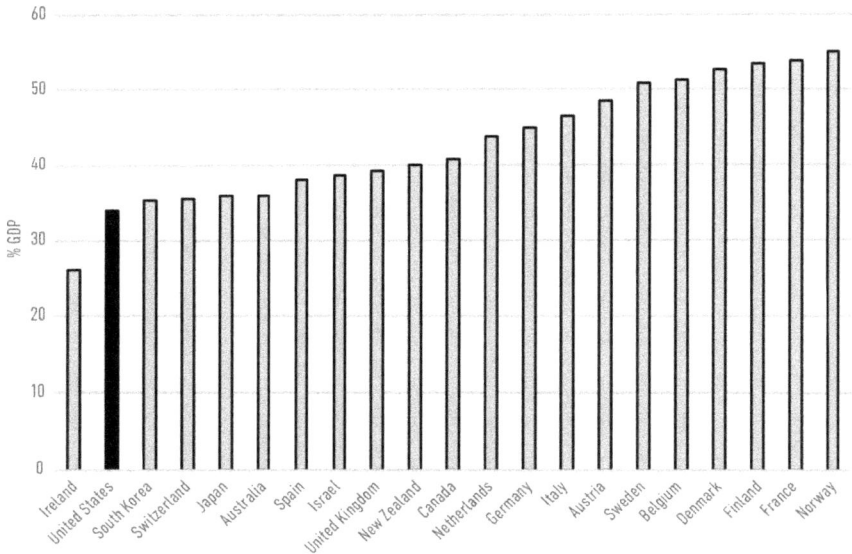

Source: OECD.Stat

Figure 10.3
Revenue/GDP: USA vs Other Advanced Nations (2017)

Cutting Welfare in America?

In considering the scope for welfare cuts, the starting point must be a
recognition that the American welfare system is extremely ungenerous.

It is a system that leaves very large numbers of people, including many children, in poverty – often *extreme* poverty. For example, the main welfare program intended to provide poor families with cash (TANF) not only provides benefits that are too low to lift most recipients out of poverty, but covers fewer than one-quarter of poor families.[5] For long-term unemployed working-age adults without children, welfare is virtually nonexistent and extreme poverty and homelessness are commonplace.[6] In a number of US cities, Brazilian-style *favelas* – shanty towns for the down-and-out – have sprung up in recent years.

The ungenerous nature of the system is reflected in the low level of welfare spending relative to most other advanced countries. Social protection expenditure – which in the international statistical classification covers welfare benefits, but not health services provided to the disadvantaged – amounts in the United States to a little under 8 percent of GDP.[7] In most continental European countries, it is more than 20 percent of GDP. In Japan and the United Kingdom, it is twice or more the American level.

In most other advanced countries, with their systems of universal health coverage, expenditure on medical services for poor people is simply part of the overall health budget. In the United States, however, there is a targeted program – Medicaid – which provides health services to poor people. Income thresholds for Medicaid eligibility have, however, histori-cally been so low that a large portion of poor people miss out. This is still the case, notwithstanding President Obama's noble efforts to address this problem through his Affordable Care Act (Garfield, Orgera and Damico, 2020).[8] The large number of uninsured people is not only a moral problem. It is also a very practical problem for society as a whole and contributed greatly to the difficulties of controlling the spread of the coronavirus during 2020.[9] Medicaid cost US governments 2.9 percent of GDP ($598 billion) in 2018.[10]

The expenditure figures alone make it clear that to make welfare cuts to offset some substantial portion of the prospective expenditure increases of more than 7 percent of GDP discussed in this book would require taking a sledgehammer to the shoddy structure of American welfare.

Despite the gross inadequacy of its social safety net, the United States is unusual in having extremely vocal and powerful forces working actively to bring about major cuts to welfare spending, under the banner of "welfare reform." These forces, which draw on the Heritage Foundation and other conservative think tanks for their intellectual muscle, long ago captured the Republican Party. They have consistently laid the blame for the country's chronic budget deficits at the door of welfare expenditure, asserting that their version of reform is essential to restoring sound public finances. Motivated by this type of thinking, the Trump administration initiated a new wave of so-called welfare reform that, as the United Nations special rapporteur on extreme poverty and human rights put it, "essentially shreds crucial dimensions of a safety net that is already full of holes" (Alston, 2017).

There is, of course, no difficulty cutting several percentage points of GDP – or more – off welfare expenditure if one has little or no regard for the suffering inflicted on poor people. In the case of certain of the cuts advocated by the most extreme anti-welfare Republicans, the destructive impact on the poor is so obvious that there is little point wasting time demonstrating it. The proposition that there should be a time limit, or a lifetime dollar limit, on Medicaid benefits is a case in point.

The main thrust of the welfare reformers' argument is, however, that it is possible to make large reductions in welfare spending without making the poor – or at least the "deserving" poor – suffer. A feeling for how far this is actually true can be obtained by looking at the principal policy measure advocated by the reformers, which is the imposition of *work requirements* as a precondition for welfare. The term "work requirements" is shorthand for rules making non-disabled working age adults (subject to limited exemptions) ineligible for welfare benefits unless they undertake a certain minimum number of hours of work or, alternatively, engage in appropriate training or volunteering. The welfare reformers have always asserted that imposing work requirements is in the best interests of the poor themselves because it gives the able-bodied among them a strong incentive to leave welfare and move to employment and self-reliance. There is nothing inherently implausible about this proposition. It is, in fact, one that the

Democrats endorsed when President Clinton signed the 1996 Personal Responsibility and Work Opportunity Reconciliation Act, which imposed work requirements on poor families receiving cash benefits under TANF.

Ever since the 1996 legislation, the welfare reformers have urged that work requirements be extended to other major programs providing non-cash benefits – specifically, to SNAP (food stamps), rental housing assistance and perhaps also Medicaid (CEA, 2018). In Congress, the most vigorous advocates of the extension of work requirements are the self-styled "Freedom Caucus" of House Republicans, who are on record as claiming that work requirements are a means of "saving money without hurting anyone" (Golshan, 2017). This group achieved a major success in 2018 when steps were taken by the Trump administration to allow state governments to introduce work requirements as a precondition for Medicaid enrollment.

The proposition that extending work requirements to welfare benefits hurts no-one is controversial (Bolen, 2016; Schott, Bolen and Fischer, 2017; Schram, Fording and Soss, 2018). The imposition of work requirements on access to medical care under Medicaid is *especially* controversial. Many view the latter proposal as morally repugnant (Katch, Wagner and Aron-Dine, 2018). The American Academy of Family Physicians considers that it would create "unacceptable barriers to care" (AAFP, 2019).

But how much could spending be reduced by the imposition of work requirements? The short answer is "not much." The slightly longer answer is that expenditure reductions would be quite small so long as work requirements were applied exactly as they are supposedly intended to be applied – in other words, as long as they excluded from benefits only those who failed the work requirement or who did not fall into certain limited exemption categories. To be specific, reductions in spending on the two big social protection programs (SNAP and rental housing assistance) would very probably be less than 0.1 percent of GDP. As for Medicaid, even on the most wildly optimistic assumptions, the maximum conceivable reduction to expenditure would be 0.4 percent of GDP (see Appendix 10.1). In practice, it would almost certainly be much less than this. Estimates by Goldman et al (2018) suggest a reduction in expenditure of only approximately 0.02 percent of GDP. Even the Heritage Foundation's leading subject-matter expert has expressed doubt that Medicaid expenditure would be significantly reduced (Rector, 2017).[11]

This book is not the place for a comprehensive review of the potential for expenditure reductions across all American welfare programs. However, the fact that the welfare reformers' claims about the potential for vast savings fail to pass muster even in respect to their flagship policy proposal underlines just how hard it is to cut meager US welfare spending significantly without causing great additional suffering.[12]

Cutting US Defense Expenditure?

It is easy to understand why many Americans want to see military spending cut. They are fed up with endless wars in remote places such as Afghanistan, and do not see why American taxpayers should bear the cost of their country's role as "policeman of the world."

Cuts to defense expenditure could well make an important contribution to funding the future spending increases identified in this book. However, the potential scale of this contribution should not be exaggerated. American military expenditure may be – with the exception of Israel – by far the highest in the advanced world, but it still "only" accounts for 3 percent of GDP. (Israel spends over 5 percent of GDP on defense but is quite obviously not going to cut spending anytime soon.) It is unclear precisely how much of this 3 percent might realistically be cut. Some indication may be provided by estimates suggesting that the average annual cost of America's post 9/11 wars has been $171 billion, equivalent to 0.8 percent of GDP (Crawford, 2019).[13] Apart from the direct costs of conducting expensive wars, a former senior defense official has recently estimated that the Defense Department could, after some upfront investment, reduce annual expenditure by $20-$30 billion (Hicks, 2020).

There are, nevertheless, major limits to how far any cuts might go. As clichéd as it may sound, America remains the protector of the free world. This role remains crucial in the current international security environment. Moreover, if our focus is on defense expenditure across the advanced world as a whole, it needs to be borne in mind that it is only because of America's high level of military expenditure that so many of its allies have been able to get away with severe under-spending. If America were to shift to an isolationist policy, the pressure on its allies to sharply boost defense spending would become irresistible.

Looking beyond welfare and defense, it would be easy to sketch a more comprehensive picture of the current American public sector by looking at the state of public schools, reminding ourselves of the severity of the country's infrastructure deficit, or examining the many other areas where American governments seriously underperform in delivering services to their citizens. None of this is, however, necessary, to see that in the low-tax, low-spending United States, the scope for compensatory spending cuts – other than those that would inflict enormous social damage – is quite limited. Faced with this stark reality, it is difficult to see how even the United States, notwithstanding its deep-rooted tradition of hostility to the state, can avoid a future of much bigger government – including significantly higher taxes.

The prominent economist John B. Taylor – president of what is perhaps the most famous international pro-small government intellectual association, the Mont Pèlerin Society – has proposed that the United States pursue a strategy of shaving government expenditure by 0.1 percent of GDP every year over the long term, to gradually reduce government expenditure/GDP and restore budgetary balance (Taylor, 2020). Taylor appears to think that such a gradual shrinking of government would be relatively painless. This is, however, a view that is only possible to take if one avoids thinking about specifically where the cuts are to be made, and if one has failed to grasp the strength of the external forces and pressure points at work to push expenditure up.

Libertarians who favor minimalist government are entitled to their ideological preferences. They are, however, deluding themselves if they believe that there is any realistic political route – whether gradual or more rapid and dramatic – by which a substantial downsizing of the modern state might be achieved in the years to come.

Raising Taxes?

The pressure to raise taxes will be considerable everywhere – not only in the United States. But one widespread illusion must be avoided – namely, the notion that all or most of the extra revenue required to finance large prospective increases in government expenditure can be raised by taxing the rich and big corporations.

Higher taxes on the rich may be a good idea, and might in many (or even most) advanced countries make a useful contribution to the financing task. Some increases in company taxes, particularly through strengthened anti-avoidance measures, would also help. However, if additional spending of the size discussed in this book were to be financed, the great majority of taxpayers would need to pay more tax – *considerably* more tax. This becomes clear when one examines the revenue potential of the specific measures for raising more revenue from the rich and corporations proposed by economists and left-wing politicians in recent years (see Appendix 10.2).

During the 2019 British national elections, the country's Labour Party – control of which was seized some years ago by Marxists and other radical socialists – proposed a package of tax measures it asserted would raise the equivalent of 3.5 percent of GDP from the rich without touching the rest of the population (Labour Party, 2019). When subjected to serious independent analysis, however, this estimate turned out to be seriously exaggerated.[14] Exactly how much Labour's tax package would have raised is unclear, but it would certainly have been considerably less than claimed. In commenting on Labour's tax package, the director of the UK's respected Institute for Fiscal Studies observed that "if you want to transform the scale and scope of the state then you need to be clear that the tax increases required to do that will need to be widely shared rather than pretending that everything can be paid for by companies and the rich."[15] This holds even more with respect to the larger long-term spending increases discussed in this book.

To raise sufficient ongoing revenue to finance large increases in spending, all advanced countries would need to become much more like the Scandinavian nations. In those countries – and several other European countries including Belgium and the Netherlands – top marginal tax rates on personal income are somewhat higher than elsewhere, at levels typically between 50 and 60 percent of income. Much more important, however, is the fact that top marginal rates kick in at a *much* lower level of income than elsewhere – concretely, at less than twice average earnings. Higher marginal rates on personal income tax are, in other words, less relevant than the fact that *average* rates of personal income tax are high. Added to this, governments in these countries also raise a large part of their revenue from value-added taxes and social security contributions, both of which are more or less flat. Basically, most people pay a lot more tax than in countries like the United States and Australia.

In advanced countries where the overall tax burden is relatively low, there would be no technical problem in modifying tax systems to raise a lot more revenue. In the United States, for example, the implementation of a value-added tax – which exists in every other advanced country – would be one of the most obvious steps (Gale, 2020). Claims by conservative pundits that significant increases in the overall tax burden would have ruinous consequences for incentives and economic activity are groundless. If they were true, Denmark would be like Romania, whereas it is in fact a robust, high-income modern economy.

Box 10.1 Compulsory Insurance Instead of Taxes?

It might be thought that an alternative to higher taxes is greater reliance on compulsory private insurance. For example, instead of raising taxes to pay for higher health expenditure, nations could shift partly or wholly to the approach of Switzerland and the Netherlands, where people pay compulsory health insurance premiums to highly regulated non-government insurers (i.e. the law requires them to be insured). The same approach could, as mentioned in Chapter 4, be used in part to fund long-term care, particularly for those facing the catastrophic scenario of dementia or other severe disability. It is, however, not clear that the politics of compulsory private insurance are any less difficult for governments than those of taxes. Swiss governments, which regulate the cost and coverage of health insurance, face ongoing major voter pressure about rising premiums. Many citizens appear to consider that government has the ability and duty to prevent premiums from constantly increasing. In light of this, it seems reasonable to assume that there is little tangible difference, in political terms, between taxes, compulsory public insurance contributions and compulsory private insurance payments. Compulsory insurance is in this respect different from compulsory contributions to personal retirement accounts (so-called second-pillar pension funding), which provokes less resistance because those obliged to pay accumulate assets that unambiguously belong to them.

The High-Tax Welfare States

At the opposite end of the spectrum from the United States are the advanced European nations with the most generous welfare systems. These can be expected to experience particularly strong pressure to make large compensatory expenditure cuts, especially to social protection. The reason is simple: these countries already have very high levels of taxation, making it difficult politically to raise taxes on the general population further.

The example of France is particularly telling. Tax levels there are the second highest in the advanced world and increased by almost 4 percent of GDP over the decade 2007-2016.[16] Voter resentment at this boiled over under the presidency of François Hollande (2012-2017).[17] Understanding how sensitive the politics of taxes had become, the government of President Macron moved quickly, after coming to office in 2017, to implement several measures to reduce the tax burden. The measures were, however, modest because of France's difficult fiscal situation and the pressure to comply with European Union fiscal rules. The modesty of these tax measures – combined with a pre-programmed increase in the carbon tax – played an important part in the violent explosion of the *gilets jaunes* movement in late 2018. The government heard the message, moving swiftly to announce significant general income tax cuts. Prime Minister Edouard Philippe declared that "we have received loud and clear the message of exasperation about taxes." The government, he told his fellow citizens, recognized that "we must reduce taxes and reduce them more rapidly." With particular reference to carbon taxes, Philippe added that it was clear that the French "want an end to taxes which tell them what to do."[18]

Even French economist Thomas Piketty has argued that, in the French context, the imposition of higher taxes on the rich should not lead to increased overall severity of taxes, but should be exclusively redistributive.[19] In other words, whatever extra revenue might be raised by increasing taxes on the rich should, in his view, be used to reduce taxes on the rest of the population.

Perhaps, however, the French are special? Significant international differences exist in the willingness of citizens to accept high taxes. Social scientists have shown that these reflect differences in levels of social trust. Scandinavians, for example, are willing to bear a high tax burden because trust and social solidarity are very high (e.g. Kleven, 2014) – and also because they feel they get a range of excellent services from the state (Wiking, 2016). France, by contrast, is characterized by an unfortunate combination of very high taxes and relatively low levels of social trust (Algan et al, 2019).

The supposed delight that Scandinavians take in paying high taxes leads to newspaper articles in the English-speaking world with titles such as "Please sir, may I pay more taxes?" The impression is given that popular support for an expansive welfare state is so strong in the Nordic countries that there is an uncomplaining acceptance of whatever levels of tax are needed to pay for it. If this is the case, then perhaps the Scandinavians at least will prove willing to accept the large tax increases required over the coming decades to finance continually improving health services, better long-term care, effective action against global warming and other worthwhile benefits?

This is far from clear. Political resistance to tax increases is alive and well even in Scandinavia. It is a key reason why tax levels, while high, are in Sweden and Finland today appreciably lower than they were at their peak several decades ago – in Sweden's case, by more than 6 percent of GDP.[20] In Denmark also, taxes are lower today than in the past, even if the reduction in tax levels is more recent and less marked.[21]

Scandinavians have, moreover, proved entirely willing to swallow cuts to social protection expenditure. Most categories of benefit – including state old-age pensions, unemployment benefits, sickness benefits, child care benefits and student allowances – have been significantly reduced over past decades in Sweden, Denmark and Finland.[22] In Sweden and Finland, these cuts started in the 1990s, in the wake of major economic crises (Hauptmeier, Heipertz and Schuknecht, 2006). The progressive scaling back of social protection has, however, been a continuing feature of public policy in all three of these countries up to present times. Since the turn of the millennium, Denmark has, among other things, cut unemployment benefits, reduced sickness benefits and strengthened associated return-to-work mechanisms (Slavina, Bouget and Vanhercke, 2016). Following Sweden, it has also substantially raised the age of access to the state old-age pension and put in place a mechanism whereby it will in future automatically rise in line with life expectancy. In Finland, further across-the-board cuts were made to social protection under the center-right government of 2015-2019. These included German-style reforms to unemployment benefits, which place considerable pressure on the long-term unemployed to accept short-term jobs and to more actively seek work. Measures taken in recent times in Sweden were mentioned in Chapter 1. In all three countries, total government expenditure/GDP is appreciably lower than in the mid-1990s as a result of cuts in welfare and other areas of government expenditure.

The welfare cuts in Scandinavia are part of a broad trend in almost all the high-tax European welfare states over recent decades (Palier, 2010; Delsen, 2012). Crucially, there is no reason to believe that this trend has exhausted itself. To the contrary, the pressure on social protection expenditure seems certain to intensify. Social protection will, in all likelihood, remain the primary target for governments keen to moderate tax increases.

One reason is that, notwithstanding all the cuts, social protection benefits remain, in many countries, quite generous. Most advanced European countries still pay unemployment benefits at a rate of two-thirds or more of prior earnings for the initial period of unemployment, which – depending on how long someone has been in the workforce – may run to 15 months or more (Asenjo and Pignatti, 2019). (In the Netherlands, for example, unemployment benefits may be paid at 70 percent of prior earnings (to a maximum of €219 per working day) for up to 38 months.) Similarly, high benefits are paid for long periods under many government-financed sickness benefits and parental benefits systems (Spasova, Bouget and Vanhercke, 2016).[23] In a number of countries, students are paid substantial living allowances irrespective of the means of their parents. Childcare is widely subsidized and, in a few countries, provided free.

While cutting welfare benefits is rarely politically easy, it seems clear that most governments find it less electorally damaging than wringing further money out of other hard-pressed areas, or than refusing periodic increases of funding for health services to meet costs arising from the continually expanding "capabilities of medicine."

In certain countries, a further factor that will contribute to future cuts is the stress placed on welfare systems by large numbers of low-skilled immigrants, many of whom remain dependent on basic social benefits for long periods.[24] This pressure has already led countries including Austria and Denmark to reduce basic benefits, either across the board or for non-EU citizens who do not meet language or other tests.

A New Era of Unsustainable Deficits?

The high-tax welfare states and the United States represent two ends of a spectrum, with other advanced countries mostly lying somewhere in between. Given the diversity of national circumstances, it is to be expected that there will be considerable variation in the responses of individual nations to the fiscal challenge of the coming decades. Some may move more aggressively than others to make compensatory expenditure cuts. Others may rely mainly on tax increases.

Looming over this is, however, a big danger. Faced with intense budgetary pressure, it will be all too easy for some advanced countries to choose – not for the first time – the path of fiscal irresponsibility. The temptation will be enormous to use budget deficits (and, in some cases, money creation) to avoid tax increases and compensatory expenditure cuts. Such imprudence would, as we have seen, lead ultimately to debt crises and/or accelerating inflation and Argentinian-style economic crisis. Although low interest rates have in recent years saved the advanced world from the consequences of earlier profligacy, even continued low rates would not save it under these circumstances. The chickens would eventually come home to roost.

The coronavirus pandemic has greatly increased this risk. Almost everyone agrees on the appropriateness of aggressive fiscal and monetary stimulus under such special conditions. Governments are spending "whatever it costs" and concerns about deficits and debt have been, quite appropriately, thrown to the wind for the time being. It will, however, be essential that, once the pandemic-induced recession is over, budget deficits are brought gradually back under control. This may not, however, be easy because of the influence of those who see the crisis response as providing a template for a future fiscal policy in which concern about fiscal sustainability is treated with contempt as a neoliberal obsession.

❖ ❖ ❖

In the long run, government is, in all advanced countries, destined to become significantly bigger. Individual countries will have some scope to determine how much bigger, but only within limits. Accepting this reality is essential if we are to work out how best to cope with the political and economic stresses of the coming era.

Appendix 10.1: Expenditure Reductions from the Extension of Work Requirements in the US

Of the three areas of spending that are the main targets of proposals for the extension of work requirements – SNAP, rental housing assistance and Medicaid – Medicaid is by far the biggest ticket item. The main text suggests that 0.4 percent of GDP would be an extremely optimistic estimate of potential Medicaid expenditure reductions from the imposition of a work requirement. This Appendix explains the basis of this estimate and then briefly considers potential expenditure reductions in SNAP and rental housing assistance.

In a 2018 report advocating the extension of work requirements to these three programs (CEA, 2018), the President's Council of Economic Advisors reported survey data indicating that 61 percent of adults enrolled in the Medicaid program were both working age and non-disabled – this being the target group of the work requirements. This 61 percent is equivalent to approximately one-third of Medicaid enrollees (many of whom are children, elderly or disabled). The question, however, is what portion of these non-disabled working-age adults could potentially be removed from Medicaid via a work requirement. Light is shed on this by a breakdown of the Medicaid population presented in Goldman et al (2018), which indicates that the population of non-disabled working-age adults was (in 2015) constituted as follows:

◆ Those who state they are seeking a job (3 percent of Medicaid enrollees, accounting for 1 percent of total Medicaid expenditure);
◆ Caregivers of a disabled person (11.9 percent of enrollees, 1.6 percent of expenditure);
◆ Parent/caregivers of a child under the age of six and pregnant women (6.4 percent of enrollees, 3.9 percent of expenditure);
◆ Full-time students (2.7 percent of enrollees, 1.8 percent of expenditure);
◆ Those who have engaged in some employment at some stage during the past survey year (7.2 percent of enrollees, 8.7 percent of expenditure).[25]

This suggests that if *all* these people were excluded from Medicaid, expenditure would be reduced by approximately 17 percent. However, the reform proposals which have been put forward do not usually envisage the exclusion of full-time students, because it is accepted that any work requirement should be designed to encourage training and education for future employment. It is also extremely difficult to see those who are caregivers of disabled persons being excluded from coverage. Once these two groups are counted out, the maximum potential reduction in Medicaid expenditure would be 13.6 percent (pertaining to 16.6 percent of enrollees), which on 2018 figures would be $81.3 billion, equivalent to 0.4 percent of GDP.

There are, however, several reasons why this should be seen as an extremely optimistic estimate. The first is that – as the leading subject-matter expert at the Heritage Foundation, Robert Rector, has pointed out (Rector, 2017) – many of those who would be denied Medicaid coverage would, when they need treatment, simply turn up at hospitals. Were they to do so, they would not be denied treatment, and much of the cost would end up being borne by the federal government (which already provides financial assistance to hospitals with large numbers of patients who cannot pay for their care).

The second reason why the figure of 0.4 percent of GDP should be seen as optimistic is that expenditure would only be reduced by this much if there was *no exemption at all* for parents and other caregivers who are looking after children at home. This is quite a large group of people. The CEA report is quite explicit in acknowledging the sensitivity of the magnitude of expenditure reductions to policy on the entitlements of parents who are caring for children. The CEA's (quite reasonable) argument for applying the work requirement to many in this group is that significant numbers of employed working-age adults have children in the same age brackets as welfare beneficiaries who are, by virtue of their parental responsibilities, exempted from work requirements. The CEA also points out that TANF already has quite tough requirements for parents. However, even were we to accept these arguments, it is clear that even a tough work requirement would exempt at least some of this group – if only those with young infants (e.g. less than one year of age).

The third reason concerns the category of people who declare themselves to be seeking a job. Work requirement advocates normally favor a limited-time exemption for such people.

Goldman et al (2018) produce estimates that imply much lower potential expenditure reductions from the imposition of a work requirement for Medicaid access. They estimate that only about 2.8 percent of Medicaid enrollees, accounting for about 0.7 percent of expenditure, would potentially be disqualified. Applied to 2018 spending levels, this suggests expenditure reductions of $4.1 billion, equivalent to 0.02 percent of GDP. The difference between this and the 0.4 percent of GDP estimate arises from the fact that Goldman et al assume that exemptions would be broad and would, for example, exclude all parents with children under the age of six.

What about potential expenditure reductions from the extension of work requirements to SNAP and housing rental assistance? In 2018, expenditure on SNAP was $68 billion and federal government expenditure on rental housing assistance was $49 billion.[26] Given the *relatively* small expenditure involved, it is not worth undertaking the same detailed analysis of the client population as for Medicaid. However, if it is assumed that the same percentage of beneficiaries would be removed as is assumed in the Medicaid estimates above – i.e. 16.6 percent – the ceiling on potential expenditure reductions would be $11.3 billion for SNAP and $8.1 billion for rental housing assistance. This figure for SNAP is quite close to the potential savings of approximately $10 billion claimed by Heritage Foundation experts (Sheffield, 2016; Rector, 2017).) These amounts, while large in absolute terms, represent only a little less than 0.1 percent of GDP.

Appendix 10.2: The Revenue Potential of Higher Taxes on Companies and the Rich

The likelihood of stiff political resistance to large broad-based tax increases and the contemporary preoccupation with the issue of rising inequality both point to a key question: *would it be possible to obtain all, or most, of the required additional revenue by taxing the rich, or by taxing companies, while leaving the vast majority of taxpayers unscathed?*

Persuasive equity arguments can be made for taxing the rich more heavily. One is that, when all taxes are taken into account, tax systems in advanced countries are on the whole regressive at the top of the income and wealth distributions (Atkinson, 2015; Piketty, 2013). The rich, in other words, generally pay less in proportionate terms than the great majority of the population. Another argument is that personal income taxes are now appreciably less progressive than they were 40 years ago (Gerber et al, 2018).

The main proposals for increasing taxes paid by the rich are higher top marginal personal income tax rates, heavier taxation of capital income and capital gains, tougher tax compliance measures, the closure of tax loopholes exploited mainly by the rich, and heavier taxation of wealth.

How much money might be raised in these ways? An indication of their revenue potential in the United States is given by a set of carefully crafted proposals targeted principally at the top 1 percent of the income distribution put forward by former Treasury Secretary Lawrence Summers and colleagues (Sarin, Summers and Kupferberg, 2020). They estimated their proposals would raise 2 percent of GPD annually, arguing that this represents "as much as is politically feasible to raise from increasing taxes on the top 1 percent of the

income distribution." (Their package does not include an annual wealth tax –
see below.)

Sarin, Summers and Kupferberg's position might be labeled as moderate left.
A good idea of what the "hard" left think could be raised by soaking the rich can
be gleaned from the 2019 election manifesto of the British Labour Party, referred
to in the main text. As noted, Labour claims of a potential revenue yield of 3.5
percent of GDP did not hold up to independent expert scrutiny. Labour also
relied on the half-truth that taxing companies is equivalent to taxing the rich.
(We return to the question of company taxes below.)

Much of the debate about the potential for higher taxes on the rich revolves
around the question of their impact on economic incentives and economic activity.
Some economists believe that much higher taxes on the rich would have seriously
deleterious effects on the economy. But others take a much more sanguine view.
The Nobel Prize winner Peter Diamond, for example, believes that capitalist economies could tolerate much higher top marginal personal income tax rates.

Wherever the truth might lie, imposing appreciably higher top marginal personal income tax rates on the rich would raise much less revenue than one might
think. In Canada, when the government in 2015 imposed a new, 4 percentage
point higher, top marginal tax rate for those earning more than C$200,000, the
estimated additional revenue was approximately C$3 billion – equivalent to 0.2
percent of GDP. In the United Kingdom, the increase in marginal rates proposed
as part of the British Labour tax package discussed above would – on Labour's
own estimates – have raised only £5.4 billion annually, equivalent to 0.3 percent
of GDP. This is despite the fact that Labour was proposing to go way beyond the
top 1 percent – its plan would have significantly increased income taxes on the
top 5 percent of British income earners.

In the United States, Representative Alexandria Ocasio-Cortez provoked vigorous debate in 2019 by proposing the imposition of a 70 percent top marginal tax
rate on those with an annual income of $10 million or more. Here again, the extra
revenue would be relatively small: the most optimistic of independent expert
estimates put it at approximately $72 billion per year, equivalent to 0.3 percent of
US GDP.[27] Even Thomas Piketty's more radical proposal for a top marginal tax
rate in the United States of 80 percent, kicking in at the lower level of $500,000
or $1 million would, he acknowledges, raise "not much money" (Piketty, 2013).
All this is notwithstanding the fact that, because the United States and United
Kingdom have income distributions more unequal than most other advanced
countries, raising top marginal rates in those two countries could be expected to
generate more revenue than almost anywhere else.

None of this is intended to suggest that raising top marginal rates is a bad idea. In many advanced countries, there is a persuasive case for including this as an element of an overall tax reform package.

Wealth Taxes

What about wealth taxes? Although these come in a variety of forms, it is the potential introduction of an *annual* wealth tax that is today attracting most attention. Decades ago, many advanced countries levied annual wealth taxes. Most, however, abolished them, and today this tax exists in only four countries. It does not raise much money – 0.18 percent of GDP in Spain, 0.22 percent in France and 0.43 percent in Norway (OECD, 2018c). Only in Switzerland is the revenue yield significantly higher, at 1.03 percent of GDP. This is, however, entirely because in the Alpine country the annual wealth tax is not a tax targeted at the rich. The asset threshold at which the Swiss annual wealth tax kicks in is so low that the tax is paid by a large proportion of taxpayers.[28]

It follows that, in order to raise large amounts of revenue, any annual wealth tax targeted at the rich would have to be levied at rates much higher than the taxes existing today.

How much revenue might be raised by an annual wealth tax that is much tougher on the rich? In the United States, advocates of an annual wealth tax targeted at the *ultra*-rich – taxpayers with assets worth tens of millions of dollars or more – have put forward a number of proposals which would, they claim, yield annual revenue of around 1 percent of GDP (Saez and Zucman, 2019; Leiserson, 2020). Critics suggest, however, that these revenue estimates are seriously exaggerated and that revenues would, in reality, be much less (Sarin, Summers and Kupferberg, 2019: 2020). These critics believe that the 1 percent estimate seriously underestimates the amount of evasion and avoidance that would occur. Lawrence Summers has described the annual wealth tax proposal as "bad economics, bad policy and built on bad data."

An even more aggressive version of the annual wealth tax was proposed during the 2019-2020 Democratic primary campaign by Senator Bernie Sanders. In his model, the wealth of the ultra-rich would be taxed annually at rates ranging from 1 percent up to a massive 8 percent. This makes the Sanders' wealth tax proposal deliberately confiscatory: in proposing such high tax rates, its explicit objective is to drastically reduce, over time, the concentration of wealth. This was made clear by the academic economists Gabriel Saez and Emmanuel Zucman who, in defending Sanders' proposal, asserted that it would cut billionaires' wealth in half, on average, within 15 years.[29] The confiscatory objective was further underlined by Sanders' accompanying plan for increases in death duties up to a maximum of 77 percent for the biggest estates.

The objective of radically reducing the inequality in the distribution of wealth may be a reasonable one. However, if one is concerned about the revenue base necessary to finance potentially very large long-term increases in government expenditure, what is most important is the ongoing revenue potential of such a tax. A crucial point here is that, whatever their short and medium-term revenue yield, confiscatory wealth taxes are not able to deliver an equivalent *permanent* expansion in tax revenues. Precisely because their aim is to drastically reduce concentrated wealth, confiscatory wealth taxes gradually undermine their own tax base, leading to a marked decline in revenue yield over the longer term. Within the timeframe of 30 years upon which we are focused in this book, this effect would be very substantial. Therefore, even if it were true that the immediate revenue yield from the Sanders wealth tax would be around 1.6 percent of GDP (again according to Saez and Zucman), it would almost certainly be *much* less than that by 2050. In this respect, confiscatory wealth taxes are like the carbon tax – by design, they undermine their own revenue base. This raises a more general point – discussed below – about the most radical proposals for "soaking the rich."

The particularly unequal concentration of wealth in the United States means that annual wealth taxes – or, indeed, almost any wealth tax proposal – could be expected to yield greater revenue there than in most other advanced countries. It is only because the tax he has in mind would have a *much* lower wealth threshold (€1 million) than those being proposed in the United States that Piketty's (2013) proposed European Union-wide annual wealth tax could possibly raise as much as the 2 percent of GDP annually that he estimates.

What about the other types of wealth tax? There are a number of other possibilities, including increasing the severity of the estate duties and inheritance taxes existing in a majority of advanced countries and the imposition of a lifetime capital receipts tax (Atkinson, 2015). But whatever approach is used to taxing wealth, the goose can only be plucked once. It is not possible to double or triple the revenue yield from wealth taxes by imposing simultaneously heavy annual wealth taxes plus one or more other type of wealth tax at high rates.

There is also a trade-off between revenue raised from wealth taxes and revenue raised from other forms of tougher taxation of the rich. In particular, raising a lot more revenue from wealth taxes necessarily means raising less from the taxation of capital income – and vice versa.

Maximizing Revenue or Fighting Inequality?

The deliberately confiscatory nature of the Sanders wealth tax proposal raises a more general point: many of the academic proponents of very high taxes on the rich do not view revenue raising as the primary policy objective. Piketty (2013), for example, explicitly endorses the view that the principal objective of wealth taxation should be to greatly reduce the level of inequality of wealth.

With respect to income taxes, Anthony Atkinson (2015) argues that fairness, rather than revenue maximization, should be the main goal when setting top marginal rates. Along the same lines, Emmanuel Saez and Gabriel Zucman have in the United States responded to arguments that Ocasio-Cortez's proposed 70 percent top marginal income tax would not be revenue-maximizing by asserting that raising additional revenue is not the "fundamental reason" for imposing such a tax rate. For them, the true objective is to reduce inequality by discouraging remuneration practices that result in a small minority of people receiving "sky-high" incomes.[30] This is also Piketty's position – he favors the imposition of a top marginal rate of 80 percent precisely to "drastically limit this type of remuneration" (Piketty, 2013). The reasoning behind this is that imposing confiscatory top marginal income tax rates would, over time, greatly reduce the numbers of people being paid astronomic levels of compensation because it would, for example, no longer make much sense for top corporate executives to bargain hard for multi-million remuneration packages (Piketty, Saez and Stantcheva, 2014; Alverado et al, 2018: 256).

Saez and Zucman have in this context explicitly compared the 70 percent marginal rate proposal with a carbon tax, saying that:

> *just as the point of taxing carbon is not to raise revenue but to reduce carbon emissions, high tax rates for sky-high incomes do not aim at funding Medicare for All. They aim at preventing an oligarchic drift that, if left unaddressed, will continue undermining the social compact and risk killing democracy.*[31]

If the reduction in inequality is the fundamental objective being pursued, it does not matter whether more revenue might be raised on a continuing basis with lower levels of wealth taxes or top marginal income tax rates. However, if one is focused on the challenge of how to raise additional revenue to finance large increases in government expenditure over the coming decades, setting taxes on the rich at confiscatory levels may not help much.

Sanders aside, it unlikely that many of the left-wing politicians who advance proposals for the steepest taxes share the Saez and Zucman perspective. For most of them, revenue-raising is by far the most important objective because the biggest challenge they face is to present voters with plausible plans for financing the large increases in spending they typically propose.

Taxing Companies More

What about taxing companies more heavily? On average across the OECD, governments raised 3 percent of GDP in taxes on corporations in 2018, of which nearly all (2.9 percent) took the form of corporate income tax (tax on corporate profits).[32] There is certainly some scope for raising additional revenue. The IMF has estimated that tax avoidance in the form of corporate profit shifting results in lost revenue in high-income countries of around 1 percent of GDP (Crivelli, de Mooij and Keen, 2016). Stories of companies such as Amazon paying no tax cause understandable outrage. It is to be hoped that a significant portion of this will be clawed back as a consequence of tax reforms currently being negotiated internationally, together with other measures taken at the national and international levels. The OECD has recently estimated that implementation of certain of the major options for reform of the taxation of multinational enterprises that are under discussion would increase corporate income tax revenue in high-income countries by slightly more than 4 percent (OECD, 2020). This would represent a little over 0.1 percent of GDP on average.

In the United States, the corporate tax reforms in the package proposed by Sarin, Summers and Knupfberg (2020) would contribute a little less than one-fifth of their estimated revenue gains – equivalent to approximately 0.4 percent of GDP annually.

Increasing company taxes should not, however, be thought of as simply another way of taxing the rich. It is basic economics that the ultimate burden of company taxes is not borne by companies themselves, but is spread in some manner between shareholders, employees and customers. Although the question of how this ultimate burden of corporate income tax is actually shared between these three groups has been endlessly debated by economists, there is no consensus on the matter and "the ultimate incidence of the tax remains somewhat unresolved" (Auerbach, 2005). It is quite plausible that the rich end up bearing a substantial part, and possibly even the majority, of the burden of the tax. It is also certainly not true that – as some conservative polemicists assert – all or most of the burden falls on workers. There is nevertheless little reason to doubt that customers and employees do end up paying some significant portion of the tax – in the form of higher prices and lower wages respectively – and that workers also pay part of it indirectly through the impact on the dividend income of their pension funds. Whatever the true story is with respect to ultimate incidence, company taxes are a poor instrument for taxing the rich.[33] Taxes on personal income and wealth are manifestly superior for this purpose.

The biggest constraint on the ability to raise company taxes is international tax competition. Any country that markedly increased its rates would have good reason to fear that this would induce an exodus of companies to lower-tax juris-dictions, and that the result could well be less rather than more tax revenue. The great majority of economists, irrespective of ideological orientations, would also agree that *very* large increases in company taxes could inflict significant economic damage. They could also be expected to induce a substantial increase in corporate tax avoidance (IMF, 2019).[34]

Proposals for increasing company tax rates are frequently justified on the grounds that governments have cut company taxes dramatically over recent decades. This is, however, not quite right. It is true that most countries have over time reduced – often quite substantially – the percentage rates at which company taxes are levied.[35] What is less widely recognized is that, at the same time, there has been a very substantial broadening of the company tax base – the measure of profits against which the tax rate is applied. The net result is that, across advanced countries generally, company tax has been broadly stable as a proportion of GDP.[36]

ACKNOWLEDGMENTS

I would like to thank the following for reviewing all or part of the manuscript and providing me with invaluable comment and advice: Eleanor Angel, Phil Laidlaw, Danièle Pralong, Edmund Robinson, Allen Schick and Peter Thurlow. Danièle Pralong provided expert advice and review of bioscience-related matter. The usual caveats apply.

I was very fortunate to have as editor Jeremy Clift, former publisher at the International Monetary Fund. Jeremy is a first-rate professional, and I am indebted to him not only for his careful editing of the manuscript, but also for knowledgeable advice on a range of content and other matters.

I'm grateful to Elisabeth Heissler for the cover, Catherine Williams for formatting, Helen Castell and Mark Swift for proofreading, and Sophie Bradshaw for the preparation of the index.

STATISTICAL ANNEX

Statistical Annex to Chapter 1

Trends in Total Government Expenditure

The following figures provide an overview of trends in aggregate expenditure (using non-interest government expenditure, all levels of government combined) for selected advanced countries.

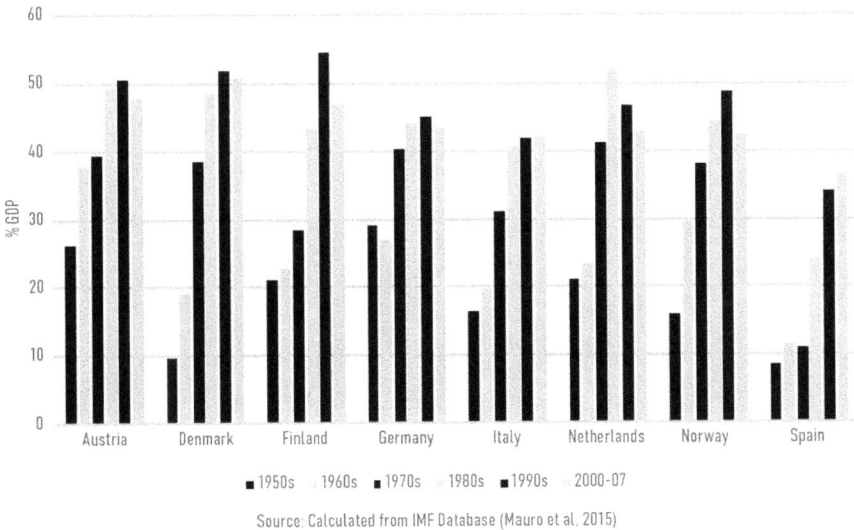

Source: Calculated from IMF Database (Mauro et al. 2015)

Figure S1.1
Non-Interest Government Expenditure/GDP: Selected Advanced Nations – Decade Averages (A)

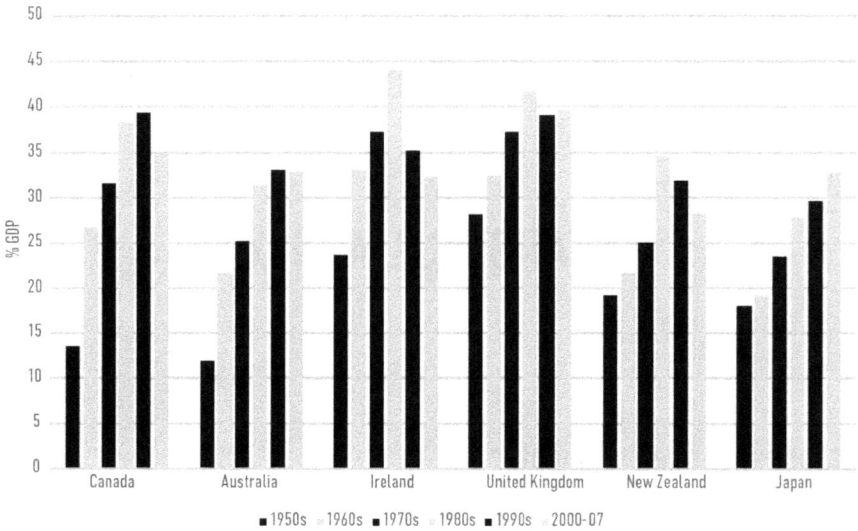

Source: Calculated from IMF Database (Mauro et al, 2015)

Figure S1.2
Non-Interest Government Expenditure/GDP: Selected Advanced Nations – Decade Averages (B)

The following figures shows trends in non-interest expenditure for US government (federal, state and local combined).

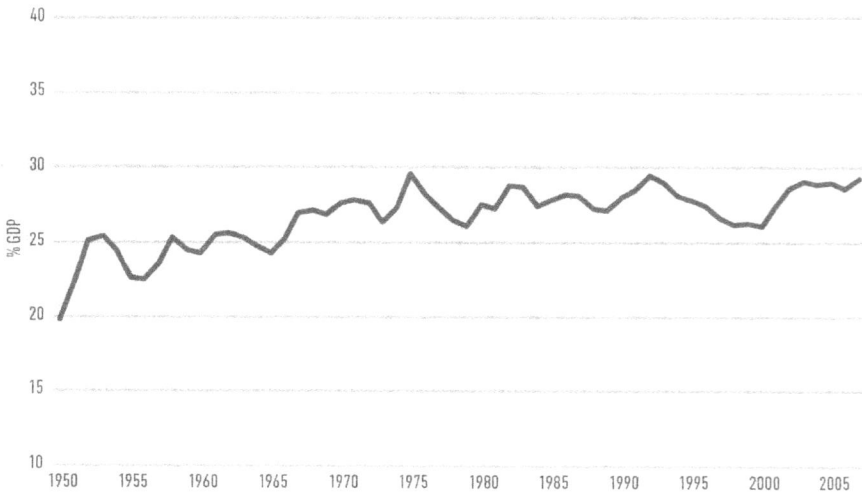

Source: Bureau of Economic Analysis, Government Current Receipts and Expenditures.

Figure S1.3[1]
Non-Interest Government Expenditure/GDP: United States (1950-2007)

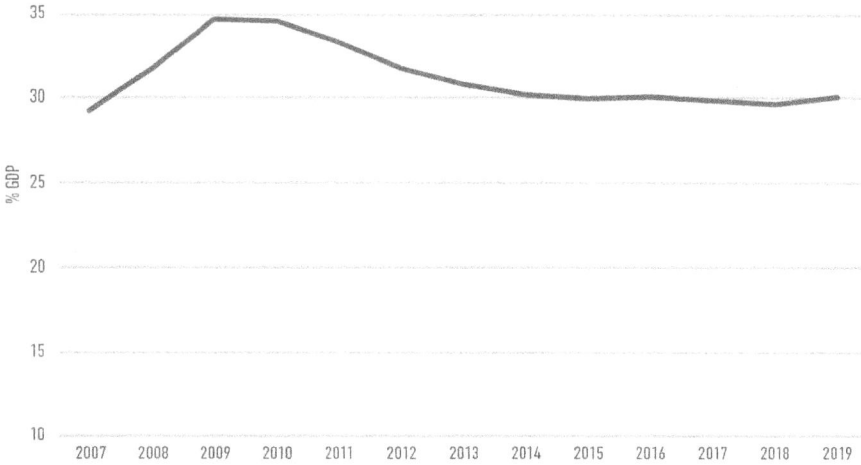

Source: Bureau of Economic Analysis, Government Current Receipts and Expenditures

Figure S1.4
Non-Interest Government Expenditure/GDP: United States (2007-2019)

Trends in Composition of Government Expenditure

Figure S1.5 shows trends in social protection spending on the elderly versus social protection spending other than for the elderly for those advanced countries for which these data are available on an internationally-consistent basis in the relevant IMF database.

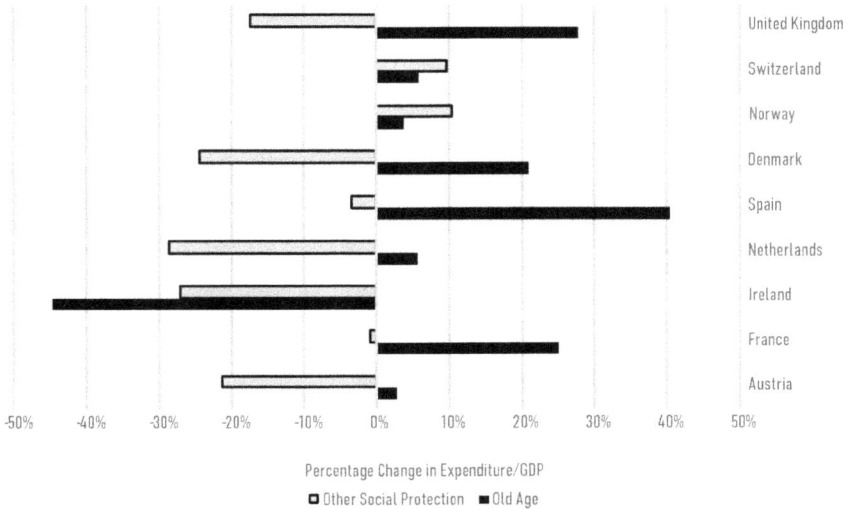

Percentage Change in Expenditure/GDP
□ Other Social Protection   ■ Old Age

Figure S1.5
Change in Social Protection Expenditure: Old Age Versus Other (1995-2018)
Percentage Change in Expenditure/GDP

Statistical Annex to Chapter 4

Population Aging — Past Trends and Projections
Figures S4.1-S4.6 illustrate the long-term aging process in advanced societies.

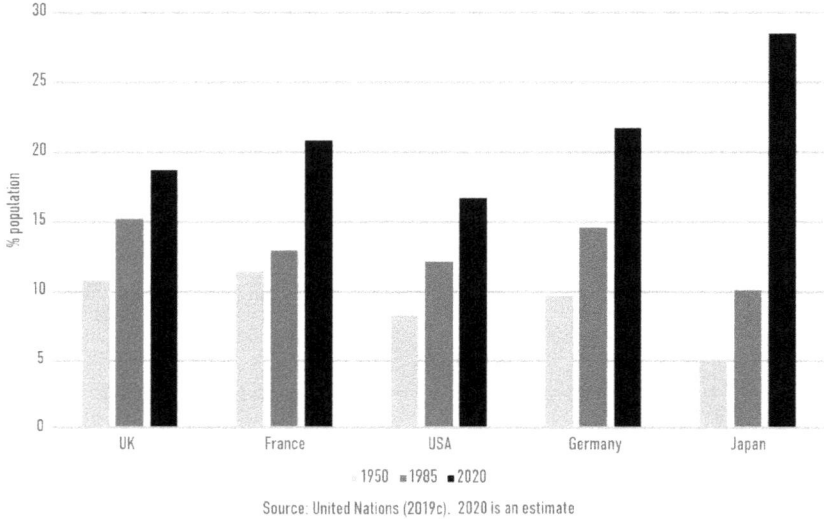

1950 ▪1985 ▪2020

Source: United Nations (2019c). 2020 is an estimate

Figure S4.1
Percentage of Population in 65-Plus Age Group (1950, 1985 & 2020)

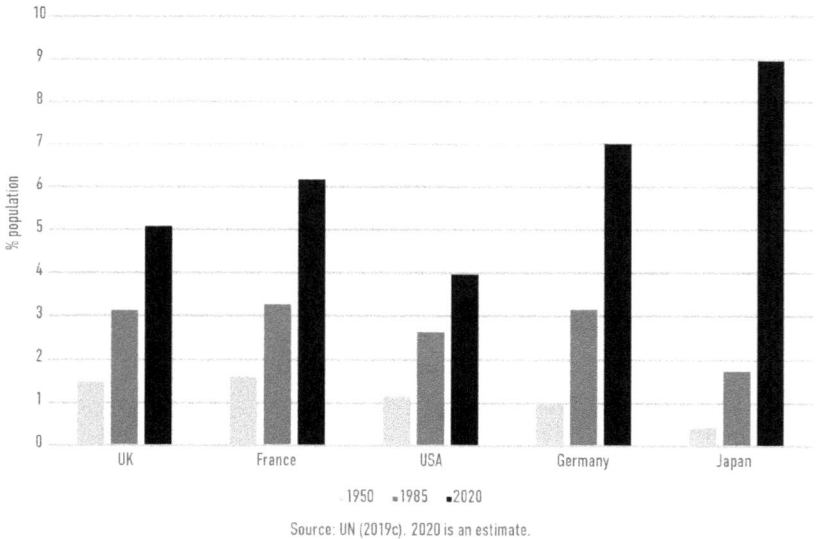

1950 ▪1985 ▪2020

Source: UN (2019c). 2020 is an estimate.

Figure S4.2
Percentage of Population in 80-Plus Age Group (1950, 1985 & 2020)

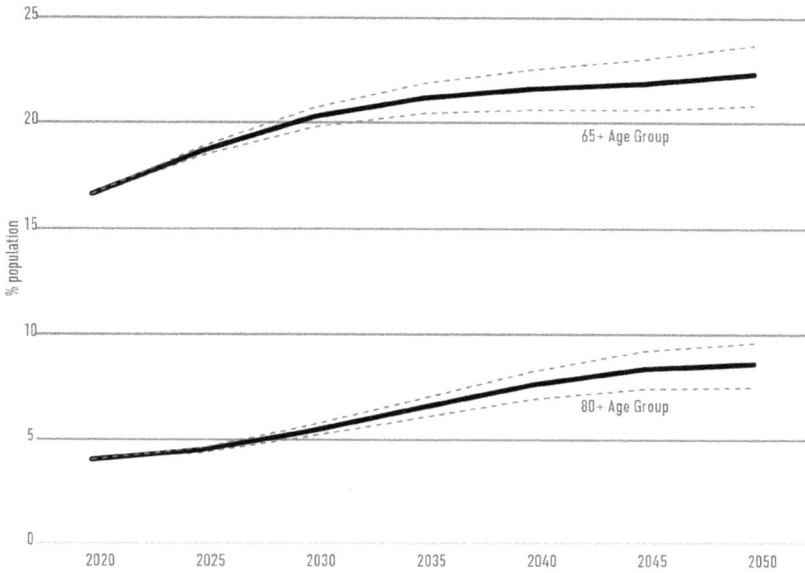

Source: UN (2019c)

For each age bracket, the median, lower and upper 80 % prediction interval projections are shown

Figure S4.3
Population Aging Projections: USA

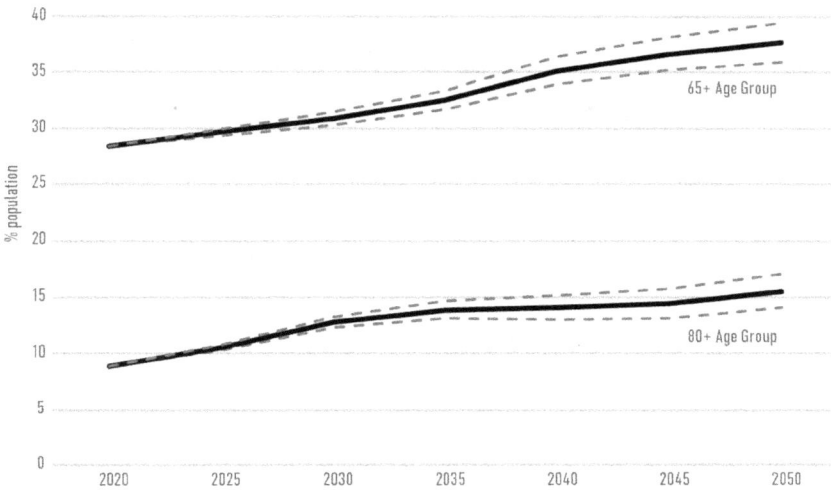

Source: UN (2019c). For each age bracket, the median, lower and upper 80 % prediction interval projections are shown

Figure S4.4
Population Aging Projections: Japan

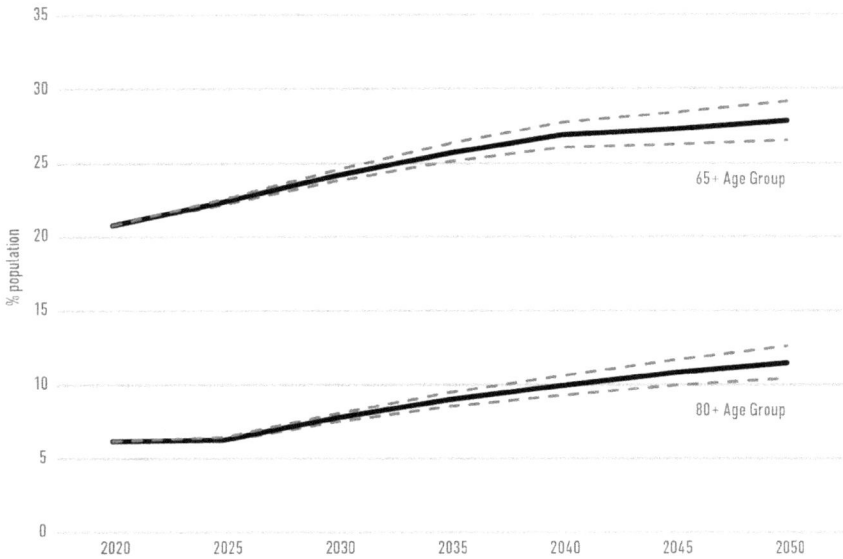

Source: UN (2019c). For each age bracket, the median, lower and upper 80 % prediction interval projections are shown

Figure S4.5
Population Aging Projections: France

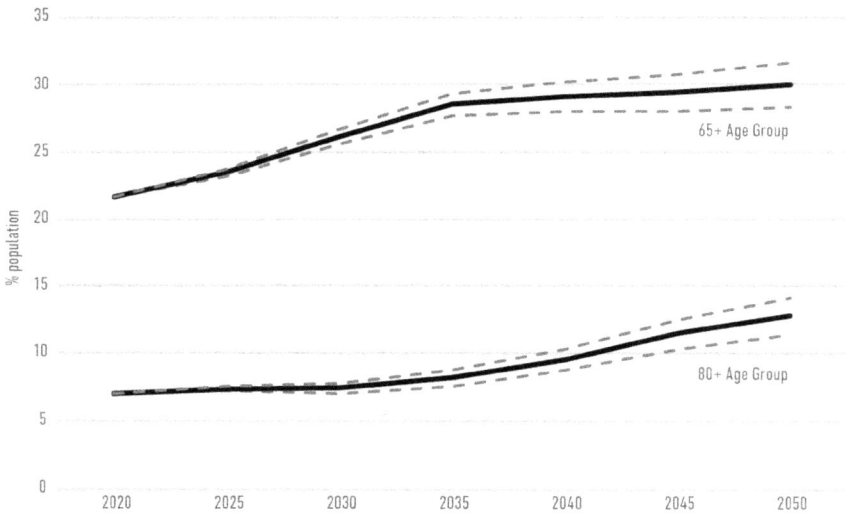

Source: UN (2019c). For each age bracket, the median, lower and upper 80 % prediction interval projections are shown

Figure S4.6
Population Aging Projections: Germany

Long-Term Care Expenditure

Reliable data on government spending on long-term care (LTC) does not appear to be available for all advanced countries. Figure S4.7 shows OECD data on government and compulsory insurance system LTC expenditure for selected advanced countries for the most recently available year.

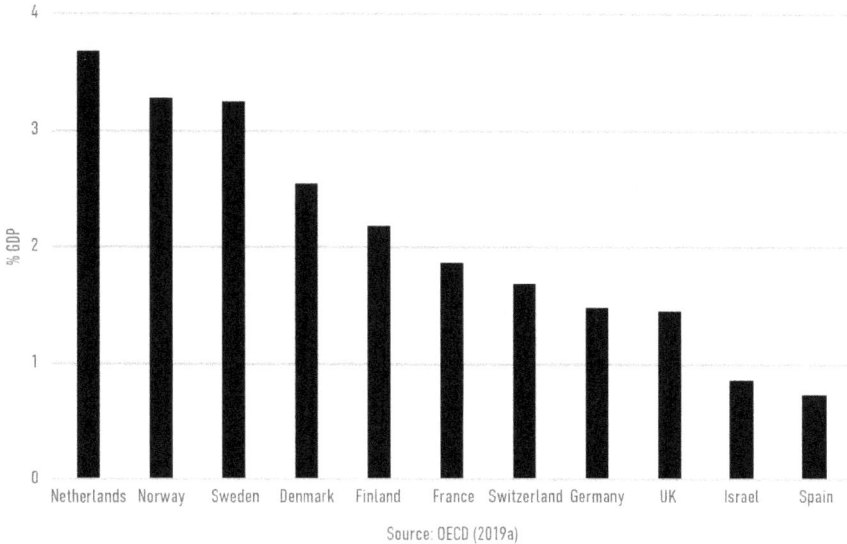

Source: OECD (2019a)

Figure S4.7
Long-Term Care Expenditure (2017)
Government and Compulsory Insurance Expenditure/GDP

In Japan, government expenditure of LTC was approximately 2 percent of GDP in 2013 (Akemura and Kojima, 2018: 550). More recent figures do not appear to be available, but with Japan's relatively generous system and the degree of population ageing in that country, the figure is probably higher now.

The numbers in Figure S4.7 include both "health" and "social" LTC expenditure for countries which report both. The US is one of the countries which reports only the health component, which according to the same OECD data was 0.6 percent of GDP in 2017. This figure of 0.6 percent is, however, probably not far off total US government expenditure, because in that country the government's role in LTC is very limited. It is essentially an adjunct to the Medicaid system and is, as such, primarily medical in its focus.

For at least some of the countries concerned, the data in Figure S4.7 may significantly understate government expenditure on LTC. The reason for this is that certain countries use tax breaks – for example, by making premium payments on private LTC insurance policies tax deductible – as an instrument to support care provision. France, for example, makes considerable use of such tax breaks (Fernandez and Nadash, 2016). Tax breaks are a cost to government, which is why they are commonly referred to by economists as "tax expenditures." The use of tax expenditures distorts expenditure data because they are not counted in official statistics on government expenditure.

Long-term projections of public LTC expenditure have been prepared both by the OECD[2] (see Figure S4.8) and by European Union member nations (using what is in principle a standardized methodology defined by the European Commission[3]) (Figure S4.9). Although neither of these correspond precisely with the 2020-2050 timeframe of this book, they suggest with a little extrapolation that few advanced countries are likely to experience an increase in expenditure of less than 1 percent of GDP over the period until the middle of the century.

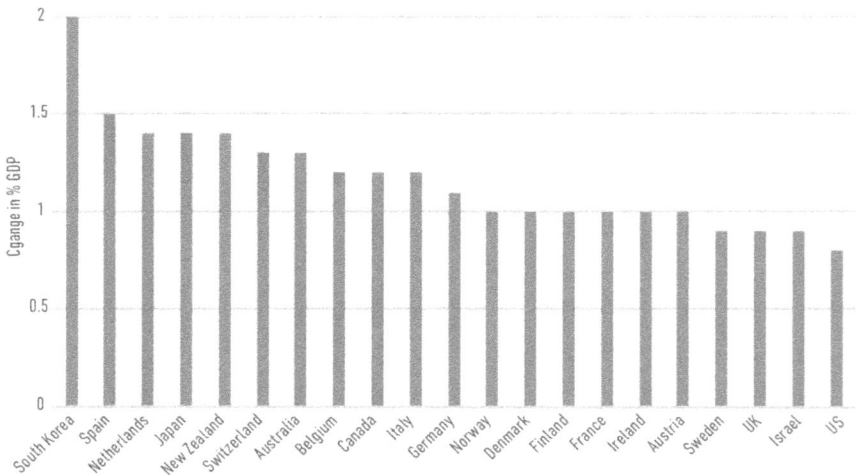

Source: Maisonneuve and Martins (2015: 86)

Figure S4.8
Projected Increase in Government Long-Term Care Expenditure (50 Years to 2060)

Using the same methodology as the European Commission, Akemura and Kojima (2018) have prepared semi-official long-term projections of public LTC expenditure in Japan for the period 2013-2060 which suggest a prospective increase of approximately 1.4 percent of GDP over that 47-year period.

Both the European Commission methodology and that of the OECD make assumptions which may be questioned, and which are on the whole likely to bias the projections downwards.[4]

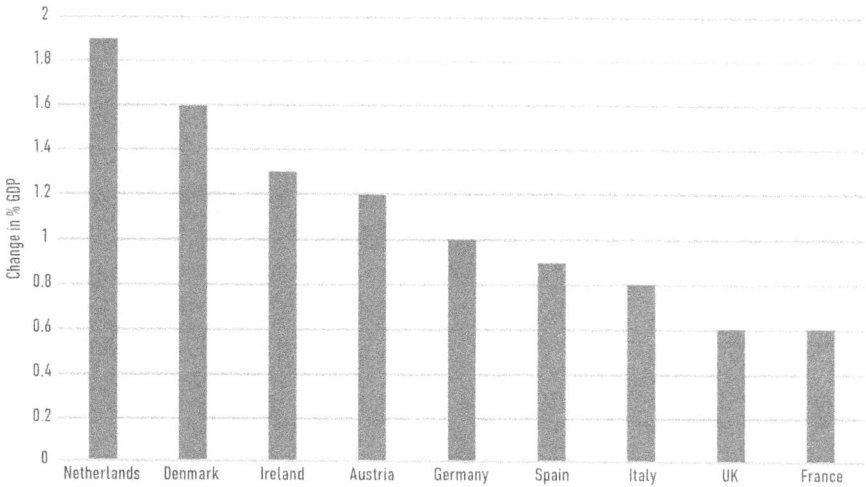

Source: 2019 Stability and Convergence Programs of respective countries (ec.europa.eu)

Figure S4.9
Projected Increases in Government Long-Term Care Expenditure (2020-2050)

Statistical Annex to Chapter 6

The International Transport Forum (affiliated to the OECD) provides interna-tionally standardized data from 1995 to the present for expenditure on "inland transport" infrastructure, and within that aggregate for both road and rail infrastructure expenditure. As mentioned in the main text, this data does not distinguish between public and private spending. Nor does it distinguish between what governments fund from budgets and what is financed by public enterprises from user charges. The following three figures show the investment levels for all advanced countries for which data are reported from 1995 to either 2016 or 2017 (whichever happened to be the latest date in the time series at the time of writing).

The US Congressional Budget Office (CBO, 2014, 2018b) has published his-torical data on "public spending on transport and water infrastructure" by US governments for 1956-2017. For some reason, the CBO report adds together investment (capital) expenditure together with maintenance and operating expenditure to derive its measure of "spending" on these categories of infrastruc-ture. However, it is possible to use supporting data provided by CBO (CBO, 2018c) to calculate the investment expenditure as a percentage of GDP, as shown in Figure S6.4.

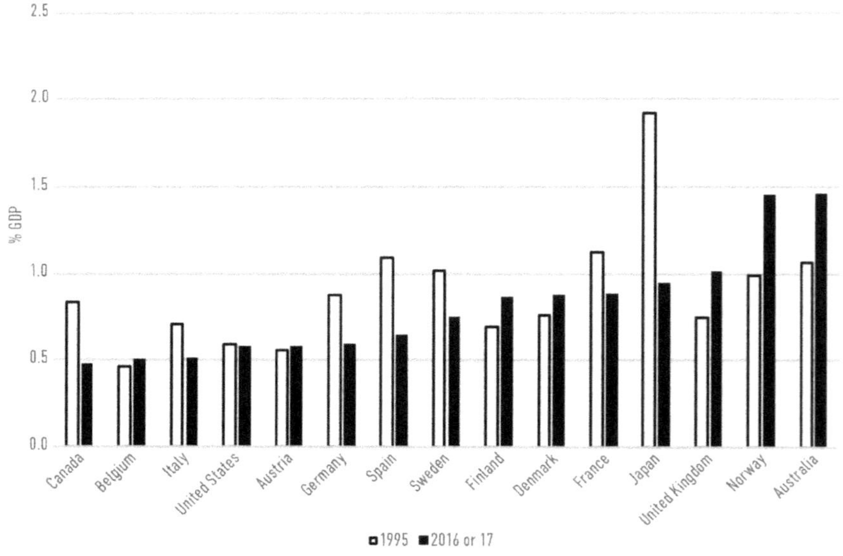

Source: International Transport Forum (ITF) Transport Statistics Database, "Transport infrastructure investment and maintenance".

Figure S6.1
Inland Transport Investment (All Sources)/GDP

STATISTICAL ANNEX 311

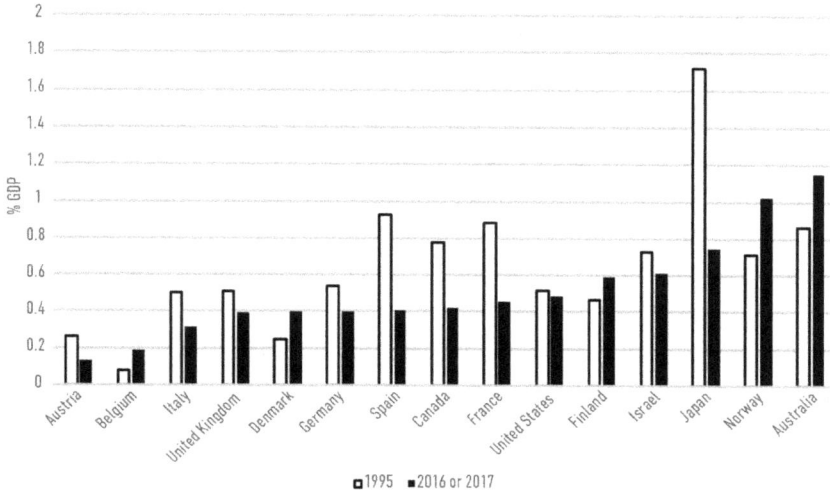

□1995   ■2016 or 2017

Source: ITF Transport Statistics Database, "Transport infrastructure investment and maintenance"

Figure S6.2
Road Investment (All Sources)/GDP

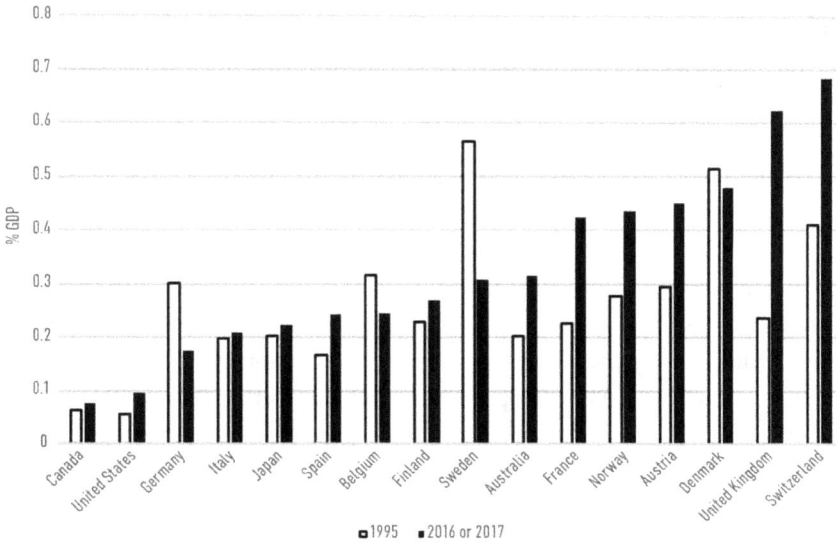

□1995   ■2016 or 2017

Data Source: ITF Transport Statistics Database, "Transport infrastructure investment and maintenance"

Figure S6.3
Rail Investment (All Sources)/GDP

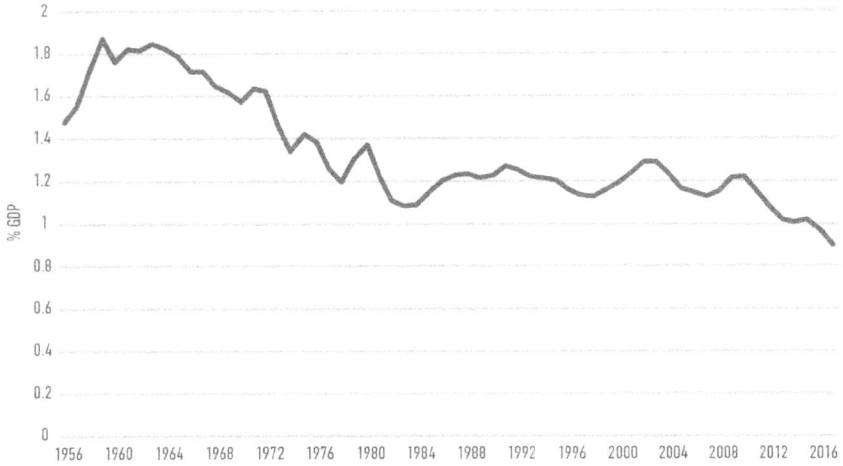

Source: calculated from data in CBO (2018c)

Figure S6.4
*Transport and Water Infrastructure Investment/GDP: United States
Government Plus Public Enterprise Expenditure*

While it is not possible to distinguish transport investment spending from water investment spending using the CBO data, it is clear that most of the combined total must have been allocated to transport. It follows that the marked downward trend in investment/GDP up to the early 1980s must apply to transport investment in isolation.

The picture in Figure S6.4 of long-term declining investment in transport and water investment up to the 1980s contrasts with the relative stability of the measure of total "spending" (again, including maintenance and operating expenditure as well as investment) which is the headline indicator used in the CBO reports. The CBO's spending measure encourages misinterpretation of the type seen in a recent 2016 RAND Corporation which claims that the relative stability of total "spending" contradicts the widespread "perception that US infrastructure needs are not being met, which animates so much of the debate over spending" (Knopman et al, 2016: xi). One of the authors of the RAND report has, in the same spirit, claimed elsewhere that "while it is conventional these days to claim that American infrastructure is falling apart because it is inadequately funded, the data shows that funding has in fact been relatively stable over the long term" (Wachs, 2020: 199). The problem with this is that it makes no sense, in this context, to add operating expenditure to maintenance and capital expenditure in the manner that the CBO has to obtain its total "spending" measure. Total spending defined in this manner might remain high even though the infrastructure is becoming increasingly dilapidated, because operating spending is increasing as the assets are worked harder – i.e. it may cost more to operate assets which are in poor condition or very outdated. While an argument could be made for adding together investment and maintenance expenditure to obtain some proxy measure of the spending devoted to sustaining the infrastructure asset base, there is no apparent rationale for also adding operating expenditure.

Trends in Government Capital Expenditure

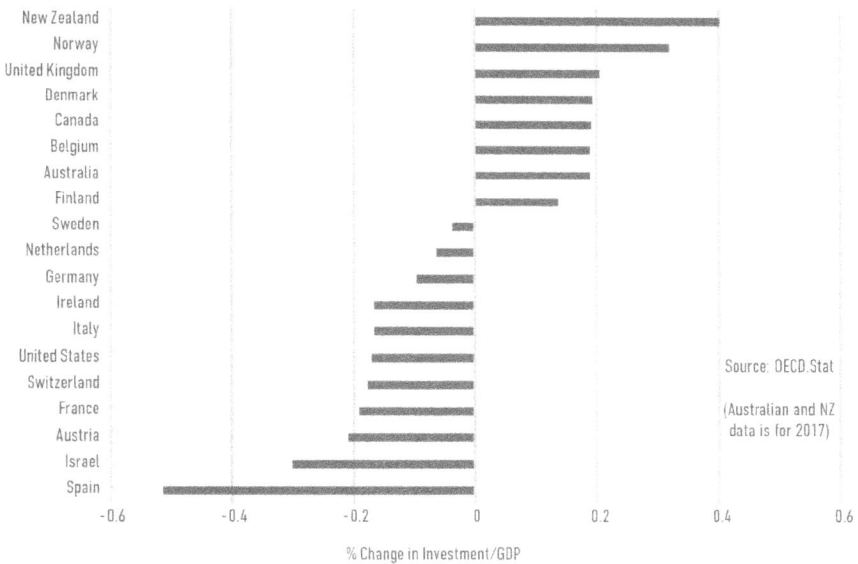

Figure S6.5
Changes in Government Capital Expenditure (1995-2018)
Percentage Change in General Government Gross Fixed Capital Formation/GDP

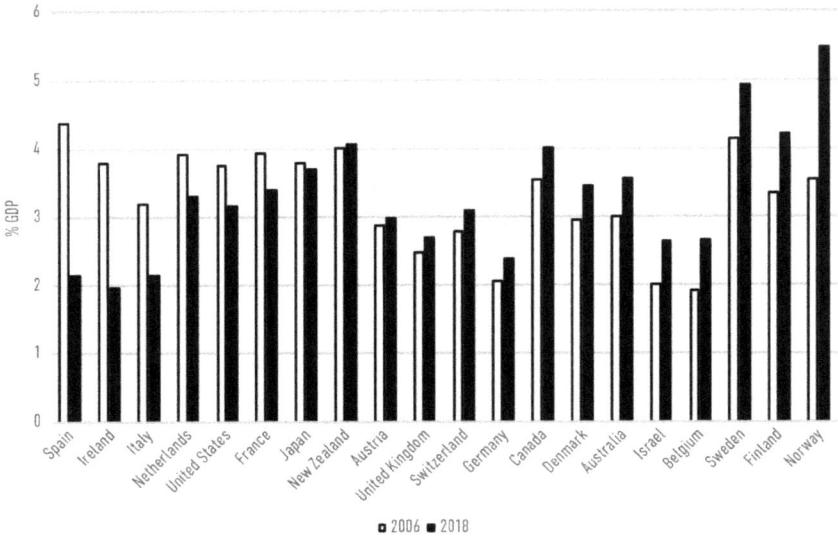

■ 2006 ■ 2018

Data source: OECD.Stat (Austalia, NZ and Japan data is for 2017)

Figure S6.6
Government Capital Expenditure (2018 vs pre-GFC)
General Government Gross Fixed Capital Formation/GDP

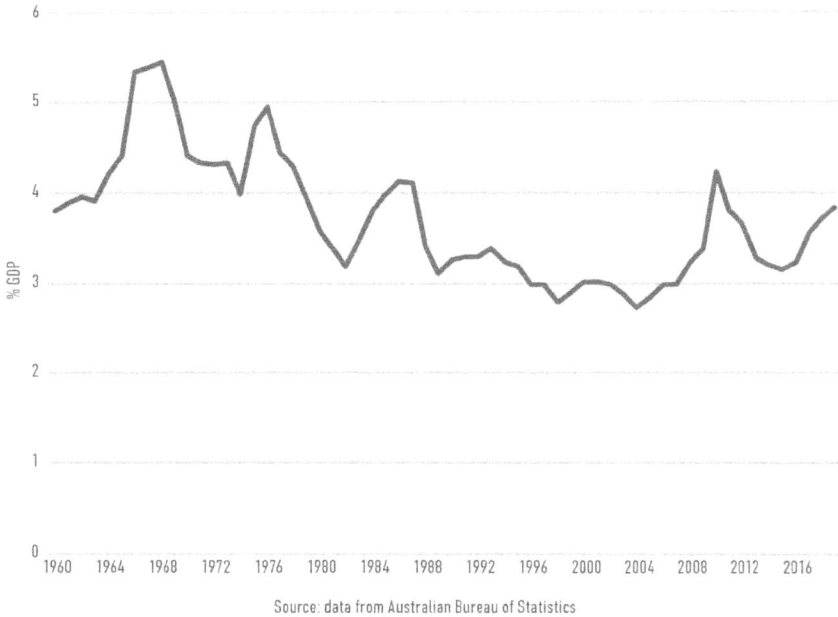

Source: data from Australian Bureau of Statistics

Figure S6.7
Government Capital Expenditure: Australia
General Government Gross Fixed Capital Formation/GDP

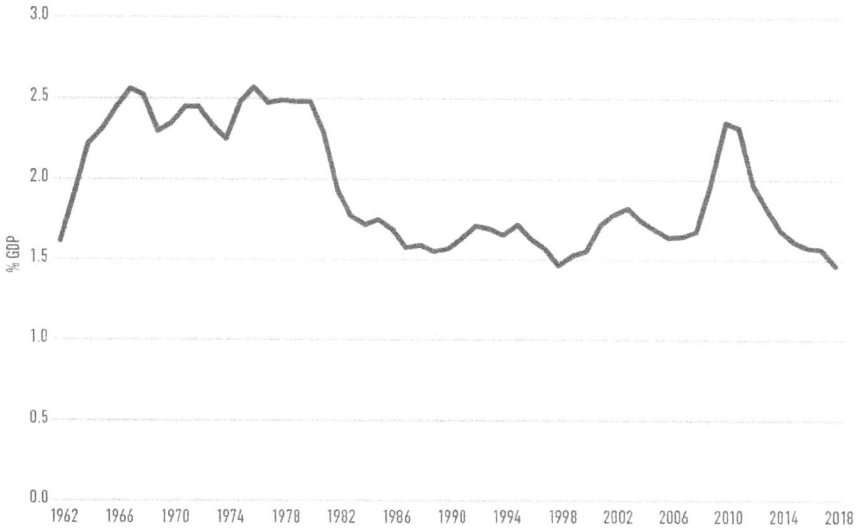

Data source: CBO (2019c)

Figure S6.8
Government Non-Defense Investment: United States
Investment Expenditure/GDP

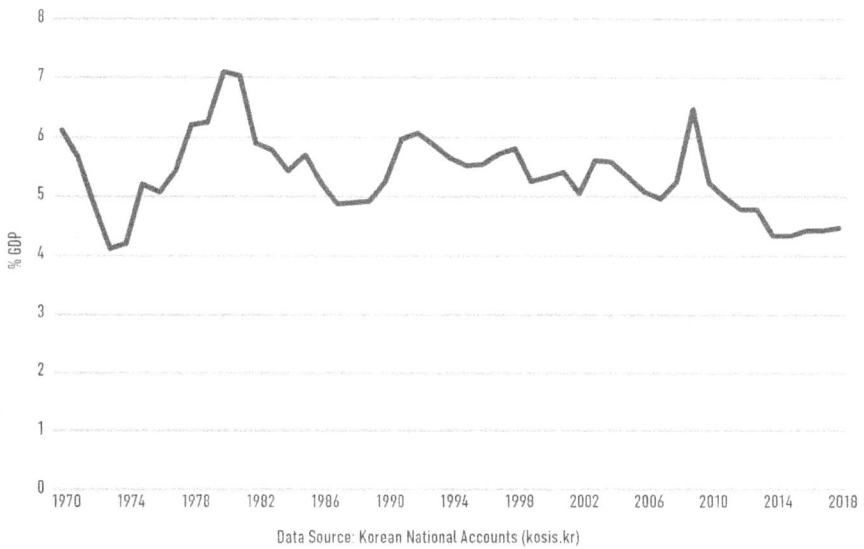

Data Source: Korean National Accounts (kosis.kr)

Figure S6.9
Government Capital Expenditure: South Korea
General Government Gross Fixed Capital Formation/GDP

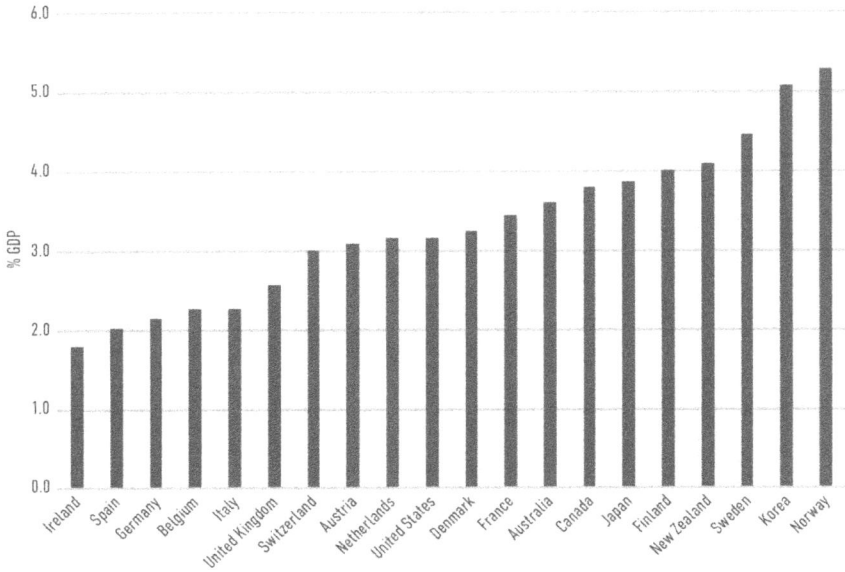

Data source: OECD.Stat

Figure S6.10
Government Investment (2017)
General Government Investment/GDP

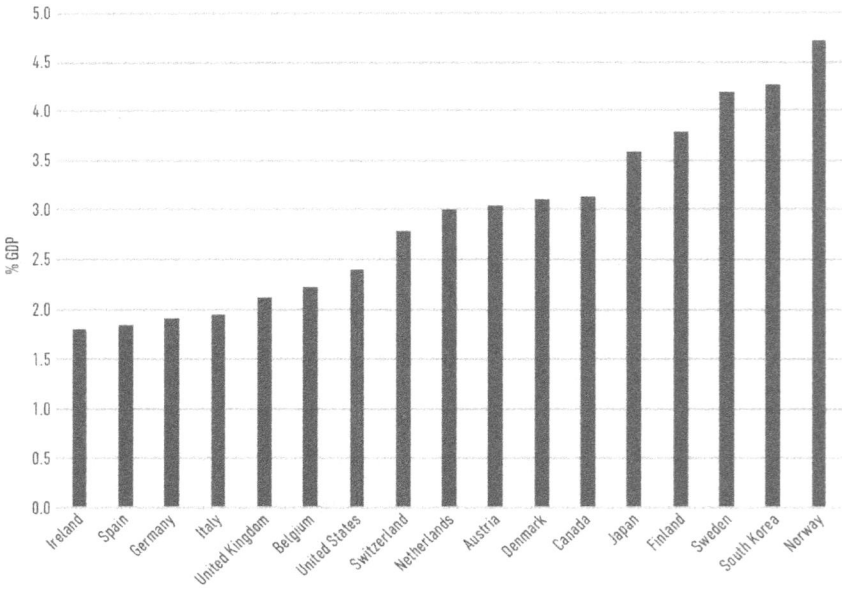

Data source: OECD.Stat (Korea data is 2016)

Figure S6.11
Government Non-Defense Investment (2017)
General Government Investment/GDP

Statistical Annex to Chapter 10

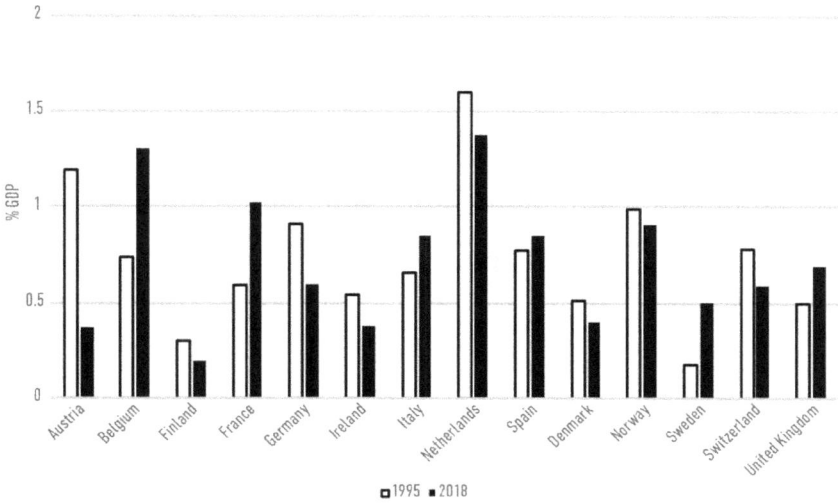

Source: IMF Data, GFS, Expenditure by Function of Government

Figure S10.1
Environment Protection Expenditure/GDP (1995 vs. 2018)

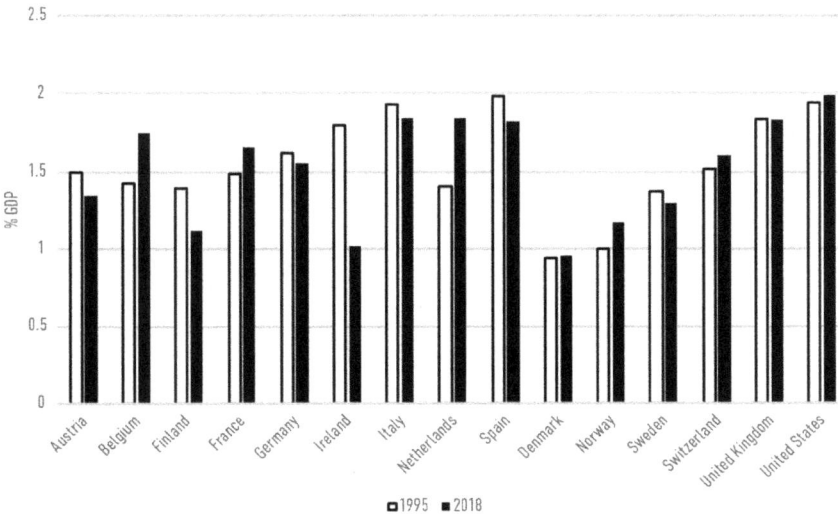

Source: IMF Data, GFS, Expenditure by Functions of Government

Figure S10.2
Public Order & Safety Expenditure/GDP (1995 vs. 2018)

NOTES

Chapter One: Big Spenders or Misers?

1   These measures are measures of "gross" debt, which is arguably less meaningful than alternative measures including "net" debt and "net financial worth."

2   For example, Facchini and Melki (2011), Magazzino and Forte (2010) and Makin, Pearce and Ratnasiri (2018).

3   Public finance data referred to in this chapter are, unless otherwise explicitly referenced, derived from the data in the IMF Public Finances in Modern History (PFMH) Database (see Mauro et al, 2015), which may be accessed at https://www.imf.org/external/datamapper/datasets/FPP.

4   Of the 21 relevant countries for which data are available in the IMF PFMH, this is true of 19. The two exceptions are South Korea and Israel. In South Korea – which did not acquire advanced country status until decades after World War II – government expenditure fell after the early 1960s as military spending was wound down after the Korean War. It did not start to increase significantly (from a low base) until the late 1980s. The data for Israel are very incomplete, but it is likely also that government expenditure was much higher in the early years after the foundation of the state of Israel than subsequently.

5   That way, we avoid being misled by the substantial increase in interest payments which occurred from the mid-1970s, and which was determined by prevailing interest rates and inherited debt.

6   This is true in 17 of the 19 advanced countries (i.e. excluding South Korea and Israel from the total count of 21 relevant countries in the IMF PFMH Database). Italy is included amongst these 17, notwithstanding that government expenditure/GDP was very marginally higher in 2006 than in 1993. It is, nevertheless, reasonable to take 1993 as peak.

7   The latest to leave the party were Japan and Spain, where non-interest expenditure peaked in the 2000s.

8   There was a temporary boost of spending in the early 1950s associated with the Korean War.

9   Qualification: it stopped everywhere except in South Korea, which was the only country where government expenditure/GDP was still growing right up to the GFC – albeit from a low base.

10   Spending reductions were also modest in Japan, where spending only peaked and started to decline in the 2000s.

11   Italy might also be regarded as an exception: non-interest expenditure/GDP peaked in 1993, fell until 2000 and then rose again until 2006 (when it reached the same level as the 1993 peak).

12   16 of 21 advanced countries experienced sharp increases in debt/GDP from the mid-1970s (or, in Italy's case, starting a little earlier). Australia, the United Kingdom, Finland, Israel, Spain and South Korea were the only countries where this did not happen.

13   References to interest rates here should be taken as references to what economists call "real" interest rates – that it, interest rates adjusted for inflation.

14   This is why expenditure/GDP rose in Ireland from 35 percent in 2007 to 65 percent in 2010.

15   The analysis which follows – and the data in Appendix 1.1 – refers to total expenditure. This does not – unlike the data used to analyze the earlier phases – exclude interest expenditure. This is for data availability reasons (there do not appear to be any internationally standardized statistics on non-interest expenditure which go back prior to the GFC). In practice, however, this makes little difference. An examination of data on net interest spending as a percentage of GDP (also available at OECD.Stat, but unfortunately only from 2009) makes it clear that interest expenditure must generally have changed only slightly over the decade from 2007.

16   Economists often use "cyclically adjusted" measures to identify underlying trends. However, given the many methodological issues surrounding such measures, it is not clear that they – where they are available – give a more reliable indication of changes in underlying spending over the decade from 2007.

17   The two outliers, where spending/GDP has increased significantly more than anywhere else, are Finland and Norway (see Appendix 1.1). In each case, however, this increase was significantly less than the very large expenditure reductions which had occurred during the retrenchment phase.

18   The two measures of debt referred to here are gross debt and net financial worth, both available at OECD.Stat.

19   In Australia's case, employees make large compulsory third-pillar investments in pension funds. Increasingly, old-age retirement income is financed from these personal pension assets, rather than from government pensions. In Switzerland, health expenditure is primarily financed by compulsory insurance.

20   At least amongst the countries for which we have statistics.

21   This Figure omits the two countries (Japan and South Korea) with the largest percentage increases in age pension expenditure, because they are literally off the graph. In Japan, there was a 95 percent increase in age pension expenditure/GDP over the relevant time period. In South Korea, the increase was 165 percent – although in absolute terms the spending levels are very low.

22   The relatively modest decline in the United Kingdom is misleading, because of major cuts to public expenditure in the 1980s. As mentioned earlier, the retrenchment phase started in that country much earlier than in most others.

23   See, for example, "La tentation du départ des médicins de l'hôpital public," Le Monde, 14 November 2019 and, in the same newspaper on 10 August 2019, "Au centre hospitalier de Lisieux, 'il y a urgence aux urgences'."

24   "Le modèle social danois sous pression," Le Monde, 2 June 2019.

Chapter Two: Why Has Health Spending Risen So Fast?

1   This has been the case in, for example, France, Germany, Austria, Japan, South Korea, Norway, Spain and the United Kingdom.

2   All the following data on the government share of health expenditure are derived from the World Health Organization's Global Health Expenditure Database (http://apps.who.int/nha/database).

3 There are also a handful of countries, including Switzerland and the Netherlands, with systems where compulsory "private" health insurance plays an important role and the role of government expenditure is thereby significantly reduced – e.g. to 40 percent in Switzerland. Because insurance is compulsory, premiums are essentially equivalent to taxes in these systems.

4 For example, in the period 1970-2017, government's share of overall health expenditure increased from 71 percent to 85 percent in Germany, from 75 percent to 83 percent in France and from 70 percent to 85 percent in Japan. Only in the United Kingdom was there a significant fall in the government's share – from 86 percent to 80 percent. (Source: OECD Statistics, at https://stats.oecd.org).

5 In Switzerland – where the health system shares certain of the fundamental flaws of the US system – a recent review panel estimated such potential savings at around 20 percent of current levels of spending (RGE, 2017), although the methodology behind this estimate is not particularly convincing.

6 A chronic condition is a disease, or a condition which predisposes towards disease (such as hypertension), that continues for a substantial period of time – usually understood as meaning for 12 months or more, although under other definitions for three months or longer.

7 Prevalence measures the number of people suffering from a given condition during the year per thousand of population (or on a percentage basis), and covers both people who have recently developed the condition and people who developed it in the past but still suffer from it. The prevalence statistics used in this chapter essentially refer to what is known as "treatment prevalence" – in which prevalence is measured by reference to individuals who have been diagnosed and are receiving treatment (or, in the case of cancers and certain other conditions, have received treatment within a defined past time frame) for conditions. Treatment prevalence does not purport to measure people who are suffering from conditions but have not been diagnosed (e.g. undiagnosed diabetes).

8 All the figures in this chapter pertaining to rates of incidence, prevalence and mortality from chronic conditions for the period 1990-2016 are, unless otherwise stated, calculated by the author from raw data available from the Global Health Data Exchange (http://ghdx.healthdata.org/gbd-results-tool). "High-income" countries in this database are defined to include Western Europe, the United States, Canada, Australia, New Zealand, Japan and South Korea, plus several other countries that do not necessarily fit the usual concept of "advanced" countries (namely Argentina, Chile and Brunei). However, the population of these latter countries is so small relative to the total that their inclusion does not significantly affect the statistics for the group, which may still be taken as representative of the advanced economies this book focuses upon.

9 Incidence measures new cases per thousand population (or on a percentage basis). Prevalence is not a good measure for cancer because people who received cancer treatment in the past are counted in the prevalence numbers for some years after treatment finishes, even if they are symptom-free. This is because it is hard to tell whether they have been cured and there is a substantial risk of recurrence. The consequence of this is that cancer prevalence statistics inevitably include significant numbers of people who turn out ultimately to have been totally cured and are therefore, in fact, not continuing to suffer from the disease.

10 This is the World Health Organization definition.

11 In Australia, the peak rate occurred earlier, in 1968, and the fall in the age-standardized CVD mortality rate from then to 2015 was 82 percent (AIHW, 2017a).

12 Calculated by the author from data in the World Health Organization's Mortality Database covering age-standardized mortality rates for ICD, chapter 9 (diseases of the circulatory system) (http://apps.who.int/healthinfo/statistics/mortality/whodpms/). For France, the data covers 1979-2014.

13   In the period 1990-2016, age-standardized CVD incidence fell 25 percent while age-standard-
      ized prevalence fell somewhat less (18 percent) due to the fact that people are surviving longer
      after a CVD event.

14   In the US, for example, the age-standardized prevalence of smoking among persons aged 25 or
      over decreased from 36.9 percent to 15.6 percent over the period 1974-2015 (NCHS, 2017).

15   Over the more recent 2000-2016 period, the age-standardized incidence of cancer has been
      approximately stable across advanced countries as a whole (i.e. a slight decline of 1.8 percent),
      but mortality rates have continued to decline (dropping 6.4 percent). Individual country expe-
      rience has varied considerably – incidence, for example, has fallen significantly in the US over
      the past decade (Siegel et al, 2018).

16   The fact that so many more CVD and cancer patients are surviving has also directly increased
      measured prevalence for both of these diseases because (as mentioned in a note above) survi-
      vors are counted in those figures for some years after their treatment. This effectively treats
      them as if they are still suffering from the disease. In the case of many CVD survivors, this
      is often literally true. For cancer survivors, including them in the prevalence statistics makes
      sense because (as, once again, was noted above) there is a significant possibility that the cancer
      will recur. It is for these reasons – as well as the fact that cancer treatment is often significantly
      more prolonged today than it was in the past – that CVD and cancer are today usually classi-
      fied as chronic diseases.

17   Statistics on life expectancy trends are difficult to find for so-called "type 2" diabetes – which,
      as discussed in the next chapter, is in fact an umbrella term for a diverse category of conditions.
      Nevertheless, increased type 2 life expectancy is clearly shown by the divergence between
      age-standardized mortality and prevalence rates for diabetes of all types, because only 5-10
      percent of diabetes is type 1 and nearly all the rest is classified as type 2. During the period
      1990-2016, the diabetes mortality rate fell by 10.4 percent, which was much more than the
      small (1.9 percent) fall in prevalence.

18   2016 data. For those in the 50-69 year age group it was 43 percent higher.

19   The results of the Chernew and Mathers studies, both of which look at the causes of increased
      life expectancy in old age, are given additional credibility by the findings of Klenk et al (2016),
      which state: (1) in nearly all advanced countries from at least the second half of the 1970s
      up to 2010, reduced CVD mortality was the most important cause of increased general life
      expectancy; and (2) these life expectancy gains occurred primarily in the 65-plus age group.
      The general proposition that falling CVD mortality has dominated increases in life expectancy
      since World War II – the period during which life expectancy increases have been mainly
      focused on older people – is also reinforced by a major international study which found that
      increases in life expectancy at birth over the period 1990-2013 in high-income countries are
      primarily due to lower mortality rates for CVD and cancer (GBD, 2015).

20   The proposition that there has been an increase in the representation of genetically slow-aging
      people in the population (Blagosklonny, 2010) is based on the view that there are natural
      genetic variations between fast-aging and slow-aging individuals. Slow-aging individuals are
      less physically robust, which makes them vulnerable in the early years of life. As a result,
      for most of human history they were far more prone to die prematurely in infancy or child-
      hood. However, whereas historically, the majority of human beings died young – usually from
      infectious disease, starvation or physical violence – this has long ceased to be the case in rich
      countries. As a result, far more slow-aging individuals are surviving childhood and reaching
      adulthood, substantially increasing average life expectancy. However, the changes in public
      health, medical treatment and living standards that so radically reduced childhood mortality
      occurred a long time ago (mainly during the second half of the 19th century and the first half
      of the 20th century). This means that the impact of increased survival rates for genetically
      slow-aging individuals must be a phenomenon of the past, not of the future.

21 For national studies rejecting the hypothesis of postponement of chronic diseases in recent decades, see Cusset (2017: 29) and Dormont et Huber (2012) for France; Walter et al (2016) for Spain; and, for the US, Crimmins and Beltrán-Sánchez (2011) and Cutler et al (2013).

22 While patterns differ between diseases, data from the Global Burden of Disease database indicate that the incidence/prevalence of the majority of major chronic conditions – including cancers, osteoporosis and diabetes – amongst elderly people in any given age bracket (e.g. 65-69, 70-74, etc.) have increased in high-income countries over the period 1990-2017. For dementia and CKD, on the other hand, they have fallen somewhat.

23 Also to extend it through the abusive use of so-called "evergreening" where they are able to get away with it.

24 Take the example of the recently developed "direct acting antivirals" developed for treatment of hepatitis C, which was previously untreatable. These are said in the US to be the most expensive oral medications in history. In Australia, which has one of the world's tougher systems for negotiating new drug prices, the cost per patient treated of these drugs was estimated in 2016 to have been in the range of A$7,700-A$9,300 (midpoint equivalent to approximately US$6,100) (Dore and Grebely, 2017). While this is much lower than the US price (which for one of the most expensive of these new hepatitis C drugs, Harvoni, is said to be in excess of $80,000), it is still very high for an oral medication.

25 Increased life expectancy is due to the fact that Kalydeco does not just treat CF symptoms, but rather blocks the operation of the underlying genetic causes of CF in the class of patients concerned, thus preventing symptoms from manifesting themselves (see next chapter).

26 The problem of scale also applies, in a different way, to orphan vaccines – that is, vaccines against infectious diseases that are quite rare, or where serious complications arising from the disease are rare. The very small number of people harmed by such diseases makes the cost of vaccination per case prevented high, particularly for new-generation vaccines with high development costs. An example is the recently developed new vaccine Trumenba, which offers protection, for the first time, against meningitis B. Although a very serious disease, meningitis B is very rare (e.g. only several hundred cases per year in the United States).

27 Definitions of specialty drugs vary, but the concept is usually used in something like the following sense: "drugs and biologics (medicines derived from living cells cultured in a laboratory) that are complex to manufacture, can be difficult to administer, may require special patient monitoring and sometimes have Food and Drug Administration (FDA)-mandated strategies to control and monitor their use. Increasingly, specialty pharmaceuticals have come to be defined by exceeding a certain threshold cost, such as $600 per month, that may place such drugs on higher cost-sharing tiers." (Health Affairs, 2013)

28 This means that when an existing treatment is replaced by a new and better treatment, productivity is considered to have increased only if the new treatment requires fewer inputs (e.g. less labor) than the old treatment. If the new treatment requires more inputs (i.e. requires more time input from doctors or requires the use of much more complex and advanced equipment), and therefore costs more, this is not considered to mean that productivity has fallen. Nor is productivity considered to have increased if inputs required per treatment remain unchanged but the quality of the treatment improves. In summary, an increase in productivity means that the inputs required per treatment have fallen without any reduction in the quality of the treatment. Improvements in quality and improvements in productivity are, in this concept of "productivity," quite distinct. This is what Baumol (2012) refers to as "quality-unadjusted" productivity and is the relevant concept for addressing the potentially cost-reducing impacts of technological change.

29 Baumol referred to these as "progressive" industries.

30 This will immediately raise the issue of so-called wage stagnation in the mind of readers.

However, wage stagnation is a proposition that concerns median wages, whereas it is average wages that are relevant to the cost disease theory. Moreover, wage stagnation has only occurred in a minority of advanced countries, of which the US is the most important (see Chapter 7).

31   Financially strained governments from time to time squeeze the remuneration of nurses and other public-sector workers, allowing it to fall behind that of the private sector. This has been the case in some countries in the wake of the global financial crisis. But such pay squeezes are unsustainable in the long term. Over time, they create major recruitment problems – such as those that currently affect Britain's National Health Service – which force government to make major upward pay adjustments. It therefore remains the case that over time public-sector wages move up as economy-wide productivity increases, although not necessarily to the same extent. (In the case of the NHS, the government actually applied a "pay cap" which held pay raises below the inflation rate for a number of years, resulting in significant reductions in real remuneration for doctors and nurses. The government was eventually forced to remove the pay in 2018 (Atkins et al, 2019)).

32   In technical language, health care is "price inelastic."

33   T. Worstall, "Bending the Health Care Cost Curve: Fire the Doctors," Forbes, September 5, 2012.

34   A WHO study estimated that in 2010, health-worker remuneration (including of self-employed doctors) accounted for approximately one-third of health expenditure in a sample of 75 countries (obviously not confined to advanced countries) (Hernandez-Peña et al, 2013). Back-of-the-envelope estimates suggest that salaried healthcare-worker remuneration may have accounted for approximately one-third of health expenditure in the US in 2016. (This calculation is derived from putting together Bureau of Labor Statistics Occupational Employment Survey Statistics (May 2017) with National Accounts statistics of the overall share of employee compensation in GDP. It does not include self-employed health-professional remuneration).

35   Australian data on the cost structure of public hospitals give a total figure of 60 percent for health-worker remuneration – including remuneration paid to non-staff doctors (AIHW, 2017b). French data give a figure of 58 percent, again for public hospitals, in 2017 (DREES, 2018).

36   An additional reason why Baumol "oversold" the cost disease theory as an explanation of the historical trend of rising health spending is that his theory is, even in principle, incapable of explaining why health expenditure would rise as a percentage of GDP. It provides, at least if we overlook the flaws identified in the main text, an explanation as to why health expenditure rises in real per capita terms. But it cannot by itself explain increases in real per capita health expenditure that are greater than the rate of growth of real per capita income (which is what is required if health spending is to increase as a percentage of GDP). Despite the bold claims made by Baumol for the cost disease theory, the only explanation for this that he provides in his 2012 book is the dubious proposition that health care is a "superior good" (discussed later in this chapter). In a simple model, the cost disease can potentially generate, at very most, a rate of increase in real per capita health expenditure equal to the rate of increase in real per capita income – i.e. health expenditure remaining constant as a percentage of GDP. Such a model would include the following (totally unrealistic) assumptions: that the healthcare industry is 100 percent labor-intensive (i.e. no other non-labor inputs used), that there is absolutely no labor productivity growth, that healthcare industry wages increase at exactly the same rate as economy-wide labor productivity, and that demand for healthcare services is completely inelastic (i.e. absolutely no reduction in the use of health services when they become more expensive). The extreme nature of these assumptions makes it clear that, even if Baumol's characterization of healthcare as technologically stagnant were correct, the cost disease would even in principle only be capable in the real world of generating a rate of increase of real per capita health spending somewhat below the rate of increase of real GDP.

37   The very widespread belief amongst economists that the cost disease affects health care, as well

as education and other labor-intensive services, showed up in a survey conducted in 2017 by the University of Chicago of its panel of US economic experts (Maiello, 2017).

38 As Smith, Heffler and Freedland (2000: 13), following Cutler (1995), put it, "productivity growth in medical services [is] defined as the efficiency with which unchanged treatment options can be delivered."

39 Other unconvincing recent attempts to provide evidence for the Baumol effect include a paper by European Commission economists (Medeiros and Schwierz, 2013) and papers by a Swiss economist (Hartwig, 2006, 2007). Both essentially assume the Baumol effect in order to prove its existence – in the case of the European Commission paper, by basing their econometric test on the completely unfounded assumption that labor productivity growth in the health sector is zero.

40 In particular, that wages generally move in line with economy-wide labor productivity growth and that the prices of non-labor inputs used by each industry remain constant in real terms. Departures from these assumptions can modify the relation between price movements and relative productivity growth.

41 Smith, Heffler and Freeland (2000) estimate that approximately half of the growth in real per capita health expenditure in the US in the period 1940-1990 was due to the introduction and diffusion of new medical technology. See also Blumenthal, Stremikis and Cutler (2013) for a summary of other quantitative research on this topic. Using somewhat different methodology, Smith, Newhouse and Freeland (2009) estimate the contribution of technology at between 27 and 48 percent. All of these papers analyze US data. However, the inherent difficulty of statistically estimating the impact of technology, combined with methodological problems affecting these studies, makes it impossible to place much reliance on the concrete numbers produced by such analysis.

42 The standard definition of a need is something that is essential or very important, rather than merely desirable.

43 This is not, of course, to deny that certain problems of access remain in all advanced countries, particularly in relation to services such as mental health care and dental treatment.

44 Most vaccines easily pass a social-benefit-cost test – meaning that their benefits (financial and non-financial) to society as a whole greatly exceed their cost (Bloom, Canning and Weston, 2005). Some vaccines – childhood immunizations and probably a few adult immunizations – also pass narrowly a financial-benefit test for society as a whole, in the sense that the cost of vaccinating their target populations is less than the financial benefits that they deliver to society (Zhou et al, 2014). However, much of the financial benefit that vaccination generates takes the form of avoidance of lost earnings and other similar savings – in other words, of savings that do not reduce health expenditure. Such limited analysis as is available (Carvalho et al, 2017) makes it appear likely that few vaccines yield savings in health expenditure that exceed their cost. (For an explicit analysis of this in the case of childhood varicella vaccination, see Coudeville et al, 2005).

45 Moreover, while it "helps" if healthcare workers are denied wage increases fully in line with economy-wide productivity growth, this in itself will in general be insufficient to prevent total health expenditure from increasing faster than national income.

46 Good surveys of this literature may be found in de Meijer et al (2013); Productivity Commission (2005) and Reinhardt (2003).

47 For some of the research on this, see McGrail et al, 2000; Spillman and Lubitz, 2000; Yang, Norton and Stearns, 2003; and Miller, 2001. More recent research in France found that 22 percent of lifetime health expenditure was concentrated in the last three years of life (Gastaldi-Ménager, Geoffard and de Lagasnerie, 2016).

48   For some of the evidence on the "proximity to death" proposition, see Zweifel, Felder and
      Meier, 1999; Howdon and Rice, 2018; Gastaldi-Ménager, Geoffard and de Lagasnerie, 2016; and
      de Meijer et al (2013).

49   Although Zweifel, Felder and Meiers (1999) found that the fertility-rate effects were not suffi-
      cient to outweigh the "proximity to death" effect during the decade 1983-1992, which was the
      focus of their study, they expressly did not rule out the possibility that they would become "an
      important driving force for future health care expenditure growth."

50   The role of fertility-rate effects is considerably more important in looking to the future, because
      their role in population aging has increased significantly over the past decade, when the baby
      boomers started moving into the elderly age bracket. An illustration of the growing relevance
      of fertility-rate effects is provided by a detailed study of French trends over three decades,
      which estimates that over the period 2000-2008, aging contributed 29 percent of growth in
      real per capita health expenditure – a significantly larger contribution than in earlier decades,
      when fertility-rate effects played a lesser part in aging (Dormont and Huber, 2012). For some
      reason, Dormont and Huber present their breakdown of the contributing factors to rising
      health expenditure in terms that fail to adjust for population growth, thus making the impact
      of changing age structure appear smaller. On this basis, they pay allegiance to generally
      accepted opinion within the health economics community by claiming that their results indi-
      cate the role of aging is "minor." But when one fails to adjust for the necessarily huge impact
      of the growing size of the total population, all other factors will necessarily appear much less
      significant than they really are. The 29 percent figure used here represents an adjustment of
      their estimates to put them on a real per capita basis. On the relationship between population
      aging and health expenditure in France, see also Hourriez (1993) and Albouy et al (2009).

51   A study by Hagist and Kotlikoff (2009) of 10 advanced countries estimated that about one-fifth
      of the growth of health expenditure/GDP over the period 1970-2002 was due to the changing
      age structure of the population.

52   This is not to suggest that direct automation has been completely absent in the health sector.
      One notable example is the replacement of most exploratory surgery by the use of imaging
      technology such as ultrasound, CT scans and magnetic resonance imaging.

53   In particular, there is a certain "endogeneity" problem in such analysis, because households
      afflicted by more sickness will tend both to spend more on health treatment and also to have
      lower incomes (Newhouse, 1992).

54   A minor qualification to this is that the concept of a superior good can also be applied to a
      group of goods that are very close substitutes, such as different leisure travel options. However,
      this does not apply to health care, where many different conditions are treated and many of the
      new treatments are very different from those already in use.

Chapter Three: The Future of Health Expenditure

1   Based on the cost of the universal coverage single-payer health plan advanced by Senator
      Bernie Sanders in the 2017 US Democratic primary, the 10-year budgetary cost, which the
      Sanders campaign estimated at $13.8 trillion. A rough calculation indicates this would be
      equivalent to about 6 percent of GDP. The prominent health economist Kenneth Thorpe esti-
      mated the cost of Sanders' health program to be $10.9 trillion higher ($24.7 trillion total).

2   In Australia, for example, the introduction of universal dental cover is estimated to carry a
      price tag of at least $5.6 billion annually (Duckett, Cowgill and Swerissen, 2019), approximately
      three-tenths of 1 percent of Australia's annual GDP.

3   The misconception that personalized medicine necessarily means treatments tailored to indi-
      vidual patients is, regrettably, widespread. For example, in a recent book on technological
      revolution in the health sector, the Swiss analyst Xavier Comtesse describes personalized

medicine as offering "therapies specifically conceived for specific patients." "Totally person-alized," he writes, "each disease and its treatment will be tailored, in a sense conceived and designed, on the basis of information specific to each person" (Comtesse, 2017). This is not only an incorrect characterization of precision medicine, but an improbable future direction for medicine.

4   Florez (2016) observes in respect to diabetes that "despite extensive epidemiological and physio-logical characterization, we have fallen short in cataloguing risk factors, identifying triggering events, elucidating pathophysiological pathways, outlining prognostic course, selecting effec-tive therapies, and predicting complications. Specific patients continue to represent diagnostic challenges, and our approach to therapy continues to be based on population averages."

5   This uses the term "epigenetic" in the broadest sense. The main type of epigenetic characteristic is a modification to a chromosome that leaves the genes unchanged but modifies the way they function. Epigenetic factors can also come into play in the case of some single-gene disorders.

6   Dr. Stéphan Eliez of the Office médico-pédagogique of Geneva, quoted in *Le Temps* (Geneva), 6 November 2018.

7   It does not, unfortunately, work for patients who suffer from the single most common CFTR gene mutation.

8   A number which is growing significantly every year with the identification of additional rare diseases.

9   Gene therapy is the insertion of genetic material into patients' cells, usually via a virus "vector," in an essentially untargeted manner (see Doudna and Sternberg, 2017: 16-20).

10   Thus the current direction of Alzheimer's research is away from the notion that there is a single condition for which a single treatment will be appropriate towards a new approach which is expected to result in "multiple treatments that target each of the different ways that it can develop and manifest" and which recognizes that "the reason the approaches we have been using to look for Alzheimer's drugs have failed is that there is not one single way that the disease develops and progresses. Instead, it now appears as if there may be many different con-tributors and pathways to the disease." ("For Alzheimer's Researchers, a Long and Frustrating Struggle to Find a Drug", *Washington Post*, 4 April 2020.)

11   In France, for example, an increase in CVD incidence amongst people under 65, probably linked to obesity and related risk factors, has already been observed (Santé Publique, 2017: 15).

12   Immunotherapy means boosting a patient's immune system to fight a disease. *Customized* immunotherapy means that the agent (e.g. vaccine) used to boost the patient's immune system is tailored specifically for that patient.

13   The OECD forecasts a demographic contribution to increased health expenditure of 0.8 percent of GDP over the period 2010-2060. The "one-seventh" referred to in the main text compares this with the OECD's "cost-pressure" projection, which forecasts an OECD average increase in spending of 6.3 percent of GDP over that period. (It disregards the OECD's alternative "cost-containment" scenario, which is an adjustment of the main "cost-pressure" scenario based essentially on wishful thinking – see note 30). In Australia, official forecasts suggest that aging will contribute only 10 percent of the projected increase over 2015-2055 in average per capita health expenditure by the national government (CoA, 2015: 62). United States estimates show a higher contribution, with population aging projected to contribute one-third of the increase in government spending on healthcare programs as a percentage of GDP over the 30-year period 2018-2048 (CBO, 2018a: 19).

14   The expenditure-increasing interactions between medical advances and population aging run in both directions. Not only will population aging amplify the expenditure impact of medical advances, but medical advances are likely to play an even greater role than in the

past in driving increases in longevity – which will, as in the past, boost spending on chronic conditions. The major contribution of medical advances to the unprecedented increase in longevity that occurred in advanced countries over the past 70 years was discussed in the last chapter. The reason that medical advances can be expected to play an even more central role in increasing longevity in coming decades is that other forces which have in the past contributed to increasing longevity – specifically, the decline of demanding physical work, the previously rapid fall in the number of smokers and the increased representation of genetically slower-aging people in the population as a delayed consequence of the conquest of infectious disease – have in large measure run their course and will probably make only a quite limited contribution to increasing longevity in coming decades. It is also hard at present to see positive lifestyle trends more generally making a net positive contribution to increasing longevity. (The obesity crisis is, in particular, working in precisely the opposite direction.) Under these circumstances, medical advances will need to shoulder even more of the burden of prolonging lifespans.

15   IMF projections for advanced economies for 2011-2030 estimate that one-third of the increase in health expenditure during that period will be due to the impact of population aging (Soto, Shang and Coady, 2012). Longer-term projections for the period 2015-2050 and 2050-2100 appear to assume a similarly large contribution from population aging, although no explicit decomposition of the projections between demographic and other factors is presented (Clements et al, 2015). The methodology underpinning the IMF's projections does not incorporate any explicit assumptions about the age profile of health expenditure. Rather, it simply assumes that a constant ratio of average per capita health spending for those aged 65 and over relative to average per capita health spending for 0-64-year-olds. This methodology may be questioned because it does not acknowledge any role for the proximity to death effect.

16   See, for example, Osterholm (2005).

17   Quoted in M. Morrell and K. Wood, "The Tragedy Is That We Knew This Was Coming," *Washington Post*, 27 March 2020.

18   "NHS Hospitals Facing Serious Shortages of Vital Equipment," *The Guardian*, 25 January 2018.

19   "Coronavirus: la mission impossible de Jérôme Salomon, directeur général de la santé," *Le Monde*, 20 March 2020.

20   This stock had been acquired several years earlier as a result of a decision by a far-sighted health minister in response to the H1N1 pandemic. In 2013 it was decided to leave the responsibility and the costs of stocking masks to individual hospitals and other public agencies. The latter failed, predictably, to do what was needed, largely because they were so short of funds. See the analysis of the problem by Aurélien Rouquet, professor of logistics at the Neoma Business School in *Le Monde*, 24 March 2020 ("Coronavirus: 'la pénurie de masques, incompetence logistique de l'Etat français'").

21   Professor Dame Sally Davies, quoted in *The Guardian*, 11 September 2019.

22   Where "robots" are defined in the most general sense as systems that integrate computers with either or both sensors and actuators.

23   The Geneva University Hospital claims, for example, to have reduced the cost of gastric bypass surgery by 27 percent through the use of the da Vinci robot. *Le News*, 15 June 2017.

24   In the UK, it has been estimated that 20 percent of general practitioner appointments and 19 percent of accident and emergency attendances are for minor medical problems that could be treated at home (Loder and Nicholas, 2018)

25   The leading AI specialist Stuart J. Russell makes the additional point that deep learning systems face the fundamental constraint in diagnostic work that, without knowing what the physiological mechanisms of diseases are, it does not work to simply "collect terabytes of data

from millions of patients and then throw that data into a black-box learning algorithm" (interview in Ford, 2018: 57).

26   Costs per case could also conceivably fall if healthcare wages were affected by broad economy-wide wage stagnation as a consequence of digital technologies dramatically reducing the demand for labor across the economy. Such an outcome is, however, improbable (see Chapter 7).

27   How far this is true for other potential transformations of the health system – such as the rather dubious prediction that "the hospital of the future will be the bedroom" (Topol, 2015) – remains to be seen.

28   In France, for example, health coverage became universal only in 2000. And even though Germany was one of the first countries to extend state-supported health coverage to most citizens (with reforms initiated by Bismarck over a century ago), it was only in 2009 that coverage became completely universal, when coverage was extended to persons on welfare benefits.

29   *The Guardian* (13 July 2018), quoting official figures, reported that in May 2018, 211,434 patients had been on the NHS waiting list for surgery for over six months. In August 2018, more than 3,000 people had been waiting for over a year (*Mail Online*, 12 October 2018).

30   These are the main ("cost-pressure") projections presented by the OECD. They are baseline estimates in the sense that they assume what the forecasters regard as the most likely trends. Alternative so-called "cost-containment" projections are also presented by the OECD, and these show much lower increases in expenditure. However, it is difficult to give any credibility to these latter projections. They are based, incredibly, on the assumption that the cost-increasing impact of the "spending residual" – which incorporates the impact of technology – gradually falls from its current level to zero by 2060. This effectively means assuming either that over coming decades technology will cease to drive up health expenditure or, alternatively, that savings from other reforms (e.g. improved efficiency through reforms to the organization of health systems) will be so big as to fully offset the cost impact of technology. The rationale presented by the OECD for presenting the "cost-containment" is simply the assertion that it is "unlikely" that governments would allow health expenditure to increase to the extent implied in the baseline forecasts. But this is wishful thinking, which disregards the fact that government health expenditure has increased massively in the past.

31   The impact of technology is not modelled as a separate variable in these or other health expenditure forecasting models. Instead it is incorporated in an omnibus category usually labelled "excess cost growth" (or in the OECD forecasts, as the "spending residual.") In the OECD forecasts, the spending residual is assumed to remain constant at levels estimated from the 15 years preceding the preparation of the forecasts. In the CBO forecasts, excess cost growth is assumed to be 1 percent from 2030, which is below past levels but is (according to Follette and Sheiner, 2008) a realistic approximation of trends adjusting for past policy and other changes.

32   The IMF forecasts assume that "excess cost growth," which again incorporates the impact of technology, will decline to zero between 2050 and 2100 (Clements et al, 2015: 7). This is similar to the assumption made in the OECD's "cost-containment" scenario (see note above) and is equally unrealistic. The IMF does not, however, assume that excess cost growth will decline in the first period of its forecasts (2015-2050).

33   The European Union's long-term projections of future government health expenditure are contained in the European Commission's annual *Aging Reports* (EC, 2018a, and previous editions), as well as in the annual stability and convergence programs of member nations. These forecasts of health expenditure, although gradually improving, lack credibility for several reasons. The rate of growth of projected government health spending is substantially lower than the average rate of growth of total health expenditure over recent decades. They present a confusing range of 12 scenarios, with no clear baseline (the so-called "AWG reference

scenario" is, by the forecasters' own admission, unrealistic (EC, 2017: 116-7)). Having failed previously to incorporate the impact of technological innovation, the latest iterations of the EC forecasts now present an explicit scenario (the "non-demographic determinants scenario") that supposedly reflects the impact of technology, institutional settings and health behaviors. However, even this scenario assumes that the impact of these factors will – for unexplained reasons – progressively decline over time (EC, 2018a: 112).

34   On the assumption that the variance between countries remains of the same order as projected in the OECD forecasts, the increases over the 30-year period would be in the range of 3.7-4.9 percent, and over the 50-year period, 6.4-8.3 percent.

35   Assuming that Belgium – the country with the lowest growth forecast in the OECD forecasts – remains below the average rate of growth of health expenditure/GDP by the same margin as in those forecasts, but nevertheless experiences 15 percent higher growth per year on average than in the OECD forecast, its 30 year growth would be 3.97 percent, and 50-year growth 6.7 percent.

Chapter Four: The Impact of Aging

1   It might be wondered why the focus of this analysis is exclusively on the percentage shares of elderly age groups in the overall population, without any mention of future trends in the much-used "old age dependency ratio" (OADR). This is because the OADR makes assumptions about the ages at which working lives commence and finish (most often, that they start at age 15 and finish at age 65) that are static and unrealistic in the light of trends for longer periods of education and the postponement of the age of retirement.

2   This refers to the UN's "median" scenario. The statistical annex supplements this with the UN's projections for several major countries.

3   For example, in the European Union, the 65-plus age group is projected to increase from 19.3 percent of the population to 28.8 percent during the period 2016-2070, while the 80-plus group is envisaged to grow from 5.4 percent to 12.5 percent (EU, 2018: 369). In the United States, the period 2016-2060 is projected to see an increase from 15 percent to 23 percent in the 65-plus age group's share of the population, while for the 80-plus group the projected increase is from 4 percent to 8 percent (NCB, 2017).

4   The UN projections to 2070 and 2100 indicate that, although many countries are looking at an eventual slowing down in the population-aging process, it is unlikely in most that there will be any significant reversal in the process over the next half-century. Japan is the big exception here. In that country, it is probable that growth in the ranks of both the 65-plus and 80-plus age groups will peak and then fall a little towards the end of the period. This reflects the fact that rapid population aging started significantly earlier in Japan than elsewhere.

5   The European Commission considers it likely that unit costs of institutional LTC will rise because of "the highly labor-intensive nature of LTC and the fact that productivity gains are expected to be particularly slow in this sector, as the services are difficult to automate or re-engineer" (EC, 2018a: 140). In the United Kingdom, official long-term forecasts of LTC expenditure prepared by the Office for Budget Responsibility make the same assumption, which translates quantitatively into the assumption that over the 50-year time horizon LTC real unit costs will increase by 2 percent per year (OBR, 2018: 147, 151).

6   See, e.g. RCAC (2019: 29). This is why, as Weaver et al (2009) stress, there is a certain PTD effect on the demand for LTC for the elderly.

7   The high costs of care for dementia patients are the main reasons why, in the United States, dementia is by far the condition with the highest treatment and care costs in the last five years of life (Kelley et al, 2015).

8   "Le décryptage éco. Emmanuel Macron souhaite créer un cinquième risque pour mieux
     prendre en charge la dépendance," *France Info*, 16 April 2018.

9   The all-party House of Lords committee, for example, recommended protection against "cata-
     strophic accommodation costs" as well as a "basic entitlement publicly funded personal care"
     (House of Lords, 2019: 5).

10   For an outline of the LTC expenditure pressures in Austria, and recent steps by government to
     increase support, see Fuchs et al (2018).

11   Although no long-term Australian government projections of public pension expenditure
     appear to be available, it is clear that spending will drop considerably beyond the 2020s. This
     will be the consequence of the major pension reforms introduced starting in the 1980s, which
     have resulted in members of the Australian workforce accumulating growing "second pillar"
     pension assets, the size of which will progressively greatly reduce dependence on "first pillar"
     public pensions (Daley et al, 2018).

12   The latest 50-year forecasts of government old age and survivor pension spending by the United
     States Congressional Budget Office (CBO, 2019b) show spending rising from 4.16 percent of
     GDP in 2018 to 5.51 percent in 4043 and then to 5.41 percent in 2068.

13   In approximately half of advanced countries, it is (using 2017 data from the IMF's COFOG
     database) one of the largest three "functions of government" in the standard COFOG classifi-
     cation of government expenditure – in almost all cases, coming third behind social protection
     and health. In the remaining countries, government expenditure on education is a little less
     than expenditure on either or both "general public services" and "economic affairs." However,
     these two latter functions are more in the nature of "grab bags" of disparate types of govern-
     ment expenditure rather than categories with a common broad purpose.

14   The 2019 stability and convergence programs of selected European Union countries fore-
     cast government education expenditure/GDP changing as follows in 2020-2050: Austria, no
     change; Denmark, increase from 5.4 to 5.6 percent; France, fall from 4.7 to 4.6 percent; Ireland,
     drop from 3.5 to 3.4 percent; Italy, decrease from 3.5 to 3.3 percent; the Netherlands, rise from
     4.9 to 5 percent; Spain, increase from 3.9 to 4.1 percent; Sweden, fall from 4.7 to 4 percent;
     the UK, decline from 4.2 to 3.8 percent; and Germany, increase from 3.9 to 4.1 percent (in
     Germany's case, each figure is the average of the two scenarios presented in the country's
     stability program).

15   This is based on data from the OECD (OECD.Stat, accessed 11 February 20), which provides
     the breakdown of government education expenditure by level of education for 16 advanced
     countries for 2017, together with government education expenditure as a percentage of GDP
     for those countries.

Chapter Five: Decisive Action on Global Warming: What Will It Cost?

1   See "Climate Change Could Be an Electoral Timebomb, Republican Strategists Fear," *New York
     Times*, 2 August 2019.

2   The main relevant form of R&D is energy related. International Energy Agency statistics indi-
     cate that advanced-country governments mostly spend only around three or four *hundredths*
     of a percent of GDP on energy-related R&D of all types. Even in Switzerland, which had one
     of the highest levels of government energy R&D spending levels, the figure was 0.06 percent
     of GDP in 2017. (International Energy Agency Energy Technology RD&D Budgets, 2019
     first edition, available at https://www.iea.org/statistics/rdd/. This is based on the "RD&D per
     thousand units of GDP" indicator reported there.)

3   The shift of the German grand coalition – comprised essentially of two conservative parties, the
     Christian Democrats and the Social Democrats – is particularly notable here. (See, for example,

"German 'Black Zero' Budget Faces €40bn Green Challenge," *Financial Times*, 19 September 2019. "Les nouveaux clivages du modèle politique allemand," *Le Monde*, 6 September 2019.)

4   Not all opposition to carbon pricing is based on political calculation. There are those who oppose the use of price-based instruments because they have an ideological dislike for market mechanisms or even for capitalism in general. From their point of view, carbon pricing represents "using the price system to try and resolve the problem created by the price system" (Nersisyan and Wray, 2019). The problem with this point of view is that, in a market economy, "price signals are critical," as the International Energy Agency (IEA/IRENA, 2017) observes with respect to carbon pricing. There are also some climate-policy specialists who argue, on grounds which are not very clear, that carbon pricing is an inferior policy instrument representing an "outdated" approach to tackling the problem (Pratt and Lilliestam, 2018).

5   For expositions of the basic case for carbon pricing, see Nordhaus (2013, 2019); Gollier (2019), Stern (2007) and Tirole (2016) (Tirole's work is available in English as *Economics for the Common Good* (Princeton University Press, 2017)).

6   The International Energy Agency estimates that by 2050 carbon prices internationally would need to be in the range of $80-190/tonne to achieve the COP21 objective of keeping global warming well below 2° (IEA/IRENA, 2017). A carbon price consistent with the 1.5° objective would need to be somewhat higher.

7   This lack of targeting based on emissions is a key reason why subsidies often have very high, and inconsistent, "implicit" costs per tonne of emission reduction (Gollier, 2019; OECD, 2018a).

8   Early retirement benefits for coal workers and others employed in the fossil fuel industries are one of the forms of adjustment assistance proposed in Elizabeth Warren's September 2019 campaign document "100% Clean Energy for America."

9   As in the cost to US governments of compulsory acquisitions of houses in coastal areas which are becoming increasingly flood prone as a result of rising sea levels (see "Trump Administration Presses Cities to Evict Homeowners from Flood Zones," *New York Times*, 11 March 2020.)

10   *The Economist*, 27 September 2019.

11   "Germany Strikes €44 billion deal to phase out coal use in energy supply," *Financial Times*, 16 January 2020; "Germany to Pay Energy Firms Begins in Coal Phaseout Plan," Deutsche Welle, 16 January 2020 (www.dw.com).

12   Germany closed its last black coal mine in 2018. However, it continues to mine considerable quantities of brown coal (lignite) for power production.

13   The climate crisis seems to be regarded as providing a license for politicians to propose even extensions of passenger public transport services for which there is unlikely to be much demand – such as proposals for new train services to sparsely populated areas; for the general reestablishment of night train services with sleepers (which would, unless massively subsidized, be prohibitively expensive for most potential travelers); or for indiscriminately wide expansions in high-speed train networks. Although good public transport is essential, it is all too easy to waste vast amounts of limited public resources on badly targeted service expansions. A graphic example of this is France's TGV (high-speed train) network. With respect to its services between major metropolises, the TGV network is a model for the world. Unfortunately, however, it has for purely vote-buying reasons also been inappropriately extended to provide high-cost fast train services to certain relatively minor towns, at a quite unjustifiable cost. This has contributed both to the accumulation of unsustainable debt by France's rail enterprise, and to the neglect of the infrastructure of the non-fast train part of the network. The very importance of good public transport networks makes it essential that close attention is paid to their financial viability.

14 Nersisyan and Wray translate these estimates in terms of 10-year investment requirements, which are on average 4.55 percent of GDP. Stretching this out over 30 years gives the figure of approximately 1.5 percent of GDP.

15 The British Department for Business, Energy and Industrial Strategy estimates the required spending to be at least 40 percent greater than does the Committee on Climate Change.

16 In addition, reporting the required annual cost as a proportion of projected GDP 30 years in the future – in 2050, when GDP is projected to have grown greatly – makes the cost look significantly smaller than reporting it in relation to projected GDP in each of the years over the forecasting period.

17 Simon Kuper, "Can the Dutch Save the World from the Danger of Rising Sea Levels?" *Financial Times*, 30 January 2020.

Chapter Six: Infrastructure Deficits

1 As presidential candidate, Hillary Clinton proposed a $275 billion taxpayer-financed five-year infrastructure spending plan.

2 As discussed there, governments will certainly need to spend significant money on infrastructure such as flood protection works and upgrading roads and train lines to cope with higher temperatures. However, a large portion of the additional public investment required to tackle climate change is not on infrastructure but in other areas such as public housing and buildings. In many countries, substantial climate-related infrastructure spending will need to be undertaken by public enterprises – e.g. state electricity companies – but this will not, at least for the most part, be tax-financed spending.

3 Governments in some other advanced countries have spent more on promoting broadband and have spent in different ways. In South Korea, the government provided financial incentives early on to speed up the establishment of the broadband network. In Australia, where the government has created a national broadband network run by a public enterprise, many analysts suggest that the government will end up bearing significant costs as a result of this endeavor not ultimately achieving its intended self-financing. Whether this is the case remains to be seen.

4 Anyone from outside the US who travels through major American airports will be well aware of how poor many of them are and may find it easy to believe that a large increase in government funding is what is needed to solve the problem. There has unquestionably been massive underinvestment in US airports relative to other advanced countries. The problem is not, however, due to American airports receiving less *government* funding than elsewhere. The key problem is that, unlike elsewhere, US airports are not largely self-financing, but are very heavily dependent on US government grants to fund investment. The government levies a tax on passengers and this tax revenue is allocated to airports in the form of grants from the Federal Aviation Administration for infrastructure investment. The FAA distributes this money in such a way that there is only a weak link between the amount of funding individual airports receive and the demand pressure they face (or, for that matter, the efficiency of their operations). Congress has, moreover, kept the level of the passenger tax artificially low for the past 20 years, thereby guaranteeing an investment funding drought. Although it might seem that the answer to the problem would be for Congress to substantially increase its financial support to airports by funding this through an increase in the passenger tax, a far better solution would be to put the airports on the same commercial basis as elsewhere and thereby end their dependence upon government funding.

5 There are those who go even further and include institutions such as the legal system as part of society's infrastructure.

6 These ratings are from the ASCE 2017 Infrastructure Report Card (https://www.infrastructurereportcard.org). Aviation (airports and air traffic control systems) gets a D, as do inland

waterways. Ports get a C+. Rail (freight and long-distance passenger) does a bit better, at B. These are ratings on a scale of A-F.

7   Deutsche Welle, "Germany Tries to Close Infrastructure Backlog," 18 August 2018 (www.dw.com).

8   The French media has reported the findings of an unpublished report of the official rail security monitoring agency identifying such widespread faults (*Le Parisien*, 20 August 2019; *Le Monde*, 21 August 2019).

9   In some countries, most of the responsibility for the road network – even including the national highways – is borne by sub-national government, and it is precisely sub-national government that has been under most financial strain due to either or both weak tax bases and cuts in financial transfers from national government (Knopman, 2016; Fratzscher et al, 2015; Sénat, 2019: 13).

10   Within that total, there has been a slight fall in road investment and an increase in rail.

11   US rail investment/GDP is much lower than in most other advanced countries. With respect to road, low investment is less obvious, given that US road infrastructure investment/GDP is roughly "middle of the pack" amongst advanced economies. However, given that the United States has a much lower population density than almost all other advanced countries, it needs to spend significantly more to have road infrastructure of the same standard.

12   $91 billion in 2015, when US GDP was $18,219 billion.

13   If urban roads are toll-free, the inevitable consequence is that there are many more vehicles on the road and fewer people use public transport. If, moreover, there is no congestion charging, peak-hour traffic inexorably worsens over time. In densely populated areas where it is impossible to continually expand the road network, the only practical means of dealing with the problem is to charge urban road users appropriately, while continuing to improve the mass transit alternatives.

14   In the United States, Congress initiated the construction of the interstate highway system in 1956. The system, as originally conceived, was declared complete in 1992. The construction of the modern Japanese highway system was also kick-started in 1956. At that time, Japan had a grossly inadequate road system in which only 23 percent of its national highways were paved. In France also, the modern system of autoroutes was constructed only after the war, with most of the work accomplished between the mid-1950s and mid-1970s.

15   Within limits, however: in China's case, analysts have suggested that the country has been over-investing in infrastructure, and spending too little on health, education and social security.

16   See the indicators of "consumer satisfaction with urban transport" at https://ec.europa.eu/ transport/facts-fundings/scoreboard/compare/people/urban-transport-consumer-satisfaction_en.

17   2017 OECD figures for general government investment/GDP (OECD.Stat, accessed 18 January 2020).

18   Even the International Monetary Fund has added to the widespread misunderstanding on this issue, claiming recently that "after three decades of decline, public investment remains at historical lows in advanced economies" (IMF, 2018: 26). However, its own data – which, incidentally, only ran up to 2013, making it five years out of date at the time this claim was made – actually showed there was no general trend in advanced countries over the relevant timeframe. In fact, in the period concerned, public investment/GDP in a majority of advanced countries either increased or remained essentially unchanged. (A detailed analysis of the underlying data (IMF Investment and Capital Stock Dataset, accessed 21 January 2020) for the 21 advanced countries shows that if one compares the average ratio of government investment to GDP in the 1980s with the average for the 2010s (i.e. the last four years of the time series, 2010-2013), government

investment/GDP increased substantially (defined as by 10 percent or more) in seven countries, and was essentially stable (defined as increasing or falling by no more than 5 percent) in five countries. In the other eight countries, the ratio fell by 14 percent or more.)

Chapter Seven: Income Support in the New Economy

1   Expressed differently, underlying poverty refers to the position of households that would be poor if they relied solely upon what economists call their "market income" – that is, income excluding welfare and other benefits and any taxes they pay. Underlying poverty differs from actual poverty to the extent that government income support, net of any taxes, increases household "disposable income" sufficiently to raise them above the poverty threshold.

2   The most common definition of relative poverty is households with an income below 60 percent of median household income (more precisely "equivalized" household income, meaning household income adjusted to what is considered to be a representatively sized household).

3   By those who refer to the new wave of technological innovation now getting under way as the Fourth Industrial Revolution.

4   It is debatable whether one might wish to push the time frame back to some point in the late 1980s. However, an important additional reason for using the 1990s as the starting point is data availability.

5   Eurostat statistics on the "at risk of poverty rate before social transfers," accessed 20 February 2019. "Significant increases" in the poverty rate means increases in excess of 1 percent. Note that most data cover the period 1995-2017, but for two countries the time series starts in 1996 (Finland) or 1997 (Norway). (The poverty cut-off point is 60 percent of median equivalized income after social transfers.)

6   Statistics prior to 1995 are more limited and less methodologically robust. However, OECD estimates for a number of advanced countries for the period 1985-1995 suggest some overall increase in underlying poverty, although with large variations between countries (i.e. the increase was small in a number of countries and quite large in others – such as Sweden, which experienced a major economic crisis in the mid-1990s) (Förster, 2000: 152).

7   OECD statistics give a time series for underlying poverty in the total population in Canada from 1980 to 2016. In 2016, the rate (19 percent) was down from the rate of nearly 20 years earlier (22 percent in 1997). (It was also higher than that in 1980 (16 percent)).

8   A time series of data on underlying poverty is available covering the period 1967-2014 using the US Bureau of Census' "supplementary poverty measure" (SPM). On this basis, the rate of poverty in the non-elderly population was essentially unchanged between 1967 and 2007 (Bivens et al, 2014: 36). The SPM is, however, not a true measure of relative poverty (it is something between an absolute and a relative measure) (Fox et al, 2018: 9; Moskowitz, Haskins and Smeeding, 2010). This means that if underlying relative poverty is measured on an international basis, it must have increased. Wimer (2013: 14) provides other estimates also pointing to the conclusion that underlying relative poverty has increased. Bivens et al (2014) report a substantial increase in underlying poverty on the SPM basis between 2007 and 2014, but this clearly has a substantial cyclical component – i.e. the lingering effects in 2014 of the global financial crisis – and cannot be taken to imply a long-term trend.

9   Two factors specific to the United States that have significantly contributed to growing underlying poverty are (1) the very large long-term increase in single-mother families (Gautié/ Ponthieux: 497) and (2) the long-term increase in the number of prime-age males outside the labor market. Neither of these factors have been present generally in other advanced countries.

10 Official definitions of long-term unemployment differ between countries. One widespread definition is, however, unemployment lasting more than six months.

11   To get an impression of long-term trends, we need to compare levels of long-term unemploy-
      ment at equivalent points in the "business cycle," so as to avoid comparing boom years with
      bust years. It makes sense from this perspective to compare long-term unemployment in 2017
      with a broadly similar year several decades ago (1989). When we do this, we see that of 14
      advanced OECD countries for which consistent data are reported by the OECD, the rate of
      long-term unemployment increased in only three (two of which were the US and Japan, where
      the increase was only approximately half of a percent). The countries where it fell – whether
      significantly or only slightly – were Australia, Belgium, Canada, Denmark, France, Ireland,
      Italy, the Netherlands, New Zealand, Spain and the United Kingdom. (Source: "Incidence
      of Unemployment by Duration," OECD.Stat, accessed 14 February 2019). Long-term unem-
      ployment is, of course, significantly higher today than in the three decades of peak prosperity
      following the Second World War, but that is irrelevant to the issue under discussion.

12   Of 11 advanced OECD countries for which consistent data are available for the period from
      1998 or 1999 through to 2017 or 2018, nine experienced either falling or stable male inactivity
      rates (Australia, Austria, Canada, Finland, Israel, Italy, Japan, New Zealand and Spain), and
      in only one country (Denmark) did the rate increase to anywhere near the same extent as in
      the United States (in the other, Belgium, the increase was quite small). Of eight other countries
      for which data are available only for a shorter period (basically from some date prior to the
      GFC through to 2017 or 2018), the rate fell in six (Germany, South Korea, the Netherlands,
      Sweden, Switzerland and the United Kingdom), was stable in one (France) and rose in only one
      (Ireland). (Source: "Inactivity Rate, aged 15-64, males" in the labor market statistics database
      at OECD.Stat, accessed 16 February 2019).

13   The only statistics available – and these are limited – concern rates of in-work poverty *after
      benefits and taxes* – and the interpretation of these is bedeviled by problems with the way
      in-work poverty is defined by the statisticians in different countries (Gautié and Ponthieux,
      2016). Moreover, EU statistics only date back to 2007. French national statistics indicate that
      the percentage of working poor as a percentage of working-age adults fell a little between
      the late 1990s and 2016 (https://www.inegalites.fr/Un-million-de-travailleurs-pauvres-en-
      France; OdI, 2018: 64). In the UK, the rate was essentially unchanged over that period (House
      of Commons, 2018: 30). However, given that the Blair government improved income support
      for working families in the late 1990s, this suggests that there may have been an increase in
      underlying working poverty. In the United States, the incidence of in-work poverty – measured
      in terms of the official Census Bureau poverty line – did not increase over the period 1986-
      2016 (Shambaugh, Bauer and Breitwieser, 2017). However, because this is based on a measure
      of absolute rather than relative poverty, it implies that the rate of relative in-work poverty
      increased. European statistics show some increase in the rate of in-work poverty over the
      period 2007-2014 (Eurofound, 2017: 16). However, the global financial crisis unquestionably
      triggered a significant increase in in-work poverty, with rates subsequently falling. The 2007-
      2014 increase is therefore likely to be in large measure cyclical.

14   The measure of in-work poverty used by the European Commission is an "after benefits"
      measure, and therefore not relevant to our analysis. It is nevertheless of interest that, accord-
      ing to a 2019 report commissioned by the European Commission (Peña-Casas et al, 2019: 23,
      A.19), in-work poverty decreased between 2012 and 2017 in six advanced EU countries, and
      increased – slightly, with the exception of Spain – in seven.

15   Low pay, like relative poverty, is a measure relative to the median. The most widely accepted
      international definition of low pay is hourly remuneration 60 percent or less of the median.

16   OECD data on low pay come from OECD.Stat ("Decile Ratios of Gross Earnings," accessed
      18 February 2019), and are based on a definition of low pay as two-thirds or less of median
      full-time earnings. For the majority of advanced OECD countries, the OECD's time series
      on low pay goes back only to the early 2000s, although for a number (including Australia,
      Italy, Japan, the UK and the US) it goes back considerably earlier. An impression of trends can

be gathered by looking at the 14 advanced OECD countries for which there is a time series starting at or sometime before 2004, and taking as the starting point the earliest point at or after 1989 (the date of a previous peak in the business cycle), and as the endpoint the latest pre-pandemic year available at the time of writing (2016 or 2017). On this basis, the incidence of low pay increased in four countries (Australia, Denmark, Ireland and Italy), fell in six (Belgium, Germany, Israel, Japan, New Zealand and the United Kingdom) and was essentially stable (i.e. rose or fell less than 1 percent) in four (Austria, Canada, South Korea and the US). In the light of its well-known experience of wage stagnation, it might seem surprising that the United States is included among the countries that over the relevant time period (1989-2017 in this case) have seen a stable rate of low pay. (Indeed, even if one goes back to the start of the OECD's US data in 1981, there was only a small increase in the rate of low pay). Data reported by Schmitt, Gould and Bivens (2018: 4) raise the possibility that there may have been a greater *longer-term* increase in the incidence of low pay in the US over the past 40 years (they report that wage movements were even less for the bottom decile than for the median worker over 1979-2017 – 8.9 percent versus 16.8 percent). But the more important point is that low pay is a relative concept – relative to median wages – so that if median wages are stagnating (as has been the case in the US) the number of people paid much less than *average* wages will increase significantly. This point is elaborated in Appendix 7.1. Note that an important limitation of the OECD data is that they pertain only to full-time workers.

17 Data published by the Brookings Institute for the period 1986-2016 indicate that in the US there has been no long-term increase in the percentage of working age adults who are poor because they are underemployed (Shambaugh, Bauer and Breitwieser, 2017). Specifically, Figure 7 in the paper shows that the number of working-age adults who are both poor and underemployed (referred to in the paper as "involuntary part-time" employment) was approximately the same in 2017 as it had been two decades earlier. While there was a large increase in the number of such people in the immediate wake of the global financial crisis, the number fell as the economy recovered. Figure 5 in the study shows that the number of poor people in "less than full-time year-round employment" in the US – which is of course not the same as underemployment, but includes the underemployed working poor – did not exhibit any trend of increase over the period 1986-2016.

18 Blundell et al (2018) report a substantial decrease in average hours worked by men in the lowest two deciles of the UK (hourly) wage distribution over the period 1994-2015, including a considerable increase in part-time work. On the other hand, there was actually a decline in the extent of part-time work for women in the lowest two deciles. So it is likely that the household poverty-increasing impact of lower hours worked by men was to at least some extent offset by increased hours worked by their partners.

19 Data are obtained from ILOSTAT (19 February 2019). For these 14 countries, data cover at least the period 2007-2017. For a number, it goes back further (e.g. Australia 1980-2017, the US 1994-2017).

20 Precarity theorists commonly treat precarious work as synonymous with irregular work. Some go further and include within precarious workers all those who are low-paid or underemployed – even when this is their continuing status and therefore has nothing to do with "precarity" in its dictionary sense of uncertainty. Some writers even deem all the working poor to be precarious workers. In Standing's (2014) work on the topic, he spends much of the first chapter supposedly defining and elaborating the concept of precarious work, without ever managing to provide a clear and succinct definition. Elsewhere in the book, he confuses the concept even further with an extraordinarily wide set of examples, some of which have no apparent relation to his "definition." These include, for example, people in jobs without the possibility of career progression, who he apparently considers to be precarious workers irrespective of how stable their employment and earnings might be. As Kalleberg and Vallas (2018: 7-8) – themselves precarity theorists, but far more careful in their analysis than Standing – note, a "source of difficulty that has bedeviled scholarship in this field [i.e. precarity theory] has involved ongoing

definitional ambiguities as to the very meaning of 'precarious work.' Instability, insecurity, and unpredictability have all been assumed to be synonyms, resulting in much conceptual slippage and confusion as to actual empirical trends."

21   In Europe, for example, two-thirds of part-time workers voluntarily chose part-time work (2014) (ILO, 2016: 104).

22   On average, across the OECD (not all the member countries of which are, of course, advanced), one-third of part-time workers were underemployed in 2017 (OECD, 2019c: 102).

23   It is also worth noting that to be poor and to work less than the equivalent of continuous full-time employment is not necessarily the same as being underemployed. Many people in this situation are unable or do not wish to work more – for example, because of health problems or family responsibilities. In the US, in 2016 only approximately one-third of the working poor who were not in full-term employment were so involuntarily (Shambaugh, Bauer and Breitwieser, 2017).

24   The data Hacker and other contributors to this debate draw upon come from the Michigan Panel of Income Dynamics survey data.

25   Because the reductions in income referred to by Hacker may, and often do, arise from factors other than the loss of a job or the voluntary reduction in working hours – such as inability to work due to illness.

26   Kenworthy (2019) interpreted the same data a little differently, finding an increase that is a little larger, but, in his words, still "isn't a massive increase." The problem with Kenworthy's trend analysis, however, is that it takes 2010 – after the onset of the GFC – as the endpoint of the time series. Because pre-tax income volatility is clearly heavily cyclical, this necessarily exaggerates the trend increase.

27   The one clear trend shown by Hacker's data is an increase in volatility in the 1970s and early 1980s. This is consistent with a study by Moffat and Gottschalk (2011), which looked at the same data set (but only with respect to male earnings) for the period 1970-2004, and concluded that there was a significant increase in this measure of income volatility from the early 1970s to mid-1980s, but that it then "remained at this new higher level through 2004." This makes perfect sense because of the major macroeconomic deterioration during that period covering most of the 1970s and the first half of the 1980s. With respect to the period after the mid-1980s, the only thing Hacker's data show clearly is the considerable cyclical fluctuations in income volatility. There is no clear trend. For example, the level of volatility was about the same immediately before the GFC (2006-2007) as in the mid-1980s. The apparent upward trend in the 2000s could easily be entirely cyclical (associated with the GFC). (One would expect that in 2014 – the end-point of Hacker's updated time series – the after-effects of the GFC were still very much present.)

28   A "significant" rise or fall is defined here as a change of more than 1 percent over the decade. On this basis, the Netherlands and Sweden saw significant increases in the job-to-nonemployment transition rate. Significant falls occurred in South Korea, Denmark, Finland, Japan, Belgium, the UK and Germany. The rate was essentially stable (i.e. it changed less than 1 percent) in the US, Italy, Australia, Austria and France. (Data on "involuntary separations" in the same report (OECD, 2019c: 100) confirm the lack of a broad trend of increasing likelihood of moving from employment to unemployment.)

29   Average job tenure is, it should be acknowledged, not necessarily a good indicator of earnings precarity, because it also reflects the extent to which workers choose voluntarily to move between jobs in search of better pay and conditions. The OECD (2019c: 97) has reported that – adjusted for relevant worker characteristics – average job tenure declined a little in most advanced OECD member countries over the period 2006-2017. Crucially, however, it found that this was probably largely because workers were choosing to move a little more frequently between jobs, rather than because they were more often being pushed into unemployment.

30   The point about taking worker characteristics into account is crucial, because if irregular workers are, for example, on average less well trained, the fact that they may on average earn less is precisely what one would expect.

31   With respect to the poorly educated (i.e. those with only high school education or less), experience has differed between countries, although it has generally been bad. Autor (2019) suggests that the US long-term trend for the real hourly remuneration of poorly educated workers to *fall* is a general international trend, and refers specifically to the United Kingdom and Germany. Curiously, however, the UK reference he cites actually shows the contrary – namely that real hourly remuneration of poorly educated workers rose in the UK from the late 1970s through to the start of the GFC. Although it fell in the wake of the GFC, it fell proportionally less than the hourly remuneration of the most educated British workers (Blundell et al, 2018: 55). The biggest trend is the long-term decline in average hours worked.

32   This is partially offset by the need for humans to design, build and maintain the robots or other new production technology. But the net effect is clearly still to reduce, over time, the demand for labor.

33   Expressed differently, this refers to the labor intensity of so-called "superior goods," as discussed in Chapter 2.

34   The question of whether automation may have weakened the *overall* demand for labor in recent decades should not be confused with the issue of its impact on the *composition* of the demand for labor – in other words, its impact on the skill and educational profile of workers who employers seek to hire. There is no question that recent technological change has impacted on the composition of the demand for labor. It has led to increased "polarization" (a.k.a. "hollowing out") of labor markets. This refers to the loss of middle-skill jobs as a result of the automation of many routine tasks (e.g. clerical and administrative office jobs) (Autor, 2019; Autor, Dorn and Hanson, 2013a). At the same time, demand for workers with high levels of skills and education has boomed. Unskilled workers at the lower end of the labor market have been less affected, both because ICT technology has had less impact on their jobs and because the supply of such workers has fallen over the long term with advances in general levels of education and training.

35   Vice President and Chief AI Scientist at Facebook and professor of computer science at New York University, interviewed in Ford (2018: 129-30).

36   Director of the Computer Science and Artificial Intelligence Laboratory at MIT, interviewed in Ford (2018: 263).

37   Elaborating on this definition, a "freelancer" is considered here to be someone whose main or only labor income is derived from tasks/project engagements (i.e. excluding people who have a traditional job but undertake some freelance work to supplement their incomes).

38   Digital platforms are, however, not the only force at work. Freelancing, and outsourcing more generally, has also been facilitated by the development of ICT tools that enable enterprises to plan production and associated labor requirements on a much more detailed and just-in-time basis, thereby permitting them to break traditional jobs into multiple distinct tasks.

39   For example, while all freelancers are by definition either temporary employees or self-employed, most temporary employees are not freelancers. Nor does being self-employed necessarily make someone a freelancer.

40   McKinsey (2016) estimated that 20-30 percent of the workforce in Europe and the United States engages in "independent" work. However, many of those concerned undertake independent worked only to supplement their main employment incomes, which excludes them from the freelancer category as defined here. Adjusting for this, the McKinsey estimate implies a range of 8.8-13.2 percent of the workforce in the freelancer category at the time of the survey.

41   Proposed by the author rather than by the OECD (which does not provide a quantitative definition of this concept).

42   For the purposes of this statement, all countries that are considered to have experienced "significant" decoupling have seen median wages grow at a rate that is both (1) 0.4 percent or more below and (2) at least 29 percent below that of labor productivity (noting that, in almost all cases, the gap between wage growth and productivity has been significantly more than 29 percent). The idea behind this definition is to exclude from the notion of decoupling countries those where wages growth was only slightly below productivity growth. (This notion of *significant* decoupling is the author's, not the OECD's.) On this basis, the countries experiencing significant decoupling were South Korea, Ireland, Canada, the Netherlands, Israel, Japan, Belgium, the United States and Australia.

43   The other six were Denmark, Sweden, Finland, Spain, Italy and New Zealand.

44   Germany, Austria and Norway.

45   In Spain, the percentage of workers engaged in temporary work fell in the period 1993-2014.

46   OECD statistics on self-employment (at OECD.Stat, accessed 13 May 2019) indicate that in almost all advanced countries the percentage of the workforce who are self-employed has fallen substantially both over the long term and more specifically over the past two decades. Australia is a typical example: in 1964, 16 percent of the workforce was self-employed; in 1990, the figure was 14 percent, and by 2017 it had fallen to 10 percent. The United Kingdom and the Netherlands are the two exceptions and have experienced significant increases over the past two decades (in the UK's case from 12 percent to 16 percent over the period 1998-2018). The rate in France remained essentially stable over the time period – 2003-2018 – for which data is reported.

47   Prior to the publication of this most recent data, Katz and Krueger (2019) suggested, in a widely noted paper, that self-employment might actually have been increasing.

48   Interestingly, the BLS also reported that on-call workers were evenly split between those who would prefer to work under a traditional arrangement and those who prefer on-call employment.

49   The BLS 2017 estimate is lower than the 2015 estimate reported by Katz and Krueger (2019) (who estimated that the percentage of workers engaged in alternative work arrangements had increased from 10.1 percent in 2005 to 15.8 percent in late 2015). However, the BLS estimates are to be preferred to those of Katz and Krueger.

Chapter Eight: Borrowing and the Printing Press

1   This should be taken as referring to the "real" interest rate – that is, the interest rate minus the rate of inflation. Inflation erodes the value of any debt and is therefore like a negative interest rate. For example, if the inflation rate is 10 percent, an interest rate of 15 percent is approximately equivalent to an interest rate of 5 percent when inflation is zero.

2   High interest rates also can result in currency appreciation that undermines export competitiveness.

3   For example, by purchasing increased amounts of government debt on the open market. To do so, it would offer higher prices for bonds, which would be equivalent to lowering interest rates.

4   All GDP growth rates referred to here and in what follows are "nominal" GDP growth rates. In other words, they do not adjust for inflation. The GDP growth rates more commonly referred to are "real" GDP growth rates, which do adjust for inflation. (For example, if the nominal GDP growth rate is 3 percent, and the inflation rate 1 percent, then real GDP growth is approximately 2 percent.) Interest rates are also nominal rates.

5   Note that these data are for *structurally adjusted* primary balances (see Appendix 8.1), and therefore exclude the impact of the GFC in temporarily pushing up budget deficits.

6   These calculations estimate the spending pressures of the coming three decades by taking as their starting point the assumption that the combined impact of additional health, long-term care and climate-related expenditure over the period to 2050 will equal at least 6 percent of GDP in all advanced countries. To this figure, projected increases (or, in a few cases, falls) in pension expenditure are added (see Chapter 4, noting that this figure is not available for several countries). (No additional amount is added for infrastructure expenditure, because of the difficulties of putting a value on the additional spending needed in the countries concerned.) This gives a rough total for additional spending, which is then added to the average structural budget balance for 2007-2018 for each country. This implicitly assumes that tax revenue (more precisely, general government revenue/GDP) remains constant. It disregards possible increases in interest payments arising from higher debt.

7   Again, this refers to the average *structural* budget balances for 2007-2018.

8   And are in fact slightly negative in some countries – although this is a situation which is clearly temporary.

9   Bean et al argue that the main factor is the high level of savings arising from the demographic aging bulge associated with the "baby boomer" generation.

10 It is actually a little more complicated than this, with several adjustments to "face" interest rates required to arrive at the effective cost to government of borrowing. This includes, for example, the deduction of the tax paid by bond holders on interest, because tax claws back some of the interest paid. Blanchard (2019a) does a very thorough job of estimating effective interest rates. Failure to take this point into account seems to be behind the claim by Mazza (2019) that the US patterns identified by Blanchard are not representative of the experience of the four largest European economies.

11 Concretely, this takes initial debt/GDP at its 2018 level of 83 percent (technically, the "debt" figures used here and in the other country examples refer to negative net financial worth), the nominal GDP growth rate as 4 percent (approximately its average over the period 2013-2018) and interest rates on government debt as 2 percent (approximately the level immediately prior to the pandemic). Net financial worth/GDP and nominal GDP growth rates are sourced from OECD.Stat (accessed 30 January 2020).

12 The average rate of nominal GDP growth over 2013-2018 was 1.43 percent (OECD.Stat, accessed 30 January 2020). The debt figure, once again, refers to net financial worth.

13 One cannot have complete confidence that very low underlying interest rates ("natural" interest rates in mainstream economic jargon) will last over the long term. Some economists doubt that long-term structural forces are driving low rates (see e.g. Hamilton et al, 2015). And even if one accepts that structural forces are at work, these will not necessarily last forever. For example, to the extent that, as Bean et al (2015) argue, they have been due to high levels of savings by the baby boomer generation, significant increases in interest rates can be anticipated when the aging bulge associated with that generation subsides in (depending on the country) several decades' time. To the extent that balance sheet repair is involved, the duration of the problem may be shorter.

14 General government structurally adjusted primary balance as a percentage of GDP, from OECD.Stat (extracted 10 August 2019). It should be emphasized once again that these estimates adjust for the fact that the primary deficit increased during the GFC for cyclical reasons.

15 Net debt subtracts from gross debt holdings of financial assets, which in Japan's case are much larger than in most other advanced countries (largely because of assets held by public pension funds). Roughly speaking, the rationale for using the net debt concept is that, if someone has $400,000 in debts (e.g. a mortgage debt and a credit card debt) but simultaneously has $150,000

in their bank accounts, it is more realistic to say that they have net debt of $250,000 rather than to focus on the $400,000 debt in isolation. The figure of 124 percent of GDP is Japan's general government (negative) net financial worth in 2017 (OECD.Stat, accessed 5 February 2020).

16   It is not actually true that, as their critics assert (e.g. Powell, 2019), MMT asserts that deficits don't matter for countries which borrow in their own currency.

17   See the letter by Green Party co-leader Caroline Lucas, MP, "Britain Needs Its Own Green New Deal," *Financial Times*, 8 June 2019. In France, it has been proposed amongst others by Jean Jouzel and Pierre Larrouturou (see Gollier, 2019: 93-6) and the influential ecologist (and former environment minister under President Macron) Nicolas Hulot (Fondation Hulot, 2011).

18   One common variant of PQE proposes that central bank money creation be used to fund a national infrastructure bank, via central bank purchases of bonds issued by the infrastructure bank. The difference between this and direct monetary funding of the government is not significant.

19   As, for example, a group of economists headed by the prominent monetary theorist Victoria Chick did in a letter to the *Financial Times* on 27 March 2015. They noted, as many others have, that in addition to the option of monetary financing of significant stimulatory government spending, it would be equally possible for central banks to create money and give it directly to households to stimulate private spending (the so-called "helicopter money" proposal). Helicopter money cannot, once again, be regarded as a variant of quantitative easing.

Chapter Nine: Trimming the Fat

1   In more precise terminology, delivering the same services (outputs) at lower cost represents an improvement in *productive efficiency*, while achieving the same outcomes at lower cost by modifying the nature of the service or mix of services represents improved *cost-effectiveness*. For convenience, we bundle the two together in our discussion under the heading of improved *efficiency*. This is the way in which some economics, including DEA analysis (discussed further below), uses the term efficiency. It also keeps the discussion simple to use this single term here.

2   In 2017, social benefits accounted for 22-50 percent of general government expenditure in advanced OECD countries. Of 22 advanced OECD countries, it exceeded 30 percent of spending in all but four.

3   Consistent with best practice, these estimates are made by extrapolating from random samples of benefit payments that are subject to very thorough and detailed investigation. "Net overpayments" refers to overpayments minus underpayments – the principle being that it is unreasonable to focus only on overpayments in estimating potential savings. Overpayments that the administration has already identified and recovered are, appropriately, not counted.

4   The SSA estimated net benefit overpayment in FY2018 at $5,625 million (www.ssa.gov/improperpayments, accessed 12 February 2020), an amount equal to 0.56 percent of benefit payments. These data shed an unflattering light on claims recently made by an influential right-wing think tank in the United States: "a substantial portion of this spending is simply wasteful, with funds going to fraudulent, erroneous, and excessive payments or to ineffective programs" (Rector and Menon, 2018: 22).

5   It may, for example, be somewhat higher in France, but it is impossible to say, because in that country no estimates of overpayments are published, other than in respect to family benefit payments. For family benefits, the relevant administration has estimated – based on a proper sample of 7,500 beneficiaries – that overpayments due to fraud represent approximately 2 percent of total benefit payments (Sénat, 2017b: 41).

6   The McKinsey study half-acknowledges this point, briefly and in passing, asserting that although external factors can have an impact on outcomes, it is what government does that is "decisive" (MGI, 2017: 16-17).

7   At least, to expenditure excluding social benefits.

8   External factors are in general only recognized in outcome-focused DEA analyses to a limited
      degree, in the form of "inputs" in the production function. This is for two reasons. The main
      one is that it is frequently the case that relevant external factors are either not measured or are
      only very imperfectly measured. The second reason is that the models have to be kept relatively
      simple and it is impractical to introduce too many input variables (resulting in the widespread
      use of composite indicators of external factors, which raise their own problems). In the OECD
      school study, for example, the only external factor recognized in the analysis is a measure of
      the socio-economic background of students. For these reasons, outcome-based DEA analysis
      is inherently prone to underestimating the impact of external factors, and consequently over-
      estimating true efficiency gaps.

9   This discussion of DEA analysis focuses entirely on outcome-based analysis. DEA analysis
      can also be used to look at output costs. Outputs are goods or services delivered by a govern-
      ment agency to, or for the benefit of, a member of the community or another external client.
      Examples are medical treatments, teaching received by a student and criminal investigations
      carried out by the police (Robinson, 2007). Regrettably, the main DEA literature – and much
      of economic theory – fails to distinguish properly between outputs and outcomes, and treats
      outcomes as just another type of output (perhaps labelled as a "higher-level" output). They are,
      however, quite different – something which the public sector performance measurement and
      evaluation literature clearly recognizes. In principle, DEA analysis is much more conceptually
      sound when applied to outputs rather than outcomes. In particular, the problem of external
      factors no longer arises. In practice, however, major difficulties also affect output-based DEA
      analysis, the most important being that of how to factor in differences in the quality of outputs,
      as opposed to recognizing only differences in the quantities of outputs delivered.

10   To be more precise, the remit of the Gershon review was to identify efficiency savings in what
      the British referred to as the "departmental expenditure limit" (DEL) part of government
      expenditure. This accounts for approximately half of government expenditure in the United
      Kingdom. The other half is what is known as "annually managed expenditure" (AME).
      Approximately 80 percent of AME is, however, social benefits expenditure.

11   See, for example, Atkins et al (2019).

12   See "An Algorithm That Grants Freedom, or Takes It Away," *New York Times*, 7 February 2020.

13   Universities, such as Oxford, which operate systems in which core teaching is based on conver-
      sations between an expert academic "tutor" and small groups of two or three students.

14   In France, for example, the starting salary of a university lecturer (maître de conference) has
      fallen from 2.4 times the minimum wage (the "Smic") in 1985 to 1.3-1.4 in 2019. This salary
      squeeze was the main factor behind an academic revolt in 2020 that led the Macron government
      to promise a major readjustment of academic salaries, part of which will increase a lecturer's
      minimum salary to at least twice the minimum wage by 2021 ("Le gouvernement annonce une
      forte revalorization du salaire des jeunes chercheurs," *Les Echos*, 22 January 2020).

Chapter Ten: Bigger Government

1   1998 is chosen as the comparison date here rather than 1995 because the latter date is some-
      what too close to the end of the Cold War (conventionally considered to have come to an end
      with the collapse of the Soviet Union in 1991), after which there was a sharp decline in military
      spending almost everywhere.

2   For which data on long-term defense spending trends unfortunately do not exist with which to
      make the comparison with 1995.

3   See "Israel, 'Start-up Nation,' Groans under Strains of Growth and Neglect," *New York Times*,
      1 March 2020.

4   This table shows all advanced countries for which the IMF database provides information going back to 1995 (the earliest date available) as well as for 2018, with one exception. This is the UK, for which the comparison between 1995 and 2018 would be misleading due to the fact that substantial spending cuts were made in the 1980s (the Thatcher era) before the data series starts.

5   In 2018, only 22 of every 100 poor families received benefits under the program (Floyd, 2020; CBPP, 2020).

6   OECD data show that the "guaranteed minimum income benefits" – in other words welfare benefits – (including any housing benefits) applying to this group of people averages in the United States a minuscule 6 percent of median disposable income. In the European Union, the average is 35 percent, which is basically the same level as in Australia and New Zealand. In the United Kingdom, the figure is 54 percent, while in Denmark it is 63 percent (2018 data from OECD.Stat, accessed 20 March 2020).

7   Based on data on social protection expenditure as a percentage of GDP in the IMF database of government expenditure by function (COFOG). It is useful to confirm this data by reference to US official data. The US National Accounts concept of "income security" expenditure is essentially equivalent to "social protection" expenditure in the international COFG classification – and as such includes old age and disability benefits (other than for government employees), and a range of welfare benefits including TANF and SNAP. Like the COFOG social protection function, it excludes medical expenditure – which in the US context means that it excludes Medicaid benefits. It should be noted that the US national accounts concept of "income security" expenditure is not the same as the narrower concept with the same name which is used in the historical budget data of the federal government. The best available measure of government income security expenditure on the national accounts basis is that reported in the Bureau of Economic Analysis Table 3.16 (Government Current Expenditures by Function). This indicates that in 2018, total government income security expenditure – i.e. covering all levels of government – was equivalent to 7.5 percent of GDP. All but a small amount of this was federal government expenditure. For completeness, it may be noted that these expenditure data do not include "tax expenditures" and, in the case of social protection, the United States also has the Earned Income Tax Credit, which provides assistance to low income people. The cost of the EITC is equivalent to 0.3 percent of GDP (TPC, 2020). The national accounts figure is broadly consistent with the data for federal government expenditure in the Historical Tables of the US federal budget. The national accounts concept of income security expenditure seems to be approximately equivalent to the sum of income security and social security expenditure, excluding retirement and disability payments to federal employees, in the Historical Tables – an amount equivalent to 6.6 percent of GDP in 2018. (Without unnecessarily going into accounting complexities here, it should be noted that the accounting basis of these two measures differs.)

8   Certain states refused from the outset to apply the provisions of this legislation, which has also been progressively undermined since Obama left office.

9   The uninsured have delayed seeking treatment, which has aggravated the spread of the disease. The jump in the number of uninsured persons due to the steep increase in unemployment has added to this effect.

10   Bureau of Economic Analysis National Accounts Table 3.12 (Government Social Benefits).

11   There is, however, one big qualification to this. There is a possibility that the imposition of tough work requirements on these programs would reduce expenditure considerably more – but only by cutting off benefits to people who should in principle remain eligible. Social policy experts point to experience showing that the imposition of the bureaucratic hurdles of the type that welfare beneficiaries would need to jump to pass the work requirement test would result in a great deal of collateral damage. They suggest many poor people who would in principle

remain entitled to benefits would miss out because, for a variety of reasons, they would have great difficulty navigating the procedural steps to obtain benefits. (This includes, for example, people who are mentally ill, have major cognitive difficulties or whose low level of education or social competence makes it difficult for them to complete the paperwork and assemble the necessary documentation in support of their claim for benefits.)

12 The goal of cutting spending often conflicts, moreover, with that of encouraging self-reliance. It has frequently been pointed out that denying poor unemployed people access to health care will make them even more unemployable. There is also the question of the "marriage penalty" – that is, the fact that benefit rules are often structured in a way that poor people receive less if they marry. To its credit, the Heritage Foundation has made the removal of the marriage penalty one of its two major themes of welfare reform (the other being the imposition of work requirements). Foundation experts have persuasively argued that this has encouraged the explosion of poor single-parent families, and that the formation of stable families should be a major goal of social protection policy. However, the elimination of all anti-marriage incentives would, in the words of the Heritage Foundation's leading expert, "be very expensive" (Rector, 2014: 5) because the main way of achieving it is by no longer reducing benefits when couples marry. This explains the scant interest in action on this front by congressional Republicans, for whom the top priority is to cut welfare spending irrespective of the consequences.

13 Estimate produced by the Costs of War Project based at Brown University. This study estimated total war-related spending and obligations for veterans over the 20-year period FY2001-FY2020 of $6,409 billion. This included two items which are manifestly inappropriate – one is the estimated interest on borrowing to finance the spending (which is not a cost of war itself but a cost of deciding not to finance it fully with taxes) and the other is homeland security spending for prevention and response to terrorism. In addition, there is a "guesstimate" of future obligations for veterans' medical and disability services in the 30 years covering FY2020-FY2059, the inclusion of which is questionable. If these amounts are deducted, the estimate is reduced to $3,430 billion, or an annual average of $171 billion. Because these are all estimates in 2020 dollars, they may be divided by 2020 GDP – which gives the figure of an annual average of 0.8 percent of GDP. If the future veteran obligations were to be included, this figure would rise to 1 percent of GDP.

14 See analysis by the independent Institute for Fiscal Studies, https://www.ifs.org.uk/election/2019/manifestos.

15 https://www.ifs.org.uk/election/2019/manifestos.

16 Tax/GDP was 49.9 percent of GDP in 2007 and had increased to 53.7 percent in 2017 (OECD. Stat, accessed 3 March 2020).

17 What former finance minister Pierre Moscovici famously referred to as a *ras-le-bol*.

18 *Le Monde,* 10 April and 13 June 2019.

19 Piketty declared on French television in 2014, when calling for much higher taxes on wealth, that "il ne faut pas augmenter les impôts. Il faut réduire les impôts sur les salaires" (one must not raise tax, one must lower taxes on salaries) ("Thomas Piketty : 'Pour réduire les inégalités, il faut taxer le patrimoine',"*France Info,* 2 May 2014, www.francetvinfo.fr). He argues broadly along the same lines in his magnum opus (Piketty, 2013), although in less categoric terms.

20 In Sweden, cyclically adjusted government revenue/GDP fell from 56.4 percent in 1995 to 54.1 percent in 2001 and was down to 50.2 percent in 2019. In Finland, the corresponding figures are 55 percent, 52.4 percent and 52.5 percent (EC, 2019). Cyclically adjusted revenue removes the impact of the weakening of revenue during recessions, so as to give a more accurate measure of revenue trends. If we look at "raw" – non-cyclically adjusted – revenue we see that at its peak (in 1987), the Swedish tax/GDP ratio was 49.5 percent. In 2018 it was down to 43.9 percent. Personal income tax peaked in 1989 at 19.4 percent of GDP and was 12.7 percent

in 2018. Social security contributions peaked in 1991 at 13.8 percent and were 9.7 percent in 2018 (OECD.Stat, accessed 3 March 2020). Tax/GDP peaked in Finland in 2000 at 45.8 percent of GDP and was 42.7 percent in 2018. Personal income tax and social security contributions have also fallen over the long term (OECD.Stat, accessed 3 March 2020).

21   In Denmark, the estimated figure was 51.6 percent in 2019, down from a peak of 56.3 percent in 2014 (taxes had in fact continued to increase in Denmark from the mid-1990s up to 2014).

22   Norway is different because of its enormous oil wealth.

23   In Sweden, for example, sickness benefits are paid by the government after the first two weeks of illness at 80 percent of salary (maximum, approximately US$78/day) for the first year, and at 75 percent thereafter.

24   See, in the case of Denmark, "Syv år er gået – nu er der 24.000 flere indvandrere i kontanth-jælpssystemet," *Berlingske*, 24 March 2017.

25   The fact that this adds up to 28.5 percent of enrollees – less than the one-third implied by the CEA estimates – is probably due to the fact that Goldman et al use 2015 survey data, whereas the CEA uses 2013 data.

26   See Historical Tables in the 2019 federal budget – specifically Historical Table 3.2 (for housing assistance expenditure) and Historical Table 11.34 (expenditure on SNAP). The same figure for SNAP expenditure (by all levels of government combined, is given in the SNAP data tables of the Food and Nutrition Service of the US Department of Agriculture (https://www.fns.usda.gov/pd/supplemental-nutrition-assistance-program-snap).

27   The respected Urban Institute estimated the revenue yield from this tax proposal as $72 billion annually (see J. Stein, "Ocasio-Cortez Wants Higher Taxes on Very Rich Americans," *Washington Post*, 5 January 2019). The Tax Foundation, by contrast, estimated the revenue yield as no more than half that amount (K. Pomerleau and H. Li, "How Much Revenue Would a Seventy Percent Top Tax Rate Raise? An Initial Analysis," 14 January 2019 taxfoundation.org).

28   The threshold for the Swiss annual wealth tax, imposed only by cantons (states) and not by the national government, varies from canton to canton. It is, for example, set at CHF50,000 (US$51,880) of family assets in the canton where the author lives. Switzerland's unusual degree of reliance on the annual wealth tax has to be seen in the light of the fact that the country has very limited taxation of capital gains for individuals.

29   T. Golshan, "Bernie Sanders' Wealth Tax Proposal, Explained," *Vox* (www.vox.com), 24 September 2019.

30   E. Saez and G. Zucman, "Alexandria Ocasio-Cortez's Tax Hike Idea Is Not About Soaking the Rich," *New York Times*, 22 January 2019.

31   See previous note.

32   OECD.Stat (accessed 2 March 2020). Revenue raised from taxes on corporations in advanced countries varied between 1.1 and 4.5 percent of GDP, with corporate income tax varying between 0.9 and 4.5 percent.

33   One of the most attractive ideas being debated is the replacement of corporate income taxes with the so-called destination-based cash flow tax (DBCFT) on companies (IMF, 2019; Hufbauer, 2019). This is an idea that was seriously floated, but not ultimately implemented, in the 2016 US congressional tax reform debate. This proposal merely highlights, however, the error of thinking of company taxes as taxes on the rich, because the actual impact of a DBCFT would be broadly similar to that of a value-added tax.

34   Given the current state of affairs, it is more realistic perhaps to aim for international agree-ment on a minimum rate of corporate income tax, which is an option currently under active negotiation.

35 A typical example is Sweden, which 20 years ago had a corporate income tax rate of 28 percent. From 2013, the rate was 22 percent, and will fall to 20.6 percent in 2021.

36 See statistics on "taxes on income, profits and capital gains of corporates, as % GDP," at OECD. Stat, Global Revenue Statistics Database.

Statistical Annex

1 Note that the BEA series does not have a "total expenditure" figure prior to 1960. However, the author has added together the relevant variables in the BEA flow statement, the only one of which is missing is "net purchases of non-produced assets." Because the data for this latter variable for the 1960s indicates that it was historically a very small number, the 1950-59 data in the Figure must be very close to accurate total expenditure figures.

2 The projections shown here are the OECD's main reference scenario (the "cost-pressure" scenario). They show projected growth from the 2006-10 average up to 2060. The OECD's estimate for Australia is consistent with than the Australian government's 2015 estimate that its spending would increase from 0.9 percent to 1.9 percent of GDP over the 40-year period from 2014-15 to 2054-55 (Commonwealth of Australia, 2015).

3 The European Commission publishes its forecasts regularly in its *Ageing Report* (see, for example, EC, 2018). EU nations use the same methodology in their annual stability and convergence program documents. The Figure uses data directly from the latter documents so as to be able to provide projections for 2050. The projections shown here are based on the so-called "base case" scenario.

4 The OECD projections assume that future demand for long-term care will be limited by a strong version of the PTD effect – in its words, the assumption is that "the prevalence of dependency per age is shifted according to the evolution of life expectancy." As discussed in the main text, this is an unwarranted and excessively optimistic assumption. Its impact, however, is to some extent offset by another questionable assumption made by the OECD which works in the opposite direction (namely, that the "income elasticity" of demand for LTC is one). Also excessively optimistic is the European Commission assumption in its reference scenario that only half of the demographic effect is felt (i.e. that the PTD effect works to reduce growth in demand for LTC to half of what it otherwise would be).

REFERENCES

AAFP (American Academy of Family Physicians) (2019), *Medicaid Work Requirements*, www.aafp.org.

Academy of Medical Sciences (2018), *Multimorbidity: A Priority for Global Health Research*, London: The Academy.

Acemoglu, D. et al (2016), "Import Competition and the Great US Employment Sag of the 2000s", *Journal of Labor Economics*, 34(1, pt. 2): S141-98.

Aden, N. (2016), "The Roads to Decoupling: 21 Countries Are Reducing Carbon Emissions While Growing GDP", World Resource Institute, 5 April, www.wri.org/blog.

AGCB (Advisory Group on Costs and Benefits) (2019), *Report to the Committee on Climate Change of the Advisory Group on Costs and Benefits of Net Zero*, www.theccc.org.uk.

Aged Care Sector Committee (2016), *Aged Care Roadmap*, agedcare.health.gov.au/aged-care-reform/aged-care-roadmap.

Agüero-Torres, H., E. von Strauss, M. Viitanen, B. Winblad and L. Fratiglioni (2001), "Institutionalization in the Elderly: The Role of Chronic Diseases and Dementia. Cross-Sectional and Longitudinal Data from a Population-based Study", *Journal of Clinical Epidemiology*, 54(8): 795-801.

AHIP (America's Health Insurance Plans) (2016), *High-Priced Drugs: Estimates of Annual Per-Patient Expenditures for 150 Specialty Medications*, Washington, DC: AHIP.

AHRQ (Agency for Healthcare Research and Quality) (2010), *Multiple Chronic Conditions Chartbook*, Rockville, MD: AHRQ.

AIHW (Australian Institute of Health and Welfare) (2014), *Healthy Life Expectancy in Australia: Patterns and Trends 1998 to 2012,* Canberra: AIHW.

AIHW (2016), *Australia's Health 2016*, Canberra: AIHW.

AIHW (2017a), *Trends in Cardiovascular Deaths*, Bulletin 141, Canberra: AIHW.

AIHW (2017b), *Hospital Resources 2015-16*, Canberra: AIHW.

Aizawa, T, R. Dekle and M. Helble (2017), "Sources of Income Inequality: Comparison of Japan and the United States", Working Paper 663, Tokyo: Asian Development Bank Institute.

Akemura, S. and D. Kojima (2018), "Japan's Long-Term Care Cost Projections: Comparison with the European Commission Aging Report", *Public Policy Review* (Policy Research Institute, Ministry of Finance), 14(4): 541-562.

Albouy V., Bretin E., Carnot N. and Deprez M. (2009), *Les dépenses de santé en France : déterminants et impact du vieillissement à l'horizon 2050*, Documents de travail de la DGTPE, 2009/11.

Alcidi, C. and D. Gros (2019), "Public Debt and the Risk Premium: A Dangerous Doom Loop", *Vox CEPR Policy Portal*, 23 May, voxeu.org.

Algan, Y., E. Beasley, D. Cohen et M. Foucault (2019), *Les origines du populisme : enquête sur un schisme politique et social*, Paris: Editions du Seuil et La République des Idées.

Allen, P. (2011), "The Singularity Isn't Near", *MIT Technology Review*. technologyreview.com.

Alston, P. (2017), *Statement on Visit to the USA, by Prof. Philip Alston, United Nations Special Rapporteur on Extreme Poverty and Human Rights*, December 15, United Nations, Office of the High Commissioner for Human Rights.

Alvarado, F., L. Chancel, T. Piketty, E. Saez and G. Zucman (eds) (2018), *World Inequality Report: 2018*, wir2018.wid.world.

An, C-B. and B. Bosworth (2013), *Income Inequality in Korea: An Analysis of Trends, Causes and Answers*, Cambridge, MA.: Harvard University Asia Center.

Anderson, G., P. Hussey and V. Petrosyan (2019), "It's Still the Prices, Stupid: Why the US Spends So Much on Health Care, and a Tribute to Uwe Reinhardt", *Health Affairs*, 38(1): 87-95.

ARTBA (American Road & Transportation Builders Association) (2019), *2019 Bridge Report*, art-babridgereport.org.

ASCE (American Society of Civil Engineers) (2016), *Failure to Act: Closing the Infrastructure Investment Gap for America's Economic Future*, Reston, Virginia: ASCE.

Asenjo, A. and C. Pignatti (2019), *Unemployment Insurance Schemes around the World: Evidence and Policy Options*, Geneva: International Labor Office.

Assurance Maladie (2016), *Améliorer la qualité du système de santé et maîtriser les dépenses : Propositions de l'Assurance Maladie pour 2017*, Paris : l'Assurance maladie.

Atkins G., et al (2018), *Performance Tracker 2019: A Data-Driven Analysis of the Performance of Public Services*, London: Institute for Government and Charted Institute for Public Finance and Accountancy.

Atkinson A. (2015), *Inequality: What Can Be Done?* Cambridge, MA.: Harvard University Press.

Atkinson, A. (2005), *Atkinson Review: Final Report. Measurement of Government Output and Productivity for the National Accounts*, Houndsmills: Palgrave Macmillan.

Auerbach, A. (2005), *Who Bears the Corporate Tax? A Review of What We Know*, Working Paper 11686, Cambridge, MA: National Bureau of Economic Research.

Autor, D. (2019), "Work of the Past, Work of the Future", *AEA Papers and Proceedings, 2019*, 109: 1-32.

Autor, D. and A. Salomons (2017), "Robocalypse Now – Does Productivity Growth Threaten Employment?", in *Investment and Growth in Advanced Economies: Conference Proceedings*, Frankfurt: European Central Bank.

Autor, D. and A. Salomons (2018), "Is Automation Labor Share-Displacing? Productivity Growth, Employment, and the Labor Share", *Brookings Papers on Economic Activity*, Spring: 1-87.

Autor, D., D. Dorn and G. Hanson (2013a), "Untangling Trade and Technology: Evidence from Local Labor Markets", Working Paper 18938, Cambridge, MA: National Bureau of Economic Research.

Autor, D., D. Dorn and G. Hanson (2013b), "The China Syndrome: Local Labor Market Effects of Import Competition in the United States", *American Economic Review*, 103(6): 2121–68.

Autor, D., D. Dorn and G. Hanson (2013c), "The Geography of Trade and Technology Shocks in the United States", *American Economic Review*, 103(3): 220–25.

Autor, D., D. Dorn and G. Hanson (2016), "The China Shock: Learning from Labor-Market Adjustment to Large Changes in Trade", *Annual Review of Economics*, 8: 205–40.

Baldwin, R. (2019), *The Globotics Upheaval: Globalization, Robotics, and the Future of Work*, London: Weidenfeld & Nicolson.

Baumol, W. (2012), *The Cost Disease: Why Computers Get Cheaper and Health Care Doesn't*, New Haven: Yale University Press.

Baumol, W. and W. Bowen (1966), *Performing Arts – The Economic Dilemma*, Cambridge, MA.: MIT Press.

Bean, C. et al (2015), *Low for Long? Causes and Consequences of Persistently Low Interest Rates*, Geneva Reports on the World Economy 17, Geneva: International Centre for Monetary and Banking Studies.

Bell, D., A. Rutherford and R. Wright (2013), "Free Personal Care for Older People: A Wider Perspective on Its Costs", *Fraser of Allander Economic Commentary*, 36(3): 69-76.

Belloni, A, D Morgan and V Paris (2016), "Pharmaceutical Expenditure and Policies: Past Trends and Future Challenges", OECD Health Working Papers, 87, Paris: OECD.

Bennett, K. et al (2006), "Explaining the Recent Decrease in Coronary Heart Disease Mortality Rates in Ireland, 1985-2000", *Journal of Epidemiology and Community Health*, 60: 322-327.

Bivens, J. et al (2014), *Raising America's Pay: Why It's Our Central Economic Policy Challenge*, Washington, DC: Economic Policy Institute.

Black, S. et al (2016), "The Long-Term Decline in US Prime-Age Male Labor Force Participation", *VOX CEPR Policy Portal,* 2 July, voxeu.org.

Blagosklonny, M. V. (2010), "Why Human Lifespan is Rapidly Increasing: Solving 'Longevity Riddle' with 'Revealed-Slow-Aging' Hypothesis", *Aging*, 2(4): 177-182.

Blanchard, O. (2019a), "Public Debt and Low Interest Rates", *American Economic Review*, 109(4): 1197-1229.

Blanchard, O. (2019b), *Public Debt: Fiscal and Welfare Costs in a Time of Low Interest Rates*, Policy Brief 19-2, Washington, DC: Peterson Institute for International Economics.

Blanchard, O. and L. Summers (2019), "Rethinking Stabilization Policy: Evolution or Revolution?", in O. Blanchard and L. Summers, *Evolution or Revolution? Rethinking Macroeconomic Policy after the Great Recession*, Cambridge, MA: MIT Press.

Bloom, D., D. Canning and M. Weston (2005), "The Value of Vaccination", *World Economics*, 6(3): 15-39.

BLS (Bureau of Labor Statistics) (2017), "The Cost of Care: New Insights into Healthcare Spending Growth", *Beyond the Numbers*, 6(7): 1-12.

BLS (2018), *Contingent and Alternative Employment Arrangements – May 2017*, News Release, 7 June.

Blumenthal, D., K. Stremikis and D. Cutler (2013), "Health Care Spending – a Giant Slain or Sleeping?", *New England Journal of Medicine*, 369(26): 2551-57.

Blundell, R. et al (2018), "Income Inequality in the Labor Market in Britain and the US", *Journal of Public Economics*, 162: 48-62.

Bobek, A., J. Wickham and S. Pembroke (2017), *Mapping Precarious Work in Ireland: A Preliminary Sectoral Analysis*, 31 March 2017 (mimeo).

Boden, M. (2018), *Artificial Intelligence: A Very Short Introduction*, Oxford: Oxford University Press.

Booth, A. and M. Wood (2008), "Back-to-Front Down-Under? Part-Time/Full-Time Wage Differentials in Australia", *Industrial Relations*, 47(1): 114-135.

Bottery, S. et al (2018), *Next Steps for Social Care Funding Reform: The Costs of Social Care Funding Options*, London: The Health Foundation.

Bowen, W. (2012), *The 'Cost Disease' in Higher Education: Is Technology the Answer?* The Tanner Lectures, Stanford University, October.

Bower, H. et al (2016), "Life Expectancy of Patients with Chronic Myeloid Leukaemia Approaches the Life Expectancy of the General Population", *Journal of Clinical Oncology*, 34(24): 2851-2857.

Breyer, F., N. Lorenz and T. Niebel (2012), "Health Care Expenditures and Longevity: Is there a Eubie Blake Effect?", Research Papers in Economics, 1: Trier: Universität Trier.

Bridges, W. (1994a), *Job Shift: How to Prosper in a Workplace without Jobs*, New York: Addison-Wesley.

Bridges, W. (1994b), "The End of the Job", Interview in *Forbes*, 19 September.

Brown, G. C. et al (2015), "Cataract Surgery Cost Utility Revisited In 2012: A New Economic Paradigm", *Ophthalmology*, 120(12): 2367-2376.

Brynjolfsson, E., D. Rock and C. Syverson (2017), "Artificial Intelligence and the Modern Productivity Paradox: A Clash of Expectations and Statistics", Working Paper 24001, Cambridge, MA: National Bureau of Economic Research.

Buchmueller, T. and J. Meliyanni (2015), "Obesity and Health Expenditures: Evidence from Australia", *Economics and Human Biology*, 17: 42-58.

Buck, T. (2018), "German Armed Forces in 'Dramatically Bad' Shape, Report Finds", *Financial Times*, 20 February.

Buiter, W. (2014), "The Simple Analytics of Helicopter Money: Why It Works – Always", *Economics*, 8 (2014-28): 1-51.

Buiter, W. (2020), "When 'Whatever It Takes' Isn't Enough", *Project Syndicate*, 17 March, project-syndicate.org.

Bunker, J. (2001), "The Role of Medical Care in Contributing to Health Improvements within Societies", *International Journal of Epidemiology*, 30: 1260-63.

Buntin, M. B., M. F. Burke, M. C. Hoaglin and D. Blumenthal (2011), "The Benefits of Health Information Technology", *Health Affairs*, 30(3): 464-471.

Busse, R. and M. Blümel (2014), *Germany: Health System Review*, Copenhagen: European Observatory on Health Systems and Policies.

Buttorff, C., T. Ruder and M. Bauman (2017), *Multiple Chronic Conditions in United States*, Santa Monica, CA: Rand Corporation.

Card, D. and J. DiNardo, (2002), "Skill-Biased Technological Change and Rising Wage Inequality: Some Problems and Puzzles", *Journal of Labor Economics*, 20(4): 733-783.

Carvalho, N. et al (2017), "Capturing Budget Impact Considerations within Economic Evaluations: A Systematic Review of Economic Evaluations of Rotavirus Vaccine in Low- and Middle-Income Countries and a Proposed Assessment Framework", *Pharmacoeconomics*, 36: 79-90.

Cawley J. and C. Meyerhoefer (2012), "The Medical Care Costs of Obesity: An Instrumental Variables Approach", *Journal of Health Economics*, 31(1): 219-230.

CBO (Congressional Budget Office) (2008), *Evidence on the Costs and Benefits of Health Information Technology*, Washington, DC: CBO.

CBO (2014), *Public Spending on Transportation and Water Infrastructure, 1956 to 2014*, Washington, DC: CBO.

CBO (2018a), *The 2018 Long-Term Budget Outlook*, Washington, DC: CBO.

CBO (2018b), *Public Spending on Transportation and Water Infrastructure, 1956 to 2017*, Washington, DC: CBO.

CBO (2018c), data file supporting exhibits in CBO (2018a) www.cbo.gov/publication/54539.

CBO (2019a), *The 2019 Long-Term Budget Outlook*, Washington, DC: CBO.

CBO (2019b), *CBO's 2019 Long-Term Projections for Social Security: Additional Information*, data downloadable from www.cbo.gov.

CBO (2019c), data file supporting exhibits in CBO, *Federal Investment, 1962 to 2018*, www.cbo.gov/publication/55375.

CBPP (Center on Budget and Policy Priorities) (2020), *Temporary Assistance for Needy Families* Washington, DC: CBPP.

CDC (Centers for Disease Control) (2017), *Long-Term Trends in Diabetes*, www.cdc.gov/diabetes/data [accessed July 2018].

CEA (Council of Economic Advisers) (2018), *Expanding Work Requirements in Non-Cash Welfare Programs*, Washington, DC: CEA.

Chazan, G. (2020), "'Groundhog Day' for German Army as Improvement Drive Stalls", *Financial Times*, 28 January.

Chernew, M., D. Cutler, K. Ghosh and M. Landrum (2016), "Understanding the Improvement in Disability Free Life Expectancy in the U.S. Elderly Population", Working Paper 22306, Cambridge, MA: National Bureau of Economic Research.

Clark, T. and A. Dilnot (2002), *Long-Term Trends in British Taxation and Spending*, Briefing Note 25, London: Institute of Fiscal Studies.

Clements, B., K. Dybczak, V. Gaspar, S. Gupta and M. Soto (2015), "The Fiscal Consequences of Shrinking Populations", IMF Staff Discussion Note, 15/21, Washington, D.C.: IMF.

CoA (Commonwealth of Australia) (2015), *2015 Intergenerational Report: Australia in 2055*, Canberra: The Treasury.

Cohen, G., J. Jalles, P. Loungani and R. Marto (2017), "Emissions and Growth: Trends and Cycles in a Globalized World", Working Paper 17/191, Washington, DC: IMF.

Colombo, F. and T. Muir (2016), "Developing a Skilled Long-Term Care Workforce", in C. Gori, J-L. Fernandez and R. Wittenberg (ed), *Long-Term Care Reforms in OECD Countries*, Bristol: Policy Press.

Committee on Climate Change (2019), *Net Zero: the UK's Contribution to Stopping Global Warming*, London: CCC.

Comtesse, X. (2017), *Santé 4.0: le tsunami du numérique*, Chêne-Bourg : Georg éditeur.

Coppola, F. (2019), *The Case for People's Quantitative Easing*, Cambridge, UK: Polity Press.

Costa, D. (2005), "Causes of Improving Health and Longevity at Older Ages: A Review of the Explanations", *Genus*, LXI (1): 21-38.

Coudeville, L., A. Brunot, T. Szucs and B. Dervaux (2005), "The Economic Value of Childhood Varicella Vaccination in France and Germany", *Value in Health*, 8(3): 209-222.

Crawford, N. (2019), *United States Budgetary Cost and Obligations of Post-9/11 Wars through FY 2020: $6.4 Trillion*, watson.brown.edu/costsofwar.

Crimmins, E. and H. Beltrán-Sánchez (2011), "Mortality and Morbidity Trends: Is There Compression of Morbidity?", *The Journals of Gerontology. Series B, Psychological Sciences and Social Sciences*, 66B(1): 75–86.

Crimmins, E., Y. Zhang and Y. Saito (2016), "Trends Over 4 Decades in Disability-Free Life Expectancy in the United States", *American Journal of Public Health*, 106: 1287–1293.

Crivelli, E. R. de Mooij and M. Keen (2016), "Base Erosion, Profit Shifting and Developing Countries," *FinanzArchiv*, 72: 268–301.

Curry, N., L. Schlepper and N. Hemmings (2019), *What Can England Learn from the Long-Term Care System in Germany?* London: Nuffield Trust.

Curry, N., S. Castle-Clarke and N. Hemmings (2018), *What Can England Learn from the Long-Term Care System in Japan?* London: Nuffield Trust.

Cusset, P-Y. (2017), "Les déterminants de long terme des dépenses de santé en France", Document de Travail no. 2017-7, Paris : Stratégie France.

Cutler, D. (1995), "Technology, health costs, and the NIH", Paper prepared for the National Institutes of Health Economics Roundtable on Biomedical Research.

Cutler, D. (2004), *Your Money or Your Life*, Oxford: Oxford University Press.

Cutler, D., K. Ghosh and M. Landrum (2013), "Evidence for Significant Compression of Morbidity in the Elderly U.S. Population", Working Paper 19268, Cambridge, MA: National Bureau of Economic Research.

Cutler, D., M. McClellan and J. Newhouse (1999), "The Costs and Benefits of Intensive Treatment for Cardiovascular Disease"", in J. Triplett (ed.), *Measuring the Price of Medical Services*, Washington, DC: The Brookings Institution.

Daley, J. and B. Coates (2018). *Money in Retirement: More than Enough*, Melbourne: Grattan Institute.

Dauth, W., S. Findeisen, J. Suedekum and N. Woessner (2014), "German Robots – the Impact of Industrial Robots on Workers", IAB Discussion Paper, 30/2017, Berlin: Institute for Employment Research.

Davis, G. (2016), *The Vanishing American Corporation: Navigating the Hazards of a New Economy*, Oakland, CA: Berrett-Koehler.

de la Maisonneuve, C. and J. Oliveira Martins (2014), "The Future of Health and Long-Term Care Spending", *OECD Journal: Economic Studies*, 2014: 61-96.

de Meijer, C., B. Wouterse, J. Polder and M. Koopmanschap (2013), "The Effect of Population Aging on Health Expenditure Growth: A Critical Review", *European Journal of Aging*, 10: 353-361.

de Vreede, A. Gorgels, G. Verstraaten, F. Vermeer, W. Dassen and J. Wellens (1991), "Did Prognosis after Acute Myocardial Infarction Change during the past 30 Years? A Meta-Analysis", *Journal of the American College of Cardiology*, 18(3): 698-706

Delsen, L. (2012), "From Welfare State to Participation Society. Welfare State Reform in the Netherlands: 2003-2010", Working Paper 12-103, Nijmegen: Niijmegen Center for Economics.

Deutch, J. (2017), "Decoupling Economic Growth and Carbon Emissions", *Joule 1* (3-9): 3-5.

Deutscher Bundestag (2019), *Unterrichtung durch den Wehrbeauftragten*, Jahresbericht 2019, Berlin: Bundestag.

Dielman, J. L. et al (2016), "US Spending on Personal Healthcare and Public Health, 1996 to 2013", *Journal of the American Medical Association*, 316 (24).

DiMasi, J., H. Grabowski and R. Hansen (2016), "Innovation in the Pharmaceutical Industry: New Estimates of R&D Costs", *Journal of Health Economics*, 47: 20-33.

Divino, V, M. DeKoven, M. Kleinrock, R. Wade and S. Kaura (2016), "Orphan Drug Expenditures in the United States: a Historical and Prospective Analysis, 2007-18, *Health Affairs*, 35(9): 1588-1594.

DOH (Department of Health) (2012), *Long Term Conditions Compendium of Information*, Third Edition, London: DOH.

Doogan, K. (2009), *New Capitalism? The Transformation of Work*, Cambridge, UK: Polity Press.

Dore, G and J Grebely (2017), "Negotiating Better Discounts for DAA Therapy is Critical to Achieve HCV Elimination By 2030", *Journal of Hepatology*, 67(2): 419-420.

Dormont, B. and H. Huber (2012), *Vieillissement de la population et croissance des dépenses de santé*, Rapport de recherche, Paris : Université Paris 1.

Dormont, B., M. Grignon and H. Huber (2006), "Health Expenditure Growth: Reassessing the Threat of Aging", *Health Economics*, 15(9): 947-963.

Doudna, J and S Sternberg (2017), *A Crack in Creation: Gene Editing and the Unthinkable Power to Control Evolution*, Boston: Houghton Mifflin.

DREES (Direction de la recherche, des études, de l'évaluation et des statistiques), *Les dépenses de santé en 2017: Résultats des comptes de la santé*, Paris: DREES.

Duckett, S., M. Cowgill, and H. Swerissen (2019), *Filling the Gap: A Universal Dental Scheme for Australia*, Melbourne: Grattan Institute.

DWP (Department for Work and Pensions) (2019), *Fraud and Error in the Benefit System*, London: DWP.

EC (European Commission) (2017), *The 2018 Aging Report: Underlying Assumptions & Projection Methodologies*, Institutional Paper 065, Brussels: European Commission.

EC (2018a), *The 2018 Aging Report: Economic and Budgetary Projections for the 28 EU Member States (2016-2070)*, Institutional Paper 079, Brussels: European Commission.

EC (2018b), *A Clean Planet for All: A European Strategic Long-Term Vision for a Prosperous, Modern, Competitive and Climate Neutral Economy*, Brussels: European Commission.

EC (2019), *Cyclical Adjustment of Budget Balances*, Spring 2019, Brussels: European Commission.

Eckel, R. et al, "Obesity and Type 2 Diabetes: What Can Be Unified and What Needs to Be Individualised?", *Journal of Clinical Endocrinology and Metabolism*, 96(6): 1654-1663.

EIB (European Investment Bank) (2016), *Restoring EU Competitiveness,* 2016 Updated Version, Luxembourg: EIB.

EIB (European Investment Bank) (2017), *Investment Report 2017/2018: From Recovery to Sustainable Growth*, Luxembourg: EIB.

Einav, L. and A. Finkelstein (2017), "Moral Hazard in Health Insurance: What We Know and How We Know It", Working Paper 24055, Cambridge, MA: National Bureau of Economic Research.

Engineers Australia (2018), *Engineering Construction on Infrastructure: 10 Years of Trends*, Canberra: Engineers Australia.

Erixon, F. and E. van der Marel (2011), "What Is Driving the Rise in Health Care Expenditures? An Inquiry into the Nature and Causes of the Cost Disease", Working Paper, 05/2011, Brussels: European Centre for International Political Economy.

Eurofound (2017), *In-Work Poverty in the EU*, Luxembourg: Publications Office of the European Union.

European Parliament (2016), *Precarious Employment in Europe: Patterns, Trends and Policy Strategies*, Brussels: European Parliament.

Eurostat (2016), *Près d'1 adulte sur 6 dans l'UE est considéré obèse*, communiqué de presse, 20 octobre.

Eurostat (2018), *2.3 Percent of EU Employees Have a Precarious Job*, press release, 9 February.

Experts in Chronic Myeloid Leukemia (2013), "The Price of Drugs for Chronic Myeloid Leukemia (CML) is a Reflection of the Unsustainable Prices of Cancer Drugs", *Blood*, 121: 4439-4442.

Facchini, F. and M. Melki (2011), *Optimal Government Size and Economic Growth in France (1871-2008): An Explanation by the State and Market Failures*, Documents de Travail du Centre d'Economie de la Sorbonne, Paris: Université de la Sorbonne.

Farbmacher, H. (2009), "Copayments for Doctor Visits in Germany and the Probability of Visiting a Physician - Evidence from a Natural Experiment", Munich Discussion Paper 2009-10, München: Volkswirtschaftliche Fakultät Ludwig-Maximilians-Universität.

Farrell, H. and A. Newman (2020), "Will the Coronavirus End Globalization as We Know It?" *Foreign Affairs*, 16 March, foreignaffairs.com.

Fazi, T. and W. Mitchell (2019), "For MMT", *Tribune* (UK), 5 June.

Felder, S. (2013), "The Impact of Demographic Change on Health Expenditure", *CESifo DICE Report*, 1(March): 3-6.

Fenoglio, C., E. Scarpini, M. Serpente and D. Galimberti (2018), "Role of Genetics and Epigenetics in the Pathogenesis of Alzheimer's Disease and Frontotemporal Dementia", *Journal of Alzheimer's Research*, 62: 913-932.

Fernandez, J-L. and P. Nadash (2016), "The Long-Term Care Financing Problem", in C. Gori, J-L. Fernandez and R. Wittenberg (ed), *Long-Term Care Reforms in OECD Countries*, Bristol: Policy Press.

Finkelstein, E., J. Trogdon, J. Cohen and W. Dietz (2009). "Annual Medical Spending Attributable to Obesity", *Health Affairs*, 28(5): w822-w831.

Finucane, M. et al (2011), "National, Regional, and Global Trends in Body Mass Index since 1980: Systematic Analysis of Health Examination Surveys and Epidemiological Studies with 960 Country-Years and 9.1 Million Participants", *The Lancet*, 377: 557-567.

Fizzala, A. (2016), *Dépendance des personnes âgées : qui paie quoi?*, Paris: DREES.

Florez, J. (2016), "Precision Medicine in Diabetes: Is It Time?", *Diabetes Care*, 39: 1085-1088.

Floyd, I. (2020), *Policy Brief: Cash Assistance Should Reach Millions More Families*, Washington, DC: Center on Budget and Policy Priorities.

Fogel, R. (2004), "Changes in the Disparities in Chronic Disease During the Course of the Twentieth Century", Working Paper 10311, Cambridge, MA: National Bureau of Economic Research.

Fogel, R. (2008), "Forecasting the Cost of US Healthcare in 2040", Working Paper 14361, Cambridge, MA: National Bureau of Economic Research.

Follette, G. and L. Sheiner (2008), "An Examination of Health Spending Growth in the United States: Past Trends and Future Prospects", in *Fiscal Sustainability: Analytical Developments and Emerging Policy Issues*, Rome: Banca d'Italia.

Fondation Hulot (2011), *Financer l'avenir sans creuser la dette*, Fondation Hulot pour la Nature et l'Homme, mimeo.

Ford, E. et al (2007), "Explaining the Decrease in US Deaths from Coronary Disease, 1980-2000", *New England Journal of Medicine*, 356: 2388-2398.

Ford, M. (2009), *The Lights in the Tunnel: Automation, Accelerating Technology and the Economy of the Future*, Acculant Publishing.

Ford, M. (2015), *The Rise of the Robots: Technology and the Threat of Mass Unemployment*, London: Oneworld Publications.

Ford, M. (ed) (2018), *Architects of Intelligence: The Truth about AI from the People Building It*, Birmingham: Packt Publishing.

Förster, M. (2000), "Trends and Driving Factors in Income Distribution and Poverty in the OECD Area", OECD Labour Market and Social Policy Occasional Papers No. 42, Paris: OECD.

Fox, L., I. Garfinkel, N. Kaushal, J. Waldfogel and C. Wimer (2018), "Waging War on Poverty: Historical Trends in Poverty Using the Supplemental Poverty Measure", Working Paper 19789, Cambridge, MA: National Bureau of Economic Research.

Fratzscher, M. et al (2015), *Stärkung von Investitionen in Deutschland*, München: PRpetuum GmbH.

Frey, C. (2019), *The Technology Trap: Capital, Labor, and Power in the Age of Automation*, Princeton, NJ: Princeton University Press.

Fries, J. (1980), "Aging, Natural Death, and the Compression of Morbidity", *New England Journal of Medicine*, 303(3): 130 – 135.

Fries, J., B. Bruce and E. Chakravarty (2011), "Compression of Morbidity 1980-2011: A Focused Review of Paradigms and Progress", *Journal of Aging Research*, doi:10.4061/2011/261702.

Fuchs, M. et al (2018), *Social and Employment Policies in Austria*, Brussels: European Parliament.

Gale, W. (2020), "Raising Revenue with a Progressive Value-Added Tax", in J. Shambaugh and R. Nunn, *Tackling the Tax Code: Efficient and Equitable Ways to Raise Revenue,* Washington, DC: The Brookings Institution

Ganascia, J-G. (2017), *Le mythe de la singularité*, Paris: Editions du Seuil.

Garber, A. and J. Skinner (2008), "Is American Health Care Uniquely Inefficient?", Working Paper 14257, Cambridge, MA: National Bureau of Economic Research.

Garfield, R., K. Orgera and A. Damico (2020), *The Coverage Gap: Uninsured Poor Adults in States That Do Not Expand Medicaid*, San Francisco, CA: Kaiser Family Foundation.

Gastaldi-Ménager, C., P.-Y. Geoffard and G. de Lagasnerie, "Medical Spending in France: Concentration, Persistence and Evolution before Death", *Fiscal Studies*, 37(3-4): 499-526.

Gautié, J. and S. Ponthieux (2016), "Employment and the Working Poor", in D. Brady and L. Burton (ed), *The Oxford Handbook of the Social Sciences of Poverty*, Oxford: Oxford University Press.

GBD (GBD 2013 Causes of Death Collaborators) (2015), "Global, Regional, and National Age-Sex Specific All-Cause and Cause-Specific Mortality for 240 Causes of Death, 1990–2013: a Systematic Analysis for the Global Burden of Disease Study 2013", *The Lancet*, 385: 117-71.

Gerber, C. et al (2018), *Income Tax Progressivity: Trends and Implications*, Working Paper WP/18/246, Washington, DC: IMF.

Gershon, P. (2004), *Releasing Resources to the Front Line: Independent Review of Public Sector Efficiency*, London: The Stationery Office.

Geruso, M. and T. Layton (2017), "Selection in Health Insurance Markets and Its Policy Remedies", *Journal of Economic Perspectives*, 31(4): 23-50.

Gething, P. et al (2010), "Climate Change and the Global Malaria Recession", *Nature*, 465: 342-345.

Giget, M. and J-P. Minster (2015), *Innovation Intelligence: Commoditization, Digitization, Acceleration. Major Pressure on Innovation Drivers*, Absans Publishing.

Gladwell, M. (2005), "The Moral-Hazard Myth", *New Yorker*, August 29.

GNDE (Green New Deal for Europe), *A Blueprint: For Europe's Just Transition*, Edition II. gndforeurope.com.

Goldin, I. et al (2018), "Why Is Productivity Slowing down?", Working Paper, Oxford: Oxford Martin Program on Technological and Economic Change.

Goldman, A. et al (2018), "Analysis of Work Requirement Exemptions and Medicaid Spending", *JAMA Internal Medicine*, 178(11): 1549-52.

Gollier, C. (2019), *Le climat après la fin du mois*, Paris : Presses universitaires de France.

Gollogly, H. E. et al (2013), "Increasing Incidence of Cataract Surgery: Population-Based Study", *Journal of Cataract and Refractive Surgery*, 39(9): 1383-9.

Golshan, T. (2017), "The Return of Welfare Reform", 30 June. vox.com.

Gordon, A. (2017), "New and Enduring Dual Structures of Employment in Japan: The Rise of Non-Regular Labor, 1980s-2010s", *Social Science Japan*, 20(1): 9-36.

Gordon, R. (2016), *The Rise and Fall of American Growth: the US Standard of Living Since the Civil War*, Princeton: Princeton University Press.

Goss, P. and J. Sonnemann (2019), *Attracting High Achievers to Teaching*, Melbourne: Grattan Institute.

Grabka, M. and J. Goebel (2018), "Income Distribution in Germany: Real Income on the Rise since 1991 but More People with Low Incomes", DIW Weekly Report, 21, Berlin: Deutsches Institut für Wirtschaftsforschung.

Graetz, G. and G. Michaels (2015), "Robots at Work", *CEP Discussion Paper No. 1335,* London: Centre for Economic Performance, London School of Economics.

Green, D. (2019), *Fixing the Care Crisis*, London: Center for Policy Studies.

Gregory, P. (2013), "Infrastructure Gap? Look at the Facts. We Spend More Than Europe", *Forbes*, 1 April.

Gregory, P. (2016), "What Infrastructure Crisis?", *Defining Ideas: A Hoover Institution Journal*, 18 August. www.hoover.org

Gregory, T., A. Salomons and U. Zierahn (2016), "Racing with or against the Machines? Evidence from Europe", Discussion Paper 16-053, Mannheim: Zentrum für Europäische Wirtschaftsforschung.

Griesi-Oliveira, K. and A. Sertié (2017), "Autism Spectrum Disorders: An Updated Guide for Genetic Counseling", *Einstein Journal of Biology and Medicine*, 15(2): 233-8.

Hacker, J. (2019), *The Great Risk Shift: The New Economic Insecurity and the Decline of the American Dream*, Second Edition, New York, NY: Oxford University Press.

Hagist, C. and L. Kotlikoff (2009), "Who's Going Broke? Comparing Growth in Public Healthcare Expenditure in Ten OECD countries", *Hacienda Pública Española/Revista de Economía Pública*, 188(1): 55-72.

Hales, C., M. Carroll, C. Fryar, and C. Ogden (2017), "Prevalence of Obesity among Adults and Youth: United States, 2015-16", *NCHS Data Brief*, no. 288, Hyattsville, MD: National Centre for Health Statistics.

Halleröd, B., H. Ekbrand and M. Bengtsson (2015), "In-Work Poverty and Labour Market Trajectories: Poverty Risks among the Working Population in 22 European Countries", *Journal of European Social Policy*, 25 (5): 473-488.

Hamilton, J., E. Harris, J. Hatzius and K. West (2015), *The Equilibrium Real Funds Rate: Past, Present and Future*, paper presented at the U.S. Monetary Policy Forum, New York City, 27 February.

Hanson, G. (2012), "The Rise of Middle Kingdoms: Emerging Economies in Global Trade", *Journal of Economic Perspectives*, 26(2): 41–64.

Harris, S. and A. Krueger (2015), "A Proposal for Modernizing Labor Laws for Twenty-First-Century Work: the 'Independent Worker'", Discussion Paper 2015-10, Washington, DC: The Brookings Institution.

Hartwig, J. (2006), "What Drives Health Care Expenditure? Baumol's Model of 'Unbalanced Growth' Revisited", KOF Working Paper 133, Zurich: Eidgenössische Technische Hochschule Zürich.

Hartwig, J. (2007), "Can Baumol's Model of Unbalanced Growth Contribute to Explaining the Secular Rise in Health Care Expenditure? An Alternative Test", KOF Working Paper 178, Zurich: Eidgenössiche Technische Hochschule Zürich.

Harwich, E. and K. Laycock (2018), *Thinking on Its Own: AI in the NHS*, London: Reform.

Hauptmeier, S., M. Heipertz and L. Schuknecht (2006), "Expenditure Reform in Industrialized Countries: a Case Study Approach", Discussion Paper No. 06-050, Mannheim: Zentrum für Europäische Wirtschaftsforschung.

Hays, P (2017), *Advancing Healthcare through Personalized Medicine*, Boca Raton, FL: CRC Press.

Health Affairs (2013), *Health Policy Brief: Specialty Pharmaceuticals*, www.healthaffairs.org.

Heger, D. and I. Kolodziej (2016), "Changes in Morbidity over Time – Evidence from Europe", Ruhr Economic Papers 640, Dortmund: Ruhr-Universität.

Helm, D. (2017), *Cost of Energy Review*, www.gov.uk/government/publications/cost-of-energy-independent-review.

Hernandez-Peña et al (2013), "Health Worker Remuneration in WHO Member States", *Bulletin of the World Health Organization*, 91: 808-15.

Hicks, K. (2020), "Getting to Less: The Truth about Defense Spending", *Foreign Affairs*, 99(2): 56-63.

High-Level Commission on Carbon Prices (2017), *Report of the High-Level Commission on Carbon Prices*, Washington, DC: World Bank.

Hourriez, J-M. (1993), "La consommation médicale à l'horizon 2010», Économie et Statistique, 265: 17-30.

House of Lords (2019), *Social Care Funding: Time to End a National Scandal*, Report of the House of Lords Economic Affairs Committee, HL Paper 392, London: House of Lords.

Howard, D., P. Bach, E. Berndt and R. Conti (2015), "Pricing in the Market for Anticancer Drugs", Working Paper 20867, Cambridge, MA: National Bureau of Economic Research.

Howden, D. and N. Rice (2018), "Health Care Expenditures, Age, Proximity to Death and Morbidity: Implications for an Aging Population", *Journal of Health Economics*, 57: 60-74.

Hufbauer, G. (2019), *Do Multinationals Pay Their Fair Share of Corporate Income Taxes?* Washington, DC: Peterson Institute for International Economics.

IEA/IRENA (International Renewable Energy Agency) (2017), *Perspectives for the Energy Transition: Investment Needs for a Low-Carbon Energy System*, Paris: IEA/OECD.

IFHP (International Federation of Health Plans), *2017 Comparative Price Report: International Variation in Medical and Drug Prices*, healthcostinstitute.org.

IHME (Institute for Health Metrics and Evaluation) (2017). *Financing Global Health Visualization.* Seattle, WA: IHME. Available from vizhub.healthdata.org/fgh (accessed 2 August 2018).

ILO (International Labour Office) (2016), *Non-Standard Employment Around the World: Understanding Challenges, Shaping Prospects,* Geneva: ILO.

IMF (International Monetary Fund) (2004), *Public Investment and Fiscal Policy*, Washington, DC: IMF.

IMF (2014), *Government Financial Statistics Manual,* Washington, DC: IMF.

IMF (2018), *Fiscal Monitor April 2018: Capitalizing on Good Times*, Washington, DC: IMF.

IMF (2019), *Corporate Taxation in the Global Economy*, Washington, DC: IMF.

IPCC (Intergovernmental Panel on Climate Change) (2018), *Global Warming of 1.5°C*, Geneva: IPCC.

IQVIA Institute (2017), *Orphan Drugs in the United States*, Parsippany, NJ: The Institute.

IRDiRC (International Rare Diseases Research Consortium) (2015), *State of Play in the Field of Rare Diseases: 2014-15*, www.irdirc.org.

IRDiRC (2018), *Progress Made in Rare Diseases Research*, www.irdirc.org/research/progress-made-in-rdr (accessed 6 August 2018).

ISSP (Insitut Scientifique de Santé Publique), *Enquête de Santé 2013 : Rapport 1*, Bruxelles : ISSP.

ITF (International Transport Forum) (2017), *Statistics Brief: Infrastructure Investment*, August, Paris: OECD.

Jemal, A. et al (2017), "Annual Report to the Nation on the Status of Cancer, 1975-2014, Featuring Survival", *Journal of the National Cancer Institute*, 109(9).

Kalleberg, A. (2011), *Good Jobs, Bad Jobs: The Rise of Polarized and Precarious Employment Systems in the United States, 1970s-2000s*, New York: Russell Sage Foundation.

Kalleberg, A. and S. Vallas (2018), "Probing Precarious Work: Theory, Research, and Politics", *Research in the Sociology of Work*, 31: 1-30.

Katch, H., J. Wagner and A. Aron-Dine (2018), *Taking Medicaid Coverage Away from People Not Meeting Work Requirements Will Reduce Low-Income Families' Access to Care and Worsen Health Outcomes*, Washington, DC: Center on Budget and Policy Priorities.

Katz, L. and A. Krueger (2019), "The Rise and Nature of Alternative Work Arrangements in the United States, 1995-2015", *ILR Review*, 72(2): 382-416.

Keane, P. and E. Topol (2018), "With an Eye to AI and Autonomous Diagnosis", *NJP Digital Medicine*, 1 (40). Doi: 10.1038/S41746–018–0048–y.

Kelley, A., K. McGarry, R. Gorges and J. Skinner (2015), "The Burden of Health Care Costs in the Last Five Years of Life", *Annals of Internal Medicine*, 163(10): 729-736.

Kelton, S. (2019), *Modern Monetary Theory is Not a Recipe for Doom*, Bloomberg Opinion, February 21.

Kemeny, T., D. Rigby, D., & A. Cooke (2014). "Cheap Imports and the Loss of US Manufacturing Jobs", *The World Economy*, 38(10): 1555-1573.

Kenworthy, L. (2019), "Stable Income and Expenses", June, lanekenworthy.net.

Khosla, V. (2012), "Data-Driven Health Care Won't Replace Physicians Entirely, but It Will Help Those Receptive to Technology Perform Their Jobs Better", *Forbes*, December 4.

Klein, M. (2016), "How Many US Manufacturing Jobs Were Lost to Globalization?", *Financial Times*, 6 December.

Klenk, J., U. Keil, A. Jaensch, M. Christiansen and G. Nagel (2016), "Changes in Life Expectancy 1950-2010: Contribution from Age- and Disease-Specific Mortality in Selected Countries", *Population Health Metrics*, 14:20. DOI 10.1186/s12963-016-0089-x.

Kleven, H. (2014), "How Can Scandinavians Tax So Much?", *Journal of Economic Perspectives*, 28(4): 77-98.

Knopman, D. et al (2016), *Not Everything is Broken: The Future of U.S. Transportation and Water Infrastructure Funding and Financing*, Santa Monica, CA: RAND.

Koo, R. (2009), *The Holy Grail of Macroeconomics: Lessons from Japan's Great Recession*, Singapore: John Wiley & Sons.

Koo, R. (2015), *The Escape from Balance Sheet Recession and the QE Trap: A Hazardous Road for the World Economy*, Singapore: John Wiley & Sons.

Krugman, P. (2019), "Don't Blame Robots for Low Wages", *New York Times*, 14 March.

Krumholz, H. M. et al (2009), "Reduction in Acute Myocardial Infarction Mortality in the United States: Risk-Standardised Mortality Rates from 1995-2006", *Journal of the American Medical Association*, 302(7): 767-773.

Labour Party (2019), *Funding Real Change*, London: Labour Party.

Laß, I. and M. Wooden (2019), "Non-Standard Employment and Wages in Australia", paper presented at the 2019 Reserve Bank of Australia Conference, Sydney, 4-5 April.

Lee, J., S. Roehrig and E. Butto (2016), "Cancer Care Cost Trends in the United States: 1998 to 2012", *Cancer*, 122(7): 1078-1084.

Lee, J.-S. and A. Fallow (2019), "The Threat of Climate Change to Non-Dengue-Endemic Countries: Increasing Risk of Dengue Transmission Potential Using Climate and Non-Climate Data Sets", *BMC Public Health*, 19(934).

Lee, R. (2003), "The Demographic Transition: Three Centuries of Fundamental Change", *Journal of Economic Perspectives*, 17(4): 167-190.

Leiserson, G. (2020), "Taxing Wealth", in J. Shambaugh and R. Nunn, *Tackling the Tax Code: Efficient and Equitable Ways to Raise Revenue*, Washington, DC: The Brookings Institution

Levine, M. and E. Crimmins (2018), "Is 60 the New 50? Examining Changes in Biological Age Over the Past Two Decades", *Demography*, 55(2): 387-401.

Libault, D. (2019), *Concertation grand âge et autonomie*, Paris: Ministère des solidarités et de la santé.

Lichtenberg, F. (2017), "The Impact of Biomedical Innovation on Longevity and Health", *Nordic Journal of Health Economics*, 5(1): 45-57.

Lindgren, B. (2016), "The Rise in Life Expectancy, Health Trends among the Elderly, and the Demand for Health and Social Care", Working Paper 142, Stockholm: National Institute of Economic Research.

Livingstone, S. J. et al, "Estimated Life Expectancy in a Scottish Cohort with Type 1 Diabetes, 2008-2010", *Journal of the American Medical Association*, 313(1): 37-44.

Loder, J. and L. Nicholas (2018), *Confronting Doctor Robot: Creating a People-Powered Future for AI in Health*, London: Nesta Health Lab.

Lohmann, H. (2018), "The Concept and Measurement of In-Work Poverty", in H. Lohmann and I. Marx (ed), *Handbook on In-Work Poverty*, Cheltenham: Edward Elgar.

Lucas, R. (2003), "Macroeconomic Priorities", *American Economic Review*, 93(1): 1-14.

Magazzino, C. and F. Forte (2010), *Optimal Size of Government and Economic Growth in EU-27*, Munich Personal RePEc Archive, Munich: Universität München.

Maiello, M. (2017), "Diagnosing William Baumol's Cost Disease", *Chicago Booth Review*, May 18.

Maître, B., B. Nolan and C. Whelan (2012), "Low Pay, In-Work Poverty and Economic Vulnerability: A Comparative Analysis Using EU-SILC", *The Manchester School*, 80(1): 99-116.

Makin, A., J. Pearce and S. Ratnasiri (2018), *The Optimal Size of Government in Australia*, Paper presented at 2018 Australian Conference of Economists, Canberra.

Marin, D. (2017), The China Shock: Why Germany is Different, *VOX CEPR Policy Portal*, 7 September.

Martikainen, P. et al (2012), "Seven-Year Hospital and Nursing Home Care Use According to Age and Proximity to Death: Variations by Cause of Death and Socio-Demographic Position", *Journal of Epidemiological Community Health*, 66(12): 1152-8.

Mathers, C. D. et al (2015), "Causes of International Increases in Older Age Life Expectancy", *The Lancet*, 385: 540-548.

Mauro, P. et al (2015), "A Modern History of Fiscal Prudence and Profligacy", *Journal of Monetary Economics*, 76: 55-70.

Mazza, J. (2019), "Is Public Debt a Cheap Lunch?", *Bruegel Blog*, 21 January.

McGrail, K. et al (2000), "Age, Costs of Acute and Long-Term Care and Proximity to Death: Evidence for 1987-88 and 1994-95 in British Columbia", *Age and Aging*, 29: 249-253.

Medeiros, J. and C. Schwierz (2013), "Estimating the Drivers and Projecting Long-Term Public Health Expenditure in the European Union: Baumol's 'Cost Disease' Revisited", *European Economy: Economic Papers*, 507.

Melberg, H. O. (2014), "Are Health Care Expenditures Increasing Faster for the Elderly Than the Rest of the Population?", *Expert Reviews of Pharmacoeconomics and Outcomes Research*, 14(5): 581-583.

Mensah, G. et al (2017), "Decline in Cardiovascular Mortality: Possible Causes and Implications", *Circulation Research*, 120: 366-380.

Merino, J. and J. Florez (2018), "Precision Medicine in Diabetes: An Opportunity for Clinical Translation", *Annals of the New York Academy of Sciences*, 1411: 140-52.

MGI (McKinsey Global Institute) (2014), *From Science to Operations: Questions, Choices and Strategies for Success in Biopharma*. McKinsey & Company.

MGI (2016), *Independent Work: Choice, Necessity, and the Gig Economy*, McKinsey & Company.

MGI (2017), *Government Productivity: Unlocking the $3.5 Trillion Opportunity*, McKinsey & Company.

Miller, R. G., A. M. Secrest, R. K. Sharma, T. J. Songer and T. J. Orchard (2012), "Improvements in the Life Expectancy of Type 1 Diabetes", *Diabetes*, 61: 2987-2992.

Miller, T. (2001), "Increasing Longevity and Medicare Expenditures", *Demography*, 38(2): 215-26.

Mir, G. and S. Storm (2016), "Carbon Emissions and Economic Growth: Production-Based Versus Consumption-Based Evidence on Decoupling", Working Paper 41, New York, NY: Institute for New Economic Thinking.

Mishel, L. (2018), *Uber and the Labor Market: Uber Drivers' Compensation, Wages, and the Scale of Uber and the Gig Economy*, Washington, DC: Economic Policy Institute.

Mishel, L. and J. Bivens (2017), *The Zombie Robot Argument Lurches On: There is No Evidence That Automation Leads to Joblessness or Inequality*, Washington, DC: Economic Policy Institute.

Mishel, L., H. Shierholz and J. Schmitt (2013), *Don't Blame the Robots: Assessing the Job Polarization Explanation of Growing Wage Inequality*, Washington, DC: Economic Policy Institute.

Mitchell, W. and T. Fazi (2017), *Reclaiming the State: A Progressive Vision of Sovereignty for a Post-Neoliberal World*, London: Pluto Press.

Moffat, M. and P. Gottschalk (2011), "Trends in the Transitory Variance of Male Earnings in the US, 1970-2004", Working Paper 16833, Cambridge, MA: National Bureau of Economic Research.

Moskowitz, D., R. Haskins and T. Smeeding (2010), *Is the Census Bureau's Supplemental Poverty Measure a Relative Measure of Poverty?* Washington, DC: The Brookings Institution.

Mueller, M., L. Hagenaars and D. Morgan (2017), "Administrative Spending in OECD Health Care Systems: Where Is the Fat and Can It Be Trimmed?" in OECD, *Tackling Wasteful Spending on Health*, Paris: OECD.

Mühleisen, M. (2000), "Too Much of a Good Thing? The Effectiveness of Fiscal Stimulus", in T. Bayoumi and C. Collyns (eds), *Post-Bubble Blues: How Japan Responded to Asset Price Collapse*, Washington, DC: IMF.

National Audit Office (2007), *The Efficiency Programme: A Second Review of Progress*, London: The Stationery Office.

NCB (National Census Bureau) (2017), *Projected 5-Year Age Groups and Sex Composition of the Population: Projections for the United States: 2017-2060. Main Series Table 3*, www.census.gov.

NCHS (National Center for Health Statistics) (2017), *Health, United States 2016*, Hyattsville, MD: NCHS.

Neild, G. H. (2017), "Life Expectancy with Chronic Kidney Disease: An Educational Review", *Pediatric Nephrology*, 32: 243-248.

Nersisyan, Y. and Wray, L. (2019), "How to Pay for the Green New Deal", Working Paper 931, Annandale-on-Hudson, NY: Levy Economics Institute.

Newhouse, J. (1992), "Medical Care Cost: How Much Welfare Loss?", *Journal of Economic Perspectives*, 6(3): 3-21.

Newhouse, J. et al (1981), "Some Interim Results from a Controlled Trial of Cost Sharing in Health Insurance", *New England Journal of Medicine*, 305(25): 1501-7.

Ng, M. et al, "Global, Regional, and National Prevalence of Overweight and Obesity in Children and Adults During 1980–2013: A Systematic Analysis for the Global Burden of Disease Study 2013", *The Lancet*, 384: 766-81.

NHS (National Health Service) (2013), *The NHS Belongs to the People*, NHS England.

NIH (National Institutes of Health) (2010), *Fact Sheet: Heart Disease*, report.nih.gov/nihfactsheets.

Noble, D. (1995), *Progress without People: New Technology, Unemployment, and the Message of Resistance*, Toronto: Between the Lines.

Nordhaus, W. (2013), *The Climate Casino: Risk, Uncertainty, and Economics for a Warming World*, New Haven: Yale University Press.

Nordhaus, W. (2019), "Climate Change: The Ultimate Challenge for Economics", *American Economic Review*, 109(6): 1991-2014.

NRC (National Research Council) (2011), *Toward Precision Medicine: Building a Knowledge Network for Biomedical Research and a New Taxonomy of Disease*, Washington, DC: The National Academies Press.

Nübler, I. (2018), "New Technologies, Innovation, and the Future of Jobs" in E. Paus (ed), *Confronting Dystopia: The New Technological Revolution and the Future of Work*, Ithaca and London: ILR Press.

Nuffield Trust (2019a), *Why a 'Risk Pool' Must Underpin a Social Care System*, London: Nuffield Trust.

Nuffield Trust (2019b), *Social Care: The Action We Need,* London: Nuffield Trust.

Oberghaus, D. and C. Reif (2010), "Total Costs and Budgetary Effects of Adaptation to Climate Change: An Assessment for the European Union", Discussion Paper No. 10-046, Mannheim: Zentrum für Europäische Wirtschaftsforschung.

OBR (Office for Budget Responsibility) (2018), *Fiscal Sustainability Report*, London: HMSO.

OECD (Organisation for Economic Cooperation and Development) (1988), *Aging Population: The Social Policy Implications*, Paris: OECD.

OECD (2010), "Health Care Systems: Getting More Value for Money", OECD Economics Department Policy Notes, no. 2, Paris: OECD.

OECD (2011), *Health at a Glance 2011*. Paris: OECD Publishing.

OECD (2016), *Health at a Glance: Europe 2016*, Paris: OECD.

OECD (2017a), *Obesity Update 2017*, Paris: OECD.

OECD (2017b) *Basic Income as a Policy Option: Can it Add Up?* Policy Brief on The Future of Work, Paris: OECD.

OECD (2018a), *Effective Carbon Rates 2018: Pricing Carbon Emissions Through Taxes and Emission Trading,* Paris: OECD.

OECD (2018b), *OECD Economic Outlook*, 2018(2), Paris: OECD.

OECD (2018c), *The Role and Design of Net Wealth Taxes in the OECD*, OECD Tax Policy Studies, 26, Paris: OECD.

OECD (2019a), *Health at a Glance 2019*. Paris: OECD Publishing.

OECD (2019b), *Pensions at a Glance 2019*. Paris: OECD Publishing.

OECD (2019c), *OECD Employment Outlook 2019: The Future of Work*, Paris: OECD.

OECD (2019d), *Education at a Glance 2019*, Paris: OECD.

OECD (2020), *Tax Challenges Arising from the Digitalization of the Economy: Update on the Economic Analysis & Impact Assessment*, presentation accompanying webcast, 13 February. Paris: OECD.

OIG (Office of Inspector General) (2018), *Hospitals Reported Improved Preparedness for Emerging Infectious Diseases after the Ebola Outbreak*, OEI-06-15-00230. Washington, DC: Department of Health and Human Services.

Ortiz-Ospina, E. and M. Roser (2020), "Trust." ourworldindata.org/trust.

Osterholm, M. (2005), "Preparing for the Next Pandemic", *Foreign Affairs*, 84(4): 24-37.

Palier, B. (2010), *A Long Goodbye to Bismarck: The Politics of Welfare Reform in Continental Europe*, Amsterdam: Amsterdam University Press.

Palmieri, L., K. Bennett, S. Giampaoli and S. Capewell (2010), "Explaining the Decrease in Coronary Heart Disease Mortality in Italy between 1980 and 2000", *American Journal of Public Health*, 100(4): 684-692.

Papanicolas, I., L. Woskie and A. Jha (2018), "Health Care Spending in the United States and Other High-Income Countries", *Journal of the American Medical Association*, 318(10): 1024-1039.

Parkin, D., A. McGuire and B. Yule (1987), "Aggregate Health Care Expenditures and National Income: Is Healthcare a Luxury Good?", *Journal of Health Economics*, 6(2): 109-27.

Patel, A. et al (2017), "Personal Protective Equipment Supply Chain: Lessons Learned from Recent Public Health Emergency Responses", *Health Security*, 15(3): 244-252.

Paul, D., K. Schaeffer and A. Coustasse (2017), "Long-Term Care Policy: What the United States can learn from Denmark, Sweden, and the Netherlands," in A. Mukherjee (ed), *Business & Health Administration Proceedings 2017.*

PBO (Parliamentary Budget Office) (2019), *Australia's Aging Population: Understanding the Fiscal Impacts over the Next Decade*, Report 02/2019, Canberra: Commonwealth of Australia.

PC (Productivity Commission) (2005), *Economic Implications of an Aging Australia. Technical Paper 5: Aggregate Studies of Agent Health Expenditures*, Melbourne: The Commission.

PC (2011), *Caring for Older Australians,* Report 53, Final Inquiry Report, Melbourne: The Commission.

Pearl, J. (2019), "The Limitations of Opaque Learning Machines", in J. Brockman (ed), *Possible Minds: 25 Ways of Looking at AI*, New York, NY: Penguin Press.

Peña-Casas et al (2019), *In-Work Poverty in Europe: a Study of National Policies*, Brussels: European Commission.

Pierce, J. and P. Schott (2016), "The Surprisingly Swift Decline of US Manufacturing Employment", *American Economic Review*, 106(7): 1632–1662.

Piketty, T. (2013), *Le capital au XXIe siècle*, Paris: Editions du Seuil.

Piketty, T., T. Saez and S. Stantcheva (2014), "Optimal Taxation of Top Labor Incomes: A Tale of Three Elasticities", *American Economic Journal: Economic Policy*, 6(1): 230-271.

Pissarides, C. (2019), *The Future of Work in Europe*, paper delivered at Brussels Economic Forum, 18 June.

Popescu, S. and R. Leach (2019), "Identifying Gaps in Frontline Healthcare Facility High-Consequence Infectious Disease Preparedness", *Health Security*, 17(2): 117-123.

Powell, J. (2019), *Statement of Jerome H. Powell, Chairman, Board of Governors of the Federal Reserve System*, Hearing before the Committee on Banking, Housing, and Urban Affairs, United States Senate, 26 February. Washington, DC: US Government Publishing Office.

Pratt, A. and J. Lilliestam (2018), "The Case Against Carbon Prices", *Joule*, 2: 2487-2510.

Putallaz, Y. and P. Tzieropoulous (2012), *Audit sur l'état du réseau (Audit Rivier)*, Lausanne: EPFL.

Putallaz, Y. et al (2018), *Audit sur l'état du réseau ferré national: rapport de la mission*, Lausanne: EPFL.

Puymirat, E., T. Simon, and P. G. Steg (2012), "Association of Changes in Clinical Characteristics and Management with Improvement in Survival among Patients with ST-Elevation Myocardial Infarction", *Journal of the American Medical Association*, 308(10): 998-1006.

QuintileIMS Institute (2017), *Understanding the Drivers of Drug Expenditure in the US*, Parsippany, NJ: The Institute.

Razin, A. and E. Sadka (2005), *The Decline of the Welfare State: Demography and Globalization*, Cambridge, MA.: MIT Press.

Razzaki, S. et al (2018), "A Comparative Study of Artificial Intelligence and Human Doctors for the Purpose of Triage in Diagnosis", *Babylon Health*, arXiv; 1806. 10698v1 [cs.AI] 27 June.

RCAC (Royal Commission into Aged Care Quality and Safety), *Medium-and Long-Term Pressures on the System: The Changing Demographics and Dynamics of Aged Care*, Background Paper 2. Canberra: Commonwealth of Australia.

Rebba, V. (2014), "The Long-Term Sustainability of European Health Care Systems", 'Marco Fanno' Working Paper 191, Padova: Università degli Studi di Padova.

Rector, R. (2014), "How Welfare Undermines Marriage and What to Do about It", Issue Brief 4302, Washington, DC: Heritage Foundation.

Rector, R. (2017), *Work Requirements and Medicaid Won't Work*, Heritage Foundation Blog, 19 March, www/heritage.org.

Reinhardt, U. (2003), "Does the Aging of the Population Really Drive the Demand for Healthcare?", *Health Affairs*, 22(6): 27-39.

Reiter, P. (2001), "Climate Change and Mosquito-Borne Disease", *Environmental Health Perspectives*, 109(Supp. 1): 141-161.

RGE (Rapport du groupe d'experts) (2017), *Mesure visant à freiner la hausse des coûts dans l'assurance obligatoire des soins*, Berne: Office fédéral de la santé publique.

Rifkin, J. (1995), *The End of Work: The Decline of the Global Labour Force and the Dawn of the Post-Market Era*, New York: Putnam.

Robert, C. et al (2017), "Role of Genetics in the Etiology of Autistic Spectrum Disorder: Towards a Hierarchical Diagnostic Strategy", *International Journal of Molecular Science*, 18(3). Doi:10.3390/ijms18030618

Robinson, M. (2007), "Results Information", in M. Robinson (ed), *Performance Budgeting: Linking Funding to Results*, Houndmills: IMF/Palgrave Macmillan.

Robinson, M. (2013), "Spending Review", *OECD Journal on Budgeting*, 2013(2): 81-122.

Rodrik, D. (2012), *The Globalization Paradox: Democracy in the Future of the World Economy*, New York, NY: Norton.

Ryan, S., C. Carlson, E. Mordecai and L. Johnson (2019), "Global Expansion and Redistribution of *Aedes*-borne Virus Transmission Risk with Climate Change", *PLOS Neglected Tropical Diseases*, 13(3).

Saez. E. and G. Zucman (2019), "Progressive Wealth Taxation", *Brookings Papers on Economic Activity Conference Drafts*, September 5–6.

Santé Publique (2017), *L'état de santé de la population en France: Rapport 2017*, Paris : Editions Dicom.

Sarin, N., L. Summers and J. Kupferberg (2020), "Tax Reform for Progressivity: A Pragmatic Approach", in J. Shambaugh and R. Nunn (eds.), *Tackling the Tax Code: Efficient and Equitable Ways to Raise Revenue,* Washington, DC: The Brookings Institution.

Scannell, J. W. et al (2012), "Diagnosing the Decline in Pharmaceutical R&D Efficiency", *Nature Reviews Drug Discovery*, 11: 191-200.

Schmitt, J., E. Gould and J. Bivens (2018), *America's Slow-Motion Wage Crisis: Four Decades of Slow and Unequal Growth,* Washington, DC: Economic Policy Institute.

Schneider, E., D. Sarnak, D. Squires, A. Shah and M. Doty (2017), *Mirror, Mirror 2017: International Comparison Reflects Flaws and Opportunities for Better U.S. Health Care*, New York, NY: The Commonwealth Fund.

Schott, L., E. Bolen and W. Fischer (2017), *Freedom Caucus 'Welfare Reform' Bill would Increase Poverty and Hardship without Helping People Succeed in the Labor Market*, Washington, DC: Center on Budget and Policy Priorities.

Schram, S., R. Fording and J. Soss (2018), "Do Work Requirements for Federal Assistance Help People Escape Poverty?", *Washington Post*, 13 August.

Schuyler, M. (2014), *A Short History of Government Taxing and Spending in the United States*. Tax Foundation Fiscal Fact No. 415, Washington, DC: Tax Foundation.

Scitovsky, A. (1967), "Changes in the Costs of Treatment of Selected Illnesses, 1951-1965", *American Economic Review*, 57: 1182-95.

Sénat (2012), *Rapport d'information au nom de la commission des finances sur l'enquête de la cour des comptes relative à l'entretien du réseau ferroviaire national*, n. 783, Paris: Présidence du Sénat.

Sénat (2017a), *Rapport d'information au nom de la commission de l'aménagement du territoire et du développement durable sur les infrastructures routières et autoroutières : un réseau en danger*, n. 458. Paris: Présidence du Sénat.

Sénat (2017b), *Rapport d'information au nom de la mission de l'évaluation et de contrôle de la sécurité social de la commission des affaires sociales sur la lutte contre la fraude sociale*, n. 599. Paris: Présidence du Sénat.

Sénat (2019), *Sécurité des ponts : éviter un drame : rapport d'information au nom de la commission de l'aménagement du territoire et du développement durable par la mission d'information sur la sécurité des ponts*, Paris: Présidence du Sénat.

Senate Democrats (2018), *Senate Democrats' Jobs & Infrastructure Plan for America's Workers*, March 7.

Shambaugh, J., L. Bauer and A. Breitwieser (2017), *Who Is Poor in the United States?* Washington, DC: The Brookings Institution.

Sheffield, R. (2016), *Welfare Reform Must Include Work Requirements*, Heritage Foundation Blog, 22 March, www/heritage.org.

Sheiner, L. and A. Malinovskaya (2016), *Measuring Productivity in Health Care: an Analysis of the Literature*, Washington, DC: The Brookings Institution.

Siegel, R. L et al (2018), "Cancer Statistics, 2018", *CA: A Cancer Journal for Clinicians*, 68(1): 7-30.

Silberman, J. et al (2015), "The Avalanche Hypothesis and Compression of Morbidity: Testing Assumptions through Cohort-Sequential Analysis", *Plos One*, 10(5). DOI:10.1371/journal.pone.0123910.

Simon, F. and G. Giovannetti (2017), *Managing Biotechnology: From Science to Market in the Digital Age*, Hoboken, N.J.: Wiley.

Smith, S., J. Newhouse and M. Freeland (2009), "Income Insurance, and Technology: Why Does Health Spending Outpace Economic Growth", *Health Affairs*, 28(5): 1276-84.

Smith, S., S. Heffler and M. Freeland (2000), *The Impact of Technological Change on Health Care Costs Spending: An Evaluation of the Literature*, Woodlawn, MD: Health Care Financing Administration.

Soto, M., B. Shang and D. Coady (2012), "New Projections of Public Health Spending, 2010-50", in B. Clements, D. Coady and S. Gupta, *The Economics of Public Healthcare Reform in Advanced and Emerging Economies*, Washington, DC: IMF.

Spasova, S., D. Bouget and B. Vanhercke (2016), *Sick Pay and Sickness Benefit Schemes in the European Union*, Brussels: European Commission.

Spence, M. (2011), "The Impact of Globalization on Income and Employment: The Downside of Integrating Markets", *Foreign Affairs*, 90(4): 28-41.

Spillman, B. and J. Lubitz (2000), "The Effect of Longevity on Spending for Acute and Long-Term Care", *New England Journal of Medicine*, 342(19): 1409-15.

Standing, G. (2014), *The Precariat: The New Dangerous Class*, London: Bloomsbury.

Stern, N. (2007), *The Economics of Climate Change*, Cambridge, UK: Cambridge University Press.

Stiglitz, J. (2015), *The Great Divide: Unequal Societies and What We Can Do About Them*, New York: Norton.

Stiglitz, J. (2018), "The Myth of Secular Stagnation", *Project Syndicate*, 28 August, project-syndicate.org.

Summers, L. (2014a), "US Economic Prospects: Secular Stagnation, Hysteresis, and the Zero Lower Bound", *Business Economics*, 49(2): 65-73.

Summers, L. (2014b), "Reflections on the New Secular Stagnation Hypothesis", in C. Teulings and R. Baldwin, *Secular Stagnation: Facts, Causes and Cures*, London: CEPR Press.

Summers, L. (2018), "The Threat of Secular Stagnation Has Not Gone Away", *Larry Summers Blog*, 6 May.

Summers, L. and N. Sarin (2019), "A 'Wealth Tax' Presents a Revenue Estimation Puzzle," *The Washington Post*, 4 April.

Susskind, R. and D. Susskind (2016), "Technology Will Replace Many Doctors, Lawyers, and Other Professionals", *Harvard Business Review*, 11 October.

Sutherland, D., R. Price and F. Gonand (2009), "Improving Public Spending Efficiency in Primary and Secondary Education", *OECD Journal of Economic Studies*, 1: 1-30.

Takeo, Y. (2018), "Bank of Japan's Hoard of Assets Is Now Bigger Than the Economy", *Bloomberg*, 13 November.

Taylor, J. (2014), "The Economic Hokum of 'Secular Stagnation'", *Wall Street Journal*, 1 January.

Taylor, J. (2020), "Restoring Fiscal Order in the United States", *Project Syndicate*, 22 January, project-syndicate.org.

Thorpe, K. (2005), "The Rise in Health Care Spending and What to Do about It", *Health Affairs*, 24(6): 1436-1445.

Thorpe, K. E. and M. Philyaw (2012), "The Medicalization of Chronic Disease and Costs", *Annual Review of Public Health*. 33: 409–23.

Thorpe, K. E., C. S. Florence, and P. Joski (2004), "Which Medical Conditions Account for the Rise in Health Care Spending?", *Health Affairs*, September, W4: 437-445.

Tirole, J. (2016), *Economie du bien commun*, Paris: Presses universitaires de France.

Topol, E. (2015), *The Patient Will See You Now*, New York, NY: Basic Books.

TPC (Tax Policy Center) (2020), *Table T20-0088: Earned Income Tax Credit and Child Tax Credit Current Law Benefits, Tax Expenditures, $Billions, 2019-28*, www.taxpolicycenter.org.

Trivedi, A., H. Moloo and V. Mor (2010), "Increased Ambulatory Care Copayments and Hospitalizations Among the Elderly", *New England Journal of Medicine*, 362(4): 320-8.

Tucker, P. S. et al (2014), "The Increasing Financial Impact of Chronic Kidney Disease in Australia", *International Journal of Nephrology*, 2014(9).

Tvinnereim, E. and M. Mehling (2018), "Carbon Pricing and Deep Carbonization", *Energy Policy*, 121: 185-89.

UN (United Nations) (2019a), *World Population Prospects 2019, Volume I: Comprehensive Tables*, New York, NY: UN.

UN (2019b), *Probabilistic Population Projections Rev. 1 based on the World Population Prospects*

2019 Rev. 1, Department of Economic and Social Affairs, Population Division. http://population.un.org/wpp.

UN (2019c). *World Population Prospects 2019*, Online Edition. Rev. 1. Department of Economic and Social Affairs, Population Division, New York, NY: UN.

Unal, B., J. Critchley and S. Capewell (2004), "Explaining the Decline in Coronary Heart Disease Mortality in England and Wales between 1981 and 2000", *Circulation*, 109(9): 1101-1107.

USGCRP (US Global Change Research Program) (2018), *Impacts, Risks, and Adaptation in the United States: Fourth National Climate Assessment*, Volume II, Washington, DC: USGCRP. doi: 10.7930/NCA4.2018

van Ark, B. (2016), "The Productivity Paradox of the New Digital Economy", *International Productivity Monitor,* 31: 3-18.

van Parijs, P. and Y. Vanderborght (2017), *Basic Income: A Radical Proposal for a Free Society and a Sane Economy*, Cambridge, MA.: Harvard University Press.

Wachs, M. (2020), "Financing US Infrastructure: Choices for the 21st Century", in A. Khan and K. Becker (eds), *US Infrastructure: Challenges and Directions for the 21st Century*, New York: Taylor and Francis.

Walter, S. et al (2016), "No Evidence of Morbidity Compression in Spain: A Time Series Study Based on National Hospitalization Records"", *International Journal of Public Health*, 61: 729-738.

Ward, Z. et al (2017), "Simulation of Growth Trajectories of Childhood Obesity into Adulthood", *New England Journal of Medicine*, 377: 2145-53.

Weaver, F., S. Stearns, E. Norton and W. Spector (2008), "Proximity to Death and Participation in the Long-Term Care Market", *Health Economics*, 18: 867-883.

Weisfeldt, M. and S. Zieman (2007), "Advances in the Prevention and Treatment of Cardiovascular Disease", *Health Affairs*, 26: 25-37.

WHO (World Health Organization) (2016), *Global Report on Diabetes*, Geneva: WHO.

Wiking, M. (2016), "Why Danes Happily Pay High Rates of Taxes", *US News*, 20 January.

Wimer, C. et al (2013), "Trends in Poverty with an Anchored Supplemental Poverty Measure", Columbia Population Research Center Working Papers, 13-1, New York, NY: Columbia University.

Winship, S. (2012), "Bogeyman Economics", *National Affairs*, 13 (Winter).

Wittenberg, R. (2016), "Demand for Care and Support for Older People", in C. Gori, J-L. Fernandez and R. Wittenberg (ed), *Long-Term Care Reforms in OECD Countries*, Bristol: Policy Press.

World Bank (2011), *Economics of Adaptation to Climate Change: Synthesis Report*, Washington, DC: World Bank.

Wray, L. (2015), *Modern Monetary Theory: A Primer on Macro Economics for Sovereign Monetary Systems*, Houndmills: Palgrave Macmillan.

Yang, Z., E. Norton and S. Stearns (2003), "Longevity and Health Care Expenditures: The Real Reasons Older People Spend More", *Journal of Gerontology: Social Sciences*, 58B(1): S2-S10.

Zhou, F. et al (2014), "Economic Evaluation of the Routine Childhood Immunization Program in the United States, 2009", *Paediatrics*, 133(4): 577-585.

Zhuo, X. et al (2014), "The Lifetime Cost of Diabetes and its Implications for Diabetes Prevention", *Diabetes Care*, 37: 2557-2564.

Zweifel, P., S. Felder and M. Meier (1999), "Aging of Population and Health Care Expenditure: a Red Herring?", *Health Economics* 8(6): 485-96.

INDEX

advanced economies 1, 17;
 debt levels 9, 12, 15;
 definition 1;
 history of 57;
 impact of Covid-19 pandemic on 230;
 recession in 13;
 support for the welfare state 23
 age-based rationing (of health care) 74–5
AGI *see* artificial intelligence
Allen, Paul 204
Alzheimer's disease 124, 327*n*10
antibiotics: resistance to 96–7
armed forces 8
artificial intelligence 3, 265;
 impact on employment 201–8, 224–5;
 in health care 87, 97–104, 206;
 in long-term care 123
aspirin 47
asthma 47
austerity 8, 15, 160, 174–5, 271
Australia 13;
 employment 193, 222, 223;
 government expenditure **314**;
 health care 29–30;
 infrastructure investment 161–2, 172;
 pensions 320*n*19, 331*n*11
autism 83
automation:
 in healthcare 51, 70–1, 98–102, 207;
 in industry 180–1, 196–9;
 in legal practice 207, 225;
 of government services 265–8

baby boom generation 38, 92, 117, 119, 124,
 131, 248
Babylon Health 100

banks: bailouts 14, 16
basic income:
 austere 216–17;
 generous 215–17;
 'lite' 217;
 universal 2, 178, 201, 215–17
Baumol, William 50–7, 64, 70–1, 102, 268
Belgium 13
benefits:
 cuts to 275–80;
 disability 20;
 'marriage penalty' 345*n*12;
 overpayment 254;
 social 17, 20, 254;
 unemployment 17, 20, 177–9, 254, 286
 see also welfare state
'big government' 1, 276;
 opposition to 10
big pharma 40
bioinformatics 78–9, 85
biologics 41
Boden, Margaret 203–4
borrowing 2, 152–3, 227–9, 233–40, 247 *see
 also* debt, government
Brexit 128
Bridges, William 214
budgets 5, 115; deficits 227–44, **246**, 249,
 287

Canada: infrastructure investment 159;
 poverty 183; taxation 292
cancer 30, 32, 33, 81;
 prevalence 321*n*9, 322*n*16;
 treatment of 34, 49, 84, 89
capitalism 195, 196, 198, 199
Carbaglu (drug) 40